GROWING
DEEP
IN THE
CHRISTIAN
LIFE

GROWING
DEEP
IN THE
CHRISTIAN
LIFE

CHARLES R. SWINDOLL

RETURNING TO OUR ROOTS

Original cover design: Walvoord, Killion, Edmonson & Hanlon, Inc.
Photography: Steve Terrill, Dave Edmonson, Photri
Editor: Larry R. Libby

GROWING DEEP IN THE CHRISTIAN LIFE
© 1986 by Charles R. Swindoll, Inc.
Published by Multnomah Press
Portland, Oregon 97266

Printed in the United States of America

Library of Congress Cataloging-in-Publication Data

Swindoll, Charles R.
 Growing Deep in the Christian Life.

 Bibliography: p.
 1. Theology, Doctrinal—Popular works.   I. Title.
BT77.S795   1986   230'.044   86-8661
ISBN 0-88070-154-4

87   88   89   90   91   –   10   9   8   7   6   5   4   3

C O N T E N T S

DEDICATION

INTRODUCTION

DOCTRINE AND DISCERNMENT

THE BIBLE

GOD THE FATHER

THE LORD JESUS CHRIST

THE HOLY SPIRIT

THE DEPRAVITY OF HUMANITY

SALVATION

THE RETURN OF CHRIST

RESURRECTION

THE BODY OF CHRIST

THE FAMILY OF GOD

This volume is affectionately
dedicated to four faithful men:

Cyril Barber
Bill Butterworth
David Lien
Bill Watkins

who serve behind the scenes at Insight
for Living, giving counsel and
encouragement to those who hurt,
finding in Scripture the foundation of
their faith. I am indebted to each man
for his unswerving commitment to
God's truth, his unselfish ministry to
people in need, his unceasing
discipline to stay at an endless task,
and his unsurpassed loyalty to my wife
and me as friends.

*B*lessed is the man who does not walk in the counsel of the wicked or stand in the way of sinners or sit in the seat of mockers.

*B*ut his delight is in the law of the Lord, and on his law he meditates day and night.

*H*e is like a tree planted by streams of water, which yields its fruit in season and whose leaf does not wither. Whatever he does prospers.

(Psalm 1:1-3, NIV)

INTRODUCTION

or years I have wanted to write a book on doctrine . . . Bible doctrine. My flesh has been willing, but my spirit has been weak. That calls for an explanation.

The need for knowledge of the Scripture is obvious. Everywhere I turn I meet or hear about well-meaning Christians who are long on zeal but short on facts . . . lots of enthusiasm and motivation but foggy when it comes to scriptural truth.

They have a deep and genuine desire to be used by God, to reach the lost, to serve in the church, to invest their energies in "the kingdom of God and His righteousness," but their doctrinal foundation is shifting sand rather than solid rock. The result is predictable: They are at the mercy of their emotions, flying high one day and scraping the bottom the next. A frustrating yo-yo syndrome.

I know. For more years than I care to remember, I, too, climbed and tumbled, soared and submerged, thought I knew the scoop, then later discovered how off target I really was. The whole miserable mess leaves a person filled with doubt and disillusionment, grossly lacking in confidence, not to mention having that awful feeling of being exposed. At that point, most Christians decide to pack it in lest they get caught again in a similar position of vulnerability. You and I may be amazed to know how many have retreated into the background scenery of passivity simply because their ignorance of the basic building blocks caused them embarrassment.

Like I said, the need is obvious. Being a fixer-upper type, I am prompted to jump in with both feet and crank out a pile of pages that will provide the doctrinal ammunition so many Christians need. That's why I said my flesh is willing. But since I am also a let's-be-realistic type, I am reluctant.

Among the last things believers need is another dull volume on doctrine. Sterile and unapplied theology interests no one living in the real world. Most of those books wind up as great (and expensive!) doorstops. They also make a good impression when the pastor drops by for a visit and sees them lying there, freshly dusted off on the coffee table. And there is nothing like wading through thick theological works late at night to cure your battle with insomnia. Who hasn't come close to fracturing his nose on an eight-pound volume while trying to make it past page 3 in the prone position?

That's why my spirit is weak. Deep within me has been this growing fear of just pumping out another thick, boring book on doctrine that looks good but reads bad.

THEOLOGY NEEDS TO BE INTERESTING

Since I am committed to accuracy, clarity, and practicality, I loathe the thought of publishing something that is anything but interesting, easily understood, creative—and, yes, even captivating. See why my desire to write a book on doctrine has been on the back burner so long? It isn't easy to communicate the deepest truths of the Bible in an interesting manner. It has taken years for me to be convinced that it can be done . . . and even more years to be convinced that I may be able to do it. The chapters that follow are my best effort at accomplishing this objective. Only time will tell whether I have achieved my desire.

If my stuff makes sense, if the average individual is able to follow my thinking, picture the scenes, grasp my logic, come to similar conclusions, and later pass on a few of those thoughts to someone else, then the book will have made the impact I desired. But if it lacks real substance, or if the reader discovers it requires a graduate degree to track my thoughts, or even if it proves to be true to the biblical text yet comes across as tedious and pedantic, then my face, I can assure you, will be as red as your nose.

THE NEED TO IMPROVE
THEOLOGY'S REPUTATION

Frankly, theology has gotten a bum rap. Just ask around. Make up a few questions and try them on for size in your church. You'll see. Many folks, if they are candid with you, will confess a distaste for sound biblical doctrines. Sound theology, like Rodney Dangerfield, "don't get no respect." You question that? Then let me suggest you do your own personal survey among some Christians. Ask things like:

- Ever made a study of the doctrines in the Bible?
- How would you respond if your pastor announced plans to bring a series of pulpit messages on several "important theological subjects"?
- Do you believe that all Christians ought to know where they stand doctrinally, or is that more the business of the clergy?
- When you hear the word "theology," do you have a mental image of something interesting and stimulating? Or do you honestly think, "Dull stuff . . . please don't bore me"?
- On a scale of one to ten (ten being most important), how high would you rate a knowledge of theology?
- Can you remember a doctrinal sermon—or one lesson on theology you were involved in—that you actually *enjoyed*?
- Choosing your preference, rearrange these topics in the order you consider most interesting and timely. Which interests you the most? The least? Give each a number from one to seven.

   ___ a biographical look at a biblical character
   ___ a verse-by-verse analysis of a book in the New Testament
   ___ a serious study of biblical doctrines
   ___ what God's Word teaches about the home and family
   ___ moral, social, and ethical issues according to Scripture
   ___ biblical principles for success and personal motivation
   ___ Proverbs made practical for today

Unless you are most unusual, the study of doctrine would be ranked toward the bottom, if not altogether in last place. Compared to success principles on the home and family, "a serious study of biblical doctrines" does not seem nearly as important or relevant to most evangelical congregations. Yet, believe it or not, at the very heart of all those other topics is a great deal of theology.

It is surprising for most Christians to hear that their doctrinal position determines their interpretation and application of Scripture—whether or not they have ever declared themselves doctrinally. What roots are to a tree, the doctrines are to the Christian. From them we draw our emotional stability, our mental food for growth, as well as our spiritual energy and perspective on life itself. By returning to our roots, we determine precisely where we stand. We equip ourselves for living the life God designed for us to live.

WHY IS DOCTRINE OFTEN SO DULL?

If all this is true, then why does the mere mention of theology turn off so many people? Why are most churches full of people programmed to think that doctrine is a synonym for dullness and boredom?

At the risk of appearing ultracritical, I'll be frank with you. Much of the problem lies with theologians who have done a poor job of communicating their subject. No offense, theological scholars, but you are notorious for talking only to yourselves. The language you employ is clergy code-talk, woefully lacking in relevance and reality. The terms you use are in-house jargon, seldom broken down into managable units for people who aren't clued in. You may be accurate and certainly sincere, but your world is like the television series of yesteryear, "One Step Beyond." Please understand that we love you and respect you. No one would dare to question your brilliance. We need your gifts in the Body and we admire your ability to stay at the disciplines of your studies. We just don't understand you.

As a result, much of what you write is kept within those cloistered chambers that intimidate people who haven't had the privilege of probing the heavenlies as you have. The majority feel a distance from you when you share your secrets. I realize that many of you wish this weren't so, but I suppose it comes with the territory.

In this book, my hope is to build a bridge of theological understanding with the common man, the uninitiated individual, the person who has never been to seminary—and doesn't care to go—but really does want to develop a solid network of doctrinal roots.

I'm interested in reaching the truck driver, the athlete, the waitress, the high school student, the person in the military service, the homemaker who has a houseful of kids at her feet, the business person whose world is practical, earthy, tough, and relentless . . . and a hundred other "types" who have the brains to absorb biblical truth but lack the time and patience to look up every sixth or seventh word in a dictionary.

I therefore make no apology for approaching various subjects in a different way than standard theologians. I want everyone who picks up this book to understand every word and grasp every principle, even if you don't agree with them. (To disagree with me is not only your privilege—I expect it. In fact, I invite it. But to misunderstand or to *fail* to understand what I'm getting at would be tragic.)

I freely confess that I want you to enjoy this journey . . . to find out that discovering doctrine and seeing its importance can encourage you like nothing else. I want us to laugh together, as well as think together, as we dig into the Book. It's been my observation for the past twenty-five years of ministry that there is no subject too deep for anyone to understand if the material is presented creatively and clearly, sparked periodically by humor, and accompanied by illustrations that let plenty of light in. All this is true of folks who really want to learn.

By the way, that brings up another reason doctrine is dull to some people. As I implied earlier, they have a built-in, longstanding *prejudice* against it. Somehow, they have convinced themselves that (a) they don't need to fuss around with heady stuff like that since they aren't doing "full-time ministry," or (b) even if they made a study of the doctrines, all that knowledge would be of little practical value. In subtle ways these two excuses tend to plug their ears and clog the learning process.

Without trying to perform an overkill, both of those excuses are totally erroneous. Because every Christian is "doing full-time ministry," being theologically informed and equipped could not be more important. And since when does a knowledge of important facts lack practical value? If I recall Jesus' words correctly, that which makes us free is knowing the truth. It's ignorance that binds us, not knowledge. Furthermore, we are left defenseless before the cults and other persuasive false teachers if we lack this solid network of doctrinal roots. As I stated earlier, it stabilizes us.

An Approach That Will Keep Things Interesting

Before we get underway, let me explain my plan of approach.

I have no intention of writing an exhaustive theological treatment on all the biblical doctrines. (If you happen to be a perfectionist, expecting every jot and tittle to be addressed in this one volume, please read that sentence again.) My plan is to offer a broad-brush approach to most of the essential points of evangelical truth. If you find certain details are not covered to your satisfaction or if you observe that some subjects of interest to you are not even mentioned, just remember that is on purpose. I'm hoping to whet your appetite for a much more intense and thorough study *on your own* once you've begun to get excited about these essential areas. Who knows? Maybe one day *you'll* be the one who will write a more thorough and analytical work. Be my guest.

And speaking of being thorough, you may stumble across a term here and there that is unfamiliar to you—or perhaps you'd like to know it's precise meaning. For your assistance I have included a glossary of terms at the end of my book (beginning on page 411) where many of the lesser-known, theologically-related terms are listed in alphabetical order and defined in an easy-to-understand manner. Don't hesitate to stop and check out any word that isn't crystal clear. The last thing I want to do is contribute more mumbo-jumbo gobbledygook that clouds the truth or leaves it indefinite and fuzzy. I hope the glossary will be well-worn by the time you finish reading these chapters.

You'll also want to keep a Bible handy. I'll try to quote as many of the main verses and passages as possible. But there will be times that I will give an additional reference or two which you might want to look up right then. If you have the time, please do that. Before too long you will begin to feel much more at home in the Scriptures. And use a good study Bible rather than a loose paraphrase or a copy of just the New Testament.

At the end of each chapter you will note several thoughts I call "Root Issues." These are simply practical suggestions designed to help you keep the doctrines out of the realm of sterile theory and in touch with the real world. To get the most out of these, I'd recommend that you purchase a handy-sized spiral notebook—your personal "Root Issues Notebook"—to record your thoughts, observations, and responses.

TEN MAJOR AREAS OF DOCTRINE

Finally, the outline I want to follow will be interwoven through the chapters. All the doctrines I want to cover will fall within these ten major categories:

- The Bible
- God the Father
- The Lord Jesus Christ
- The Holy Spirit
- The Depravity of Humanity

- Salvation
- The Return of Christ
- Resurrection
- The Body of Christ
- The Family of God

As I mentioned earlier, the list is purposely not exhaustive, but there is plenty here to get our roots firmly in place. In fact, the better-known historic creeds down through the ages have included these ten areas. While considering this recently, I decided to write my own doctrinal credo, a statement of my personal faith. What it may lack in theological sophistication I have tried to make up for in practical terminology.

As I return to the roots of my faith, I am encouraged to find the time-honored foundations firmly intact:

- I affirm my confidence in God's inerrant Word. I treasure its truths and I respect its reproofs.
- I acknowledge the Creator-God as my heavenly Father, infinitely perfect, and intimately acquainted with all my ways.
- I claim Jesus Christ as my Lord—very God who came in human flesh—the object of my worship and the subject of my praise.
- I recognize the Holy Spirit as the third member of the Godhead, incessantly at work convicting, convincing, and comforting.
- I confess that Adam's fall into sin left humanity without the hope of heaven apart from a new birth, made possible by the Savior's death and bodily resurrection.
- I believe the offer of salvation is God's love-gift to all. Those who accept it by faith, apart from works, become new creatures in Christ.
- I anticipate my Lord's promised return, which could occur at any moment.
- I am convinced that all who have died will be brought back from beyond—believers to everlasting communion with God and unbelievers to everlasting separation from God.
- I know the Lord is continuing to enlarge His family, the universal Body of Christ, over which He rules as Head.
- I am grateful to be a part of a local church which exists to proclaim God's truth, to administer the ordinances, to stimulate growth toward maturity, and to bring glory to God.

With confidence and joy, I declare this to be a statement of the essentials of my faith.

That's where I stand . . . sort of a preview of coming attractions. Now it's time for you to dig in and discover where you stand. With God's help I think you will find this study one of the most important and interesting projects you have ever undertaken. You may even get so "fanatical" about your faith that your whole perspective on life changes.

Come to think of it, that's exactly what Christianity is supposed to do . . . change our lives.

I wish to express my thanks to Larry Libby and Brenda Jose at Multnomah Press for their untiring commitment to and competent assistance in this rather involved project. And, once again, I thank my long-term, splendid secretary as I have so many times before. Helen Peters has done it again. Without regard for her own needs and preferences, she has deciphered my hand scratching, typed and retyped my manuscript, verified my footnotes, corrected my spelling, and helped me meet my deadlines. "Thank you" seems hardly sufficient to declare the depth of my gratitude.

And now let's dig in. You have stumbled your way through shifting sand long enough. May this book on Bible doctrine give you just the help you need so that you can stand firmly and finally on a foundation that is solid as rock.

Charles R. Swindoll
Fullerton, California

But his delight is in the law of the Lord
and on his law he meditates day and night ...

Doctrine and Discernment

"And this is my prayer: that your love may abound more and more in knowledge and depth of insight, so that you may be able to discern what is best . . ." (Philippians 1:9-10 NIV).

THE VALUE
OF KNOWING
THE SCOOP

*J*osh Billings was a humorist in the nineteenth century. On one occasion he said, "It is better not to know so much than to know so many things that ain't so." Which I suppose could be paraphrased, "Whatever ya know oughta be so!"

Jaime O'Neill, on the other hand, is a teacher in the twentieth century. The man has taught for about fifteen years in community colleges and currently teaches in a college in the state of Washington. Over the years O'Neill has become increasingly concerned about the lack of knowledge among so many of his students. It's not that he was concerned about their lack of technical knowledge or complex facts, but that so many of the general "facts" they thought they knew just "ain't so."

One day he decided to do something about it. Hoping to demonstrate to his students just how lacking they were in the basics—not simply to expose or to take pot shots at their ignorance, but to help them see that they had a problem and they could hide it no longer—he devised an eighty-six-question quiz on general knowledge. He gave it to his college English class.

There were twenty-six people in the classroom, ranging in age from eighteen to fifty-four, all of whom had completed at least one quarter of college work. Remember now, these eighty-six questions were not what you would call complex, technical, or tricky. They were simple facts about the world around them—facts about people, facts about geography, facts about life in general. Professor O'Neill was so startled by what he discovered that he recorded his findings and later wrote about them in *Newsweek* in an article entitled "No Allusions in the Classroom." Here's a sampling of what he found that "ain't so."

> Ralph Nader is a baseball player. Charles Darwin invented gravity. Christ was born in the 16th century. J. Edgar Hoover was a 19th-century president. . . . "The Great Gatsby" was a magician in the 1930s. Franz Joseph Haydn was a songwriter who lived during the same decade. Sid Caesar was an early Roman emperor. Mark Twain invented the cotton gin. . . . Jefferson Davis played guitar for the Jefferson Airplane. Benito Mussolini was a Russian leader of the 18th century; Dwight D. Eisenhower came earlier, serving as a president during the 17th century. . . . Socrates [was an] American Indian chieftain. . .

He adds:

> My students were equally creative in their understanding of geography. They knew, for instance, that Managua is the capital of Vietnam, that Cape Town is in the United States, and that Beirut is in Germany. Bogotá, of course, is in Borneo (unless it is in China). Camp David is in Israel, and Stratford-on-Avon is in Grenada (or Gernada). Gdansk is in Ireland. Cologne is in the Virgin Islands. Mazatlán is in Switzerland. Belfast was variously located in Egypt, Germany, Belgium and Italy. Leningrad was transported to Jamaica; Montreal to Spain.

> And on and on it went. Most students answered incorrectly far more often than they answered correctly. Several of them meticulously wrote "I don't know" 86 times, or 80 times, or 62 times. . . .

> As I write this, the radio is broadcasting the news about the Walker family. Accused of spying for the Soviets, the Walkers, according to a U. S. attorney, will be the Rosenbergs of the '80s. One of my students thought Ethel Rosenberg was a singer from the 1930s. The rest of them didn't know.

> As we enter the postindustrial "information processing" age, what sort of information will be processed? . . . [1]

As I smiled, shook my head, and laughed my way through that article, I was suddenly seized with the realization that general knowledge is fast slipping from us. For many, many years Americans have been considered a people who are supposed to be fairly well educated. No longer can we make this assumption. This makes me nervous. I get a little fearful over the ignorance that sweeps our television-addicted generation—the attitude that if someone doesn't do it for me, I'm not interested . . . or if someone doesn't think for me, I am not desirous of learning for myself.

IGNORANCE IS NOT BLISS

I want to state openly and forcefully that ignorance is not bliss—that ignorance, even in the general, secular realm, is the breeding ground for fear and prejudice, leading ultimately to superstition and slavery. An uneducated country is a defenseless country at the mercy of an educated country. Although I study every week, after reading that article I suddenly wanted to study harder. I love to read and do research, but I found myself wanting to drink deeper at the fountain of knowledge.

Before going one step further, let me address all of you who make your living in the world of education. I have four words of encouragement: *Press on—never quit!* And to you who are in the process of getting an education, I offer the same counsel: Press on. Never stop studying. Never stop reading. Never stop learning. Don't believe something just because someone says it. Find out for yourself!

I read recently that an education is nothing more than going from an unconscious to a conscious awareness of one's ignorance. There is so much to be discovered!

What is true in the realm of general knowledge is equally true in the realm of spiritual knowledge. Talk about knowing things that "ain't so," I am constantly amazed at the level of *biblical* ignorance in these United States. Aren't you? I was watching the presidential elections in 1984. A well-known news commentator wanted to make reference to the Old Testament book of 2 Chronicles. His notes, no doubt, used the Roman numeral two (II). As he read the line from the script, he called it "eleven Chronicles." The man may be culturally suave and politically sophisticated, but he has no idea how many Chronicles there are! He doesn't mean to sound foolish; he just cannot hide the fact that he is ignorant of the Scriptures.

That's bad enough for a person who doesn't claim to be a Christian, but how about you?

What if someone gave you a piece of paper with eighty-six questions on it—just basic information about your faith? How would you do? Or what if someone came rapping at your door tomorrow morning and said, "I would like to talk with you about this wonderful class we have. We're meeting with some of your neighbors and we're studying the Bible together. We'd like you to attend the class with us." The more the two of you talk, the more you realize this person is not from your church and doesn't represent your faith. Later on, the same individual makes these comments, "Oh, I understand where you're coming from. You must really live under the delusion that Jesus is God. Do you realize . . . ?" And then he and his partner quote three or four verses that seem to contradict the deity of Christ.

How would you do in that situation? Could you stand alone and convince them otherwise?

Or perhaps you've picked up a very convincing piece of literature that makes an attack against the Scriptures and says, in effect, "Really, it's the work of man. Those men who wrote the Scriptures were zealous and sincere, but not actually 'inspired.' That which has been passed on to us really isn't that credible." As you read those words, could you convince yourself the information was unreliable? To do so requires knowing the scoop. Do you?

There is a great section of Scripture in the New Testament that contains some words of exhortation about our growing up as we learn and discover truth for ourselves.

> *And who is there to harm you if you prove zealous for what is good? But even if you should suffer for the sake of righteousness, you are blessed. And do not fear their intimidation, and do not be troubled, but sanctify Christ as Lord in your hearts, <u>always being ready to make a defense</u> to everyone who asks you to give an account for the hope that is in you, yet with gentleness and reverence; and keep a good conscience so that in the thing in which you are slandered, those who revile your good behavior in Christ may be put to shame* (1 Peter 3:13-16, emphasis mine).

The first-century recipients of Peter's letter were hurting. They were suffering people. So Peter writes to encourage them, lest they become intimidated and fearful. That's why, in the midst of this word of encouragement, he drops a comment about their being able to "make a defense" of their faith. And it isn't just a casual comment exclusively reserved for ancient Christians. It is truth for all Christians in every generation. It's a command.

Look closely at verse 15 once again:

> *But sanctify Christ as Lord in your hearts, always being ready to make a defense to everyone who asks you to give an account for the hope that is in you, yet with gentleness and reverence.*

The words "make a defense" come from the Greek term *apologia*. We get our word "apologetic" or "apology" from it. Not in the sense of apologizing or saying you're sorry for something. The idea of "apology" carries with it the thought of a formal justification, a convincing defense. Let's use those words: "Always being ready to make a formal justification or to give a convincing defense to any one who asks." Not only for our sakes, but for younger and less mature Christians who may not be able to defend themselves. God often exhorts His people to have a good deal of biblical savvy.

KNOWING THE SCOOP
IS OFTEN EMPHASIZED IN SCRIPTURE

Let me take you on a brief scriptural safari. This journey will take us quickly through the Scriptures. In the ancient days under Moses, God was so concerned that His people know His truth that He, with His finger as it were, wrote His laws into stone. Moses brought the stone tablets down from a mountain in his arms. He presented them to the people and explained that these words were to be a guide for their lives. God wanted His people to know His truth.

Before the people marched into Canaan, Moses pulled the Israelites aside for a final review. The book of Deuteronomy contains his sermons [*deutero*, "second"; *nomos*, "Law" or "a repetition of the Law"]. It is a book in which Moses repeats and applies the Law as he delivers no less than seven sermons to the people of God. In the sixth chapter of Deuteronomy he tells the fathers and mothers to take the truth of God and instruct their children in it, because the children were soon to be exposed to a whole new lifestyle that would cut across the grain of their belief and faith in one God. They would soon be moving into a land characterized by idolatry and polygamy. They would be exposed to a whole new way of thinking. So Moses said ahead of time, "These children must *know* the truth. Teach them." Pause and read Deuteronomy 6 for yourself—great chapter!

As early as the days of Samuel, a school of the prophets had been established. Such a school was made up of a body of men who were interested in honing their skills and becoming spokesmen for God. They trained at the feet of Samuel and other men of God. They became known as prophets of God who knew God's truths.

In the days of captivity, God's continual reproof to His people was, "You did not act upon what you knew. You acted in ignorance."

They failed to apply the theology they had been taught, hence, they fell into captivity in a foreign land.

In the days of Jesus, how often our Lord looked at the scribes and Pharisees and rebuked them with the words, "Do you not *know*? Have you not *read*?" He said that to the clergy of His day. "Why are you ignorant of what the scrolls say?"

When Jesus departed from the earth, He left the Church in the hands of the apostles. They wrote letters to both churches and individuals. The letters contain truth for us to read, to learn, to put to use, to pass on to others. Frequently, we find words like "know this" and "stand fast" and "I would not have you to be ignorant about" and "be ready to defend your faith" threaded through those letters. Throughout the Bible God's repeated command to the people of God is "learn, study, grow, equip your mind with My words so that you can defend your position when asked about it or when faced with attack."

Just this past week I did a brief analysis of church history. As I surveyed the subject, I was encouraged and refreshed all over again by the lives of men and women who took the Book seriously and, when necessary, laid down their lives for it. Some of them wrote our creeds which exist today. Some of them gave us the dogma upon which we stand. They systematized our theology. Others gave us our hymns so that we could sing our faith. And, in fact, they wrote catechisms for the young so that children might be cultivated in a knowledge of the truth. Our own American heritage finds many of our principles rooted in the pages of Scripture. It wasn't uncommon for higher education to be interwoven with biblical truth.

Do you know how long it was that our forefathers stayed on this continent before they established a school of higher learning? A mere sixteen years. They survived those bitter winters. They built their houses. As early as possible they established their government. Some then devoted themselves to establishing an educational center in a little place called Newtown, which was later changed to Cambridge. And they named that school, the first American school of higher learning, after a thirty-one-year-old clergyman who had died prematurely. He had left his library and half his estate to the school. His name was John Harvard.

Ever read the cornerstone at Harvard University? When I ministered at Massachusetts, back in the mid 1960s, I remember driving down to that campus. It was during a harsh winter storm that I stood knee deep in snow near the wall that contained the etched cornerstone. I wiped the ice and snow off the bronze plate and copied these words:

> After God had carried us safe to New England and wee had built our houses, provided necessaries for our livelihood, reared convenient places for God's worship, and settled the civil government, one of the next things wee longed for and looked after was to advance learning and perpetuate to posterity, dreading to leave an illiterate ministry to the churches when our present ministers shall lie in the dust.

Think of it! The very first institution of higher learning was established to give to the colonies a literate ministry, a body of thinking, devoted, biblically committed believers who would stand in the gap, who would have a knowledge of the truth that was strong and firm and courageous against the attack of the enemy, for surely such attacks would come. How essential it is that we who claim to love the Lord and commit ourselves to the truth in His Word *know* where we stand!

SIX BENEFITS OF BEING SPIRITUALLY INFORMED

Why is it so important to be well grounded in the truth of God? Why bother to know the scoop? Why not leave that responsibility to the missionary and minister? Let me suggest six specific reasons. There may be many more, but these six are essential. Each one is something we must personally enter into.

1. *Knowledge gives substance to faith.* On what do those who do not know the truth rely? On emotion, on feelings, on someone else's opinion, on a book, on tradition, or some other empty, humanistic hope. And the result? Their faith lacks substance. That is especially revealing when they are under attack or when testing comes. That thought introduces the next benefit.

2. *Knowledge stabilizes us during times of testing.* When we know what God has said, and then we go through a period of pain when the bottom virtually drops out of our life, we don't panic, we don't doubt, we don't ship the faith. The knowledge we have gained stabilizes us and equips us with essential, calming fortitude when the tests come.

3. *Knowledge enables us to handle the Bible accurately.* By knowing the general themes of Scripture, we are better able to handle the Scriptures intelligently and wisely. A working knowledge of the doctrines, for example, gives us confidence in using Scripture.

4. *Knowledge equips us to detect and confront error.* As I mentioned earlier, when you know where you stand spiritually, no one can get

you off course. When you're hearing erroneous information, you don't need someone to nudge you and say, "Did you get that? Listen to that. That's not true, is it?" Or, "You know, in light of what Scripture teaches, what he just presented is out of whack." Why? Because you have gone to the trouble to know the scoop. You can't be intimidated. Your antennae have been sensitized.

5. *It makes us confident in our daily walk.* Show me a person who stumbles along in the Christian faith, and I'll show you a person who isn't exposing himself or herself to a consistent intake of the Scriptures. The learning process has somehow been stifled, interrupted, or put on "hold." Biblical knowledge and personal confidence are like Siamese twins, inseparably linked together.

6. *A good foundation of spiritual truth filters out our fears and superstitions.* How important! I think we would all be amazed if we knew how many people operated their lives from superstition and fear. God's truth has a way of silencing those erroneous voices that would otherwise siphon our inner energy and immobilize us.

Before proceeding any further, let's take the time to meditate on two passages of Scripture. I will quote the first from the Modern Language Bible: Hosea 4:1-6. The other will be a paraphrase from The Living Bible: Amos 8:11-13. Both are from minor prophets who had a major message for their times and ours as well.

> *Listen to the word of the Lord, sons of Israel; for the Lord has a charge against the dwellers of the land, because there is no fidelity, no kindness, no knowledge of God in the land. There is swearing, lying, murder, theft, adultery, violent outbreaks, bloodshed after bloodshed. Wherefore the land mourns, and everything living in it languishes. . . .*

> *Even at that, let no one enter complaint; let no one bring accusation, for My people are like their priestlings. You priests! You stumble by day; the prophet, too, stumbles with you by night, . . . My people perish for lack of knowledge, and because you have rejected knowledge, I reject you from being priest to Me. Since you have forgotten the law of your God, I, too, will forget. . . .* (Hosea 4:1-6, MLB).

> *"The time is surely coming," says the Lord God, "when I will send a famine on the land—not a famine of bread or water, but of hearing the words of the Lord. Men will wander everywhere from sea to sea, seeking the Word of the Lord, searching, running here and going there, and will not find it. Beautiful girls and fine young men alike will grow faint and weary, thirsting for the Word of God"* (Amos 8:11-13, TLB).

Even though those two prophecies are many centuries old, they slice through the fog of our times and speak with incredible relevance today. Is there not a devastating famine in our land? Is there not a thirst for the unadulterated truth of God?

Periodically, I am invited to speak to groups of people who wish to know more of what God's Word teaches. I have, on certain occasions, begun those sessions by saying, "I am here today because there is a famine in the land—but not the kind of famine sweeping across India or sections of Africa. This famine is in America and most other places on earth. Not a famine of food or water . . . not a famine of churches or religious ministries. This is a famine like the ancient prophets mentioned—a famine of hearing the truth of the Word of God." To support those statements, I will often read the prophesies from Hosea and Amos.

Invariably, heads begin to nod in agreement. After such sessions I have interacted with people who respond to those words by relating how starved they are for the life-giving, encouraging, enlightening instruction of Scripture.

The teaching of biblical doctrine is as rare as it is valuable! Yet I'm not suggesting that such doctrinal knowledge is an end in itself, but a means to an end. Those who hope to survive with any measure of emotional sanity and mental stability must have a solid diet of sound biblical theology, clearly understood, consistently digested, regularly put into action.

SOUND DOCTRINE IS INVALUABLE

For the next few moments, let's consider some equally vital words written to a young pastor named Timothy. The letter is 1 Timothy, chapter 4. This chapter, written to a minister at a local church in the city of Ephesus, contains special instructions on various subjects related to the ministry. The first six verses have to do with that which will occur in later times. Certainly, our own times would be included in that phrase, "in later times."

> *But the Spirit explicitly says that in later times some will fall away from the faith, paying attention to deceitful spirits and doctrines of demons, by means of the hypocrisy of liars seared in their own conscience as with a branding iron, men who forbid marriage and advocate abstaining from foods, which God has created to be gratefully shared in by those who believe and know the truth. For everything created by God is good, and nothing is to be rejected,*

if it is received with gratitude; for it is sanctified by means of the word of God and prayer. In pointing out these things to the brethren, you will be a good servant of Christ Jesus, constantly nourished on the words of the faith and of the sound doctrine which you have been following (1 Timothy 4:1-6).

The writer (Paul) begins rather forcefully: "But the Spirit explicitly says . . ." Before proceeding, pause long enough to understand the force of those five opening words, especially the term *explicitly*. Why would he add "explicitly"? Why wouldn't he just say, "the Spirit says," or "thus says the Lord"? Because "explicitly" adds emphasis to what is to follow. The term *explicitly* (and it's used only here in all the New Testament) means "expressly, most assuredly in stated terms." It is introducing an unequivocal fact. Not merely a hunch or a pretty good idea that will probably occur. No, this is absolutely reliable information.

I thought of that word "explicitly" while I was reading about earthquakes some time ago. While doing some research on those horrible experiences that our southern neighbors in Mexico City endured, I came across these lines:

> In this country, geologists say that a major earthquake not only can but will strike somewhere in California with appalling loss of life and enormous property damage. A quake of a magnitude greater than 8.0— . . . has a 50-50 chance of happening on the southern section of the San Andreas fault within the next 30 years, according to estimates prepared for the National Security Council. Estimates are that it will kill between 3,000 and 13,000 people, depending on the time of day.[2]

Geologists, in the words of 1 Timothy 4, explicitly state that a major earthquake will hit California, which happens to be my place of residence! It isn't simply a theory. It isn't an exaggerated scare tactic based on some fanatic's hunch or a haunting idea; it is fact.

By the way, when I was reading that article, someone on the second floor of our home cranked up the vacuum cleaner. I will never forget that moment! I almost lost it when the very moment I read that frightening fact I began hearing noises and feeling vibrations. I experienced *explicit* panic!

The Spirit *explicitly* states that something is a fact . . . a fact that is even more sure than the prediction of a California earthquake. What? "That in later times some will fall away from the faith." The Greek term translated "fall away" is the same word we use in English—*apostasize,* "abandon, withdraw from, leave." In today's terms: "In later times, some will bail out theologically."

Why? Why would someone want to leave something as marvelous as the Christian faith? Why would anyone choose to defect in doctrine? We are told why: "Because they will begin to pay attention to deceitful spirits"—that's the *style* of teaching they'll get exposed to, "and doctrines of demons"—that's the *source* of such teaching. We don't like to call it that. In our devil-ignoring, demon-denying era, we're reluctant to suggest such radical thoughts (and nothing could delight our adversary more!), but Scripture clearly states that he is behind the scenes of spiritual apostasy. It is satanic in source. There will be doctrines that come from the pit, but they will be deceitfully displayed as truth—convincingly so.

How? Verse 2:

> *by means of the hypocrisy of liars seared in their own conscience as with a branding iron.*

False teachers have no qualms about leading people into the realm of error. They're convinced that what they are teaching is true. Along with an abundance of charisma, they have the ability to persuade others to buy into their position. And they have what they call "facts" to pull you away from where you stand. Again, this is not some superficial scare tactic from a wild-eyed fanatic . . . it is true. Remember the Spirit *explicitly* warns of such.

And to go a step further, Paul, the writer, mentions the teaching of one of the first-century heresies: gnosticism. Gnostics taught that matter was evil, and that whatever was physically pleasing to humans was spiritually displeasing to God—which would include things like marriage and eating certain foods. So they taught, "You're not to marry, and you shouldn't eat certain foods."

> *men who forbid marriage and advocate abstaining from foods, which God has created to be gratefully shared in by those who believe and know the truth* (v. 3).

Interestingly, we don't find the apostle Paul biting off his nails and churning within, wondering, "How do I respond to these things? Could they be true?"

He simply says, "But that's not true!"

How could Paul be so sure that what the Gnostics taught wasn't true?

> *For everything created by God is good, and nothing is to be rejected, if it is received with gratitude; for it is sanctified by means of the word of God and prayer* (vv. 4-5).

He was confident and calm in the face of heresy because he knew the theological scoop. In fact, he gives wise, needed counsel to all who are ministers of the gospel. In verse 6 he says:

In pointing out these things to the brethren, you will be a good servant of Christ Jesus. . . .

In other words, Timothy, here's how you're to spend much of your time:

constantly nourished on the words of the faith and of the sound doctrine which you have been following.

Isn't that helpful? That one statement gives ministers (especially pastors) a large part of their job description. We are responsible for nourishing ourselves in the Book, consistently and faithfully. And the longer we are in ministry, the more we *need* to be nourished, because the greater the pressure, the more the problems, the more the temptations, the more the calendar will get filled with other things.

Today I could not be more thankful for the doctrinally sound graduate school where I studied, for mentors who loved the truth and helped me understand it, for parents who taught me the way, for a wife who helped put me through the earlier years of my higher education, for congregations who patiently prayed and believed and encouraged me as I forged out my theology right up to this present moment. I am grateful for so many who had a hand in my learning, growing experience. By the way, it is still going on!

My question to you is this: Where are *you* in the learning process? Are you learning your way through God's Book? Is doctrine important to you? Or do you think of it as dull, irrelevant stuff? Hopefully, by the time you've worked your way through this book, you will be more convinced than ever that doctrine—rather than being dull—is downright essential and exciting. We must never stop learning and growing in our faith!

Let me make it even more practical. Would you ever think of going to a physician who had decided to stop studying? I doubt it. I don't think anyone would ever say to his wife who was in need of medical help, "Just check the Yellow Pages, honey. Any one of those guys with 'M.D.' after his name is fine." Never! We select only the ones we respect. And even then, we may get a second and sometimes a third opinion. We check into their credibility, their credentials, their reputation. Why? We want to know if the physician diagnosing our ailment is still growing, if he or she is still learning, still practicing good medicine. The same could be said for an attorney who takes our complicated case and defends us before a court of law. Because we are at the mercy of the person's intelligence, integrity, and knowledge of law, we want to be certain of his or her practice.

One of my major objectives in this book is to help equip you to stand firm amidst the strong and subtle currents of our day. In Paul's words, to explain "the words of the faith" and to offer reliable instruction in "sound doctrine" (1 Timothy 4:6). In the pages that follow I want to help you realize the value of knowing the scoop about the Bible, the Trinity, our Heavenly Father, the Lord Jesus, His Son, the Holy Spirit, mankind, sin, justification by grace through faith apart from works, the subject of salvation, the return of Christ, the resurrection of the dead, the universal Church as well as the local church, its ordinances, and the family relationships that should be enjoyed among Christians. I'll do my best to keep it interesting and clear if you will do your best to concentrate—mentally devoting yourself to each subject.

But just at this very point, a warning is in order. An intellectual knowledge of doctrine—by itself—can be dangerous.

KNOWLEDGE ALONE CAN BE DANGEROUS

As I conclude this chapter, I should warn us against some of the dangers of knowledge. I can think of at least four:

1. Knowledge can be dangerous when it lacks scriptural support—intelligent, biblical support. Knowledge just for knowledge's sake is a heady thing and can turn into pride. God's Word frequently warns us about being full of knowledge and feeling "puffed up" because of it.

2. Knowledge can be dangerous when it becomes an end in itself. God gave us His truth so that we may put it into practice, not simply store it up.

3. Knowledge can be dangerous when it isn't balanced by love and grace. Such knowledge results in arrogance, which leads to an intolerant spirit . . . an exclusive mindset.

Ever been around a group of people who think they've got a corner on the truth? I call this "the Bible club" mentality. And because you're not in it, you're out to lunch and they're cool. That's a dangerous thing. When knowledge leads to an intolerance of other people, it has gone beyond proper bounds. Knowledge that isn't balanced with love and grace is truth gone to seed.

4. Knowledge can be dangerous when it remains theoretical—when it isn't mixed with discernment and action. More on that in the next chapter.

Now, I know there are some who are thinking, "Hey, Chuck, give me a break, man. I'm getting up in years. I've paid my dues. You minister-types can get all excited about that truth, but it's enough to know I'm saved. I'm not going to hell. I know I'm gonna be with Jesus when I die. Just don't make me think. I'm tired. Just tell me, and I'll believe it."

Do you know the problem with that kind of response, my friend? It's that you've forgotten that you have people around you who respect you and need you to stand firm. They look up to you. And they rely on you to know. You may not like to read this, but in some ways you're their theological defense. They *need* you to know the scoop.

I love the way C. S. Lewis put it:

> If all the world were Christian it might not matter if all the world were uneducated. But, as it is, a cultural life will exist outside the church whether it exists inside or not. To be ignorant and simple now—not to be able to meet the enemies on their own ground—would be to throw down our weapons, and to betray our uneducated brethren who have, under God, no defense but us against the intellectual attacks of the heathen.

Then he concludes:

> Good philosophy must exist, if for no other reason, because bad philosophy needs to be answered. The cool intellect must work not only against cool intellect on the other side, but against the muddy heathen mysticisms which deny intellect altogether. Most of all, perhaps, we need intimate knowledge of the past . . . the learned life then is, for some, a duty.[3]

Our problem is not that we know so many things, it's that we know so much that just "ain't so." My hope is that this book will help clear that out of the way so we can find out what *is* so.

For most of us that's more than a nice idea. It's a duty.

1. Picture in your mind a friend or relative who is younger in the faith than you—perhaps still wrestling with some of the basics of belief in Christ. Picture this individual experiencing a sudden tragedy or crushing disappointment—or perhaps an encounter with a deceptive false teacher. Your friend, really struggling, looks to you for help. Is your grip on Bible knowledge strong enough to help your friend cope? Could you point him or her in the right direction? As you begin this book pray, "Lord, for the sake of _____, I commit myself to this study." Write that person's name on a piece of paper and use it for a bookmark. It will be a reminder that a return to your roots may help others who look to you, as much as it helps yourself.

2. Look again at Deuteronomy 6:4-9. If you are a parent of young children, visualize each of the "teaching opportunities" mentioned in verse 7. How might some of these opportunities be captured for God in your home and in your schedule? Note that this verse speaks specifically of teaching your children "on the way." In those early biblical days there was a great deal of time to talk as people walked from place to place. How might this same principle translate into our fast-paced, freeway-driving culture? Write these ideas in your personal notebook.

3. First Timothy 4:6 speaks of being *"constantly nourished on the words of the faith and . . . sound doctrine."* What can you change in your daily schedule that would make it easier to draw this kind of nourishment from God's Word? It may be a matter of eliminating time-wasters, or it may be simply a matter of substituting "the best" in place of "the good." Nail down your thoughts by writing them out in your notebook.

DON'T
FORGET TO ADD
A CUP OF
DISCERNMENT

or many people life is two-dimensional—rather plain and drab. It lacks depth and color. Like staring at a blank wall.

There was a period of time in my life when that was true. During that time the most important thing to me was simply the gaining of knowledge. It's not that there was something wrong with that. It's just that something terribly important was missing during that period of my life. My interest was strictly in getting hold of biblical facts . . . gaining a thorough knowledge of scriptural doctrines. I wanted to know what God's Book was all about. I wanted to understand how it fit together. In my pursuit of knowledge, I diligently probed the Bible much like Sergeant Friday in the old "Dragnet" television show. I wanted the facts, "just gimme the facts."

Thanks to the teaching of a very persuasive and powerful minister whose stated desire was to communicate the doctrines of the Bible, I became virtually brainwashed with his approach and system of thinking. And all who sat under his ministry for very long had the same mind-bending experience. A knowledge of doctrine became our watchword. Everyone outside our circle was judged on the basis of how much they knew. And since they never seemed to know as much as we did, we looked down our noses at them! I don't believe I was ever more legalistic than during those years, even though all of us in the group would never have admitted such a thing. I mean, legalism was something *other* people demonstrated, not us.

I absorbed an enormous amount of information, some of which I came to realize later was spurious. But I did begin to grasp a measure of truth, and that was stimulating to me because I was so blatantly ignorant of how the Scriptures fit together. As I look back and reflect on those days, I must confess I grew, not only in knowledge, but every bit as much in pride . . . a pride so hideous it was like a growing cancer in my life. What I gained in knowledge I lacked in compassion and care for others. There was a lack of tolerance for people who would not agree with my system of thought. Other Christians became increasingly less important to me. In addition, non-Christians were virtually outside the scope of my inner radar screen.

While I was growing in biblical facts, I was diminishing in what we might call the third dimension of life; color, depth of character, a broader appreciation for the whole of living. My joy was conspicuous by its absence as I became more demanding, more rigid. And I'm not the rigid type! I became more structured. And I am not that much of a structured person in my personality. Furthermore, very little creativity flowed through my mind. My world was reduced to a spectrum of blacks and whites and a very few grays. No color. No beauty. No cushion. No room for people who happened to disagree. Not much laughter and, most unfortunately . . . not much love. God became a lifeless deity to be studied, a sterile caricature put together in an outline of theological topics, well systematized and perfectly memorized.

Looking back on all that, what I gained was intellectual knowledge and what I lacked was wise discernment. And rather than cultivating an open mind to new truth and open arms for new people, I pushed them away. I realize now, with much regret, that I became a blind slave to a system of thought rather than a discerning servant of the living God, committed not only to His principles but also to His people.

I had grown in knowledge . . . but not in grace.

Now, why do I unload all this? Because I want to save you from the same pitfall. And because I want you to remember all the way through this book on doctrine that these truths are to enhance our walk with God and our relationship with others, not *hinder* it. To borrow from Solomon, let's learn wisdom and understanding along with biblical facts. Let's learn a fear of the Lord as well as the Word of the Lord.

Please don't misunderstand. I plan to deal with facts. I hope they will be interesting. I hope they will be presented in a logical, believable, and easily understood manner. I want you to understand as best you can what Scripture is teaching. But I want you to mix with these facts a full cup of discernment. The last thing I want to happen is that we become a body of strict, narrow-minded, exclusive people who have no room for folks who are not as "informed" as we. If in the process of reading these chapters you become less concerned about the person without Christ, something is missing. Consider it an alarm signal going off in your head. Life was never meant to be two-dimensional. It's multidimensional, because our God is full of beauty, color, variety, depth, and grace. Yes . . . always grace.

LET'S START WITH A FEW DEFINITIONS

Perhaps the best place to start is with several definitions . . . not dictionary definitions but practical, spiritually related definitions.

First of all, what do I mean when I talk about *knowledge*? By knowledge I mean an acquisition of biblical facts, principles, and doctrines. When I write about gaining knowledge, I have in mind an understanding of the great themes and principles of Scripture so that they fit together into a system of thought that assists us in accurately interpreting the whole of Scripture. Knowledge doesn't get emotionally involved. Knowledge alone lacks action. It lacks feelings. Knowledge has to do with the gaining, the gathering, and the relating of facts. And all of this can remain theoretical . . . if you let it.

Turn to 1 Corinthians, chapter 13. Let me show you a place where knowledge appears in this light. Interestingly, it occurs in a chapter on love.

> *If I speak with the tongues of men and of angels, but do not have love, I have become a noisy gong or a clanging cymbal. And if I have the gift of prophecy, and know all mysteries and all knowledge; and if I have all faith, so as to remove mountains, but do not have love, I am nothing* (vv. 1-2).

You remember these words. They begin the most wonderful treatise on love in all of literature. They cannot be improved upon. The reference to "knowledge" in these verses is a factual, doctrinal, theological, biblical kind of knowledge. But don't miss the emphasis: "Let there be love with knowledge!" Without love, all those facts leave us empty . . . "I am nothing."

Turn to 2 Corinthians, chapter 10. Same group of people—first-century Corinthians. Written a little bit later by the same writer, Paul. Second Corinthians 10:3-5 reads:

> *For though we walk in the flesh, we do not war according to the flesh, for the weapons of our warfare are not of the flesh, but divinely powerful for the destruction of fortresses. We are destroying speculations and every lofty thing raised up against the <u>knowledge</u> [there's our word] of God, and we are taking every thought captive to the obedience of Christ [emphasis mine].*

The writer is referring to a knowledge of God, a knowledge about God, a knowledge of His Holy Word. Paul's point is well taken— such knowledge is often the target of our enemy's attack.

So much for knowledge. Next, what do I mean by *discernment?* This is the ability to detect, to recognize, to perceive beyond what is said. Now this may seem a little vague because it's not quite as exact and objective as knowledge. Discernment is the ability to "sense" by means of intuition. It is insight apart from the obvious, outside the realm of facts. People with discernment have the ability to read between the lines.

Think of being with a salesman who wants to sell you a car. In the process of listening to the person for a while, you sense in his presentation that he's not telling you the truth. Obviously, he doesn't have a three-by-five card sticking out of his upper pocket with bold print, reading, "I am a hypocrite. I do not tell the truth." But you say to yourself, "I don't trust this guy—something's not right." Why don't you trust him? Because you have perceived, you have *discerned* something that's either present or lacking in his words, or perhaps in his lack of eye contact or by the way he handles your questions.

Spiritually speaking, discernment enters into the realm of wisdom—the wisdom of God. Solomon specifically prayed for such wisdom.

> *So give Thy servant an understanding heart to judge Thy people to discern between good and evil* . . . (1 Kings 3:9).

"I'm not asking You to make me rich," Solomon was saying. "I'm not asking You to make me famous. I'm not asking You to expand my territory. But I do ask You, O God, to give me discernment, to help me understand, to help me perceive beyond the realm of the visible and the audible."

Discernment includes the idea of sizing up a situation or a person correctly. Spotting evil that's lurking in the shadows. Sensing something that's missing. But it doesn't always have to do with matters of evil. Discernment also helps us sense truth and good. You discern when you are with certain individuals or listening to certain teachers that the person has character. Or that there is a lot of depth in that person's life. You detect that the person is presenting only a bit of what he or she really knows. You sense that there's a lot more behind the counter. Discernment signals such a message when we're with resourceful individuals.

In the second chapter of Proverbs we read about "discerning the fear of the Lord." In the fourth chapter of 1 John it appears again—although not in those precise words:

> *Beloved, do not believe every spirit, but test the spirits to see whether they are from God; because many false prophets have gone out into the world* (v. 1).

A lengthy paraphrase in today's terms might read: "Don't believe everything you hear. Put it to the test. Check it out. Mull it over. Talk it through. Think it out. Check it with Scripture. Be selective. Don't be gullible." Just because a man wears a collar doesn't mean he's to be considered "a godly man." Just because he speaks on radio or television or because he "seems so sincere" doesn't mean that he should be trusted and have your support. Just because he writes religious books or has charisma and presents his material in a persuasive, intriguing, interesting manner doesn't mean he is reputable. The New Testament commands us to test the spirits!

Look next at the first chapter of Philippians. It is verse 9 that interests me, Paul's prayer for the Philippians.

> *And this I pray, that your love may abound still more and more in real knowledge and all discernment.*

This is the only time in the New Testament that the noun "discernment" appears in the *New American Standard Bible.* The original Greek verb means "to perceive." He's praying, in effect, "That you may grow not only in complete knowledge, but in a broad range of perception."

I really wish I could describe to you how that happens, but I simply cannot. I don't believe there's a course you can take in some university on how to become more intuitive. Neither do I believe anyone can spell out the process in a step-by-step, one-two-three-four fashion. Discernment isn't taught as much as it's caught. But it can happen if you let it . . . if you seek it . . . if you spend time with those who model it.

Looking back at my earlier years once again, it's clear now that I didn't bother to cultivate discernment in my life. I was young. I was impressionable. I was caught up in the emotion, the momentum, the brilliance and persuasion of the teacher. I was swept into it along with hundreds of others. Maybe it is more accurate to say thousands. I silenced questions of doubt. I ignored a few inner reservations. Though in my heart I knew some things weren't right, I rationalized around them. I bought the whole package. My reservoir of knowledge was growing . . . but at the expense of my discernment.

Now, thank God, I'm growing in both. I wish I could dispense discernment to you in an easy-to-get fashion so that it could suddenly blossom in your life. I admit again, I cannot. Perhaps the warning is all that's needed to begin with. Be warned! Beware that if you drink at just one fountain, you will lose a great deal of the perspective that God wants to give you. It's like eating one food, or enjoying only one kind of entertainment, or reading only one author, or participating in only one exercise, or wearing only one color. How restrictive, how drab! Remember what Paul wrote: "I pray that you will grow in full knowledge *and discernment*."

There is a third term we need to define. I'm referring to *balance*. Although I haven't stated its importance, balance has been interwoven through most of this chapter. Frankly, it is a major objective of my life. What do I mean when I refer to balance? I have in mind remaining free of extremes, being able to see the whole picture— not just one side or a small part of it.

Maintaining one's spiritual equilibrium is another way to describe balance. Balanced Christians are realistic, tolerant people, patient with those who disagree. Serious when necessary, yet still having fun, still enjoying life. They are less and less intense, free from fanaticism. Furthermore, they are not afraid to say, "I don't know." They're still discovering. They listen to and value another opinion, even one with which they may disagree. They uphold the dignity of others, refusing to put them down. They are not easily threatened. Why? They're *balanced*! They realize they don't have all the truth. They're open to the possibility of alternative positions that give new slants and fresh perspective.

I read somewhere, many years ago, that heresy is nothing more than truth taken to an extreme. Check that out. Trace the heresies and you will find that they began with a certain truth that was pushed to an out-of-balance extreme.

SOME EXAMPLES FROM SCRIPTURE

In the Scriptures we find both positive and negative examples of this quality called "balance." The New Testament puts a red flag on individuals as well as churches where balance has gone out the window—instances where knowledge overshadows discernment. On the other hand, we find some examples where knowledge and discernment coexisted in beautiful balance.

Let's look at the negative examples before we focus on the positive.

Some Negative Examples

Tucked away in the obscure letter of 3 John is a classic example of one who lacked discernment. He has been called by some authors a first-century "church boss." A self-appointed authority. His name was Diotrephes. Here is a vivid pen portrait of an unbearable man. (There are a few in almost every church to this day. Rather than changing or softening in their older age, they simply *remain* unbearable.) Diotrephes is openly exposed and criticized by the apostle John in verses 9 and 10:

> *I wrote something to the church; but Diotrephes, who loves to be first among them, does not accept what we say. For this reason, if I come, I will call attention to his deeds which he does, unjustly accusing us with wicked words; and not satisfied with this, neither does he himself receive the brethren, and he forbids those who desire to do so, and puts them out of the church.*

In today's terms, the man was running the show. He became a dangerous savage on the loose in a congregation. Apparently he was well-read and well-versed in the Old Testament Scripture. It is worth noting that there's not a word about his lacking knowledge. That could have been the reason he was brought to power and given leadership in the early church. But he became so overbearing in his leadership, so lacking in discernment (totally unaware that he was missing tact and grace and love) that John was forced to declare that Diotrephes was way out of line.

A lack of discernment is something like blindness. A crippling handicap. In the process of growing up in God's forever family, I plead with you to remain perceptive and gracious and tolerant with others in the same family! Gain knowledge, certainly. But as you do, guard against becoming blinded by your own importance. Diotrephes failed at that very point. He lost his perspective. He lost his balance. He was in serious danger of bringing judgment upon himself.

The New Testament also cites a *church* that lacked discernment. The Corinthians—what a carnal corral of Christians! But don't misunderstand, those people were intellectually bright. They had lots of knowledge. They were open and extremely well taught. They knew their way around the block theologically. And they were cultured. The problem was that they couldn't get along with each other, which led to all kinds of difficulties. Their lack of spiritual equilibrium erupted into chaos. But before we get to that, look at a few verses in 1 Corinthians, chapter 1:

> *I thank my God always concerning you, for the grace of God which was given you in Christ Jesus, that in everything you were enriched in Him, in all speech and all knowledge, even as the testimony concerning Christ was confirmed in you, so that you are not lacking in any gift . . . (vv. 4-7).*

What a place in which to worship during those early days! Talk about good teachers! And knowing the scoop! The Corinthians had a marvelous heritage. They had gained an understanding of the truth from Paul, their founder. Those truths were watered by Apollos, a gifted preacher, and nurtured by Christ. That little isthmus in Greece contained a magnificent and exciting body of "with-it" people . . . the Corinthian church.

Ah, but look at verses 10 and 11. Those same people who possessed all that knowledge had made a royal mess of things.

> *Now I exhort you, brethren, by the name of our Lord Jesus Christ, that you all agree, and there be no divisions among you, but you be made complete in the same mind and in the same judgment.*
>
> *For I have been informed concerning you, my brethren, by Chloe's people, that there are quarrels among you.*

Quarrels? Among people with knowledge? Yes, quarrels. Because they weren't able to keep their knowledge in balance. They lacked the discernment to see what was happening. They missed the danger signals. As they grew in knowledge, they didn't grow in grace—a massive blind spot still found in churches today. They didn't perceive the dangers. They failed to add a cup of discernment to their bowl of knowledge.

Look a little further on in chapter 1, verse 12, for example.

> *Now I mean this, that each one of you is saying, "I am of Paul," and "I of Apollos," and "I of Cephas," and "I of Christ."*

There were cliques. One group followed the teachings of one individual to the exclusion of anyone else . . . first-century groupies who lived their so-called Christian lives out of balance. Not one but four distinct cliques. And obviously each of the four groups lacked discernment.

Chapter 3, verses 3 and 4:

> *for you are still fleshly. For since there is jealousy and strife among you, are you not fleshly, and are you not walking like mere men?*
>
> *For when one says, "I am of Paul," and another, "I am of Apollos," are you not mere men?*

What is Apollos . . . and what is Paul? They're servants. Gifted men, but only men called by God to be spiritual leaders, not religious Pied Pipers.

Lest I overdraw the point, I'll restrain myself from going any further. But there is one thought I must underscore. You who are new in the Christian faith must constantly guard against getting all your food from one source. You need to vary your diet. You need to determine first if the teacher you are following is presenting biblical truth. But even if he or she is, you must always guard against believing it just because that one person says it—even if the person was the one who led you to Christ.

No one person has a corner on the truth. Never forget that!

And if you follow just one, you may very likely live to see the day you become disillusioned as that person reveals his or her feet of clay. I hope you will remember my warning for the rest of your life.

But later in the first Corinthian letter we find these words:

> *Now concerning things sacrificed to idols, we know that we all have knowledge. Knowledge makes arrogant, but love edifies. If any one supposes that he knows anything, he has not yet known as he ought to know (8:1-2).*

Mark that well. If we think we've got it all together in knowledge, then, spiritually speaking, we hardly understand what knowledge is about. What's worse, such arrogance will cause us to lack dependence upon the Lord. And before the ink is dry on that warning, Paul goes on to describe the importance of restraining liberty for the sake of weaker brothers and sisters in the family of God who wouldn't understand.

Once again, please note it takes discernment to gauge one's

actions. You don't simply gain a great deal of knowledge about liberty and then run wild with little concern about others. Your lifestyle speaks! A person with knowledge *and discernment* thinks about his lifestyle. Weighs his words and actions. Cares about others. That's all part of growing up in a balanced manner.

Some Positive Examples

Enough negatives! Let's look at a couple of positive examples. In the book of Acts, chapter 18, we find a courageous, zealous young man named Apollos. At the end of that chapter we read of his ministry. Here was a bright, capable man, greatly gifted and wonderfully available. His theology, however, was a little thin at one point. And he listened to some people who knew more than he knew—an admirable trait!

> *Now a certain Jew named Apollos, an Alexandrian by birth, an eloquent man, came to Ephesus; and he was mighty in the Scriptures* (v. 24).

Did he know what he was talking about? You bet. Was he able to preach? With all his heart. Did anyone listen? Indeed. He was apparently quite an orator. In today's terms we'd say, "he had it together."

> *This man had been instructed in the way of the Lord; and being fervent in spirit . . .* (v. 25).

Fervent? The word means "boiling"! So he was a passionate speaker. He had an electric, compelling delivery.

> *. . . he was speaking and teaching accurately the things concerning Jesus, being acquainted only with the baptism of John* [so there were limitations in his knowledge]; *and he began to speak out boldly in the synagogue. But when Priscilla and Aquila heard him . . .* (vv. 25-26).

This was a husband-wife team who had been trained by Paul in Corinth, and later sent on to Ephesus to minister to a group of people there. Apollos traveled from Alexandria to Ephesus where the couple lived. He spoke openly of Christ. Aquila and Priscilla went to the meeting and heard him speak. As they listened, however, they *discerned* something was lacking. They must have loved his delivery. They, no doubt, appreciated his emphasis. But they realized he needed to know more. He didn't know about the ministry of the Holy Spirit. He only knew about salvation through Christ. He lacked a full knowledge of the truth. And perhaps they invited the young evangelist to come home with them that evening. Here's how it happened:

> *and he began to speak out boldly in the synagogue. But when Priscilla and Aquila heard him, they took him aside and explained to him the way of God more accurately* (v. 26).

Apollos must have felt like a little puppy getting fresh food and water, encouragement and love. He loved it! He was teachable. He discerned they knew what they were talking about. They discerned he needed to know more. So the discernment mixed with knowledge as the three of them met and melted together.

We're not told how much time they spent together—but apparently it was long enough to help Apollos develop what was missing in his theology. I am so impressed with his teachable spirit. Not many great preachers are open to the counsel of others. It's wonderful when you meet one who is willing to listen to another side, especially when he's willing to listen to others who point out what may be missing in his message.

After a period of time, Apollos was ready to leave.

> *And when he wanted to go across to Achaia, the brethren encouraged him and wrote to the disciples to welcome him; and when he had arrived, he helped greatly those who had believed through grace; for he powerfully refuted the Jews . . .* (v. 27).

I would love to have heard Apollos, especially after his theology fell into place. Once he got that part of his theology honed to perfection he delivered the goods!

> *for he powerfully refuted the Jews in public, demonstrating by the Scriptures that Jesus was the Christ* (v. 28).

Because he mixed his knowledge with discernment, he was even better equipped. No one could refute him!

I don't care how gifted, how capable, how eloquent you may be, how widely used in your ministry; you can always benefit from the help of someone else—to hone, to sharpen you. Leadership requires accountability. You never get too old to be taught a new truth. Discernment says, "I know that my knowledge is limited. Others can help me. I am open and ready to learn."

Another example worth remembering is the church mentioned in chapter 17, verse 10 of the same book, the book of Acts. The Berean church. This church had discernment.

> *And the brethren immediately sent Paul and Silas away by night to Berea; and when they arrived, they went into the synagogue of the Jews.*

And what about those people in Berea? Read very carefully:

> *Now these were more noble-minded than those in Thessalonica, for they received the word with great eagerness, examining the Scriptures daily, to see whether these things were so* (v. 11).

What does it mean when we read they were "more noble-minded" than those in Thessalonica"? Does that mean sophisticated? No. Were they closed, maybe suspicious? No. Everett Harrison writes:

> The nobility consisted in this, that instead of having a suspicious attitude which was ready to reject out of hand what was set before them they actually "received the word with great eagerness."[1]

There's a fine line between discernment and suspicion. These Bereans, when they heard the men who came to them with the truth, perked up, listened, and they remained open to what was presented. And did you notice what they did?

> *. . . for they received* [the term means "welcomed"]—*the word with great eagerness, examining the Scriptures daily, to see whether these things were so* (v. 11).

That's discernment. "Good truth, Paul! Great sermon, Silas! Man, they make a great dynamic duo. Those men can really preach. Now, let's go home and see if what they taught squares with the truth. Let's dig through the Scriptures and let's compare what they taught with what God's Word teaches. Let's make sure that that's really what we believe. We respect them. We know God has anointed them. His hand is certainly on their lives. But we don't believe it just because they said it. We believe it because it is in agreement with what God has written."

The Bereans added that necessary cup of discernment.

I certainly do not want to imply that all of us must become detectives, looking for clues of wrongdoing in another's life or teaching. It's one thing to be suspicious people who question everything we hear . . . and another thing entirely to be discerning, alert, perceptive. There is a very real need on our part every time we hear the Word proclaimed, that we listen closely, think it through, sift it out, compare it with other Scriptures and other material we've been taught.

THREE PRINCIPLES
WE MUST NEVER FORGET
■

Before wrapping up this chapter, I want to mention three timeless principles. You may want to write them in the margin of your Bible alongside the comments we just read about the church at Berea.

1. *No one person has all the truth.* Healthy Christians, young and old alike, maintain a variety in their diet. They draw truth from here and they draw it from there. They grow from this person and from that one . . . from this ministry and from that one. They realize there is not only wisdom but safety in a multitude of counselors.

2. *No single church owns exclusive rights to your mind.* Maybe I ought to broaden the word "church" to "ministry." No single *ministry* owns exclusive rights to your thoughts. We are not to commit intellectual suicide when we become a part of any ministry. If we do, we're on our way to trouble. I think that might be the major reason God allowed a Jonestown. What a living memory in all our minds! So many of those sincere followers committed intellectual suicide as they absorbed and embraced only one man's message simply because he said it. In subtle ways he stole their allegiance, which belonged to Christ. Our submission is ultimately to one Head—the Lord Jesus Christ. We bow to the lordship of Christ, not the headship of some minister. To respect human leaders is commendable, but to follow them, *regardless*, is to flirt with danger.

3. *No specific interpretation is correct just because a gifted teacher says so.* If the Bereans felt Paul and Silas were worth comparing with Scripture, surely that says something about teachers and preachers today.

Well, there you have it. I really want you to live a fuller life than you now live, especially those of you who have settled for tunnel vision, lacking imagination. In fact, I don't want you to wind up your Christian life as I started mine, sacrificing the beauty and color, perception and creativity. For that reason I want to close this chapter with a story you'll never forget.

There were once two men, both seriously ill, in the same small room of a great hospital. Quite a small room, just large enough for the pair of them—two beds, two bedside lockers, a door opening on the hall, and one window looking out on the world.

One of the men, as part of his treatment, was allowed to sit up in bed for an hour in the afternoon, (something that had to do with draining the fluid from his lungs) and his bed was next to the window.

But the other man had to spend all his time flat on his back—and both of them had to be kept quiet and still. Which was the reason they were in the small room by themselves, and they were grateful for peace and privacy—none of the bustle and clatter and prying eyes of the general ward for them.

Of course, one of the disadvantages of their condition was that they weren't allowed much to do: no reading, no radio, certainly no television—they just had to keep quiet and still, just the two of them.

They used to talk for hours and hours–about their wives, their children, their homes, their former jobs, their hobbies, their childhood, what they did during the war, where they had been on vacations—all that sort of thing. Every afternoon, when the man in the bed next to the window was propped up for his hour, he would pass the time by describing what he could see outside. And the other man began to live for those hours.

The window apparently overlooked a park with a lake where there were ducks and swans, children throwing them bread and sailing model boats, and young lovers walking hand in hand beneath the trees. And there were flowers and stretches of grass and games of softball, people taking their ease in the sunshine, and right at the back, behind the fringe of the trees, a fine view of the city skyline.

The man on his back would listen to all of this, enjoying every minute—how a child nearly fell into the lake, how beautiful the girls were in their summer dresses, and then an exciting ball game, or a boy playing with his puppy. It got to the place that he could almost see what was happening outside.

Then one fine afternoon, when there was some sort of parade, the thought struck him: Why should the man next to the window have all the pleasure of seeing what was going on? Why shouldn't he get the chance?

He felt ashamed and tried not to think like that, but the more he tried, the worse he wanted to change. He'd do anything!

In a few days he had turned sour. He should be by the window. And he brooded and couldn't sleep, and grew even more seriously ill—which none of the doctors understood.

One night, as he stared at the ceiling, the other man (the man next to the window) suddenly woke up coughing and choking, the fluid congesting in his lungs, his hands groping for the button that would bring the night nurse running. But the man watched without moving.

The coughing racked the darkness—on and on—choked off— then stopped. The sound of breathing stopped—and the man continued to stare at the ceiling.

In the morning, the day nurse came in with water for their baths and found the other man dead. They took away his body, quietly, no fuss.

As soon as it seemed decent, the man asked if he could be moved to the bed next to the window. And they moved him, tucked him in, and made him quite comfortable, and left him alone to be quiet and still.

The minute they'd gone, he propped himself up on one elbow, painfully and laboriously, and looked out the window. It faced a blank wall.[2]

As I said earlier, for several years my life faced a blank wall. I lacked any imagination. Life was comprised of blacks and whites— neatly boxed, tightly sealed. I was very little help to anyone else.

Today, your life may literally face a blank wall, and the only thing you can draw on is the beauty and depth and color prompted by God's Book. You need more than knowledge, you need a new infusion of creativity from the Spirit of God Himself. In a word, you need discernment.

Don't miss it. Add a full cup of it to your knowledge. Mix it well, and you'll never lose your balance.

1. Gaining biblical knowledge seems to have at least two built-in dangers
   . . . the danger of pride and the danger of becoming rigid and narrow-
   minded. In what ways can you guard yourself against these twin
   spiritual hazards as you seek to grow in your knowledge of the truth?

2. Take another look at Paul's wholehearted prayer for the Philippian believers in Philippians 1:9-11. What does it mean to "love with discernment"? How does this "way of seeing" affect your relationship with the
   world? With your family? With fellow believers? Take time to think and
   pray through a situation in your own life where you might apply this
   truth.

3. From how many different sources are you drawing your spiritual
   nourishment? If you find that number is low, list in your notebook
   three to five additional sources that might help to balance your intake
   of truth. Your list could include books, booklets, radio broadcasts,
   tapes, church-sponsored Bible studies, or other sources that come to
   your mind. Choose at least one from which you might begin receiving
   benefit this week. There is safety in a multitude of counselors!

The Bible

"I affirm my confidence in God's inerrant Word. I treasure its truths and I respect its reproofs."

GOD'S BOOK—
GOD'S VOICE

hat is your final authority in life?

I mean, when you're cornered, when you're really up against it, when you're forced to face reality, upon what do you lean?

Before you answer too quickly, think about it for a few moments. When it comes to establishing a standard for morality, what's your ruler? When you need an ethical compass to find your way out of an ethical jungle, where's north? When you're on a stormy, churning sea of emotions, which lighthouse shows you where to find the shore?

Let me get even more specific. While getting dressed one morning you notice a dark mole on your side, just above your beltline. A few days later you observe that it is surrounded by red, sensitive flesh. It's becoming increasingly more sensitive to touch. You're disturbed about it. You finally talk yourself into seeing a physician. The surgeon probes and pushes, asks some pertinent questions, takes a few X rays, and finally says to you with a frown, "I don't like the way this looks. And I don't like the way it feels. I'll have to remove it— we'll do a biopsy." You churn inside while he talks. After the procedure he pays a visit to your room and tells you that his report isn't good. In fact, he quietly informs you, "It is melanoma." The worst kind of cancer. How do you handle that? To whom or to what do you turn? You need something solid to lean on. What is it?

Here's another: It's between one and two o'clock early one morning when your phone rings. It's a police officer. He tries to be tactful, but it's obvious that someone you love very much has been in an automobile accident—a terrible head-on collision. The victim—your loved one—suffered a tragic death. He tells you he has the unenviable and unfortunate responsibility of asking you to come and identify the body. What do you do in the hours that follow? How do you handle your grief? What gives you the courage to accept the truth . . . to go on?

Here's another: You've worked very, very hard in your own business. Your diligence has been marked by integrity, loyalty, sacrifice. You've given up a lot of personal desires and comforts so that the business might grow. You've plowed what little bit of profit you've made right back into the operation. And you've never once compromised your principles. But during the last few hours you've discovered that your product, which has taken the best years of your life to perfect, will soon be obsolete, thanks to a recent technological breakthrough. In fact, it appears that within the next few months you may lose everything. The awful reality of financial bankruptcy suddenly looms like a massive shadow. Where do you turn? How do you stay on your feet?

Just one more: You've been married a little over twenty-five years. You and your partner have reared three now-adult children. One will soon finish college, and the other two are gone, both happily married. You're thinking that the future will soon reward you with relief and relaxation. You have been faithful to your mate. You've worked hard and you've given yourself to this marriage. Out of the blue one evening your partner sits down beside you and begins by saying, "I . . . can't keep something from you any longer. There's someone else in my life. In fact, I don't want to be married anymore. I . . . I don't love you. I don't want to be in this home anymore. I want out of the marriage. I'm divorcing you." What gives you the stability you need to continue your life? How do you keep from becoming bitter? Where do you turn to find hope amidst such rejection?

I've worked with people for more than twenty-five years. And I've seen them in the worst kind of crises. I've seen some who could not take it. They ultimately took their lives, and I buried them. I've seen others who lost their minds. Some lost their will to go on. Others became physically ill or attempted to dodge the reality of the pain through drugs or alcohol abuse. I've visited with them, and tried to help them through it.

COMMON CRUTCHES PEOPLE LEAN ON

It has been my observation through the years that people usually

$$
\begin{array}{r}
5{\overline{\smash{\big)}\,60.00}}
\end{array}
$$

12 books of 5.00 each

$$
\begin{array}{r}
12 \\
5 \\
\hline
60
\end{array}
$$

PRAYER & PRAISE
June 7, 1995

MISSIONARIES
-Tim & Cheryl Perry - IV - Bloomington, IL - pray
that students will not be apathetic to the ministry,
that leaders would set an example of commitment,
for students to gain a deeper interest in the
scriptures
-David & Connie Johnson - B. G. F. M. - Brazil -
pray for their financial needs; for Connie, who has a
lump on her back that needs to be examined
-David & Lois Martin - CEF - Cyprus - for
someone to cook & clean for the Institute, for visa
clearance for students going to Cyprus, for
scholarship funds to come in
-For strength, wisdom, and grace for all our
missionaries

FAITH BAPTIST CHURCH
-Church Boards - PRAY for new board members,
for wisdom, unity, & commitment of each as they
serve the Lord through the church
-Staff Needs - Sunday School teacher for 3-5 yr.
old class and one more teacher for children's church

HEALTH
-Our Young at Heart, Shut-Ins, and Nursing
Home residents
-Mary Horgan - strength and encouragement as she
continues going through chemotherapy

-Lillian Jones - for healing for her knee problems
-Stephanie Barthelemy - out of the hospital, but still recovering
-Ron Devore - not feeling well
-all those with ongoing health problems

OTHER
-The effective outreach of Faith Baptist Church ministries and individuals: AWANA, Jail, Nursing Homes, Sunday School, Ladies Prayer Group
-for VBS this week: that kids will see their need for Christ, rather than just a fun time
-Youth Mission Project - that needed funds would be supplied & those participating would grow spiritually from the experience.

PRAISE
-Praise the LORD, O my soul; all my inmost being, praise his holy name.
-Praise the LORD, O my soul, and forget not all his benefits
-who forgives all your sins and heals all your diseases
-who redeems your life from the pit and crowns you with love and compassion
-who satisfies your desires with good things so that your youth is renewed like the eagle's
-The LORD works righteousness and justice for all the oppressed.

do one of four things when they are faced with information like this. I think of these responses as common crutches on which people lean. The first I would call, for lack of a better title, *escapism*. Most people, at least initially, escape the reality of the pain. They run. They either run away emotionally or they literally run in physical ways through travel or affairs or chemical dependence. They deny the horror of what has happened. They refuse to let reality run its course and take its toll on them. They escape.

Secondly, I've noticed many people turn to *cynicism*. They not only face their troubles, they become preoccupied with them. And they grow dark within. Surprise leads to disillusionment. And they let that fester into resentment and finally bitterness. Often they spend the balance of their lives trying to take revenge. They become victims of their own lack of forgiveness. They begin to live out the message on the bumper sticker: "I don't get mad . . . I get even." Whether their hostility is directed toward God, or some other person, they turn to cynicism. More often than not, the cynic ships the faith as bitterness wins the final victory.

Third, there is the crutch of *humanism*. They listen to the counsel of some other person, rather than God. They get their logic and their reasoning from a man or a woman or a book. They turn to self-help, people's opinion, self-realization. They try human reasoning, which inevitably is based on the horizontal wisdom of man. And it leaves them empty, it leaves them lacking. Or they try meditation, which fails to satisfy. And they do not really come to terms with the truth of what they could learn through the whole experience.

Fourth, the crutch of *supernaturalism*. This may be mild or maddening. Some people turn to mediums. They seek information from the other world. They get in touch with witches and wizards with the assurance of demonic powers. Some begin to try astrology and others turn to superstition. More and more connect with the occult as they are trying to cope with their world of pain.

Popular though these four crutches may be, escapism, cynicism, humanism, and supernaturalism do not provide any sense of ultimate relief and satisfaction. They leave the victim in quicksand—more desperately confused than at the beginning. None of the above is an acceptable "final authority."

So I return to the question that opened this chapter: What is your final authority in life? What holds you together when all hell breaks loose around you?

There can be no more reliable authority on earth than God's Word, the Bible. This timeless, trustworthy source of truth holds the key that unlocks life's mysteries. It alone provides us with the shelter we need in times of storm.

THE BIBLE:
THE ABSOLUTELY TRUSTWORTHY CRUTCH

If I could have only one wish for God's people, it would be that all of us would return to the Word of God, that we would realize once for all that His Book has the answers. The Bible *is* the authority, the final resting place of our cares, our worries, our griefs, our tragedies, our sorrows, and our surprises. It is the final answer to our questions, our search. Turning back to the Scriptures will provide something that nothing else on the entire earth will provide.

Psalm 119 speaks of a man who knows what it means to hurt. He needs help outside himself. The specifics may be different from what I've described thus far, but he is no stranger to suffering. He's going through hard times. He says,

> *My soul languishes for Thy salvation;*
> *I wait for Thy word* (v. 81).

In other words, "I wait for the truth of Your Word to come to pass, Lord. I wait for help to return. I wait for the promises to become a reality. I wait for the wisdom to take shape and to make sense in my life." That's what the psalmist means when he writes, "I wait for Your Word." Notice he waits for God's Word, not human reasoning, not his own feelings, and not for a chance to get even.

Let's read on:

> *My eyes fail with longing for Thy word,*
> *While I say, "When wilt Thou comfort Me?"* (v. 82)

God's assistance is not always immediate. He doesn't come swiftly every time we cry out for help. Most Christians I know are currently "longing for Thy word" to bring needed relief in at least one major area of life. Read verses 85-87:

> *The arrogant have dug pits for me,*
> *Men who are not in accord with Thy law.*
>
> *All Thy commandments are faithful;*
> *They have persecuted me with a lie; help me!*
> [Here is a man being criticized. He's under the gun.]
>
> *They almost destroyed me on earth,*
> *But as for me, I did not forsake Thy precepts.*
> ["I come back to Thy word, O God."]

Then verses 89 and 90:

> *Forever, O Lord,*
> *Thy word is settled in heaven.*

> *Thy faithfulness continues throughout all*
> *generations. . . .*

And finally, verse 92. I love it!

> *If Thy law had not been my delight,*
> *Then I would have perished in my affliction.*

Isn't that the truth! If I hadn't had the eternal foundation of the Book of God on many an occasion, my very life would have been finished.

In a world of relativism, the Bible talks in terms of right and wrong, good and bad, yes and no, true and false. In a world where we're encouraged to do it "if it feels good," the Bible addresses that which is sinful and holy. Scripture never leaves us with a bewildered look on our faces, wondering about the issues of life. It says, "This is the way it is. That is the way it is not to be. This is the way to walk; do not walk there." It tells us straight. It provides the kind of solid foundation you and I need.

WHY THE FOUNDATION IS SO DEPENDABLE

But wait. We need to understand why. Why is it that this Book qualifies as our final authority?

Its Identity

First, I think it will help us to know something about the identity of the Bible. By the way, the term *Bible* is never once found in Scripture. It's not a biblical term. So what does the Bible call itself? What is its identity?

Let's take a look into the Gospel by Luke, chapter 24. Jesus is speaking with two men on the road to Emmaus. In verse 27 we read of the outcome of that historic walk together:

> *And beginning with Moses and with all the prophets, He*
> *explained to them the things concerning Himself in all the Scrip-*
> *tures.*

Jesus verbally worked His way through the Old Testament, called here "the Scriptures." A little later on, the two men related to their friends what had happened:

> *And they said to one another, "Were not our hearts burning within us while He was speaking to us on the road, while He was explaining the Scriptures to us?"* (v. 32).

Again, they referred to "the Scriptures." Very interesting term, "Scriptures." It is a translation of the Greek term *graphe*. (We get our word "graph" from it.) It means "that which is written." In other words, the sacred writings. When we rely on the Bible, we rely on that which has been *written*. I linger here because I think it's significant that God didn't simply *think* His message. He didn't simply *speak* His message or reveal it in the clouds or through dreams to men and women in biblical times. No, He saw to it that His Word was actually written down. He put it in the language of the people so that people in all generations could read it and grasp its significance. He "graphed" His Word. We're grateful we have a book that contains the very mind of our God—the Scriptures—in written form. And, in addition, it is in our own language.

Moving from Luke's Gospel let's look next into the seventeenth chapter of John. This entire chapter is a prayer. It's the longest recorded prayer of the Lord Jesus Christ in all the Bible. While praying He says to the Father:

> *I have given them Thy word; and the world has hated them, because they are not of the world, even as I am not of the world. I do not ask Thee to take them out of the world, but to keep them from the evil one. They are not of the world, even as I am not of the world. Sanctify them in the truth; Thy word is truth* (vv. 14-17).

I am so grateful those verses are in the Bible. Look again at that closing comment. What an absolute statement from the lips of Jesus! "Thy Word is truth." In four monosyllabic words we find the basis of our belief in the veracity, the reliability of Scripture. This is not human counsel, it is truth—divine counsel. It is honest. It has integrity. It is as absolute as it is timeless. "Your Word, O God, is truth."

I appreciate what James Montgomery Boice once wrote regarding the relevance of this claim:

> We talk about the Word of God as truth. We are right to do so. But we have to acknowledge when we speak along those lines

that the world of our day no longer strictly believes in truth. The great apologists of our time are all saying that. C. S. Lewis said it very well in the opening pages of *The Screwtape Letters*, where the devil's henchman, tempting his patient on earth, is advised not to talk about truth and falsehood because people don't operate on that basis anymore, but rather to talk about what's useful or what's practical. "That's the way to get through," says the devil.

Francis Schaeffer has said the same thing in more philosophical terms. He's pointed out quite rightly that today, unlike previous generations, people, though they speak of truth and falsehood, are not speaking of truth in the biblical sense or even in the traditional sense to mean that which is true now and will always be true universally. Rather they mean that which is true now but not necessarily tomorrow or yesterday; or it is true for me but not necessarily for you. In other words, truth for contemporary men and women is relative.

But here we have truth embodied in the Scriptures. . . .

Here the efficacy of the Word of God comes in: the fact that God really uses the Word to accomplish his purposes, whether men and women believe in the Word of truth or not.[1]

Talk about a familiar line of logic! We've heard such reasoning, haven't we? "A thinking person shouldn't cut off his head when he starts getting serious about religion. There are lots of things out there that we have to consider . . . lots of stuff beyond the bounds of this Book." Certainly, there are. But truth, real truth, truth you can rely on, truth that will never turn sour, that will never backfire, that's the truth in this Book. That's what this Book is about. That's why this Book provides us with *the* constant and *the* needed crutch.

By the way, do *you* turn to it for the truth you need? The longer I live the more I realize that most people on this earth have an amazing ability to twist truth . . . to change things so that right isn't really right, it's partially right. And wrong isn't really wrong, it's sort of unfortunate . . . somewhere between okay and I'm not really sure. The world system talks about truth, but it doesn't ever identify it. I have to make up my mind with my own moral standard or my own ethical compass. I'm left to choose the direction I want to go. And no one is going to lay any trip on me, because nobody else knows where the boundaries are. And therefore I am left not free—definitely not free—but quasi-paralyzed between bewilderment and confusion. That, my friend, is bondage!

What does it take to free us? It takes truth. Yes, the truth. It was

Jesus Himself who once promised, "You shall know the truth and the truth shall make you free" (John 8:32).

I was born in 1934. I have now lived over fifty years—long enough to realize that I desperately need truth in my life. I've been exposed to just enough human intelligence to be dangerous! I've gotten just enough of man's wisdom not to trust in it. I don't need more of those things in my life. I need truth. I need God's "yes" and God's "no," God's light and God's mind. That explains why I appreciate the Scripture so much. His Word provides the truth I need. It erases the doubts, it gives a sure footing even though I am surrounded by people in a swamp of uncertainty.

It's interesting that in all of my research for this book, I did not find one source that made much of the next verse I want us to look at. And it's surprising, because it's one of the most helpful on this subject. I'm referring to 1 Thessalonians, chapter 2. I find in one verse (verse 13) that the Scripture is "God's message." That it is, in fact, "God's Word."

> *And for this reason we also constantly thank God that when you received from us the word of God's message, you accepted it not as the word of men, but for what it really is, the word of God, which also performs its work in you who believe.*

"When I stood to speak," Paul is saying, "and I delivered to you God's message and I unrolled the scrolls and pointed out the truth of what Moses had written and what Jeremiah had said and what Amos had pointed out . . . when I presented that to you, you didn't take that as the word of man. You saw it for what it really was—the very word of God."

Frankly, that does something to you. When you realize that the print on the page you are reading is, in fact, God's message, God's Word, it stands alone. Absolutely unique . . . in a class by itself. Think of it this way: God's Book is, as it were, God's voice. If our Lord were to make Himself visible and return to earth and speak His message, it would be in keeping with this Book. His message of truth would tie in exactly with what you see in Scripture. His opinion, His counsel, His commands, His desires, His warnings, His very mind. When you rely on God's voice, God's very message, you have a sure foundation.

Now one more thought regarding identity—and it's the practical side of the subject. Let's look at 1 Peter, chapter 1, verses 22-25. Referring to the same writings, the same truth, the same message of God, Peter writes:

Since you have in obedience to the truth purified your souls for a sincere love of the brethren, fervently love one another from the heart, for you have been born again not of seed which is perishable but imperishable, that is, through the living and abiding word of God. For,
  "All flesh is like grass,
  And all its glory like the flower of grass.
  The grass withers,
  And the flower falls off,
  But the word of the Lord abides forever."
And this is the word which was preached to you.

Here is another reference to the everlasting nature of God's message.

Do you realize there are only two eternal things on earth today? Only two: people and God's Word. Everything else will ultimately be burned up—*everything* else. Kind of sets your priorities straight, doesn't it?

I smile understandingly at the story that Charlie "Tremendous" Jones tells about walking down into his basement after the Youngstown flood had left its damage. As the water receded and left thick mud and gunk almost waist deep, he walked into his basement where he had displayed all of his awards and all of his plaques and all of his honors, now under four feet of mud. His response went something like this: "I stood there, staring in disbelief as I heard the voice of God. He said, 'Charlie "Not-So-Tremendous" Jones, don't worry about all this, I was gonna burn it all up anyway!'"

The stuff we place on the shelf, the things we put frames around, the trophies and whatnots we shine and want to show off, the things we're so proud of . . . it's all headed for the final bonfire. But not God's Book! Peter reminds us that the truth will "abide forever." Grass will come, it will flower . . . and then it will wither and die. But His written message, the truth, will abide forever.

Its Inerrancy

But wait. How can anyone get so excited about something that was written by men? We have no problem with the Giver of truth. He gave it . . . but wasn't the truth corrupted when He relayed it to earth through the hands of sinful men?

This is the perfect moment for you to become acquainted with three doctrinal terms you need to remember. It wouldn't hurt for you to commit them to memory: revelation, inspiration, and illumination. *Revelation* occurred when God gave His truth. *Inspiration* occurred when the writers of Scripture received and recorded His truth. Today, when we understand and apply His truth, that's *illumination.* That would include discovering new truth for our lives, understanding it, and implementing it.

Revelation has ceased. Inspiration has ceased. But illumination is going on right up to this moment!

Isn't that a great thought? Right now as you hold this book in your hands and as you grasp what I am writing regarding Scripture, the Holy Spirit is incessantly at work instructing you and affirming your thoughts and giving you new hope and clear direction.

Now then, thinking back over those three terms, you realize that the most critical of the three is inspiration.

In the same way, the critical point of your confidence in the Bible is directly related to your confidence in its inspiration. How then can we be sure that God's Word is free from error and therefore deserving of our trust?

There is great help in 2 Timothy, chapter 3. (We visited with Timothy earlier in this book.) You'll recall that Timothy has just been exhorted to maintain his godly priorities regardless of the times in which he lived—days which were marked by difficulty and depravity and deception (verses 1-13).

Then these words appear:

> *You, however, continue in the things you have learned and become convinced of, knowing from whom you have learned them; and that from the childhood you have known the Scriptures* [graphe, there's our word again for sacred writings] *which are able to give you the wisdom that leads to salvation through faith which is in Christ Jesus. All Scripture is inspired by God and profitable for teaching, for reproof, for correction, for training in righteousness . . .* (vv. 14-16).

Having said that about the Scriptures, Paul verifies His confidence in inerrancy, "Timothy, all *graphe*, all the writings of God, all Scripture is 'inspired of God.'" If you use the New International Version of Scripture, you see it as literally as we can render it in English: "God breathed." When God revealed His truth for human writers to record, He "breathed out" His Word. It says in verse 16 that all Scripture is inspired because it has been miraculously "God breathed." Not inspired like a Picasso, not inspired like a sculpture by Michelangelo, not inspired like a great composition by Handel or Brahms, not inspired like a literary master work by Shakespeare, but inspired, as in "God *breathed*." All Scripture has been "breathed out" by God.

Now, wait a minute. This still doesn't fully answer your question, does it?

When I breathe out my message to my secretary, she takes it and she writes it down and goes back over it with me and then types it and gives it to me so I can sign the letter. The process is called taking dictation. Did the writers of Scripture take dictation?

If you know much about the Bible, you realize that it includes different personalities. Peter doesn't sound a lot like John. And John doesn't sound like David. And David's writings aren't like Paul's. And Paul is altogether distinct from Jude or Peter or, for that matter, any of the other apostles. So somehow there was the preservation of each writer's personality without corrupting the text. That rules out the idea of dictation. So we have a Bible full of human personality and style, and yet it's God who breathed out His message. And it came in written form from the pens of men who differed in style.

Then how did He do it? How did He make that happen? Second Peter 1, verses 19-21:

> *And so we have the prophetic word made more sure, to which you do well to pay attention as to a lamp shining in a dark place, until the day dawns and the morning star arises in your hearts. But know this first of all, that no prophecy of Scripture is a matter of one's own interpretation, for no prophecy was ever made by an act of human will. . . .*

Let me interrupt. Paul didn't sit down one day and think, "Let's see, I think I'll write 2 Corinthians." Or, "I feel like Galatians. I'll write Galatians today." No prophecy ever came to pass because of the impulse or the inner urging of the will of man. No, in contrast to that, the key word in verse 21 is *moved*.

> *. . . but men moved by the Holy Spirit spoke from God.*

This English word *moved* is translated from an ancient Greek nautical term. In extrabiblical literature it was used to describe ships at sea. When a ship had lost its sails and its rudder, and it was at the mercy of the winds and the waves and the currents of the sea, it moved along apart from its own power. It remained a ship, but it was without its own power and energy. That's the word used here . . . not referring to ships at sea but writers of Scripture. They were moved outside their own power and energy as they wrote His truth.

So what we have is the preservation of an inerrant text. God breathed out His message to human writers, who, without losing their own style and personality, wrote His truth under His divine control. And because He superintended the process in its entirety, no error was present right down to the very words of the original text. What Scripture says, God says—through human agents, without error.

I appreciate professor Paul Feinberg's insightful comment:

> Inerrancy means that when all facts are known, the Scriptures in their original autographs and properly interpreted will be shown to be wholly true in everything that they affirm, whether that has to do with doctrine or morality or with the social, physical, or life sciences. . . .[2]

Can I rely on it? Is it reliable when I go through those experiences I wrote about at the beginning of this chapter? Absolutely and unreservedly.

Its Reliability

We started in Psalm 119. Let's end in the same chapter. Interwoven through this magnificent psalm is one theme, "I rely on Your word, O God." God has established His precepts, and the psalmist again and again declares their reliability. He's given us a morality to follow. He helps us with our greed, with ethics, with integrity, with verbal attacks from others, feeling lonely, and on and on. We could read right through this psalm, and we would uncover most of life's major battles. Each time the writer returns to the same throbbing theme and says, "I rely on Your Word . . . I find Your Word dependable . . . I realize it has never once failed me."

And it is still true today. Amazing, isn't it? This ancient, inerrant Book is reliable right up into these closing days of the twentieth century. I like what an old Baptist scholar named A. T. Robertson once wrote with tongue in cheek, "One proof of the inspiration of Scripture is that it has withstood so many years of poor preaching." It's remarkable that this Book is still around after the way some of us have been handling it . . . sometimes *mishandling* it. I'll say more about that in the next chapter.

BENEFITS OF RELYING ON THE BIBLE

In this same psalm we find three wonderful benefits of relying on the Bible. They are recorded in Psalm 119:98, 99, and 100. What benefits come my way when I rely on this marvelous Book? Verse 98:

Thy commandments make me wiser than my enemies,
for they are ever mine.

First benefit: *stability* in the midst of storm. I realize you have not been immune to stormy times in your life. No doubt you bear the marks and the scars, the hurt and the pain in your face. And if you could see me, you'd see them in mine. That's part of being in the human race. But the wonderful thing about relying on God's Book is that it gives you stability. It gives you that deep sense of purpose and meaning, even when you get the phone call in the middle of the night, even when your mate says, "It's over," even when, for some unrevealed reason, bankruptcy comes unexpectedly and leaves you financially vulnerable. No other counsel will get you through in the long haul like the stability that comes from God's Book.

Verse 99:

I have more insight than all my teachers, for Thy
testimonies are my meditation.

Here's a second benefit: *insight.* Students love verse 99! But it doesn't mean you can pull rank on your prof (I'd not suggest that you try that.) It says you will have *insight* rather than *intimidation.* There are few scenes more intimidating than the scholarly world. But the interesting twist to that is this—people who really know their Bibles aren't intimidated. Scholarly arguments designed to paint Scripture in a poor light don't pin you to the mat. Nor can you be battered in such a way because you realize that what they are saying isn't really truth—it's a misuse of Scripture. But I've observed when people really get a knowledge of the Scriptures and they begin to rely on that knowledge and see it work in their lives, they are less and less threatened by such attacks. They can face criticism and important people and strong words and even be outnumbered in an educational scene, but not intimidated, because they have the truth which gives them insight . . . the ability to see beyond the obvious.

By the way, the Bible will always be under attack in secular schools of higher learning. One scholar explains why.

> Satan does not waste his ammunition. Professors, who are being paid to teach philosophy, English, biology, mathematics . . . often take time from their class periods to undermine the

Bible and orthodox Christianity. Why are they not doing the same with the sacred books of other religions? The answer is that Satan, the original liar, is sympathetic with books that lie. His real enmity is directed against the book of truth because it contains the dynamite for his defeat.[3]

A third benefit is seen in verse 100:

I understand more than the aged,
because I have observed Thy precepts.

We gain *maturity* beyond our years by relying on Scripture. I don't meet too many people who say, "I'm very satisfied with my level of maturity." Most people I talk to say, "I'd love to grow up. I'd love to be stronger in my faith. I'd love to learn from the dumb mistakes I have made and not keep making them . . . I'd love to be mature." The hope for such maturity is in God's Word. You will have "understanding more than the aged" as you rely on this Book.

I wrestle with a basic question: How do I close a chapter as full as this one? Perhaps with this one thought: It is the simple truth that holds you together in the most complex situations. Not simplistic, but simple. The profound truth that the Bible gives us is like a warm blanket wrapped around us on a cold night.

Let me conclude with three quick questions: Do you want stability? Would you like insight? Is it your desire to have maturity? Of course! Absolutely. All that—and so much more—can be found in God's reliable Word. Even if you have spent most of your years questioning God's authority, wondering about God's Book, question and wonder no longer.

Return to this taproot of truth. Lean on it. Start today. It will hold you up and keep you strong. When it comes to a "final authority" in life, the Bible measures up.

1. Does the Bible serve as a shelter for you when the storms rage in your life? It's no good to try and construct a shelter *after* the storm descends . . . you need one ready *before* the winds begin to howl. Take some time to identify at least five "shelter" verses from Scripture—promises of God's unfailing love and sustaining power. (Your pastor or a mature Christian friend might enjoy helping you locate these verses if you're not sure where to start.) Ask your spouse or a friend to hold you accountable to memorize those verses in a reasonable length of time.

2. Only people and God's Word are eternal. That's all! Carefully evaluate your activities over the past week. What portion of your time and energies were devoted to either personally interacting with biblical truth or building that truth into the lives of others? What small (but significant) steps could you take over this coming week to move that percentage toward eternal priorities? Remember to capture these insights in your notebook.

3. How long has it been since you've joined with another person—or perhaps a small group—to work through a Bible study together? If you're uninvolved, consider scheduling a weekly time with one or more believers to search through a portion of God's Word together. Ask the folks at your local Christian bookstore for help in selecting some material suited to your needs.

HANDLING
THE
SCRIPTURES
ACCURATELY

ife has many disappointments. But I doubt if there is one any greater than the realization that you have been abused. Webster defines abuse as ". . . a deceitful act . . . a corrupt practice or custom, improper use or treatment."

Ours is a day of abuse: sexual abuse, emotional abuse, verbal abuse. But what about *biblical* abuse? By that I mean being deceived by the improper use of Scripture. Who of us has not witnessed someone twisting Scripture, forcing it to mean something it does not mean? Those who don't know better start believing it with all their heart, only to discover later on that both the interpretation and the application were fallacious . . . perhaps dangerous to their spiritual health and growth.

We hear about all kinds of abuse in this generation, but seldom do we hear from victims of biblical abuse, though they number into the thousands. In my opinion, it is one of the major problems among Christians today. I think it's not an exaggeration to call it "the ultimate rip-off." Can you imagine the disillusionment following the realization that the information you were given from the Bible, which you believed to be true, was in fact erroneous . . . the result of gross mishandling of Scripture?

THE PROBLEM: MISHANDLING THE BIBLE

Now this has nothing to do with *sincerity*. Many, perhaps most, people who mishandle the Word are very sincere. And it really has little to do with *theology*. Some who have their theology fairly well in place can still mishandle Scripture. It also has nothing to do with *personality*. There are gifted teachers dripping with charisma who can sway an audience and hold them in the palm of their hand, yet be guilty of mishandling Scripture. It certainly has nothing to do with *popularity*. Famous, highly visible personalities in Christian circles who can draw large listening audiences can (and often *do*) mishandle Scripture. So let's put to bed, once for all, the idea that if a person just "loves the Lord," he or she will be preserved from mishandling Scripture. No, even those of us who believe in the inerrancy of Scripture and affirm the importance of sound doctrine can be guilty of biblical abuse.

Most likely there are problems of Scripture abuse unique to each country. Our problem in America is not the availability of Scripture. We have numerous copies of the Bible. I looked on the shelf in my study the other day and counted sixteen Bibles! Among them were about twelve different versions or paraphrases of the Scriptures in various sizes, print styles, and with a selection of study notes from reputable scholars. And that doesn't include those in my home. There are probably several copies of the Scriptures in your home as well.

No, our problem in this country is not a lack of Bibles; it is a lack of people who carefully handle the Word of God, both privately and publicly. I'm convinced that we should not simply be students of the Scriptures—sound in our theology—but that we must also be careful in our interpretation of the Scriptures. And the more we teach, the greater that need!

This is nothing new. You will find the problem of biblical abuse mentioned often in the New Testament. It may not have been called that, but it went on, nevertheless.

OUR NEED: MAINTAINING THE MEANING

On several occasions in the New Testament, people are mentioned who failed to maintain the meaning of Scripture. And in each case they were people who knew better. Are you ready for a surprise? Many of them were professional clergymen—the scribes and the Pharisees—people in the first century who took the Scriptures seriously. They were not theological liberals, nor were they people who were soft on divine revelation. On the contrary, they devoted their lives to the Scripture . . . but they mishandled it.

Look first at Matthew 9:10-12:

And it happened that as He was reclining at the table in the house, behold many tax-gatherers and sinners came and were dining with Jesus and His disciples. And when the Pharisees saw this, they said to His disciples, "Why is your Teacher eating with the tax-gatherers and sinners?" But when He heard this, He said, "It is not those who are healthy who need a physician, but those who are sick."

Didn't Jesus have a marvelous way of addressing the real issue? With incredible insight He never failed to cut through all the fog. But now the point. In verse 13 He quotes Hosea, chapter 6, to the Pharisees:

But go and learn what this means, "I desire compassion, and not sacrifice," for I did not come to call the righteous, but sinners.

Notice the veiled rebuke. It was as if He said, "Go and learn the meaning of the verse you know by heart!: 'I desire compassion, and not sacrifice.'" I'm sure they had taught that verse from the prophet Hosea, along with many other related passages. I'm sure they had it neatly tucked away in their hearts. Yet they didn't even know the meaning of it! So, he said, in effect, "Go and learn what it means, men!"

Next, take a look at Matthew 12. We'll see a similar situation. As you read this account, notice Jesus' question, "Have you not read?"

At that time Jesus went on the Sabbath through the grainfields, and His disciples became hungry and began to pick the heads of grain and eat. But when the Pharisees saw it, they said to Him, "Behold, Your disciples do what is not lawful to do on a Sabbath." But He said to them, "Have you not read what David did, when he became hungry, he and his companions; how he entered the house of God, and they ate the consecrated bread, which was not lawful for him to eat, nor for those with him, but for the priests alone? Or have you not read in the Law, that on the Sabbath the priests in the temple break the Sabbath, and are innocent? But I say to you, that something greater than the temple is here. But if you had known what this means, 'I desire compassion, and not a sacrifice,' you would not have condemned the innocent. For the Son of Man is Lord of the Sabbath" (vv. 1-8).

Look back and underscore Jesus' exhortation: "If you had known what this means . . . you would not have condemned the innocent."

Strange words! An extremely reliable New Testament scholar observes:

> Our Lord does not deny that rest on the Sabbath is commanded, and He does not stay to protest against the rigor which would make plucking and eating corn a violation of the command. He points out that every rule has its limitations, and that ceremonial regulations must yield to the higher claims of charity and necessity.[1]

But they hadn't thought that through. They had learned a line from the scroll. They had, no doubt, committed it to memory. And then they went about the business of looking for people who were breaking the letter of the Law. Pharisees and scribes were notorious for omitting the spirit of the Law. Because they missed the deep meaning of the passage of Scripture, because they failed to handle it wisely, they committed biblical abuse. And that is precisely what goes on today by well-meaning, sincere people. May we never forget Jesus' observation, "If you had known what this means . . . you would not have condemned the innocent."

Look next into Matthew, chapter 15. The intensity increases:

> *Then some Pharisees and scribes came to Jesus from Jerusalem, saying, "Why do Your disciples transgress the tradition of the elders? For they do not wash their hands when they eat bread." And He answered and said to them, "And why do you yourselves transgress the commandment of God for the sake of your tradition? For God said, 'HONOR YOUR FATHER AND MOTHER,' and 'HE WHO SPEAKS EVIL OF FATHER OR MOTHER, LET HIM BE PUT TO DEATH.' But you say, 'Whoever shall say to his father or mother, "Anything of mine you might have been helped by has been given to God," he is not to honor his father or his mother.' And thus you invalidated the word of God for the sake of your tradition. You hypocrites, rightly did Isaiah prophesy of you, saying,*
>
>> *'THIS PEOPLE HONORS ME WITH THEIR LIPS,*
>> *BUT THEIR HEART IS FAR AWAY FROM ME.*
>> *BUT IN VAIN DO THEY WORSHIP ME.*
>> *TEACHING AS THEIR DOCTRINES THE*
>> *PRECEPTS OF MEN.'"*
>
> *And after He called the multitude to Him, He said to them, "Hear and understand. Not what enters into the mouth defiles*

the man, but what proceeds out of the mouth, this defiles the man" (vv. 1-11).

Talk about severe! "The Scripture says, 'Honor your father and mother,' but you have taken the very lines of Scripture and you have twisted them so that they fit what you want them to say. And I'm calling your hand on it," implies our Lord. Don't miss His pointed rebuke: "You invalidate what the Scripture says for the sake of your tradition." And then He calls them hypocrites!

I love the statement made by His disciples:

> *Then the disciples came and said to Him, "Do You know that the Pharisees were offended when they heard this statement?" (v. 12).*

Isn't that great? "Do you realize You made them angry?" I doubt very seriously that Jesus ever lost much sleep over making people like that angry.

> *But He answered and said, "Every plant which My heavenly Father did not plant shall be rooted up. Let them alone; they are blind guides of the blind* [wow!]. *And if a blind man guides a blind man, both will fall into a pit" (vv. 13-14).*

Strong counsel! I enjoy reading these verses to folks who mistakenly think of Jesus as a wimp—sort of a human doormat. On the contrary! Don't miss what our Lord felt so strongly about. He despised the way those hypocrites mishandled the Word. In effect, He said, "They have My Book, and they're making it say something it was never meant to say."

Maybe you don't need such a warning, but perhaps someone you know does. Just because a person opens the Scripture and calls himself or herself a teacher of the Bible doesn't guarantee the message. Just because they are well-known, just because people hang on their every word, just because they have great followings, and just because they travel the world over, carrying a Bible and teaching from the Bible, none of that guarantees they're right. Be careful about people who lift lines from the Scriptures and adapt them to what they want those passages to say. Scribes and Pharisees live on today. Their problem? They may quote Scripture correctly, but they fail to maintain the correct meaning of God's Word.

Now, sometimes it's the *hearer's* fault. And that is a completely different problem. Over in Matthew, chapter 16, we find a case in point. Jesus didn't mishandle the Scripture; those who heard Him misinterpreted what He said. Read Matthew 16:5-7:

> *And the disciples came to the other side and had forgotten to take bread. And Jesus said to them, "Watch out and beware of the leaven of the Pharisees and Sadducees." And they began to discuss among themselves, saying, "It is because we took no bread."*

Note: That's not at all what Jesus meant. They misunderstood Him. Keep reading:

> *But Jesus, aware of this, said, "You men of little faith, why do you discuss among yourselves that you have no bread? Do you not yet understand or remember the five loaves of the five thousand, and how many baskets you took up? Or the seven loaves of the four thousand, and how many large baskets you took up? How is it that you do not understand that I did not speak to you concerning bread? But beware of the leaven of the Pharisees and Sadducees"* (vv. 8-11).

Then it "clicked." It took them a while, but they finally put the pieces of the puzzle together.

> *Then they understood that He did not say to beware of the leaven of bread, but of the teaching of the Pharisees and Sadducees* (v. 12).

Now the reason I linger over this is because the same thing occurs today. Sometimes teachers and preachers work extremely hard to speak the truth from Scripture and to maintain its meaning. There are occasions when Scripture is a bit symbolic. And there are hearers who take things so directly, so painfully literal, that they miss the meaning behind the symbol—the significance of what the passage is teaching, even though the teacher tries to keep that from happening. Hearers (like the disciples) either miss it altogether or they twist part of it so that the meaning becomes confused. The disciples said He was talking about literal bread. He was talking about the leaven (a symbol of evil) of the Pharisees. Let's not forget our goal: It is always to *MAINTAIN THE MEANING OF SCRIPTURE.*

May I pass along one of the major secrets of accomplishing that goal? When you study or when you teach or when you hear, *pay attention to words.* Now you might be thinking, "How elementary can you get? Of course you pay attention to words." No, a lot of people don't. A lot of people speak in vague paragraphs . . . they roll together a lot of thoughts and ideas like kneading dough. And you have to dig through it to figure out what's there. But the best teachers, like the best students, are ever conscious of words.

One of the finest things I've ever read on handling the Scriptures with accuracy came from an article written by Dr. Bernard Ramm. In this fine piece he talks about being sensitive to words.

> The good interpreter never looks at a word without a question mark in his mind. He may consult his Greek lexicon, or his Webster's, or a commentary, or a concordance. But he fusses around among his books till the word upon which he has fixed his attention begins to glow with meaning.
>
> An experienced doctor has a wonderful sensitivity in his fingers. He has spent a lifetime feeling lumps, swellings, growths, tumors, and wens. He knows their textures, their shapes, and their peculiarities. Where our fingers tell us two things, a doctor's fingers might tell him a dozen things. Just as a doctor's fingers have a feel for lumps and growths, so a Bible teacher must have a feel for words. He must pass the fingers of his mind over their shapes, textures, and peculiarities.
>
> This means sensitivity to *phrases*, *clauses*, *paragraphs*, and *idioms*. A good Bible teacher is restless; he takes nothing for granted. He is the detective whose victim *is the meaning* and the words in their various combinations of phrases, sentences, and paragraphs are the clues. Out of the various configurations of the words he delves for the meaning. He looks for the train of thought (i.e., the sequence *in meaning*) and tries to follow it throughout the passage. He works, digs, meditates, ruminates, and studies *until the meaning of the biblical text shines through*.
>
> It is right at this point where the poor teacher fails. He is content with his efforts even though his thoughts are vague and his impressions are indistinct. As soon as he gets a good exhortation or practical application, he's content and rests at that point. He does not sit with a restless mind and dig and sweat, until he has achieved the meaning of the text.[2]

When you study the Bible, always pay close attention to words. Never miss the significant ones. Pull out your dictionary; trace the meaning of key words. Talk the words through; think the words through. Compare that word with another word and another place in Scripture where a similar word is used so that you will begin to see the meaning of the passage. John R. W. Stott refers to the importance of concentrating on words like a dog worrying over a bone.

AN EXAMPLE: EZRA AND THE SCROLL

Dr. Ramm's advice is vividly illustrated in the Old Testament book of Nehemiah, chapter 8. Here is one of the clearest examples in all of the Scriptures where the Bible was handled accurately, where its words, their meaning, and overall application were correctly rendered for the people. Here is biblical exposition at its best.

Before I point out four observations from this passage as it relates to Ezra and the scroll, let's allow Scripture to set the stage.

And all the people gathered as one man at the square which was in front of the Water Gate, and they asked Ezra the scribe to bring the book of the law of Moses which the Lord had given to Israel. Then Ezra the priest brought the law before the assembly of men, women, and all who could listen with understanding, on the first day of the seventh month. And he read from it before the square which was in front of the Water Gate from early morning until midday, in the presence of men and women, those who could understand; and all the people were attentive to the book of the law. And Ezra the scribe stood at a wooden podium [this is the first place in all the Bible where even a passing reference is made to a pulpit] *which they had made for the purpose* (vv. 1-4a).

Got the picture? Lots of people. A priest named Ezra. The scroll of God—an ancient copy of the Hebrew Scripture. A pulpit. Great interest in what God's Word had to say. So much for the background. Now for the four observations, each having to do with the careful manner in which God's Word was handled. No abuse here!

First: *Accurately handling the Scriptures starts with the reading of Scripture.* You will observe that Ezra read from the book of the law, and that those who listened "were attentive to the book of the law" (v. 3). And in verse 5:

He opened the book in the sight of all the people for he was standing above all the people. . . .

Now the reason I emphasize that is because I want you to notice that the focus was upon the Book of God, not some performer, not some program that they came to applaud, not even the opinion and wisdom of this man Ezra, though he was certainly a wise, godly, greatly respected man.

When reading from the Book of God, it is terribly important that everyone realize its importance. And if we're going to handle the Book of God accurately, then the Scripture must form the basis of our thoughts—not someone's idea, not the teacher's lesson plan, not even a preacher's opinion. Let Scripture speak for itself! And that's what those people focused on when they heard the Scriptures read. That's what they gave attention to. First, there must be the reading of Scripture.

> . . . and when he opened it, all the people stood up (v. 5).

Second: *Accurately handling the Scriptures includes having respect for the Scriptures.* This needs to be underscored again and again. They were attentive to the book, and when Ezra opened the book in their sight, all the people stood up. Those things illustrate respect. Furthermore, there was a podium, which seems to emphasize an attitude of authority. They showed reverence when they stood, and as they listened "from early morning until midday." And verse 6 tells us of their submissive response:

> Then Ezra blessed the Lord the great God. And all the people answered, "Amen, Amen!" while lifting up their hands; then they bowed low and worshiped the Lord with their faces to the ground.

This isn't just casual listening (like planning the menu for the week while the Scripture is being presented). This is focused attention and full concentration upon the Book of God. What an awesome sight it must have been!

For the next few moments I invite you to come into my study with me. When I begin to prepare a biblical message, a sermon or a scriptural talk, I begin not with *Time* or *Newsweek* magazine, not with the newspaper, not with someone's comment that was made to me, not even some book about the Bible. Nor do I start with an event I saw on television or something I've read on an airplane that week (as important as those things may be for illustration). My first place of reference is the open Bible. What does it actually say?

I often read the passage aloud. I read it repeatedly. I read it with emphasis and feeling. I pause. I think. I take some time to pray over that section. I think it through as best I can until it becomes very familiar in my mind. I read it over and over and over again so that the focus of my concentration is upon Scripture. I become so familiar with it that I can "see" it in my mind without having to look at it all the time.

I am occasionally surprised to meet men in the ministry who don't do that. They come to a passage with a bias or with an idea of something they want to say, and they start looking for a verse that says it for them. And it's amazing—they'll find it! That's called "proof texting." You can prove anything (yes, anything!) you want to prove from Scripture if you just stop reading soon enough and don't finish the thought, or if you twist a term here and there, "spiritualizing" the meaning. Or if you start in the middle of a paragraph and don't consider the context, you can make it say what you want it to say. And every time you do . . . you abuse! But those who refuse to commit biblical abuse don't go about it that way.

As we've already noticed, that's certainly not what Ezra did. He said to the people, as it were, "Let's hear from God. Let's unroll the scroll." And they stood to their feet. And he read from the law of God. And they said, without any comment from him, "Amen, Amen! We believe it. That's the Book. That's the truth. We care about what God says." But he didn't stop there. When God's Book was opened (remember the title of my previous chapter?), it was as if God were speaking.

Third: *Accurately handling the Scriptures means that the truth is explained so that all can understand.* Now I'm glad to say, we've come to one of the clearest verses on biblical exposition in all the Old Testament.

> *And they read from the book, from the law of God, translating to give the sense so that they understood the reading.*

Go back to those words and find the the term "translating." Don't go any further. Let's be like the dog and worry over this bone for a few moments. The original term meant "to make distinct, to separate." An acceptable paraphrase: "to take apart for the sake of making something clear and understandable so that the truth would fall in place."

But why was there a need to translate? Stop and think. Who were those people? They were Hebrews. In what language was the scroll written? In Hebrew. But where had the people been? According to Jewish history, they'd been in captivity for seven decades. Some of them didn't know what life was like *outside* captivity. They had been born in captivity, having lived their entire lives among the Babylonians. Their whole frame of reference was Babylonian or Chaldean. Their language was Chaldean. They thought in Chaldean. Their culture, their lifestyle was Chaldean . . . but the Book of God was written in Hebrew. Not only were they removed from the truth by centuries since its writing, they were removed from the truth culturally and linguistically. All the more reason to "to translate to make distinct."

In other words, when Ezra and his scribes built the bridge of understanding in the minds of the people, they took the Hebrew Scriptures and made them distinct to a Chaldean mind. That is always the job of the Bible teacher . . . building a linguistic and cultural bridge from Scripture's original setting to today's audience.

Today we are even further removed from the days of the Bible. So the Scripture is not only nineteen centuries old, it's from another continent. It's also from another culture. The careful student of Scripture will keep that uppermost in mind.

Please observe next, they gave "the sense." They translated "to give the *sense*." The original term means "insight, to see into something." They shed light on that which was otherwise unclear to the listener. And the result? The people understood the reading.

For many years I have believed that the greatest test of good biblical communication occurs a day or two after people have heard what is taught . . . when they can sit down at their kitchen table and go back through that passage—and can pretty well explain what it meant in that day and how it applies today.

Now for the fourth and final observation: *Accurately handling the Scriptures results in obedience to the Scriptures.* Bible study, like any theoretical knowledge, is not an end in itself. It is a means to an end. Accurately handling the Scriptures results in specific, personal acts of obedience to the Scriptures. Let's watch that happen! Take your time and read through these verses:

> *Then Nehemiah, who was the governor, and Ezra the priest and scribe, and the Levites who taught the people said to all the people, "This day is holy to the Lord your God; do not mourn or weep." For all the people were weeping when they heard the words of the law. Then he said to them, "Go, eat of the fat, drink of the sweet, and send portions to him who has nothing prepared; for this day is holy to our Lord. Do not be grieved, for the joy of the Lord is your strength." So the Levites calmed all the people, saying, "Be still, for the day is holy, do not be grieved." And all the people went away to eat, to drink, to send portions and to celebrate a great festival, because they understood the words which had been made known to them.*
>
> *Then on the second day the heads of fathers' households of all the people, the priests, and the Levites were gathered to Ezra the*

scribe that they might gain insight into the words of the law. And they found written in the law how the Lord had commanded through Moses that the sons of Israel should live in booths during the feast of the seventh month. So they proclaimed and circulated a proclamation in all their cities and in Jerusalem, saying, "Go out to the hills, and bring olive branches, and wild olive branches, myrtle branches, palm branches, and branches of other leafy trees, to make booths, as it is written." So the people went out and brought them and made booths for themselves, each on his roof, and in their courts, and in the courts of the house of God, and in the square at the Water Gate, and in the square at the Gate of Ephraim. And the entire assembly of those who had returned from the captivity made booths and lived in them. The sons of Israel had indeed not done so from the days of Joshua the son of Nun to that day. And there was great rejoicing. And he read from the book of the law of God daily, from the first day to the last day. And they celebrated the feast seven days, and on the eighth day there was a solemn assembly according to the ordinance (vv. 9-18).

They heard what God said and they did it. Rather plain and simple, huh? But that's obedience—doing what God says.

Allow me to return one more time to Bernard Ramm's comments:

I feel that I have experienced a good session of Bible study:
__ when I felt the teacher took me right into the text and not around it.
__ when I felt we interacted with the text itself and not with the party-line beliefs of the teacher. [You've had that experience, haven't you?]
__ when I felt that I had a better understanding of the text than when I came into the session.
__ when I felt that the time was basically spent in meanings and not in a miscellany of religious platitudes.
__ when I felt challenged, comforted, encouraged, and practically instructed.[3]

TOOLS FOR THE TRADE

Some of you are getting downright serious about Bible study.

Good for you! Since that is true, you need to get hold of some tools that will help you do that. I call these tools abuse busters!

First, you need a *Bible concordance*, which is an alphabetical listing of all the words in the Bible. The bigger the concordance, the more the words. Some are exhaustive, meaning they include every word that appears on every page of the Bible. No serious student of the Scriptures should be without a copy of a reputable concordance.

Second, you need a *Bible dictionary*. Like an English dictionary, this book defines and describes the major terms, places, and people in Scripture. Numerous dictionaries are available. Take your choice. Talk to your local Christian bookstore and have the manager show you the options.

Third, you need a *Bible atlas* which gives you maps and helpful geographical observations of the world in biblical days.

Fourth, you need some *Bible commentaries*. Initially, you need to have one that covers the whole of Scripture in one volume. Then you should begin to purchase individual commentaries on the individual books in the Bible. Serious Bible students get serious about purchasing biblical tools. Be forewarned: They're not 98-cent booklets. So don't drop by a store with $1.50, planning to buy two or three of them!

WARNING FOR THE WISE

At the beginning of this chapter, I referred to being biblically abused. One of the interesting (albeit tragic) facts of child abuse in our day is the fact that most parents who abuse their children were themselves abused. I find the same is true of scriptural abuse. My warning? People who were abused biblically tend to abuse others biblically. If you happened to have been abused, how about breaking the trend? Just face the fact that you were ripped off. And rather than sending hate mail to your teacher of yesteryear and wasting hours of valuable time resenting what you were taught, just commit yourself to change. Forgive him or her and pay no more attention to those old teachings. Get away from the former error and commit yourself to God's Word afresh and anew. Set up a reading program so that you can begin to absorb the Scripture. Begin to build a new respect for the Bible. Use helpful tools as you seek a clear, careful understanding, ultimately living obediently in keeping with God's Word.

SOME PRINCIPLES: RULES TO REMEMBER
■

Want some help on breaking the old syndrome? How about five simple rules? Each includes a different word—what, who, why, where, and when.

1. WHAT. *Never forget what you are handling.* And what is that? It is the Word of God. God's Book—God's voice. That will keep you *sensitive*.

2. WHO. *Always remember who has the authority.* That's the Lord Himself. That'll keep you *humble*. I was speaking with some Christians recently, and they commented on a particular Bible teacher they had heard. The thing that disturbed them the most about this person was an air of arrogance. Nothing wrong with his competence or his theology or his years of experience. But there was an unattractive arrogance about his style. Confidence is essential, but proud arrogance has no place whatsoever in Bible teaching. When I hear an arrogant teacher, I realize I'm listening to a person who has forgotten who has the authority. Those who remember who has the authority don't have a big battle with pride.

3. WHY. *Keep in mind why you are teaching.* This will keep you *accurate*. Why study . . . why teach? To capture the original meaning and then today's application of the Scriptures. Would it help if I drilled it home with a couple of "nots" or negatives?

First, your desire is not to impress. Don't try to "wow" others with your scholarship. If you've got it, they will notice it and be impressed on their own. No reason to toss in Hebrew or Greek words unless they really help clarify the subject. If it doesn't really help your case, forget the original language barrage. If it does, refer to it sparingly. It confuses an English audience to wade through a lot of Greek or Hebrew verbiage dangled in front of them in rapid-fire fashion.

Second, try not to ride a hobbyhorse. Now I realize everybody has a few. I've got 'em . . . you've got 'em. Sometimes I get on 'em, I confess. But when I do I realize later that I rode away from my point rather than toward it.

Try to remember those two negatives as you keep in mind why you are teaching. Accuracy is always the underlying goal of Bible study and Bible teaching.

4. WHERE. *Think about where people are.* That'll keep you *interesting*. If you're dealing with people in southern California, it takes one kind of approach. If you're dealing with people in the Northeast, it takes another kind of approach. The Deep South calls for yet another. If you're dealing with folks on the mission field, yet another kind of approach is best. Or with prisoners, another. If

you're dealing with folks in a situation where there's very little knowledge of Scripture, your presentation will be more interesting if you'll remember where they are. They're not as far along as others in another circle. To keep it interesting . . . remember where.

5. WHEN. *Focus on when the teaching ends.* That'll keep you *practical.* When the teaching is all over, when the Bible study that you've been involved in is history, what difference will it make?

I never intended this chapter to be so long . . . but the deeper I got into the subject, the more I felt needed to be said. After all, there are few things more important than handling the Scriptures accurately.

Those who are committed to these principles, those who put them into action, will become part of the solution to biblical abuse.

1. How can you guard against "biblical abuse" as you teach others—or even as you represent God and Scripture in casual conversation? If you realize that you have been using Scripture in a "proof text" manner, determine right now to *always* study the context so that you will *maintain the meaning.*

2. If the Bible you use is full of notes and comments from an unreliable source, perhaps you need to purchase another Bible. By starting over with clean, unmarked pages, you will be able to reconstruct a fresh path to the truth.

3. Commit to memory the "what, who, why, where, and when" statements you just read. Review them until they are fixed in your mind. Remind yourself of them each time you study the Scriptures.

God the Father

"I acknowledge the Creator-God as my heavenly Father, infinitely perfect and intimately acquainted with all my ways."

KNOWING GOD: LIFE'S MAJOR PURSUIT

rophets are not easygoing people . . . never have been, never will be. They are notorious for making us uncomfortable. But they never fail to make us think. Interestingly, most prophets have not been spawned in seminaries, nor have they spent all their lives in churches. Some were first farmers or fishermen. A few of them came from such unlikely places as political arenas and prison wards. One in our generation was both politician and prisoner before he emerged as a prophet.

I'm referring, of course, to Chuck Colson, former White House assistant during Richard Nixon's presidency. You know Colson's story . . . from the President's confidant to a prison cell, only to emerge as a clear-thinking prophet for our times.

I think the man received some of his best insights while behind bars. And some of the things he writes today that stir us into action found their origin during those lonely months he spent in prison. While reading one of his works not long ago, I came across a few paragraphs that speak for themselves. Hold on tight! Like all other prophets, Chuck Colson doesn't mess around.

> For a generation, Western society has been obsessed with the search for self. We have turned the age-old philosophical question about the meaning and purpose of life into a modern growth industry. Like Heinz, there are fifty-seven varieties, and then some: biofeedback, Yoga, creative consciousness, EST, awareness workshops, TA—each fad with an avid following until something new comes along.

Popular literature rides the wave with best-selling titles that guarantee success with everything from making money to firming flabby thighs. This not-so-magnificent obsession to "find ourselves" has spawned a whole set of counterfeit values; we worship fame, success, materialism, and celebrity. We want to "live for success" as we "look out for number one," and we don't mind "winning through intimidation."

However, this "self" conscious world is in desperate straits. Each new promise leads only to a frustrating paradox. The 1970s self-fulfillment fads led to self-absorption and isolation, rather than the fuller, liberated lives they predicted. The technology created to lead humanity to this new promised land may instead obliterate us and our planet in a giant mushroom cloud. Three decades of seemingly limitless affluence have succeeded only in sucking our culture dry, leaving it spiritually empty and economically weakened. Our world is filled with self-absorbed, frightened, hollow people. . . .

And in the midst of all this we have the church—those who follow Christ. For the church, this ought to be an hour of opportunity. The church alone can provide a moral vision to a wandering people; the church alone can step into the vacuum and demonstrate that there is a sovereign, living God who is the source of Truth.

BUT, the church is in almost as much trouble as the culture, for the church has bought into the same value system: fame, success, materialism, and celebrity. We watch the leading churches and the leading Christians for our cues. We want to emulate the best-known preachers with the biggest sanctuaries and the grandest edifices.

Preoccupation with these values has also perverted the church's message. The assistant to one renowned media pastor, when asked the key to his man's success, replied without hesitation, "We give the people what they want." This heresy is at the root of the most dangerous message preached today: the what's-in-it-for me gospel.

The "victorious Christian life" has become man's victorious life, not God's. A popular daily devotional quotes Psalm 65:9, "The streams of God are filled with water," and paraphrases it, "I fill my mind to overflowing with thoughts of prosperity and success. I affirm that God is my source and God is unlimited." This is not just a religious adaptation of the look-out-for-number-one, winner-take-all, God-helps-those-who-help-themselves gospel of our culture; it is heresy.[1]

Woven through the fabric of those penetrating words is the revelation of an invisible, insidious disease that has infected and crippled our once-strong nation. It is commonly called "me-ism" . . . a subtle yet consuming passion to please one's self, to exalt "I, me, mine, myself."[2]

Shirley MacLaine, the award-winning actress granted an interview to the *Washington Post* back in 1977. In that interview she tipped her hand:

> The most pleasurable journey you take is through yourself . . . the only sustaining love is with yourself . . . When you look back on your life and try to figure out where you've been and where you're going, when you look at your work, your love affairs, your marriages, your children, your pain, your happiness— when you examine all that closely, what you really find out is that the only person you really go to bed with is yourself. . . . The only thing you have is working to the consummation of your own identity. And that's what I've been trying to do all my life.[3]

At the risk of sounding terribly narrow and simplistic, I have a message today that represents not just a different approach—but an *opposite* one. I am more convinced than ever that life's major pursuit is not knowing self . . . but knowing God.

As a matter of fact, unless God is the major pursuit of our lives, all other pursuits are dead-end streets, including trying to know ourselves. They won't work. They won't satisfy. They won't result in fulfillment. They won't do for us what we think they're going to do.

You never really begin the process of coming to know yourself until you begin the process of coming to know God. The by-product of such a process is discovering the peace you long for so desperately.

THE WAIL OF A WEEPING PROPHET

Let's leave a modern-day prophet, step into the time tunnel, and return to an ancient prophet named Jeremiah. He spoke and wrote 2,500 years ago. Perhaps I should say he wept 2,500 years ago. So much so that to this day he's called "the weeping prophet." Dear Jeremiah! If tears had been ink, I think Jeremiah would have had more to write than all the other prophets put together. Here was a man of God who saw way ahead of his times (most prophets do, by the way). He found himself surrounded by a polluted stream of human depravity, lamenting the condition of his people—people who knew better, who had been instructed for centuries to know and walk with their God. But they had deliberately and willfully turned away from the word of their God. Instead of turning to Him, they went after their own pursuits, which resulted in a downward spiral of self-destruction. They had disintegrated into a weak nation, soon to be destroyed by a greater power.

He wrote these tragic words in chapter 9 of the biblical book that bears his name:

> *O that my head were waters, and my eyes a fountain of tears, that I might weep day and night for the slain of the daughter of my people!* (v. 1).

The scene the prophet paints isn't pretty—but it is realistic. He says, in effect, "My people are goners! They're a pack of wimps. Those who were once known as strong for their God are now weak, emaciated, and about to be destroyed."

If you want to know what Jeremiah really wished to do, read verse 2:

> *O that I had in the desert a wayfarers' lodging place; that I might leave my people, and go from them!* (v. 2a).

In today's terms, "Oh, that I could escape to a condo in Palm Springs and get out of this mess, this moral filth and carnal pollution in which I'm living." He really wished for the ability to escape.

Why? Disease was everywhere! He names a few of the symptoms. Not the disease yet, just the symptoms:

> *For all of them are adulterers, an assembly of treacherous men. "And they bend their tongue like their bow; lies and not truth prevail in the land;"* [in today's terms the way it would read is "because they are going from bad to worse"] (vv. 2b-3a).

Jeremiah wails, "Everywhere I turn I seek for truth and I hear lies. I look for faithfulness and I find unfaithfulness. I look for people who are gentle, kind, encouraging, and I find treachery, murder, assault, rape. I look in vain to find the things that are to characterize the people of God."

Now the disease—here's the foundational cause:

". . . And they do not know Me," declares the Lord, (v.3b).

That may seem like a very simple answer, yet it's profound. A little later the prophet continues to quote his Lord.

> . . . *"Let not a wise man boast of his wisdom, and let not the mighty man boast of his might, let not a rich man boast of his riches . . ."* (v. 23).

Now wait. Just pause right there.

You want to know what people pursue when their eyes are on themselves? You've got it right in that statement. They embrace a "counterfeit value system"—the same dead-end pursuit that Chuck Colson described in his book. Human wisdom . . . human might . . . human riches.

I ask you, is this relevant or what? Does that description sound like today's world? Stop on most any university campus and ask, "What is your goal? What is your plan? Where are you going?" Sometimes the answers will surprise you.

I was on a university campus not long ago. I asked a student, "Where are you going?" He said, "Lunch." I was expecting some great philosophical answer. But aside from a simple answer like that, you will probably hear, "I want to be resourceful" (human wisdom). "I want to be influential" (human might). "I want to be powerful" (human riches). "I want to be successful. I want to wind up top in my company. I want to run things. I want to control people. I want to be in charge. I want to make a name for myself."

We don't read a single comment in verse 23 about the living God. But in the next statement (verse 24) the solution emerges:

> *but let him who boasts boast of this, that he understands and knows Me. . . .*

Now there's the cure—plain, brief, and simple. What is it that will make an unfaithful man faithful? What is it that will make an influential man who's controlling people a servant? What is it that will cause an individual who has turned to treachery to become gentle and gracious and giving, demonstrating a heart for God? It is understanding and knowing the living God.

Allow me a few moments to take those words apart. (Remember my last chapter? Words are of utmost importance.) The first word, *understand,* in verse 24, comes from a verb in the original text that means to have correct "insight" into the nature of the object. In this case, the object is the living God. It also includes the idea of "conducting oneself wisely and dealing prudently." Harris, Archer, and Waltke add, "conforming one's life to the character of God."[4] It's as if he is writing: "To the one who would otherwise turn to his own might and wisdom and riches I offer an alternate plan." It isn't popular. You'll never be in the majority. But you will find the happiness you're pursuing. You'll discover what life is about if you have correct insight into the nature of and conform your life to the character of the living God.

Second, look again at the word *to know*. It is a knowledge gained by the senses, not one gained in a rational manner. It's not a knowledge that you can put your hands on, or that you can prove in an experiment or observe with the naked eye. It is a kind of knowledge that involves the inner faculties of the mind, being focused on and motivated by the living God. It's hard to put that in practical terms. It's a faith-kind-of knowledge. When you put the two terms together, *understand* and *know* fully express all the powers and faculties of a human mind being focused on the living God.

Now, how many people do that? I think a better question is: How many people *want* to do that? Start with yourself—do you?

I often look into the faces of successful businessmen and career women, wondering, "Is that person really pursuing a knowledge of God?" I'm occasionally in touch with individuals who are at the top in their companies. And I often meet people who are on their way up that competitive corporate ladder. And I meet students who are making their plans and fitting their education into their ultimate objectives. Frequently, I think: "Does that person really want to know God?"

How about you? Do you really want to understand His ways? I'm not referring to the kind of understanding and knowledge that is merely intellectual theology. Not that. I have in mind men and women who see life through the eyes of God, who understand life's circumstances through the lens of God's plan, who accept and believe that whatever is happening has been given by God, permitted by God, and continues under God's personal surveillance . . . that kind of God-understanding and God-awareness.

Now I need to confess something to you. When I sat down to write this chapter on God the Father, I thought, "What can I say?" Returning to this theological root is an awesome journey. Much of it is beyond our comprehension.

Reminds me of the time I got a phone call from Goodwill Industries. They wanted me to speak to their group of people. I said to the lady, "What do you think would be a good subject?" She rather flippantly said, "Oh, how about God and the universe and various subjects?" I thought, "Well, that boils it down to basics, doesn't it? God and the universe."

How can I limit the subject of the living God to a brief chapter in a book? So I decided I wouldn't take the normal approach on this. Most books on doctrine offer page after page after page on God's attributes. That's helpful and needed, yet most of us have heard such things since we were little kids in Sunday school. So I've decided to approach this subject in a much more practical way. I want to write about the importance of knowing Him. And having done that, I'm going to trust the Spirit of God to motivate you to change your course in life, if that is necessary. And, lest you get the mistaken idea that everything ends with knowing Him, I will address the flip side in the next chapter . . . loving Him.

THE IMPORTANCE OF KNOWING GOD

I am convinced that there is nothing more important about us than what we think about God. Here are just a few of the reasons I believe that.

___ It shapes our moral and ethical standards.
___ It directly affects our response to pain and hardship.
___ It motivates our response toward fortune, fame, power, and pleasure.
___ It gives us strength when we are tempted.
___ It keeps us faithful and courageous when we are outnumbered.
___ It enhances our worship and prompts our praise.
___ It determines our lifestyle and dictates our philosophy.
___ It gives meaning and significance to relationships.
___ It sensitizes our conscience and creates the desire to be obedient.
___ It stimulates hope to go on, regardless.
___ It enables me to know what to reject and what to respect while I'm riveted to planet Earth.
___ It is the foundation upon which EVERYTHING rests!

God has given us a *general revelation* of Himself in the heavens. So much so that more than once in the New Testament letter to the

Romans it states that we're without excuse. He has written His handiwork in the heavens.

The heavens are telling of the glory of God; and their expanse is declaring the work of His hands (Psalm 19:1).

You look up into the starry skies and you realize, if you make any kind of serious study of those stars, they didn't just tumble into space. The rising of the tide and the lowering of the tide; the dropping of seed into the ground and the growing of plants; the climates, the wind, the weather, the torrential wind currents that sweep across this earth—those things don't "just happen." They are so obviously from the hand of the living God that you have to train yourself *not* to think that way.

In fact, I personally believe you have to teach a child *not* to believe in God. The most natural thing in the world in the heart of a child is to believe that someone outside himself arranged things and keeps them in motion. If you question that, you haven't listened to children lately.

But there's more. There is also *special revelation* in history as well as in Scripture. God specifically reveals Himself in both. All this brings me to capitalize on five reasons it's important to know God.

1. *Knowing God gives us the desire to be like Him.* Read again Jeremiah's words:

. . . *"But let him who boasts boast of this, that he understands and knows Me, that I am the Lord who exercises loving kindness, justice, and righteousness on earth; for I delight in these things," declares the Lord* (Jeremiah 9:24).

Interesting, isn't it, that when the Lord talks about Himself, He reveals His attributes, His character traits: lovingkindness, justice, righteousness.

Over in 1 Peter we read that the Lord is holy. In fact, we even read the command, "You shall be holy, for I am holy" (1:16).

The most natural thing in the world is to become like our parents, even when we don't want to become like our parents! Isn't it amazing? I've heard people say, "When I grow up, I'm not gonna be like my father!" Or, "I'm not going to be like my mother." Yet when they grow up, they are just like their father or mother. Why? Because they know their parents; they've been around them. Their mother's or father's thumbprint is indelibly imprinted on their lives.

That's the way it is with God our Father. The more I get to know my God, the more I become like Him. I discover He's holy; I want to be holy. I discover He's good; I want to be better. I discover He's strong; I want to be more confident. I discover He's in control; I don't want to panic my way through life. I don't want to ricochet from one event to another; I want to move through life calmly, consistently. I want to be like my Father. And in order to be like Him, I need to know what He is like.

2. *Knowing God reveals the truth about ourselves.* A glance into the sixth chapter of Isaiah will help support this fact. What a great section of Scripture!

King Uzziah had died. I take it that Isaiah was close to Uzziah the king. He was grieving over his death. And as a result, he went to the place of worship—the same year, perhaps near the same time that Uzziah had died. And while in worship, he observed the living God. Imagine the scene:

> *In the year of King Uzziah's death, I saw the Lord sitting on a throne, lofty and exalted, with the train of His robe filling the temple. Seraphim stood above Him, each having six wings; with two he covered his face, and with two he covered his feet, and with two he flew* (Isaiah 6:1-2).

Here are six-winged creatures, fluttering about the throne of heaven, giving praise to God. And they are saying, "Holy, Holy, Holy, is the Lord of hosts." One is standing saying it, and another answers in antiphonal voice. Still another praises, and another responds. This group praises, and that group responds. The whole throne is filled with His glory.

And having seen the Lord high and lifted up, Isaiah suddenly got a glimpse of *himself.*

> *Then I said, "Woe is me, for I am ruined! Because I am a man of unclean lips, and I live among a people of unclean lips . . .* (v. 5).

Perhaps Isaiah struggled with profanity. He was certainly surrounded by a profane-speaking people. And when he saw the holiness of God in all of His splendor, he clapped his hand over his mouth and thought, "How could I be His spokesman with these unclean lips?"

When we study the Lord God we discover He's holy and we're unholy. It doesn't hurt us to know that; it helps us. We discover that He's perfect and we're imperfect . . . He's strong and we're weak . . . He's patient and we're impatient . . . He's impartial, yet we're prejudiced. He's in control, and our lives are often fractured by fear and worry. And something occurs in that contrast that causes His character to overshadow our need. The result is marvelous—the knowledge of the Holy One equips us to see the truth and to change. I cannot explain how it works; I just know it does.

Do you change by spending time with people? Very little. Only a few people can impact you sufficiently to result in your changing for the good. Most people will tell you that you're so far ahead of others that you don't have anything to work on—"nothin' to worry about." Trust me, God won't leave you with that information! He'll help you see yourself—your strengths and certainly your weaknesses. And every time you turn to His Word, you'll see another flaw, another need, another weakness that needs to be addressed. God always tells us the truth. And it is the truth that sets us free! When we see ourselves as we really are, we are prompted to lean on Him and to trust Him to make us like He is.

3. *Knowing God enables us to interpret our world.* Toward the end of the fourth chapter of Daniel, we bump into a rather remarkable individual. The man's name is Nebuchadnezzar. He is the king of Babylon. In great arrogance the king lived as though he needed no one else. Full of conceit, he is strutting around the kingdom with his thumbs under his suspenders saying, "How great I am. How wonderful I am. Look at this kingdom I've built. What a magnificent person I have become. Everybody, together, say it with me again and again, 'Nebuchadnezzar.' Let's all say together . . ." Then, very suddenly, he lost his mind.

> *Immediately the word concerning Nebuchadnezzar was fulfilled; and he was driven away from mankind and began eating grass like cattle, and his body was drenched with the dew of heaven, until his hair had grown like eagles' feathers and his nails like birds' claws* (Daniel 4:33).

It means just what it says. This once-great man is reduced to a wild beast, living out in the field through day and night, with claws like an eagle and long hair. What a terrible, insane existence!

I can't fully explain my next statement . . . I can only tell you it's often true: For some people, it takes insanity to come to the end of themselves and to find God. That's the way it was with Nebuchadnezzar. Not all breakdowns are the end of a person's life. Sometimes they are the beginning, which means we should perhaps call them break-*ups*. One day the Nebuchadnezzar-beast paused in the midst of its grazing and looked up toward heaven. A shaft of light broke through into the darkened mind. As the king described it:

But at the end of that period I, Nebuchadnezzar, raised
my eyes toward heaven, and my reason returned to me, and I
blessed the Most High and praised and honored Him who lives
forever; [he used to praise and honor himself];
> *For His dominion is an everlasting dominion,*
> *And His kingdom endures from generation to*
> *generation.*
> *And all the inhabitants of the earth are*
> *accounted as nothing,*
> *But He does according to His will in*
> *the host of heaven*
> *And among the inhabitants of earth;*
> *And no one can ward off His hand*
> *Or say to Him, "What hast Thou done?"*

At that time my reason returned to me . . . (Daniel 4:34-36a).

It's the thirty-fifth verse that interests me.

> *And all the inhabitants of the earth are*
> *accounted as nothing,*
> *But He does according to His will in the*
> *host of heaven*
> *And among the inhabitants of earth;*
> *And no one can ward off His hand*
> *Or say to Him, "What hast Thou done?"*

Once Nebuchadnezzar saw God in all His sovereignty and glory, his whole perspective changed. He saw the earth as under God's control. His pride vanished as he realized that God was the One calling the shots, not himself.

I remember that during my pastoral internship many years ago I happened to come across Daniel 4. That summer I was studying the book of Daniel. And I'll never forget struggling over the sovereignty of God. I battled with it. I wrestled with God about it. I'd been taught to reject it, to resist it, to turn it off as heresy . . . yet, here in Daniel 4 I had to face it.

And you know what? I could resist it no longer. In fact, I finally embraced it.

I began to experience a peace like you can't believe. A calm swept over me. I distinctly remember saying to Pastor Ray Stedman of the church where I was an intern, "I gotta tell ya, Ray, that doctrine has changed my life this summer." Ray, who had long since come to realize that same truth, grinned from ear to ear and said, "Chuck, that is wonderful! It will be a comfort to you throughout your ministry." He was right.

When you get hold of the knowledge of God and begin to see that He is in charge, you won't panic every time you read the paper. You won't give up hope because there's an earthquake somewhere. You won't live in the fear of terrorism or possible disease.

In fact, you'll be able to sort of sing your way through the business section, editorial page . . . even the sports page! Why? Because you know the God who is in control of all things.

People have this weird idea that God is tentatively sitting on the edge of heaven going, "Ooh! Oh, no! How am I gonna handle this? HELP!" My friend, that's *not* the God of the Scriptures. That isn't the living God who holds everything in His hands. He may be invisible, but He's in touch. You may not be able to see Him, but He is in control. And that includes *you*—your circumstances. That includes what you've just lost. That includes what you've just gained. That includes all of life . . . past, present, future.

4. *Knowing God makes us stronger and more secure.* Goodness knows, we need this! Daniel 11:32 says:

> *And by smooth words he will turn to godlessness those who act wickedly toward the covenant, but the people who know their God will display strength and take action.*

This verse emerges from a tough setting. It's a scene of conflict and warfare. There's a battle going on between good and evil. And right in the middle of the verse, Daniel inserts:

> *. . . but the people who know their God will display strength and take action.*

James Boice writes these words about the strength of our God.

> We do not have a strong church today nor do we have *many* strong Christians. We can trace the cause to an acute lack of sound spiritual knowledge. Why is the church weak? Why are individual Christians weak? It's because they have allowed their minds to become conformed to the "spirit of this age," with its mechanistic, godless thinking. They have forgotten what God is like and what He promises to do for those who trust Him. Ask an average Christian to talk about God. After getting past the expected answers you will find that his god is a little god of vac-

illating sentiments. He is a god who would like to save the world but who cannot. He would like to restrain evil, but somehow he finds it beyond his power. So he has withdrawn into semiretirement, being willing to give good advice in a grandfatherly sort of way, but for the most part he has left his children to fend for themselves in a dangerous environment.

Such a god is not the God of the Bible . . . the God of the Bible is not weak; He is strong. He is all-mighty. Nothing happens without His permission or apart from His purposes—even evil. Nothing disturbs or puzzles Him. His purposes are always accomplished. Therefore those who know Him rightly act with boldness, assured that God is with them to accomplish His own desirable purposes in their lives.[5]

I want to ask you a direct question. Isn't it true, more often than not, that the God you picture in your mind is old, has a long beard—and maybe leans on a cane? Isn't that true? You picture Him standing in the North with His cheeks pushing out as He blows real hard, right? Sure you do. He wears a robe, has big toes, sandals. He's not too sure about modern things like advanced nuclear physics, dense packs, laser beams, and electronic computers. He's more of a kind old grandfather that is gonna be there when you need Him, and you can trust Him because He is wise and generous. He could handle things yesterday and maybe He could handle most things today. But He's sort of losing touch.

If that's your God, then listen to me: THAT IS HERESY!

It is nothing short of HERESY to think of God like that. He isn't old; He is eternal. He isn't intimidated; He is omnipotent. Computers don't bother Him; He is omniscient! The nuclear warheads don't have Him worried! He is sovereign.

So things aren't out of hand! He's in control. He can handle it. And what's more, He can handle you. He knows you thoroughly . . . He even knows the number of the hairs on your head (and for some of you, that's no big deal). He's got everything wired! He's got it all together! He is the sovereign God of the universe and He's never once lost control. He strengthens and He secures His people. Those who know their God operate in such a context of confidence, they can face whatever . . . and "display strength and take action."

See the value of knowing God? See what it does to your perspective? See how much calmer you become? Lift your eyes. Behold His glory high and lifted up. Worthy is the Lamb that was slain to give power and authority over this place. His kingdom will not fail. That's our God.

Now, I've saved the best till last. Why is it important to know Him?

5. *Knowing God introduces us to the eternal dimension of existence.*
Look at John 17:3. Jesus is praying to the Father as He says:

> *And this is eternal life, that they may know Thee, the only true
> God, and Jesus Christ whom Thou has sent.*

Knowing God introduces me to the invisible world of God's kingdom.
I see through eyes that aren't given to everyone. We read elsewhere:

> . . . *Things which eye has not seen and ear has not heard, and
> which have not entered the heart of man, all that God has pre-
> pared for those who love Him* (1 Corinthians 2:9).

The natural person isn't born with this kind of insight. It's given
at the new birth. That's why I often talk about coming to know Jesus
Christ, believing in the Lord Jesus Christ, turning one's life over to
Christ, coming to one's heart's door, opening it by faith, and saying,
"Jesus Christ, come into my life. Take charge." Because when He
comes in, He introduces us to an eternal dimension for living. And
that perspective lifts the mind ABOVE the present, irksome details
of life. What we gain is an eternal dimension of life.

THE PRESENCE OF INCOMPREHENSIBLE SUBJECTS

As we have considered five reasons to know God, I must confess
to a little fear. My fear doesn't relate to what I've communicated—
but to what you might do with it. You might have the idea that if you
take pen in hand and open the Bible and start in Genesis and work
your way through to Revelation, you'll have it all put together. You'll
not only understand everything about God, you'll understand all
the mysteries, right? Wrong!

> *Oh, the depth of the riches both of the wisdom and knowledge of
> God! How unsearchable are His judgments and unfathomable
> His ways!* (Romans 11:33).

Remember those words when you travel down the road in hopes of
understanding and knowing your God. Realize in advance that you
will come to some streets that are mysterious and unfathomable. Don't
let the mystery surprise you or disturb you. God planned it that way.
It occurs to me that there are several theological thoughts that
are incomprehensible. Four come to mind.

1. *Trinity.* There is one God yet three distinct persons. The Godhead is co-equal, co-eternal, co-existent: God the Father, God the Son, God the Holy Spirit. Much of that remains a profound mystery. Don't lose sleep if you cannot unravel the truth of the Trinity.

2. *Glory.* The Trinity has to do with the *person* of God. Glory has to do with the *presence* of God. It has something to do with light—with blinding brilliance. The people sensed His presence in the tabernacle and the temple because the light of His glory was there. That same glory of God was later lifted from the place of worship and removed because of the unbelief of the people. There is something terribly mysterious about the glory of God, revealed through Scripture. Don't weary yourself trying to unscrew the inscrutable.

3. *Sovereignty.* This has to do with the *plan* of God. Certainly, he is in control of all things; yet, even though He is perfectly holy, sin is present. He permits it. He allows it. Without being contaminated by the sin, our Holy God is working out His plan. If you want to engage in a futile study, try to reconcile those things. No, seriously, quit trying to reconcile it! Take it by faith!

4. *Majesty.* This relates to the Father's *position.* He is unseen and will remain unseen throughout eternity. I'm not sure if we will ever see God the Father, even in a glorified state, and yet He's there in all of His glory. His majestic position will never be diminished—and yet I'm sure we'll never be able to grasp it on this earth. Just believe it. And bow before His almighty majesty.

FINALLY, SOME ESSENTIAL FACTS

But there are some things we *can* understand that are very practical and absolutely essential. Let me close this chapter with them. None of these things are mysterious. They can be grasped and applied.

- *God is pleased when we walk by faith.* The Bible is full of that fact. Nothing pleases the Lord more than when we walk by faith.
- *God is glorified when we worship in truth.* When I come across something that I can't handle or explain, He's pleased when I trust Him to get me through it. And when I gather in an assembly with other believers—or all alone—and I worship my God, He's glorified in it.
- *God is our Father when we believe in His Son . . . and not until.* Scripture never teaches that God is the Father of everyone, even though He graciously gives rain and sun to all on this earth. By grace, He becomes the Father of those who believe in His Son.

If you read this chapter and go out and buy a big study Bible and start to work on discovering just the *facts* about God, you've really grasped only part of what I've tried to communicate.

True knowledge affects the way we live, affects our attitude, affects our heart, our response, and it changes our direction. It alters the way we make decisions. It even takes away our worries. It brings us face to face with the truth of God and what He says about Himself. Perhaps that best explains why God's prophets have always been so intense and so unbending . . . and why their message has never failed to cut through the veneer of all the things that keep us from knowing the living God.

Knowing God is life's major pursuit, but that's only half the story. Loving God is our ultimate response. And that's what the next chapter is all about.

ROOT ISSUES

1. Schedule a lunch or dinner with a close Christian friend or your spouse (no kids along, please). The agenda? Thinking out loud about the major goals and *direction* of your life. Are you *really* growing in your knowledge of God as the days and weeks slip by? Are you *honestly* walking more closely with Jesus Christ? If not, why not? What might be keeping you from making this goal number one? What would have to change in your life and schedule to shift your focus and perspective in the coming months? Record these thoughts in your notebook. Be honest, practical . . . and don't forget to reserve some time in your evening for prayer.

2. Scripture often condemns people because there is "no room for God in their thoughts." Now, let's get down to the nitty-gritty. How often do WE think about our God during the course of a regular, garden-variety work day? How often do you pause (if only for a moment) to consider the reality and nearness and loving concern of your Lord? Talk to several Christians whom you respect about how *they* do it. Be sure to have your notebook handy so that you can save these valuable insights.

3. Spend some extended time in the Word (you'll probably have to schedule it in advance) reading and reflecting on the power and sovereignty of our great God. Select from passages such as: Isaiah 6, 40; Job 38-41; Psalms 8, 19, 24, 31, 46, 47, 91, 95, 100, 103, 104, 121, 148; Hebrews 1; Revelation 1, 4, 15, 19, 21, 22. You might try reading a number of these passages in a paraphrased version such as The Living Bible. As you read, ask the Lord to help you catch a new vision of who He is . . . what He demands . . . and what He can accomplish in and through your life as you trust Him.

LOVING GOD:
OUR ULTIMATE RESPONSE

here are not enough people who encourage us in life. As a matter of fact, I find that a majority of people have a way of discouraging us rather than affirming us and offering us fresh confidence to go on.

John Powell tells a true story that vividly illustrates this fact. It happened to one of his friends who was vacationing in the Bahamas.

> He saw a large and restless crowd gathered on a pier. Upon investigation he discovered that the object of all the attention was a young man making the last-minute preparations for a solo journey around the world in a homemade boat. Without exception everyone on the pier was vocally pessimistic. All were actively volunteering to tell the ambitious sailor all the things that could possibly go wrong. "The sun will broil you! . . . You won't have enough food! . . . That boat of yours won't withstand the waves in a storm! . . . You'll never make it!"

> When my friend heard all these discouraging warnings to the adventurous young man, he felt an irresistible desire to offer some optimism and encouragement. As the little craft began drifting away from the pier towards the horizon, my friend went to the end of the pier, waving both arms wildly like semaphores spelling confidence. He kept shouting: "Bon voyage! You're really something! We're with you! We're proud of you! Good luck, brother!"[1]

Can't you picture that scene? Everybody on the pier saying, "You'll never make it, man . . . that boat of yours is sure to sink!" And here stands one fellow waving his arms, shouting, "Go for it! You can do it! We believe in you!"

What's true about life in general is also true about the Christian life in particular. You and I are in the little boat. And that little boat has put out to sea. We are on our journey toward knowing and obeying God. Have you noticed how few there are who stand alongside as we push out into the sea, saying, "Good for you! Go for it! You can make it! You're on the right track! God be with you!"

I feel like we need many more who say such affirming things to all who desire to grow in their knowledge of God and the doctrines of His Word. In fact, as I write this book I think of myself on the pier cheering you on . . . because I believe in your journey. And I believe that if you have made the decision to know God fully and to walk with Him obediently and to learn His truths thoroughly, He will honor that decision. He, too, applauds your determination to return to your theological roots and discover the ocean of truth that stretches out before you. Never lose that love for knowledge! Never stop exploring in this adventure of faith! My hope is that each of these chapters will encourage you as well as inform you.

We have spent a chapter thinking about the importance of knowing God, which I've called life's major pursuit. Let's consider the other side of the same coin—loving God, which is clearly our ultimate response.

Tucked away in the fifth book of the Bible is a profound statement and a wonderful command. I want you to see both statement and command together in Deuteronomy 6, verses 4 and 5. The command is preceded by the statement. Let's look first at the statement, which talks about *knowing* God, and then let's observe the command, which addresses the importance of *loving* God.

Deuteronomy 6:4 is one of the most familiar statements in all of Jewish liturgy:

> *Hear, O Israel! The Lord is our God, the Lord is one!*

You can't see it in the English, but in the Hebrew that word *one* conveys the idea of "one in multiple," one as in a "cluster" or "group." *Echad* is the Hebrew word . . . it's the term for one, as in a cluster of grapes. "The Lord our God is one—one in Father, one in Son, one in Spirit." Moses says, "Hear, O Israel, and come to know Him as your only God." That statement had to do with knowing God. Now, the command:

And you shall love the Lord your God with all your heart and with all your soul and with all your might (v. 5).

How significant was this? He now explains its importance:

And these words, which I am commanding you today, shall be on your heart; and you shall teach them diligently to your sons and shall talk of them when you sit in your house and when you walk by the way and when you lie down and when you rise up. And you shall bind them as a sign on your hand and they shall be as frontals on your forehead. And you shall write them on the doorposts of your house and on your gates (vv. 6-9).

God is saying, "This is something I want you to put on your heart, men and women. And then as I bring children into your family, these are the things I want you to teach them. Not simply as an intellectual exercise, but I want it to be in the warp and woof of your lives. I want it to take place when you lie down at night and when you get up. When you walk, when you play, when you work. I want these things to characterize your lifestyle. I want you to model knowing Me and loving Me with all your heart, with all your soul, with all your might. And I want your children to absorb the same convictions, so that they will have that impression even when you're gone."

Every once in a while my wife and I talk about how life will be in our family when both of us are gone. I'm sure you who are parents have discussed the same. Cynthia and I are in agreement. We are in great hopes that our children will have learned by our model that there was nothing on earth more important to their mother and dad than knowing God and loving Him with all their heart and soul and might. If they will have gotten that impression, we will have accomplished a major part of our job. You see, children don't automatically realize the value of knowing God and loving Him. They need it modeled. They need those things woven into the fabric of their childhood memories.

How important was it for the Israelites? A brief history lesson will be worth the effort. Those people were right on the verge of the land of Canaan—the land that "flowed with milk and honey," the promised land. But what you may not remember is that it was crawling with idolaters. An idolatrous atmosphere covered the territory where they would soon be living. Shortly, Moses would die leaving only the memory of his instruction in their minds. Once they invaded and conquered Canaan, they would begin to rear their families in homes they didn't build, eating from vineyards they didn't plant, drinking from cisterns they didn't dig. From a nomad-like existence they would gain instant affluence.

So Moses is concerned that those simple people who had culti-vated a simple walk of faith might be blown away by the impact of idolatry and affluence, which could diminish their love for God. That explains why he told them to print His words on the doorposts of their houses, to write them on their hands and foreheads. He didn't want them ever to forget that they were people who knew and loved Jehovah God.

> . . . and He brought us out from there in order to bring us in, to give us the land which He had sworn to our fathers. So the Lord commanded us to observe all these statutes, to fear the Lord our God for our good always and for our survival, as it is today (vv. 23-24).

Let me make a suggestion: Underscore those last two preposi-tional phrases in red, "for our good" . . . "for our survival."

I don't know how many people I've met who lived under the false impression that when God makes a command He's trying to take away our fun. On the contrary, when God gives us a command, it's always for our good—and it's often for our survival. If you want to do what is good and if you want to do what will help you survive, then get to know your God and love Him with all your heart and soul and mind.

You'll remember in my previous chapter that I didn't give you six steps on how to know God. That was on purpose. Knowing God doesn't occur like that. It isn't a mechanical, step-by-step process. It's a lifetime pursuit. What it really requires is a day-by-day commit-ment in one's head and one's heart. A commitment that says, "Today I'm going to know God better. Today I'm going to love God more. This is going to become a regular, major pursuit of my life."

And piece by piece, little by little, day after day, it will begin to permeate your whole frame of reference. That's what Moses wanted for the Israelites, and that's what God wants for us.

GOD OF GRACE, GOD OF MERCY

Let's turn our attention from Deuteronomy to the Psalms, from history to poetry, four hundred years later, during the reign of King

David. Deuteronomy looked ahead, the Psalms look back. Moses anticipated the things on the horizon, and David responded by recording a number of the events that transpired.

I told you at the beginning of this book that this would not be your basic book on Bible doctrine. Here is a case in point. Take time to let your heart be encouraged in God. In the next few pages I want us to graze through several psalms. We'll see God at work as He came to the people's rescue for their good and for their survival. And then later on, we'll focus on the poet himself—David. We'll see how God brought him through difficult personal situations. And we'll see how David's heart welled over in response to this great love of God.

My hope is that these few pages we spend in the Psalms will stir up your faith and whet your appetite to trust God as you have never trusted Him before. After all, no one is more trustworthy than He! What will stand out in the Psalms is that the people, in every case, had no other one to lean on but God. They had no bank account. They had no visible shield of protection. They had no arsenal of weapons. They had no defense, not even a flag to fly. All they had was the living, trustworthy, faithful God! And the psalmist talks about how He came through time after time after time. The absence of all other substitutes forced them to lean hard on their God. When they did, He showed Himself strong in grace and glory.

Psalm 31. This is a good place to start. Look at the protection God provided:

> *In Thee, O Lord, I have taken refuge; let me never be ashamed; in Thy righteousness deliver me. Incline Thine ear to me, rescue me quickly; be Thou to me a rock of strength, a stronghold to save me. For Thou art my rock and my fortress; for Thy name's sake Thou wilt lead me and guide me. Thou wilt pull me out of the net which they have secretly laid for me; for Thou art my strength* (vv. 1-4).

Notice there is no other strength, no other source of encouragement, no other protection—only the Lord. Hence, David says, "It's You, Lord, I turn to."

A little later on he writes this prayer:

> *Be gracious to me, O Lord, for I am in distress; My eye is wasted away from grief, my soul and my body also. For my life is spent with sorrow, and my years with sighing; my strength has failed because of my iniquity, and my body has wasted away. Because of all my adversaries, I have become a reproach . . .* (v. 9-11a).

Ever had this experience? Just read on and you'll feel it with him.

> . . . *I have become a reproach, especially to my neighbors, and an object of dread to my acquaintances; those who see me in the street flee from me. I am forgotten as a dead man, out of mind, I am like a broken vessel. For I have heard the slander of many, terror is on every side; while they took counsel together against me, they schemed to take away my life* (vv. 11-13).

Look at the man. "Lord, I am at Your mercy. I have no defense. I am outnumbered. I am surrounded. And in myself, I am intimidated." But the point here is this, "But, Lord, O God, I know You. I trust You to get me through this." Read on.

> *But as for me, I trust in Thee, O Lord, I say, "Thou art my God." My times are in Thy hand; deliver me from the hand of my enemies, and from those who persecute me* (vv. 14-15).

Haven't you experienced holding on to things, gripping things, keeping them near, playing your cards close to your vest, protecting them, not wanting God to take them? They were important things to you, things you'd leaned on for strength, almost as if they were idols, right? And slowly, agonizingly, the Lord pried your fingers loose and you had to let go. I love how Corrie ten Boom used to put it. She used to say, "Vell, I've learned to hold every ting loosely, because it hurts ven God pries my fingers apart and takes tem from me."

An anonymous poet said it this way:

> One by one God took them from me,
> All the things I valued most,
> Till I was empty-handed,
> Every glittering toy was lost.

> And I walked earth's highways grieving
> In my rags and poverty
> Til I heard His voice inviting
> "Lift those empty hands to Me."

> So I turned my hands toward heaven,
> And He filled them with a store
> Of His own transcendent riches
> Till they could contain no more.

And at last I comprehended,
With my stupid mind and dull
That God could not pour His riches
Into hands already full.

Let it go. Trust Him. Love Him. Remind yourself that He's trustworthy. He won't hang you out to dry. Let others slander. Let them say those things against you. He knows you have integrity. Release your defense. Quit trying to fight back—give the battle to the Lord! That's the message of Psalm 31. Trust in no substitutes, seek no other refuge, lean on no other crutch but the living God. Love Him as you love no one else on earth. I dare you!

Psalm 37. Here is another grand statement of faith in this gracious, glorious God. Consider the inner strength, the peace that He alone gives. Let's work our way through the first nine verses.

> *Do not fret yourself because of evildoers, be not envious toward wrongdoers. For they will wither quickly like the grass, and fade like the green herb* (vv. 1-2).

Ever find yourself envious of the evildoers? Isn't it amazing how those who do wrong get away with murder, and you and I who do right can't even get away with taking a dime out of the phone booth? Isn't it remarkable? Somehow God zaps us with such guilt we have to return and stick the dime back in the slot so we can live with ourselves.

> *Trust in the Lord, and do good; dwell in the land and cultivate faithfulness. Delight yourself in the Lord; and He will give you the desires of your heart. Commit your way to the Lord, trust also in Him, and He will do it. And He will bring forth your righteousness as the light, and your judgment as the noonday* (vv. 3-6).

You see, our God knows us so well. When we begin to fret because of one who prospers in wickedness, then anger replaces peace. That anger boils over into wrath, and wrath begins to consume us. So He says again, "Do not fret yourself. It leads only to evildoing" (v. 8). How much better to focus on letting God do our defending.

> *For evildoers will be cut off, but those who wait for the Lord, they will inherit the land* (v. 9).

Observe an illustration David uses:

I have seen a violent, wicked man spreading himself like a luxuriant tree in its native soil (v. 35).

Can't you picture it? "I've seen this big hulk of a man, evil in his ways, with blood dripping from his fingers, planning wickedness, doing wrong, growing larger, more powerful, more intimidating."

Then he passed away, and lo, he was no more; I sought for him, but he could not be found. Mark the blameless man, and behold the upright; for the man of peace will have a posterity. But transgressors will be altogether destroyed; the posterity of the wicked will be cut off. But the salvation of the righteous is from the Lord; He is their strength in time of trouble. And the Lord helps them, and delivers them; He delivers them from the wicked, and saves them, because they take refuge in Him (vv. 36-40).

What magnificent words of hope! I have a feeling they increase your pulse as you read them. Here's why. You don't walk close to God very long before you become the face on someone's dart board, the object of someone's resentment and wrath, even though you really did no wrong to that person. For all the right reasons and the purest of motives, you did what you did and you have been misunderstood. It's a very tender place to be.

Here's the major point of this psalm: Your knowledge of God and your love for God will be on display in how you respond to the other person's treatment. Rather than diminishing His glory, let your light shine! God will honor such a response.

Psalm 46. We cannot—we *dare* not—ignore this, another statement of faith.

God is our refuge and strength, a very present help in trouble (v. 1).

My favorite word in that opening line is "present." "A very *present* help." Right now.

Therefore we will not fear, though the earth should change, and though the mountains slip into the heart of the sea; though its waters roar and foam, though the mountains quake at its swelling pride [Selah] (vv. 2-3).

Someone has suggested that each time the word "Selah" appears in the Psalms it's time to think, "pause and let that sink in . . . drink that in." Drink what in? This:

God is our refuge and strength, a very present help in trouble.

My sister Luci was, for some time after she graduated, a field representative for her alma mater. And while she was traveling around the Southwest making contact with potential students, she of course had a number of interesting experiences as a single woman.

On one unforgettable occasion she noticed that she was being followed by a vehicle. Since it was getting dark and she was all alone, she became increasingly more uneasy. She decided she would turn in for the night, and so she drove into this rather small town and began searching for a motel. She noticed that the car behind her did the same. As she made several unusual turns, the car following her did too. So she knew for sure she was being followed. She quickly pulled into a motel, got out, and registered. She noticed the lights of the other car down the road about a half a block away. Her heart was beating in her throat. After quickly signing the register, she got the key and jumped into her car, drove around to the room, grabbed her bags and ran inside. She quickly locked every possible lock there was on the door and then breathed a sigh of relief.

While preparing herself for bed, she needed to take a shower. While she was stepping out of the shower, she noticed that the venetian blind was up a little on one end, and she suddenly had this horrible sense of fear that she was being watched, that this person who followed her was right outside the window. And Luci later said to me, "I didn't know what to do. I was defenseless, I was all alone. If he were outside and if he had broken in, I couldn't have protected myself. Then for some strange reason I looked down and noticed that someone had slipped a piece of paper under the glass on top of the chest of drawers."

These words were written on that paper:

> *Come to Me, all who are weary and heavy laden, and I will give you rest. Take My yoke upon you, and learn from Me, for I am gentle and humble in heart; and you shall find rest for your souls* (Matthew 11:28-29).

She said when she saw those verses, she was enveloped with an enormous sense of relief that surged over her. With the towel wrapped around her, she marched over and yanked that venetian blind down, put on her pajamas, turned the lights off, got into bed, and immediately fell asleep . . . zzzzzzzz! And not another thing happened that night.

There is something *remarkable* about the Word of God when it's taken literally and applied to your situation. It works, friends! It works! It isn't voodoo. It isn't magic. It isn't some kind of divine aura you place on someone else. It is the living and abiding Word of God. It is His *present* help. It is the testimony of His strength in your life. It's as if He is pleading, "Take it. Believe it. Apply it. Love Me for it." And it works! Stories like that could be multiplied all over the family of God.

When we make the Lord alone our single source of protection or solitary refuge, He shows Himself strong, doesn't He? And then who gets the glory? When He comes through, all you can do is say, "Praise be to the Lord . . . He did it again!"

Now, the best part of the whole process is this: As He proves Himself strong when we need Him, the most natural response on our part is love, "Oh, how I love this One who sees me through. He is truly worthy of my worship. My Maker, Defender, Redeemer, and Friend!"

MAN OF GRATITUDE, MAN OF LOVE

Now I want to show you how this grateful man responded to his Lord's gracious dealings. I'm referring, of course, to David.

Psalm 18. He has been delivered from the hands of his enemies. He has been rescued from Saul's pursuit again and again. He is now safe in some forlorn place. I don't know if he's in the open wilderness or in a narrow cave, but the best part of all is this: He is safe. And once safe, he *has* to write a song, he *has* to testify of his gratitude in song. All who write music can understand such an impulse of praise. He begins:

I love Thee, O Lord, my strength (v. 1).

Here is why he loved his Lord so passionately:

The Lord is my rock and my fortress and my deliverer, my God, my rock, in whom I take refuge; my shield and the horn of my salvation, my stronghold. I call upon the Lord, who is worthy to be praised, and I am saved from my enemies. The cords of death encompassed me, and the torrents of ungodliness terrified me. The cords of Sheol surrounded me; the snares of death confronted me. In my distress I called upon the Lord, and cried to my God for help; He heard my voice out of His temple, and my cry for help before Him came into His ears (vv. 2-6).

The response of love concludes the same psalm:

The Lord lives, and blessed be my rock; and exalted be the God of my salvation, the God who executes vengeance for me, and subdues peoples under me. He delivers me from my enemies; surely Thou dost lift me above those who rise up against me; Thou dost rescue me from the violent man. Therefore I will give thanks . . .
(vv. 46-49a).

He said at the beginning, "I love You, O Lord." He says toward the ending, "I thank You, Lord."

Now the scene isn't always that simple and objective. Sometimes we will do wrong. Sometimes our situation is deserved. Sometimes we will fail . . . we will stumble. David stumbled terribly.

When I mention the name David, unfortunately many people think first of his failure—and it is a glaring one. At the height of his career, he stumbled into lust. The lust turned into open adultery, the adultery led to murder, the murder led to deception—in fact, almost a year of lying to his people. Don't you know the word spread in his kingdom? Can't you imagine how they whispered about him in the alleys and in the homes around the palace? It was obvious he had married Bathsheba. And it was obvious as they counted back over the months that she had had the baby in less than nine months, in those days a slanderous thing. All of that was clear to the people. During those awful months, he slumped into an enormous depression.

When he came out on the other side, after he repented, he wrote another song.

Psalm 32. He has compromised his walk with the Lord, he has given into lust, murder, deception. We can hardly imagine his misery. Verse 3:

When I kept silent about my sin, my body wasted away through my groaning all day long.

Ever had that happen? Ever been so stubborn in your iniquity that you refused to confess it, resulting in your beginning to suffer physically for it? How many illnesses really can be traced to sin!

For day and night Thy hand was heavy upon me; my vitality was drained away as with the fever heat of summer. [Selah] I acknowledged my sin to Thee, and my iniquity I did not hide; I said, "I will confess my transgressions to the LORD"; and Thou didst forgive the guilt of my sin [Selah] (vv. 4-5).

Now look back at verses 1 and 2. You'll read the response of a forgiven man.

How blessed is he whose transgression is forgiven, whose sin is covered! How blessed is the man to whom the Lord does not impute iniquity, and in whose spirit there is no deceit!

"How blessed I am, how forgiven, how clean!"

You know what's happened? He's claimed God's cleansing. He's experienced God's forgiveness. And as a result, his love is expressed in gratitude. "I see my wrong. I accept it as wrong, and I lay it before You." Don't dare overlook the fact that God took away the guilt as well as the sin.

Psalm 40.

I waited patiently for the Lord; and He inclined to me, and heard my cry. He brought me up out of the pit of destruction, out of the miry clay . . . (vv. 1-2a).

This "pit of destruction" can mean many things to us today. It may mean a depression. It may represent a period of time where you wandered. It may be a period of unexplainable sorrow in your life . . . a series of losses and grief. It may be the loss of health, a terminal illness. You put *your* pit in this situation. David left it undefined.

He brought me up out of the pit of destruction, out of the miry clay; and He set my feet upon a rock making my footsteps firm. And He put a new song in my mouth, a song of praise to our God; many will see and fear, and will trust in the Lord.

How blessed is the man who has made the Lord his trust . . . (vv. 2-4).

I'm thinking of that grand hymn:

Guide me, O Thou great Jehovah,
Pilgrim through this barren land;
I am weak, but Thou art mighty;
Hold me with Thy pow'rful hand;
Bread of heaven, Bread of heaven,
Feed me till I want no more,
Feed me till I want no more.[2]

The last part of the third stanza says, "Songs of praises, songs of praises, I will ever give to Thee." The heart that loves God is a heart that bursts forth in songs of praise. It is marvelously spontaneous. It is wonderful to have your heart so in love with your Lord that the only way to express it is to sing it. "Songs of praises I will ever give to Thee." What a response of love!

FOR THOSE WHO TRULY LOVE GOD

Let me suggest three observations of those who truly love God.

1. *You who truly love the Lord have experienced His power to deliver, so your fears are gone.* You could write your own chapter. You could sing your own song of praise. Your fears have been taken away. Perfect love casts out fear, doesn't it?

2. *You who truly love God have received His peace and forgiveness, so your guilt has been relieved.* And what a relief it is! You don't spend your days washing around in how wrong or how badly you feel. You have claimed His mercy. You're free of guilt.

3. *You who truly love God have felt His presence through affliction and your faith has been strengthened.* You're stronger now. You know what's happened in the process? You and your Lord have become close friends . . . so close that the relationship can't really be explained in human terms. You have linked yourself with the Almighty and you and He are in league together. You're walking together. And nothing breaks that fellowship. That's the way it is with God. He's on that basis with His children.

Playwright Moss Hart once recalled a childhood Christmas when his father took him shopping, hoping to buy the boy a present he would like. The two walked the New York streets, inspecting the merchandise displayed on scores of pushcarts. Hart's eyes, as a little boy, were drawn to chemistry sets and to printing presses. But the father, a very poor man, had less expensive things in mind.

Each time they would find something the boy wanted, the father would ask the vendor's price, shake his head, and move on. Occasionally he would pick up a smaller, less expensive toy and try to attract his son's attention. But there was no meeting of the minds. Eventually they came to the end of the line of pushcarts without a purchase.

Hart writes:

"I heard [my father] jingle some coins in his pocket. In a flash I knew it all. He had gotten together about seventy-five cents to buy me a Christmas present, and he hadn't dared say so in case there was nothing to be had for so small a sum. As I looked up at him I saw a look of despair and disappointment in his eyes that brought me closer to him than I had ever been in my life.

I wanted to throw my arms around him and say, "It doesn't matter . . . I understand. . . . This is better than a printing press . . . I love you." But instead we stood shivering beside each other for a moment—then turned away from the last two pushcarts and started silently back home . . . I didn't even take his hand on the way home, nor did he take mine. We were not on that basis. Nor did I ever tell him how close to him I felt that night— that for a little while the concrete wall between father and son had crumbled away and I knew that we were two lonely people struggling to reach each other.[3]

You need to know that God wants to be on that basis with us. God wants our arms around Him. God wants to hear us say, "I love You, Father. I trust You. Whatever You want to give me I accept. I need You. I cling to You. I walk with You. I adore You."

The better you get to know your God, the more comfortable you will be with that kind of response. And as you gain comfort in that kind of response, express it. Sing your songs. Lay your burdens on Him. Trust Him with all your heart and might. He'll be honored as you do that.

1. Who are you *encouraging* in the Christian life? Are there one or more individuals who feel the courage to dig deeper, hang on tighter, or look heavenward because of your regular counsel and concern? How about someone *outside* your family circle? Who, for instance, could you encourage with a note or letter? Make it a goal to write such a note this week. It doesn't need to be elaborate . . . just an appropriate Scripture, or a thought about the love and faithfulness of the Lord—and your genuine expression of support. "I care" goes a long, long way.

2. If you have children, project yourself ahead to that day when they will be on their own—even when you may be off the scene. What will they have learned about the priority of loving God by *observing* the lives of their mom or dad? If you find yourself troubled by your "glimpse into the future," discuss your concerns with your spouse or a close Christian friend. How can you better *model* the priority of loving God?

3. Review Psalm 40, especially the first three verses. Can you remember the last "pit" you found yourself in . . . knee-deep in the muck . . . your heart almost breaking (v. 12)? Do you recall how the Lord heard your cry and reached down to deliver you? Why not follow David's example and *write* about it? There is something uniquely powerful about *writing* one's praise and gratitude to God—even if you and God are the only ones who ever see it! Open your notebook to a fresh page and take time to actually write a special letter to God, just pouring out all your joy and appreciation for what He has done. And even if you *still* find yourself in a pit, write to your Father about it. Open your heart to Him. Tell Him how you're trusting Him to deliver you. This is one letter that will be received and read!

The Lord Jesus Christ

※ ※ ※

"I claim Jesus Christ as my Lord—very God who came in human flesh—the object of my worship and the subject of my praise."

MARY'S LITTLE LAMB

istory tells us that early in the nineteenth century the whole world was watching with bated breath the campaigns of Napoleon. There was talk everywhere of marches, invasions, battles, and bloodshed as the French dictator pushed his way through Europe. Babies were born during that time. But who had time to think about babies or to care about cradles and nurseries when the international scene was as tumultuous as it was? Nevertheless, between Trafalgar and Waterloo there stole into this world a veritable host of heroes whose lives were destined to shape all of humanity. But again I ask, who had time to think about babies while Napoleon was on the move?

Well, someone should have.

Let's take the year 1809. Internationally, everyone was looking at Austria, because that was where blood was flowing freely. In one campaign after another that year, Napoleon was sweeping through Austria. Nobody cared about babies in 1809 . . . but when you check the record, you realize the world was overlooking some terribly significant births.

Take, for example, William Gladstone. Gladstone was destined to become one of the finest statesmen that England ever produced. In that same year Alfred Tennyson was born to an obscure minister and his wife. Tennyson would one day greatly affect the literary world in a marked manner. Oliver Wendell Holmes was born in Cambridge, Massachusetts, in 1809. And not far away in Boston, Edgar Allan Poe began his eventful, albeit tragic, life. It was also in that same year—1809—that a physician named Darwin and his wife named their child Charles Robert. And it was that same year that the cries of a newborn infant could be heard from a rugged log cabin in Hardin County, Kentucky. The baby's name? Abraham Lincoln.

If there had been news broadcasts at that time, I'm certain these words would have been heard: "The destiny of the world is being shaped on an Austrian battlefield today." Or was it?

Funny, only a handful of history buffs today could name even two or three of the Austrian campaigns. Looking back, you and I realize that history was actually being shaped in the cradles of England and America as young mothers held in their arms the shakers and the movers of the future. No one could deny that 1809 was, in fact, the genesis of an era.

The same could be said of the time when Jesus of Nazareth was born. No one in the entire Roman Empire could've cared less about the birth of that Jewish infant in Bethlehem. Rome ruled the world. *That's* where history was being made! Or was it?

Dr. Luke was as careful with his study of history as he was with his practice of medicine. In the Gospel that bears his name, he provides for us several dependable, helpful facts. We can look up these facts and realize that if never before, at least at that time, God chose things that seemed to be terribly insignificant to put to shame the things that seemed highly important.

Background Behind Jesus' Birth

Now it came about in those days that a decree went out from Caesar Augustus, that a census be taken of all the inhabited earth (Luke 2:1).

To what days does Luke refer? What was the scene? It wasn't Napoleon in Austria, it was Caesar. And it wasn't only Caesar, it was all of Rome in all her power and splendor. The Roman Empire had stretched its real estate to maximum proportions. Its western boundary was the Atlantic Ocean. Its eastern boundary was the Euphrates. It reached as far north as the Danube and the Rhine and as far south as the Sahara desert. And there was one name prominent and paramount over all of this land. The Caesar. His name was Augustus.

Now in the midst of this great, powerful structure known as the kingdom, the Roman kingdom, there was a little finger of land that struggled for existence and identity along the easternmost shores of the Mediterranean—the land of Palestine. But somehow God had graciously provided its security through the years . . . even to this day that is true. There had been raised from lowly birth a young man who came to be known as Herod the Great. He had been given tacit approval by Caesar Augustus to give a measure of guidance over the Jewish people in the land of Palestine, specifically, for our interest, Judea.

At the time of Herod the Great's death, he wrote a will that was, for the most part, honored by Caesar. Herod's territory would be given to his three sons. One was named Archelaus, a brutal tyrant. Archelaus would get Judea. He was anti-Semitic from the crown of his head to the sole of his feet. And for a decade—ten uninterrupted years—he ruled over the Jews with a brutal iron fist until finally, so many complaints came to the attention of Augustus that he banished Archelaus to Gaul. It was there he died in disgrace.

At that same time Augustus put his approval on a young man named Publius Quirinius, who lived in Syria serving as its president or governor (to use the words of Luke). And Quirinius, though unfamiliar with Judea, was brought down to the land of Judea to change things around. In other words, Caesar was designing a plan to put into operation the machinery that would make Judea a Roman province for the first time. In order to do this he had to take care of two things: (1) He had to move the power structure (the power of life and death was taken out of the hands of the Jews and placed into the hands of Rome), and (2) he had to tax the people heavily to get them in line with the rest of the empire.

Those two things, it seemed to the world, were most unfair, and of maximum significance. But looking back, how insignificant they really were. The significant event was the birth of a baby in Bethlehem . . . but who could care about a baby born in Judea during a time when Caesar was expanding his kingdom? Who could care about a crying little infant when taxation was being increased?

And for the first time the Jews had no direct representative in Rome. At this juncture, it seems fitting that we leave Luke 2 and listen to a prophet's prediction for a moment. His name was Micah. I smile when I write that name because Micah was not even *known* by the Roman Caesar. It is doubtful that he had even a passing interest in the writings of that obscure Jewish prophet. But Micah's prediction, written eight hundred years (did you get that?—eight *centuries*) before Caesar made his taxation decree, before he'd announced, "Archelaus, be gone! Quirinius, move in! Let's tax the world!" was about to be fulfilled. Caesar's decree made it necessary for a Jewish couple living in Nazareth to make a rugged eighty-mile journey from Nazareth to Bethlehem for the purpose of signing that taxation census. Participating in such a census required that a man go back to what, today, we would call his family "county seat." Now look back to Micah 5:2:

> But as for you, Bethlehem Ephrathah, too little to be among the clans of Judah, from you One will go forth for Me to be ruler in Israel. His goings forth are from long ago, from the days of eternity.

Beth-le-hem means "house of bread" in Hebrew. Insignificant as a tiny loaf of bread . . . yet the Lord through the writing of a minor prophet eight centuries earlier puts his finger on Bethlehem and announces that this place will be famous. Why, that's like the President addressing Muleshoe, Texas, or Pea Ridge, Arkansas, saying, "From you there will come forth a great person." In fact, it seems so insignificant that for centuries men questioned the writings of Micah. How could it be that Bethlehem, "the house of bread," insignificant as a grain of wheat, would be the seed plot—the birth place of one who

> . . . will arise and shepherd His flock . . . and . . . be our peace
> (vv. 4, 5).

You see, no one cared about the writings of Micah. I can picture pompous Augustus sitting securely on his throne, in charge of the Roman world, thinking he had made a decision that was altogether original and unique. But looking back, we realize he was running the errands of a minor prophet named Micah. Augustus had no earthly idea that a teenaged pregnant girl named Mary living in Nazareth with Joseph, her carpenter husband, was about to bear a son named Jesus, who would be the Savior of the world. But the world was about to find out that infant named Jesus was really the significance of that era, not Caesar. The spotlight of redemption's history would fall on Bethlehem, not Rome.

Luke tells us:

> . . . that a decree went out from Caesar Augustus, that a census be taken of all the inhabited earth. This was the first census taken while Quirinius [there's our man] was governor of Syria (Luke 2:1-2).

And so Quirinius cranked up the machinery that would put taxation into motion. I'm sure he went about his duties in a matter-of-fact fashion, knowing absolutely nothing of Micah's prophesy. As the dominoes began to bump up against one another, it became necessary for Mary and Joseph to travel from Nazareth to Bethlehem.

And all were proceeding to register for the census, everyone to his own city (v. 3).

It looked like history was being made in the magnificent house of Caesar, but in actuality it was soon to be made in the lowly house of bread.

A capable journalist-author named Jim Bishop wrote a fairly reliable analysis of Jesus' birth in his book, *The Day Christ Was Born*. His description of Mary, the young mother-to-be, bears repeating:

> She no longer noticed the chafe of the goatskin against her leg, nor the sway of the food bag on the other side of the animal. Her veiled head hung and she saw millions of pebbles on the road moving by her brown eyes in a blur, pausing, and moving by again with each step of the animal.
>
> Sometimes she felt ill at ease and fatigued, but she swallowed this feeling and concentrated on what a beautiful baby she was about to have and kept thinking about it, the bathing, the oils, the feeding, the tender pressing of the tiny body against her breast—and the sickness went away. Sometimes she murmured the ancient prayers and, for the moment, there was no road and no pebbles and she dwelt on the wonder of God and saw Him in a fleecy cloud at a windowless wall of an inn or a hummock of trees, walking backward in front of her husband, beckoning him on. God was everywhere. It gave Mary confidence to know that He was everywhere. She needed confidence. Mary was fifteen.
>
> Most young ladies of the country were betrothed at thirteen and married at fourteen. A few were not joined in holiness until fifteen or sixteen and these seldom found a choice man and were content to be shepherds' wives, living in caves in the sides of the hills, raising their children in loneliness, knowing only the great stars of the night lifting over the hills, and the whistle of the shepherd as he turned to lead his flock to a new pasture. Mary had married a carpenter. He had been apprenticed by his father at bar mitzvah. Now he was nineteen and had his own business.

It wasn't much of a business, even for the Galilean country. He was young and, even though he was earnest to the point of being humorless, he was untried and was prone to mistakes in his calculations. In all of Judea there was little lumber. Some stately cedars grew in the powdery alkaline soil, but, other than date palms and fig trees and some fruit orchards, it was a bald, hilly country. Carpentry was a poor choice.[1]

The story in Luke proceeds:

And Joseph also went up from Galilee, from the city of Nazareth, to Judea, to the city of David . . . in order to register, along with Mary, who was engaged to him, and was with child (vv. 4-5).

If we could step into the time tunnel and return to those days, Luke's papers would be laid aside as rather bland and insignificant. After all, it was taxation that was important, not the birth of some little baby. It would have seemed as insignificant as the birth of an Oliver Wendell Holmes, an Edgar Allan Poe, or an Abraham Lincoln when Napoleon took Austria. But looking back on the scene, *nothing* was more important than Mary and Joseph's journey to Bethlehem. Within days, Messiah would be born!

THE SCENE IN BETHLEHEM

It will help you to realize that at that time Bethlehem was a confusing jungle . . . a hubbub of people. Not only did this taxation move Mary and Joseph from their home in Nazareth, it moved hundreds, perhaps thousands, of others as well. And the little town wasn't set up with motels and hotels as we are today. The best they had was what was known as a *caravansary*. It was like an ancient bus depot . . . where weary travelers in caravans would move in, be refreshed for a brief period, and then move on. But even the caravansary was full.

They tried other areas, but they were also full. No signs swung brightly after dark, reading, "Travelers welcome here for the night." Historians tell us that it was possible that the travelers slept all over the street during this heavy taxation time.

That was the harsh scene that met them when they came into Bethlehem. In fact, in verse 7, it says with a great deal of emotion, "there was no room for them in the inn." No room—not a single place for Messiah to be born.

Have you ever traveled from one city to another, knowing no one at the place of your destination? Most people I know have. And the pain was only intensified when, upon arriving, you found no room.

I'll never forget when Cynthia and I moved in 1957 from Houston to San Francisco. We had heard about its being a beautiful, picturesque, romantic city. And we found it to be so, after awhile. But at first glance there was no room anywhere to stay. We searched and searched for an apartment—*any* apartment. It took us over a week of constant searching . . . and that was pretty quick. The search can be a terribly depressing experience.

I think perhaps one of the most moving stories of no room, besides this one that Luke gives us, is the one that a pastor friend of mine tells of his beginning days in the pastorate in a city back East many years ago. He tells of the time when he moved with his family—his wife, a little baby, and a couple of other small children. They had accepted the pastorate of a church in a city where they knew no one.

When they arrived it was *Halloween night*—Saturday night. He was to preach his first sermon to his new flock the next morning. You should hear him describe the scene when they arrived! "Every fool was in the streets of that city on Halloween night. What a place!" It seemed as though no one even knew this pastor and his family were coming. No plans had been made. No one met them. No open house. No warm reception. No provision for his family. Not even a room at a hotel for that first night. So he pulled up to a pay phone and dialed the number of the one name he had. The fellow answered with a startled surprise, "Oh, yes, you *are* coming . . . that's right." The man drove over to meet him and then took him and his family to an attic at an old abandoned theater. If you can believe it, that's where he began his pastorate—wrinkled clothes, crying baby, bottles, formula, and makeshift beds in a theater attic. That's where he prepared his first sermon. Talk about having to overcome first impressions!

But it was far worse for Mary. She was now only minutes removed from delivery. Exhausted from the long journey, she came to Bethlehem, and there was not one place to stay except in an animal enclosure by an inn. But who cared about a baby? The whole talk around the city was the problem of taxation and Caesar and Quirinius and Archelaus . . . and Herod, who started it all. And the crying of that little infant was another irritant in the ears of the people wanting sleep, because they were bothered to be in that strange place. Nobody cared, and there was no room.

So she had her little baby all alone. Only Joseph was near.

The sheep corral, filthy as only an Eastern animal enclosure can be, reeked pungently with manure and urine accumulated across the seasons. Joseph cleared a corner just large enough for Mary to lie down. Birth pains had started. She writhed in agony on the ground. Joseph, in his inexperience and unknowing manly manner, did his best to reassure her. His own other tunic would be her bed, his rough saddlebag her pillow. Hay, straw, or other animal fodder was nonexistent. This was not hay- or grain-growing country. Stock barely survived by grazing on the sparse vegetation that sprang from the semidesert terrain around the town.

Mary moaned and groaned in the darkness of the sheep shelter. Joseph swept away the dust and dirt from a small space in one of the hand-hewn mangers carved from the soft limestone rock. It was covered with cobwebs and debris fallen from the rock ceiling. There, as best he could, he arranged a place where Mary could lay the newborn babe all bundled up in the swaddling clothes she had brought along.

There, alone, unaided, without strangers or friends to witness her ordeal in the darkness, Mary delivered her son. A more lowly or humble birth it is impossible to imagine. It was the unpretentious entrance, the stage entrance of the Son of man— the Son of God, God very God in human guise and form— upon earth's stage.

In the dim darkness of the stable a new sound was heard. The infant cry of the newborn babe came clearly. For the first time deity was articulated directly in sounds expressed through a human body. Those sounds brought cheer and comfort and courage to Mary and Joseph. These peasant parents were the first of multiplied millions upon millions who in the centuries to follow would be cheered and comforted by the sounds that came from that voice.

God is come. God is with His people. Immanuel.[2]

And she bundled Him in wrappings, little makeshift clothes, and put Him in the manger . . . her firstborn—Mary's little Lamb.

Every mother reading these words can identify with Mary. Remember your firstborn? My wife tells me of the occasion when our first child was born. She was fully conscious. She said, "There is no feeling at all like the feeling when they have taken the baby and cut the cord, then laid him alongside you. In fact, (referring to our firstborn) they laid him right across my tummy. He stretched out, and I reached down and felt him. I thought, 'Oh, dear God, *life* from *me!* '"

MARY'S LAMB

Joseph cleaned up from the birth and put that little tiny life into a rough feeding trough. Mary looked down and saw *God* by her side. But nobody cared. One poet wrote:

> They all were looking for a King
> To slay their foes and lift them *high*:
> Thou cam'st a little baby thing
> That made a woman cry.[3]

And another:

> A baby's hands in Bethlehem
> Were small and softly curled.
> But held within their dimpled grasp
> The hope of all the world.[4]

The most significant event of the centuries took place in an enclosed patio made into a stable in an insignificant "loaf-of-bread" city, Bethlehem. I wonder what Mary thought? Haven't you wondered that when you have read the story? Haven't you wondered what went through her mind as she saw that little one? The most significant thing that happened didn't happen in Caesar's court or Quirinius's palace or among the plans of the Jewish zealots to overthrow Rome. The most significant thing happened in a manger. As Mary held that baby, I wonder if she thought about Isaiah's words? Surely she knew them.

Therefore the Lord Himself will give you a sign: Behold, a virgin will be with child and bear a son, and she will call His name Immanuel (Isaiah 7:14).

She was holding in her arms Immanuel . . . "God with us." Or maybe she remembered the angel who had visited her nine months earlier and said, "Don't be afraid."

Just like the Lord, isn't it? You see, God doesn't make edicts like man does. The Caesar makes a decree . . . it is announced and the world jumps to attention. But God's first concern is the feeling of the one that will hear the message, so He says, "Don'tⱼbe afraid, Mary. Something amazing is going to happen. Behold, not knowing a man, you will conceive in your womb. You will bear a Son, and you will call His name Jesus." A never-to-be-repeated event! A virgin will have a baby . . . even though most people will never believe it.

I wonder if God gave her a passing premonition of John the Baptizer, who, in years to come, would look at Jesus and point that prophetic finger in His direction and say, "Behold, the Lamb of God who takes away the sin of the world"? Yes, Mary had a little Lamb that night. And her precious little Lamb was destined for sacrifice.

I think the Lord seems to underscore this as Luke records for us those who heard the announcement. You notice He didn't send angels to Rome. He didn't send them to Judea or Syria, or to other places of honor and significance. He sent the angels to a group of lowly shepherds (verse 8) who were staying out in the fields, keeping watch over their flock by night.

What flock? If it is true what I read in preparing my thoughts for this chapter, this was a very significant flock of sheep kept near Bethlehem. These sheep were set aside, destined for sacrificial altars. These were "slaughter sheep." And what a perfect group to announce the message of the gospel to, to tell those who were watching the sheep, "The Lord has come!"

There was a tiny Lamb in Bethlehem who was destined for Golgotha's altar.

In fact, Luke's record reads:

> And in the same region there were some shepherds staying out in the fields, and keeping watch over their flock by night. And an angel of the Lord suddenly stood before them, and the glory of the Lord shone around them; and they were terribly frightened (2:8-9).

Have you ever pictured what that must have been like? Here were half-asleep shepherds out keeping a flock of little woolies in the field, just like any other night, then suddenly it was brighter than high noon.

The Old Testament uses a word several times that is called the *shekinah*, which seems to describe the light that flows from heaven, giving brilliance to the place where God is. That light filled the holy place of the tabernacle. It later filled the temple where God's presence could be felt before His Son came to earth . . . burning light—resplendent, blinding light—the same light perhaps that struck

Paul blind. That night this same light fell upon those shepherds. They saw the light, and naturally they were afraid. They had no idea what was going to be announced.

What had they been talking about? Like everyone else, they were talking about taxes, the change of government, the increased Roman rule that would impact the Jews—what it would mean to their families, the loss of freedom, the helplessness they felt, the fear. Those were the issues of that day. Suddenly, without any warning, the Lord spoke through the voices of the angels:

> . . . *"Do not be afraid; for behold, I bring you good news of a great joy which shall be for all the people; for today in the city of David there has been born for you a Savior, who is Christ the Lord"* (v. 10).

THE SIGNIFICANCE OF THE INSIGNIFICANT

There is a small verse in the book of 1 Corinthians that is a fitting motto for all that we have read in these first eleven verses of Luke 2. It goes like this:

> *But God has chosen the foolish things of the world to shame the wise, and God has chosen the weak things of the world to shame the things which are strong* (1:27).

If I could add my own kind of paraphrase, "And God has chosen the Lamb of Mary to bring to nothing the authority of Rome."

Things haven't changed much, have they? Every Christmas season the significance seems to get lost among the insignificant. How often have you heard from people on the street, behind the counters, or outside the church, of the wonderful yet simple story of Jesus Christ? If you have heard it once or twice, you are very rare. Apart from Christian friends, it is remarkable if you hear that the Christmas message is Jesus Christ—His virgin birth, His incarnation, His coming to this earth. Because, you see, our world continues to be caught in the web of insignificant things like busy commerce—the profit-and-loss issues of life.

And Christ? Well, who can worry too much about Him when history is being made at the cash register. Or is it?

One true story I read recently told of a commercial venture of one of the largest department stores in our nation. It proved to be disastrously unsuccessful. It was a doll in the form of the baby Jesus. It was advertised as being unbreakable, washable, and cuddly. It was packaged in straw with a satin crib and plastic surroundings, and appropriate biblical texts added here and there to make the scene complete.

It did not sell. The manager of one of the stores in the department chain panicked. He carried out a last-ditch promotion to get rid of those dolls. He brandished a huge sign outside his store that read:

JESUS CHRIST—
MARKED DOWN 50%
GET HIM WHILE YOU CAN

My friend, Jesus is God's Lamb, the Son of God. He didn't come to be packaged and offered for half price where, if you hurry, you can get Him. He came as very God. And the world in its tinsel and tarnish has just about ruined the picture. As in the days of Rome, our God is not panicked over the scene of America or other nations of the world. Are you wise enough to see the significant in the midst of the insignificant?

Has there been a time in your personal life when you have asked Christ Jesus to occupy your heart, as He once occupied the manger? Honestly now, does He have first place? The Lord Jesus Christ is available in the same form He has been for centuries—the Son of God who died for you, who paid the price for your sin, who was raised from the dead, who is living. If you will, by personal invitation, ask Jesus to become the Lord of your life; He will come in. In the solitude of this quiet moment, make room in your heart for the Lord Jesus. Set the book aside and tell Him you take Him . . . you give Him the place of honor and authority in your life. I invite you to do that now.

Wise men still seek Him, you know.

1. Luke 2 and Matthew 1:18-2:23 may comprise "the greatest story ever told." Don't limit this magnificent account to Christmas Eve! It's too important, too encouraging to be put on the shelf as a "yearly tradition." Read one or both of these passages out loud—either to yourself or to your family. Reflect on what it meant for God to become a baby . . . and a Man. Come, let us adore Him—today!

2. If it is near the Christmas season as you read these words, carefully think about how you might make better use of these days when so many non-Christian men and women, boys and girls think about the Babe, a manger, and Bethlehem. How might you grasp this special opportunity to introduce neighbors and relatives to Mary's Lamb—the One who was born to die for *all* the sins of *all* mankind? Could you compose a Christmas letter that includes a clear testimony of your faith—or perhaps the simple plan of salvation? How about an "open house" when you could invite in the neighbors for casual conversation and Christmas goodies? (It might open a door for you to speak about your Lord at some future time.) Groups such as SEARCH Ministries offer many creative and practical suggestions for planning such informal gatherings.

3. The headlines of today's newspaper and the covers of *Time* and *Newsweek* trumpet what the world considers the "major news" of the day. Actually, what transpires between you and your neighbor or you and your associate at work could have much deeper *eternal* significance. How long has it been since you actually prayed that the Lord would give you the privilege of speaking to someone about your Savior? "You shall be My witnesses," He tells us in Acts 1:8. A witness simply reports what he or she has seen and experienced—doesn't have to be a "sermon" or a dumptruck load of information. Just a word at the right time about the greatest Hope in all the world. The *big* news is the Good News. Write down your prayer request in your notebook and date it.

WHEN THE
GOD-MAN
WALKED
AMONG US

ho is Jesus Christ? You may be surprised to know that that question has continued to be asked ever since the first century when He walked on earth. His identity has never failed to create a stir. Who exactly is this Jesus? The answers have varied from demon to deity.

It is imperative that we know the right answer. Otherwise, we do not know how to interpret what He has done. And if we are unable to interpret what He has done, we will never be able to give ourselves to Him as He invites us to do.

WHO IS JESUS CHRIST?

Even during the days of Jesus' earthly pilgrimage, there were many opinions. Let's travel through Matthew's Gospel and find out how varied the opinions really were.

The Wise Men

We come first to a group of men called magi or, more popularly, the wise men. Jesus has been born in Bethlehem. The magi had seen the star, which prompted them to journey a long distance. Finally, they arrived at Jerusalem, anxious to discover His whereabouts.

> *Now after Jesus was born in Bethlehem of Judea in the days of Herod the king, behold, magi from the east arrived in Jerusalem,*

saying, "Where is He who has been born King of the Jews? For we saw His star in the east, and have come to worship Him" (Matthew 2:1-2).

There was no question in their minds, the birth of Jesus represented the birth of a king. The star was "His star." Clearly in their minds, He was "King of the Jews," and they had come to bow down before Him in worship.

God the Father

At the age of thirty, Jesus was baptized by John in the Jordan River. Coming up out of the water, a voice broke through the clouds of heaven, announcing His identity:

And after being baptized, Jesus went up immediately from the water; and behold, the heavens were opened, and He saw the Spirit of God descending as a dove, and coming upon Him, and behold, a voice out of the heavens, saying, "This is My beloved Son, in whom I am well-pleased" (Matthew 3:16-17).

There was no question in God's mind. "I have given you My beloved Son."

Later, at what we know as the transfiguration on a mountain with some of His disciples, the same voice spoke yet again, making the same announcement: "This is My beloved Son, with whom I am well-pleased; listen to Him" (Matthew 17:5).

The wise men, along with God the Father, had no question. "He is the King of the Jews." "He is My Son." But when it came to people on earth, in the milieu of everyday life, there were many who did not agree. Let's hear from several of them.

The Pharisees

The best that the Pharisees ever said of Him was that He was a teacher, a rabbi.

And it happened that as He was reclining at table in the house, behold many tax-gatherers and sinners came and were dining with Jesus and His disciples. And when the Pharisees saw this, they said to His disciples, "Why is your Teacher eating with the tax-gatherers and sinners?" (Matthew 9:10-11).

That was, no doubt, the most respectable title they ever used of Jesus—"Teacher." They realized He instructed His followers, He spent time discussing spiritual things. At best, they viewed Him as "Teacher."

But things degenerated quickly for the Pharisees. That same group of men later said, "He casts out the demons by the ruler of the demons" (9:34). In other words, "He represents the enemy. His power comes from the pit . . . from hell itself."

You may be surprised to know that not all of those who were confused over Jesus' identity could be listed among what we would call His enemies.

John the Baptizer

Many people are very surprised when they discover that the one who baptized Christ became so despondent and disillusioned that he questioned His identity—yes, John—John the Baptizer!

> *Now when John in prison heard of the works of Christ, he sent word by his disciples, and said to Him, "Are You the Expected One, or shall we look for someone else?"* (Matthew 11:2-3).

I find that rather startling. Here is the same man who baptized Him. Here is the forerunner . . . the one who had paved the way for His arrival, who earlier declared: "Behold, the Lamb of God who takes away the sin of the world!" (John 1:29). This was John, the humble prophet who admitted that Jesus was the Christ, saying, "the thong of whose sandal I am not worthy to untie" (John 1:27). This was the same John who, having compared himself to Jesus, had said, "He must increase . . . I must decrease" (John 3:30).

But things have changed. He is now saying that he has serious doubts. With severe concern John asked, "Are You the Expected One, or shall we look for someone else?" (Matthew 11:3). In other words, "I don't know who You are. Your works don't seem to square with the things that You're supposed to do as Messiah. I'm beginning to wonder myself—just who are You?"

Jesus' Neighbors and Immediate Family

If that isn't strange enough, consider Jesus' own family and friends in the neighborhood where He was raised. This scene is captured in Matthew 13.

> *And it came about that when Jesus had finished these parables, He departed from there. And coming to His home town He began teaching them in their synagogue, so that they became astonished, and said, "Where did this man get this wisdom, and these miraculous*

*powers? Is not this the carpenter's son? Is not His mother called
Mary, and His brothers, James and Joseph and Simon and Judas?
And His sisters, are they not all with us? Where then did this man
get all these things?" And they took offense at Him . . .* (Matthew
13:53-57).

That certainly puts the knife to the fallacious doctrine of the perpetual
virginity of Mary. Matthew's record assures us that Mary had other
children. He even records a few names. Jesus was the firstborn, of
course, but His neighbors were unconvinced that He was anything
special. The neighbors, in effect, were asking: "Isn't this the kid my
kids were raised with? Isn't He the one who, years ago, played hide 'n
seek with them around the corner? Isn't this the same One we saw
grow up in His father's carpenter shop? Isn't He the One who repaired
our cabinet? He's the same Jesus, isn't He? Where in the world did He
get these miraculous powers? Why does everybody applaud and respect Him? He's just one of us!"

They were confused. "Where did he get all these things?" Verse 57
says, "They took offense at Him."

"How dare You call Yourself the Son of God. You're just the son of
Joseph!"

If that doesn't surprise you, just take a quick glance at Mark, chapter
3. I want you to zero in on His immediate family. It's bad enough to
come home and be a prophet without honor, but to return to His own
family and to hear them question His authority would be insult added
to injury. Yet that is precisely what happened.

*And He came home, and the multitude gathered again, to such an
extent that they could not even eat a meal* (v. 20).

Now watch:

*And when His own people heard of this, they went out to take cus-
tody of Him; for they were saying, "He has lost His senses"* (v. 21).

Tell me, were you aware that there was a time in Jesus' earthly life
when His own flesh and blood considered Him insane?

Herod the Tetrarch

One of the officials in Jesus' day feared that He was John the
Baptizer, risen from the dead.

At that time Herod the tetrarch heard the news about Jesus, and said to his servants, "This is John the Baptist; he has risen from the dead . . ." (Matthew 14:1-2).

Herod was haunted with thoughts of John, because John had been the one who had said to him earlier, "You're living in sin," while Herod was living with his brother's wife. John is the one whose head Herod required after watching Salome dance. And when word reached him about Jesus, he thought, "Oh no, the ghost of John has come to haunt me. This isn't Jesus—this must be John the Baptizer raised from the dead!" Almost like Edgar Allan Poe's moving short story, *The Tell-Tale Heart* (which still sends chills up my back). The murderer thinks he hears the heartbeat of the man he had murdered and buried in the basement . . . thump . . . thump . . . thump . . . thump . . . thump. . . . That pumping heart haunts him. In actuality it is his *own* heart. That's what Herod was living with: "This isn't any Messiah. This is John, back from beyond. I can't escape him."

The General Public's Opinion

Jesus later dialogued with his disciples, asking about His identity. The disciples, I think, rather calmly yawned and said:

"[Oh,] . . . Some say John the Baptist; and others, Elijah; but still others, Jeremiah, or one of the prophets" (Matthew 16:14).

This casual conversation occurred in a brief moment. Matthew slips this information in to show us more evidence that when it came to Jesus' identity, many folks didn't have a clue.

What a mixture! Here's Herod saying, "He's John raised from the dead." Here's John the Baptizer in prison, bewildered and impatient, asking, "Are You really the Coming One?" Earlier there were magi, saying, "He's the King of the Jews." God the Father, saying, "My beloved Son." And now a group of people are saying, "Oh, He's Elijah . . . He's Jeremiah . . . He's one of the prophets back from beyond." Interestingly, some people actually agreed with Herod. "You really must be John," they were saying.

Peter, the Disciple

That same conversation continues:

He said to them, "But who do you say that I am?" And Simon Peter answered and said, "Thou art the Christ, the Son of the living God" (Matthew 16:15-16).

This was one of Peter's greatest moments. He could not have been more correct.

The Citizens in Jerusalem

You might think that most of the people in the city would know that Jesus was Messiah; certainly they would as He entered the city on the back of a donkey, fulfilling prophecy. But they didn't. Even at His triumphal entry, there was a group of people who had no idea who He was.

> And when He had entered Jerusalem, all the city was stirred, saying, "Who is this?" And the multitudes were saying, "This is the prophet Jesus, from Nazareth in Galilee" (Matthew 21:10-11).

There were a few who cried, "Hosannah to the Son of David. Blessed is He who comes in the name of the Lord. Hosannah in the highest!" (v. 9), quoting from the prophet. But there were many who stood back, scratching their bearded faces and saying, "We don't have any idea who that man is. I don't even know who He *thinks* He is. Honestly, I don't know."

Caiaphas, the High Priest

After being betrayed by Judas, Jesus was placed on trial. Not one trial, but six trials. All of them kangaroo courts. The most farcical series of trials in the history of jurisprudence were the trials of Jesus—every one illegal. He was brought to a man named Caiaphas, who was the high priest. And Caiaphas, looking into His eyes, pressed Him for His identity.

> But Jesus kept silent. And the high priest said to Him, "I adjure You by the living God, that You tell us whether You are the Christ, the Son of God" (Matthew 26:63).

Christ means "Anointed One." When reading the Bible you can always think "Messiah" when you come to the word "Christ."

"Tell us whether You are the Anointed One, the Son of God," the priest demanded. "We don't know who You are. We heard who You claimed to be. You tell us."

> Jesus said to him, "You have said it yourself; nevertheless I tell you, hereafter you shall see the Son of Man sitting at the right hand of Power, and coming on the clouds of heaven." Then the high priest tore his robes, saying, "He has blasphemed! What further need do

we have of witnesses? Behold, you have now heard the blasphemy; what do you think?" They answered and said, "He is deserving of death!" Then they spat in His face and beat Him with their fists; and others slapped Him, and said, "Prophesy to us, You Christ; who is the one who hit You?" (vv. 64-68).

After such hostile indignities, they hustled Him off to Pilate.

Pilate

Now Pilate was an interesting study. He was in a Catch-22 situation. He was already suspect in the eyes of the Romans. And he was so anti-Semitic that he was hated by the Jews. So much so that there had been more than one insurrection against his rulership as a governor of Judea. So he was in hot water. When it came to Jesus, Pilate couldn't win.

So the Jewish officials pushed Jesus before Pilate. He was forced to deal with the identity of this man who claimed He was the Son of God (which meant nothing to him as a Roman since he had many gods). So he had to interpret the problem through their ears and eyes. And he couldn't ignore them. If he did there would be another insurrection and he'd be gone. But, you see, they needed Roman authority to put Jesus to death, because the Jews couldn't perform capital punishment; that was strictly a Roman act. So they were forced to plead their cause through Pilate. He didn't want to deal with it, but he had to.

> *Now Jesus stood before the governor, and the governor questioned Him, saying, "Are You the King of the Jews?" And Jesus said to him, "It is as you say"* (Matthew 27:11).

Hold your place and go now to John's Gospel. The same question, the same interrogation, is recorded here in John 18:

> *Pilate therefore entered again into the Praetorium, and summoned Jesus, and said to Him, "You are the King of the Jews?" Jesus answered, "Are you saying this on your own initiative, or did others tell you about Me?" Pilate answered, "I am not a Jew, am I? Your own nation and the chief priests delivered You up to me: what have You done?" Jesus answered, "My kingdom is not of this world. If My kingdom were of this world, then My servants would be fighting, that I might not be delivered up to the Jews: but as it is, My kingdom is not of this realm." Pilate therefore said to Him, "So You are a king?" Jesus answered, "You say correctly that I am a king. For this I have been born, and for this I have come into the world, to bear*

witness to the truth. Every one who is of the truth hears My voice."
Pilate said to Him, "What is truth?" (vv. 33-38).

So Pilate, in good Shakespearean fashion, finally washed his hands of
the thing . . . "I'll have nothing to do with Him. You take Him and do
with Him as you please. I find no fault in Him." With that, they prepared Jesus for the cross. Even though Pilate was convinced of Jesus'
innocence, he lacked the courage to stand by his convictions.

They painted a sign. It was the custom in those days to put a sign
on the top of a criminal's cross. Much like you would know the
reason a person would go to the gas chamber or an electric chair. In
those days the reason was spelled out so that all who passed by could
read it, for capital punishment was done in a public place so as to
deter further crimes. Jesus' sign was painted, according to John
19:19:

JESUS THE NAZARENE, THE KING OF THE JEWS

Now that's what Pilate wanted to appear on the sign to be nailed on
Jesus' cross. But the Jewish officials said, "Wha . . . wh . . . we don't
want that! No!" When the Jews read it, they saw it was done in Hebrew, Latin, and Greek. But they disapproved of the wording.

> *And so the chief priests of the Jews were saying to Pilate, "Do not
> write, 'The King of the Jews'; but that He said, 'I am King of the
> Jews'" (John 19:21).*

"There's a lot of difference," the priests were saying. "When you put
that sign on the cross, you're making a statement—'He is.' We want
everybody who passes by to know this is what He *claimed*, but that is
definitely not what He was. He was not our king." The One the
magi had pursued, because they viewed Him as a king, was crucified
because the people refused to believe He was a king. What an irony!

Jesus Himself

When you get to Luke 24, Jesus has gone to death and beyond. He's
come out of the grave. He has victoriously risen in bodily form, and
He is speaking to His disciples. I find it most intriguing that in Luke
24:44, Jesus goes back into the Old Testament and mentions words
out of the Old Testament, words concerning Himself:

> *Now He said to them, "These are My words which I spoke to you
> while I was still with you, that all things which are written about*

Me in the Law of Moses and the Prophets and the Psalms must be fulfilled."

This is one of the few times Jesus took people through the Scriptures and explained Himself to them from the Law, from the Psalms, and from the Prophets. "You see that? That was a reference to Me. You see this? That's spoken of Me. You see what the prophet said? I fulfill this."

> *Then He opened their minds to understand the Scriptures, and He said to them, "Thus it is written, that the Christ should suffer and rise again from the dead the third day; and that repentance for forgiveness of sins should be proclaimed in His name to all the nations, beginning from Jerusalem. You are witnesses of these things* (24:45-48).

"Men, you have had a unique privilege—to have lived during transition. You've seen Me carry these things out. Now I've come back from the grave. And I'm declaring to you, 'This is truth. I am who I claim to be, *undiminished deity, true humanity, in one person.'*"

Or as John writes, "The Word became flesh, and dwelt among us." The word *dwelt* is the word for "tabernacled" or "pitched a tent." I've heard the verse paraphrased, "The Word became flesh and pitched His tent among us for thirty-three years." And John, the disciple, testified:

> . . . *and we beheld His glory, glory as of the only begotten from the Father, full of grace and truth. John bore witness of Him, and cried out, saying, "This was He of whom I said, 'He who comes after me has a higher rank than I, for He existed before me.'" For of His fulness we have all received, and grace upon grace* (John 1:14-16).

"The Word became flesh. God became man. And as man, He lives among us, and we give Him glory. No question, He is the Son of God."

C. S. Lewis puts his finger on the real issue:

> I am trying here to prevent anyone saying the really foolish thing that people often say about Him: "I'm ready to accept Jesus as a great moral teacher, but I don't accept His claim to be God." That is the one thing we must not say. A man who was merely a man and said the sort of things Jesus said would not be a great moral teacher. He would either be a lunatic—on a level with the man who says he is a poached egg—or else he would be the Devil of Hell. You must make your choice. Either this man was, and is, the Son of God: or else a madman or something worse. You can shut

Him up for a fool, you can spit at Him and kill Him as a demon; or you can fall at His feet and call Him Lord and God. But let us not come with any patronising nonsense about His being a great human teacher. He has not left that open to us. He did not intend to.[1]

Here you are, sitting and reading this information—perhaps realizing for the first time that the evidence is undeniable. Or you may be thinking, "Mmmm, okay, Chuck, you've at least gotten my attention. I can see enough by what you've written that they were confused, yet I need more evidence to be convinced." So for your sake, I want to take one example from each of the four Gospels where Jesus Christ revealed Himself as both God and man.

EXAMPLES OF HUMANITY AND DEITY

I want to mention four examples in which Jesus demonstrated His humanity—then immediately on the heels of that displayed His deity. Maybe you've never made such a study. Let's limit it to one per each Gospel writer.

And immediately He made the disciples get into the boat, and go ahead of Him to the other side, while He sent the multitudes away. And after He had sent the multitudes away, He went up to the mountain by Himself to pray (Matthew 14:22-23a).

We see Jesus' humanity as we find Him in prayer. You will never read of a place recorded in Scripture where God prays. Deity has no needs. Prayer is an act of mankind. Humans pray. Prayer is an expression of need. It is a declaration of adoration. God adores no one. There is no one higher to adore. He is self-contained, self-sufficient. All glory resides in Him. But mankind prays because of an expression of a need to worship, to ask for strength, to request assistance, guidance, or whatever. And that's what Jesus is doing. In praying He shows Himself man. His deity is displayed in the next scene:

. . . and when it was evening, He was there alone. But the boat was already many stadia away from the land, battered by the waves; for the wind was contrary. And in the fourth watch of the night He came to them, walking upon the sea (14:23b-25).

It seemed to the disciples that Jesus came out of nowhere, walking toward them on the water. And they looked across the sea and saw Him coming and they were scared to death. They screamed: *"Phantasma!*

Phantasma!" That's the word Matthew uses. It is from that word we get our word "fantasy" or "fantastic" or "phantom." It's as if they yelled "It's an apparition! It's a ghost! Look!"

And so naturally Peter says, "If that's the Lord walking on the water, I'm going to try it, too!" So he stumbles out into the water, and he soon goes under. He can't pull it off. Later, a very significant conversation occurred:

> *And when they got into the boat* [both of them—one was wet and the other one dry, I might add], *the wind stopped.* [That in itself is remarkable!] *And those who were in the boat worshiped Him, saying, "You* [singular] *are certainly God's Son!"* (vv. 32-33).

Only man prays. Only God walks on water. According to Matthew, Jesus Christ did both.

Mark records another occasion where humanity and deity were seen together.

> *And a leper came to Him, beseeching Him and falling on his knees before Him, and saying to Him, "If You are willing, You can make me clean"* (Mark 1:40).

I don't know if you've ever seen leprosy. I have. While in the Orient during my days in the Marine Corps, it was customary for my military outfit to visit a leprosarium once or twice a year. We went to entertain and encourage them. I have never seen such help-less, tragic sights. The hands and feet of those poor folks are often-times just bleeding stumps. No shoes of any kind can be worn, and it's obvious some of them don't even have feet or toes.

I can imagine this tragic man, with his bleeding stumps, saying to Jesus, "If you're willing, cleanse me."

Scripture never speaks of leprosy being cured or healed—always *cleansed,* because leprosy is the biblical picture of sin. We are never cured or healed of sin. We're cleansed of it. The leper says, "You can do it. Ah, I know You can heal me if You're willing. I know You can cleanse me." That's the word he used. "You can make me clean!"

As a man, the Lord Jesus is moved with compassion over a fellow human being in need. Years ago the original King James Bible (before the New King James Bible came out) spoke of one being moved "deep within his own bowels of mercies." It's the best expression the Old Eng-lish had of that pit of the stomach where you churn. One writer calls it our "churning place." He churned down deep (if I may) in His "gut." Man does that. Woman does that. When you walk by a scene that is tragic or when you view one on the television screen or read of one in a magazine or a newspaper, you are moved with compassion. That's human mercy expressed over human misery. That's an example of Jesus' humanity. But He doesn't stop with just humanity.

And moved with compassion, He stretched out His hand and touched him, and said to him, "I am willing; be cleansed." And immediately the leprosy left him and he was cleansed (vv. 41-42).

Only *God* can do that. For all we know there were suddenly toes on the feet, fingers on the hands. The ache ended, the hemorrhaging stopped. And God in man had done His work.

Another great story occurred on the sea, according to Dr. Luke.

Now it came about on one of those days, that He and His disciples got into a boat, and He said to them, "Let us go over to the other side of the lake." And they launched out. But as they were sailing along He fell asleep . . . (Luke 8:22-23a).

I've not done a great deal of sailing, but the little sailing I've done, I've usually fallen asleep. It's the most natural response to the rhythm of the sea as it massages the weariness of my bones. Most humans I know would agree—easy-going sailing and restful sleeping are meant for each other! But, in Scripture, it's never said that God sleeps. In fact, it specifically says, "He who watches over Israel neither slumbers nor sleeps." Yet man sleeps. Humanity must sleep.

Here, as a man, weary from the day, according to this passage, He falls sound asleep in the boat. That's when things started to happen:

and a fierce gale of wind descended upon the lake, and they began to be swamped and to be in danger. And they came to Him and woke Him up, saying, "Master, Master, we are perishing!" (vv. 23b-24a)

"Master, wake up, wake up! We're gonna die!" Now isn't that something?

They've already witnessed the feeding of the five thousand. And each one had a basket of food left over . . . but they hadn't learned the lesson of His power.

They'd seen Him walk on water and cleanse a leper . . . but they hadn't connected either with His deity.

So here they are in a boat with God in flesh, and they say, "We're gonna sink." You can't sink with God on the same boat! And suddenly, with a word, everything is calm. Only God could do such a thing!

And being aroused, He rebuked the wind and the surging waves, and they stopped, and it became calm (v. 24b).

I may not have done much sailing, but I have certainly done a lot of fishing in my day, and I can tell you I have occasionally seen the sea become what we fishermen usually call "a slick." It's an eerie sight—especially in the ocean. The water is so smooth that if you flipped a penny into it you could count the ripples. But never in my life have I seen a slick occur *suddenly*. Yet in this case a storming, raging, sea—with incredible wind velocity—instantly became a slick. You could hear your own breath. Their boat may have taken a few minutes to stop rocking . . . but the sea was calm as glass.

Look again at the disciples' response. It's great.

> . . . *And they were fearful and amazed* [they spent half their lives fearful and amazed, didn't they?], *saying to one another, "Who then is this, that He commands even the winds and the water, and they obey Him?"* (v. 25).

Doesn't that sound like strong, believing followers? "Who is this?" Can't you see Peter, the fisherman, mumbling under his breath, "Even the winds and the waves obey Him." This is GOD. Yes, Peter, the One you woke up a moment ago is indeed God. HE IS GOD.

Never doubt it, my friend. In the tragic storms of life He specializes in calming waves and silencing winds. It'll just shock you sometimes. How can Jesus Christ do such a thing? He is God!

The last scene we want to relive has to do with Jesus' friend, Lazarus, who became ill and died shortly thereafter. Finally Jesus arrives on the scene of death. He meets up with blame since He hadn't dropped everything and earlier come alongside the grieving family. It's bad enough to be blamed.

> . . . *"If you had been here, my brother would not have died"* (John 11:32).

But to face the grief of His friends—

> *When Jesus therefore saw her weeping, and the Jews who came with her, also weeping, He was deeply moved in spirit, and was troubled* (v. 33).

You'll never read of God's being troubled. Not like this. That's the *man* part of Jesus . . . humanity on display.

... *"Where have you laid him?" They said to Him, "Lord, come and see." Jesus wept* (vv. 34-35).

Neither will you read of God's weeping in the heavens. Tears are a human trait, not divine. He wept as He grieved, not only because of their unbelief, but over the loss of His friend and the sorrow of His companions. It was a scene where any one of us would cry.

Jesus therefore again being deeply moved within, came to the tomb. Now it was a cave, and a stone was lying against it. Jesus said, "Remove the stone." Martha, the sister of the deceased, said to Him, "Lord, by this time there will be a stench; for he has been dead four days." Jesus said to her, "Did I not say to you, if you believe, you will see the glory of God?" And so they removed the stone ... (vv. 38-41).

You don't argue much with Jesus, you notice. Maybe one line. That's all. "I said, 'Move the stone.'" So they moved it.

Jesus, you see, is not going to resurrect Lazarus, He will resuscitate Him. If He would have resurrected Him, the stone could have stayed, because in the resurrection state the whole molecular structure of one's body changes and you can pass through wood, stone, glass, or space with no resistance. It's a whole different makeup. But you must move the stone out of the way if you are going to bring a man back from beyond and resuscitate him. So He says, "Move the stone."

And so they removed the stone. And Jesus raised His eyes, and said, "Father, I thank Thee that Thou heardest Me. And I knew that Thou hearest Me always, but because of the people standing around I said it, that they may believe that Thou didst send Me." And when He had said these things, He cried out with a loud voice, "Lazarus, come forth" (vv. 41-43).

I love the country preacher's comment, "If He hadn't limited that command to Lazarus, every corpse in the graveyard would have come forth!" It was as if He said, "Just Lazarus, this time, just Lazarus." Some day He'll bring them all back!

A great scene follows. We've got a mummy staggering out of the tomb.

He who had died came forth, bound hand and foot with wrappings; and his face was wrapped around with a cloth. Jesus said to them, "Unbind him, and let him go" (v. 44).

Isn't that an electric moment! Wouldn't you love to have had supper with Lazarus that night? "How was it, Lazarus?"

Only man can weep in grief. And Jesus did. Only God can raise the dead. And Jesus did.

G. Campbell Morgan, when wrestling with the mystery of Christ's incarnation, once wrote:

> He was the God-man. Not God indwelling a man. Of such there have been many. Not a man Deified. Of such there have been none save in the myths of pagan systems of thought; but God and man, combining in one Personality the two natures, a perpetual enigma and mystery, baffling the possibility of explanation.[2]

The apostle John's final comment in his Gospel goes like this:

> *This is the disciple who bears witness of these things, and wrote these things; and we know that his witness is true. And there are also many other things which Jesus did, which if they were written in detail, I suppose that even the world itself would not contain the books which were written* (John 21:24-25).

"I could have gathered up materials the world over and would not have had enough paper to write the stories with convincing, irrefutable evidence that He is who He claimed to be—namely, very God come in human form to die, to be raised, that you might see how magnificent He really is!"

Who is Jesus Christ? The God-man—the most unique Person who ever lived. The awesome Son of God!

Some time ago a lady wrote me a true story of an event that happened in a Christian school:

> A kindergarten teacher was determining how much religious training her new students had. While talking with one little boy, to whom the story of Jesus was obviously brand new, she began relating His death on the cross. When asked what a cross was, she picked up some sticks, and fashioning a crude one, she explained that Jesus was actually nailed to that cross, and then He died. The little boy with eyes downcast quietly acknowledged, "Oh, that's too bad." In the very next breath, however, she related that He arose again and that He came back to life. And his little eyes got big as saucers. He lit up and exclaimed, "Totally awesome!"

You don't know the full identity of Jesus if your response is "Oh, that's too bad." You know His identity only if your description is "TOTALLY AWESOME!"

1. Review Matthew 13:53-57 and Mark 3:20-21. Jesus knew what it meant to be misunderstood by friends and family. Have you experienced the pain of being misunderstood recently? What clues can you find in 1 Peter 2:18-23 about our Lord's response to unfair treatment? Look a little further on in 1 Peter 3:8-18a for even more encouragement!

2. Memorize Hebrews 1:3 and John 1:1-3 and/or John 14:9 so that you will have an answer for those you meet who say, "Jesus may have been a great teacher—but He wasn't God." When someone says, "Well, who do *you* say He is?" be ready with a reply!

3. Remember my plea for color and imagination in chapter 2? Reread Matthew 14:22-33. Only this time, *put yourself there*. This is no fairy tale—it really happened. Do your best to visualize the whole scene in vivid detail . . . the surging waves, that eerie night, the sight of a figure in the distance walking on the water. As soon as you have the opportunity tell that story to a child to help that little one understand "who He really is." (TOTALLY AWESOME.) Or, visualize a similar scene in Luke 8:22-25. This time describe to an adult how Jesus—as God!—specializes in calming the waves and winds that come into your life.

CHANGING LIVES
IS
JESUS' BUSINESS

t was Karl Marx, the father of modern socialism, who said, "Philosophers have only interpreted the world differently; the point is, however, to *change* it."

After serving the Lord for some fifteen years in Pakistan, missionary Warren Webster was invited to speak at the now famous Urbana Missionary Conference. He spoke very candidly about his days in Pakistan, but part of his message that his listeners will never forget are these words:

> If I had my life to live over again, I would live it to change the lives of people, because you have not changed anything until you have changed the lives of people.

Changing the world requires changing the lives of people.

While thinking through this chapter, I drifted back to the year 1973 and remembered the most famous musical our generation of Christians ever heard and sang. It's that immortal piece of music the Bill Gaither ministry composed—"Alleluia, A Praise Gathering for Believers."

I thumbed through the musical and came across the part of the narration that mentions changing lives. The narrator breaks into the familiar melody, "Something beautiful, something good, all my confusion He understood . . . " with:

> Well, down through history, changing lives has been His business. He's changed the rich—changed the poor. He's changed

the high and the mighty and He has changed the meek. He's changed my life, maybe He's changed yours. But if He hasn't, it can happen for you—right now! Today! . . ."[1]

Marx, Webster, Gaither—talk about three unlikely bedfellows! Yet a socialist, a missionary, and a composer agree at one point. They may be poles apart in philosophy and coming at the subject of change from different cultures, but all three agree, and we do too, that the key to changing our world is changing people. That is not optional, it is essential.

When I think about that which keeps me going in my ministry, it is the hope of *change*. When I meet with people who have struggled through the battles, the valleys, and the swamps of their experiences, and I search for reasons they hang on and keep growing, I discover that it is the hope of *change*. It is the inner conviction that God is at work, changing them and working through them to change others.

Just think about yourself for the last ten years. You're not the same person, are you? In fact, if you go back even further, and if you were completely candid, you'd have to admit that your life today compared to twelve, fifteen, eighteen years ago, doesn't even resemble the same person. Why? You are changing—and if it's for the better, I commend you!

SCRIPTURAL STATEMENTS REGARDING CHANGED LIVES

Before we analyze three lives Jesus changed, let's take a brief look at the Old and New Testaments and trace the idea of change. We are going to discover that the concept was of major significance to the Lord our God. His specialty is changing people.

The Old Testament

Let's look first into the book of Jeremiah, chapter 18. Glance over the first four verses from that chapter.

The word which came to Jeremiah from the Lord saying, "Arise and go down to the potter's house, and there I shall announce My words to you." Then I went down to the potter's house, and there he was, making something on the wheel. But the vessel that he was making of clay was spoiled in the hand of the potter; so he remade it into another vessel, as it pleased the potter to make.

If you have never seen a potter at work, your education isn't complete. You owe it to yourself to take the time to observe an artist at work on the wheel. It's fascinating!

Several years ago my wife and I visited a local university campus during their art festival. We had the privilege of slipping behind the curtain and watching a potter at work. She was quite skilled in the art—a pleasure to watch. She was finishing the top part of a vase. As the wheel was spinning, her fingers and thumbs were smoothing, shaping, pulling, pushing . . . she never looked up at those who were watching her.

While finishing the process, a part of the top of the vase displeased her. It looked fine to me, but not to her. In the simplest of ways, she reached over, and with a little instrument she peeled off that part and remade it. Still it wasn't the way she wanted it. Again it looked excellent to me, but it wasn't what she liked. I was tempted to say, "That looks fine. Leave it alone!" But I'm glad I didn't. She remade it yet again . . . and it was more beautiful than ever. As she pulled out the clay ever so slightly, what finally resulted was this delicate flare at the top of the vase. She gave a slight nod, as if to say, "There, that's what I wanted it to look like." Then she left it alone. Finally, she looked at us and smiled as we quietly applauded.

When we observed her artistry, we were impressed with the care she had demonstrated. No detail was unimportant. The clay had to be just right.

That's what Jeremiah witnessed as he saw the potter at work. Then the Lord drew an analogy for His prophet.

> *Then the word of the Lord came to me saying, "Can I not, O house of Israel, deal with you as this potter does?" declares the Lord. "Behold, like the clay in the potter's hand, so are you in My hand, O house of Israel" (vv. 5-6).*

You see change written there without even finding the word.

"You're like a lump of clay to Me, Israel. And I can shape you and hollow you out and thin your walls and flare the top. I can make you decorative, or I can reshape you and start all over again, because change is My specialty. And you are the object of My attention and affection!"

From Jeremiah, we turn back to another prophet, Isaiah is his name.

> *But now, O Lord, Thou art our Father, we are the clay, and Thou our potter . . . (Isaiah 64:8).*

Can you recall which gospel song came from this verse of Scripture?

Have Thine own way, Lord!
Have Thine own way!
Thou art the Potter, I am the clay.
Mold me and make me after Thy will,
While I am waiting yielded and still.[2]

Once again, it is the idea of our Lord's shaping us and changing us whichever way He pleases.

Would it help to see a living flesh-and-blood example of that? His name was Saul. He became a king. Shortly after being appointed the first king over the nation Israel, Saul heard these words:

Then the Spirit of the Lord will come upon you mightily, and you shall prophesy with them and be changed into another man. And it shall be when these signs come to you, do for yourself what the occasion requires; for God is with you. And you shall go down before me to Gilgal; and behold, I will come down to you to offer burnt offerings and sacrifice peace offerings. You shall wait seven days until I come to you and show you what you should do.

Then it happened when he turned his back to leave Samuel, God changed his heart; and all those signs came about on that day (1 Samuel 10:6-9).

Now I wish all changes were that rapid and that easy. Usually, changes take time and pain on our part—and much patience on God's part. But God is committed to our being changed, no matter how long or how painful the process. Never forget that! While being changed we may feel like a shapeless mass. We can't understand His reasons, like I couldn't understand the potter as she worked on her vase. But trust the Father. He's changing you. He knows what He's about.

Let's look at one more example from the Old Testament—a wonderful promise from the proverbs of Solomon. When you think about the political scene of our day, you will find great peace in this verse.

The king's heart is like channels of water in the hand of the Lord;
He turns it wherever He wishes (Proverbs 21:1).

When God is ready to change a heart, it gets changed, whether it's a proud king, a stubborn husband, a strong-willed athlete, one of your own family members, or you. He turns it wherever . . . *wherever* He wishes. No one is an "impossible case" to God. Not even *you*!

The New Testament

In the New Testament we have more familiar passages of Scripture. It shouldn't take us long to survey a few of these. There is no way we can bypass Romans 8. I love this passage!

> *And in the same way the Spirit also helps our weakness; for we do not know how to pray as we should, but the Spirit Himself intercedes for us with groanings too deep for words; and He who searches the hearts knows what the mind of the Spirit is, because He intercedes for the saints according to the will of God. And we know that God causes all things to work together for good to those who love God, to those who are called according to His purpose. For whom He foreknew, He also predestined to become conformed to the image of His Son, that He might be the first-born among many brethren* (vv. 26-29).

God is committed to the task of conforming you and me to the image of His Son. Not physically—He's not making us look like Jesus looked physically—but inwardly: in character, in patience, in gentleness, in goodness, in grace, in truth, in discipline. He's committed to conforming our lives to the inner character of His Son.

Years ago I worked as an apprentice in a machine shop. One of the lathes I learned to operate was a tracer lathe. It had an air-controlled "finger" that traced its way along a fixed template. The template was an exact pattern of what was to be turned out on the lathe. And as this very sensitive little finger followed along the template, its every movement caused the tool that was cutting the metal to cut that exact shape. When I finished, I had a finished product from the lathe that was a precise replica of the template.

Again, that is the Father's specialty. He places His finger on the template—His Son. And He watches over His workmanship. At times the tool bites in, causing the heat to increase because of the friction. We squirm and may even try to get away. But we are His workmanship and the Father won't let us go. He holds us tightly in the lathe of His will. His goal is that we bear the image of His Son. That's the Father's task. He's committed to it. He's changing us.

Speaking of our being the Father's workmanship, look at Ephesians 2:10. Another verse brimming with encouragement!

For we are His workmanship, created in Christ Jesus for good works, which God prepared beforehand, that we should walk in them.

Look again at those first five words: "For we are His workmanship." We're His project. He's got His eye on us. He knows what our tomorrow holds. Early every January He knows what the year will hold for us. And He is working on His project all year long. He's shaping and molding and making us like He wants us to become.

Let's glance at just one more before we look more closely at three people whose lives were changed by Jesus. Lest you think He's going to give up, lest you think He's going to back off (even though you beg Him to) this verse says He won't:

For I am confident of this very thing, that He who began a good work in you will perfect it until the day of Christ Jesus (Philippians 1:6).

What God starts, God finishes. He's never been known to walk away from an individual and say, "He's just too stubborn for Me. He is too much of a job." Kind of like some do with their teenagers. "They're just too much. I'll just leave 'em with the Lord." Well, He'll never say that. He's never met a teenager that's His match. He's never met a thirty-year-old that's His match. Any ministers reading this? He's never met a *preacher* that's His match. How about someone in their eighties or nineties? He's never met a senior citizen that's His match. God will complete what He starts—including you. It may seem unfair, it may be painful, it may involve changes that cause you to question His goodness. But He knows what is necessary.

When God wants to drill a man,
And thrill a man,
And skill a man,
When God wants to mold a man
To play the noblest part;
When He yearns with all His heart
To create so great and bold a man
That all the world shall be amazed,
Watch His methods, watch His ways!
How He ruthlessly perfects
Whom He royally elects!

How He hammers him and hurts him,
And with mighty blows converts him
Into trial shapes of clay which
Only God understands;
While his tortured heart is crying
And he lifts beseeching hands
How He bends but never breaks
When his good He undertakes;
How He uses whom He chooses,
And with every purpose fuses him;
By every act induces him
To try His splendor out—
God knows what He's about.[3]

THREE LIVES JESUS CHANGED

I find in the Gospel by John three gripping illustrations of people who were changed. They were as different as snowflakes, but all three were like pieces of clay on the potter's wheel. And in each slice of life that is revealed in John's Gospel, we witness a remarkable change.

There's hope here. If our Lord could change them, He can do the same today. Who were they? One, a wayward woman; another, a blind beggar; and a third, a doubting disciple. There are differences here in sex, physical ability, age, marital status, and occupation. I've chosen different ones on purpose so that we'll be able to identify with at least one of the three.

A Wayward Woman: John 4

The scene occurs by a well in Samaria. The two people who meet have never met before. One is a woman and the other is a man. The woman is never named here or elsewhere in Scripture. It happens at noon. The Samaritan sun is burning down. And Jesus, hot from His journey, sits down alone by a well. His disciples have gone for food. A woman walks up to draw water. She's in for a change and doesn't know it . . . not yet, that is.

That's the way it happens, by the way. That's what makes life exciting. You think tomorrow is going to be your basic dull, bland tomorrow. It's not. It's very possible that a change is on the horizon.

Here's a woman who has no idea of who or what is in front of her.

As she walks up to the well she hears a Jew—a *Jew*, mind you—speaking to her, a Samaritan.

"Give Me a drink," He says.

Now you can't appreciate that, not being Jewish (and certainly not being Samaritan). You haven't seen prejudice like they knew it then. I mean, if a Jew were going to go from his homeland in Judea up north, instead of going through Samaria he went all the way around Samaria and then went further in his journey. It's sort of like going from Texas to Kansas, but choosing to travel *around* Oklahoma. Anything to keep from encountering Samaritans!

I gave that illustration some time ago. When I finished my talk I had three huge fellas corner me. All three were from Oklahoma. Almost in unison—and with a smile—they said, "We jus' want you to know we ain't got any Samaritans livin' in Oklahoma!" I've never felt more in the minority!

Remember now, His disciples had gone into the city to get something to eat, which left Jesus alone with this woman by the well.

> *The Samaritan woman therefore said to Him, "How is it that You, being a Jew, ask me for a drink since I am a Samaritan woman?" (For Jews have no dealings with Samaritans)* (John 4:9).

She was bewildered! "Not only are You speaking to a woman on the street, you're speaking to a *Samaritan* woman. And not only are You a man . . . You're a Jewish man!" Jews in Samaria stood out like a uniformed sheriff from Savannah would stand out walking through the back alleys of Harlem.

Jesus being in Samaria would be sort of like our President and his wife spending their vacation in a P.L.O. camp. That's how amazing, actually how ridiculous it seemed to the Samaritan woman. "What are You, a Jew, doing in *my* territory? And of all things, You're asking me for a drink. What's with You?"

> *Jesus answered and said to her, "If you knew the gift of God, and who it is who says to you, 'Give Me a drink,' you would have asked Him, and He would have given you living water." She said to Him, "Sir, You have nothing to draw with and the well is deep; where then do You get that living water? You are not greater than our father Jacob, are You, who gave us the well, and drank of it himself, and his sons, and his cattle?" Jesus answered and said to her, "Everyone who drinks of this water shall thirst again; but*

whoever drinks of the water that I shall give him shall never thirst; but the water that I shall give him shall become in him a well of water springing up to eternal life." The woman said to Him, "Sir, give me this water, so I will not be thirsty, nor come all the way here to draw" (vv. 10-15).

She said, "I'll take it. Pipe it into my house. I'll take that 'living water.' I don't like walking down here and hauling it back with this jug on my head. I'd love to have you bring the water to me." She misses the point completely.

He says to her, "Go and call your husband. . . ."

She answers, hesitatingly, "I . . . I . . . I have no husband."

. . . *"You have well said, 'I have no husband'; for you have had five husbands, and the one whom you now have is not your husband; this you have said truly"* (vv. 17-18).

Now that was in a day when having had five husbands was scandalous . . . in a time when living with a man outside of wedlock was considered shameful. In one sentence, Jesus exposes the truth as He unveils her life.

I have discovered as a minister of the gospel that there are many, many people who have secrets they don't want anybody to know—even though they may do impressive things and look heroic. All of us have feet of clay.

I read some time ago about a fellow who went into a fried chicken place in Long Beach, California, and bought a couple of chicken dinners for himself and his date late one afternoon. The young woman at the counter inadvertently gave him the proceeds from the day—a whole bag of money (much of it cash) instead of fried chicken.

After driving to their picnic site, the two of them sat down to open the meal and enjoy some chicken together. They discovered a whole lot more than chicken—over $800! But he was unusual. He quickly put the money back in the bag. They got back into the car and drove all the way back. Mr. Clean got out, walked in, and became an instant hero.

By then, the manager was frantic. The guy with the bag of money looked the manager in the eye and said, "I want you to know I came by to get a couple of chicken dinners and wound up with all this money. Here." Well, the manager was thrilled to death. He said, "Oh, great, let me call the newspaper. I'm gonna have your picture put in the local paper. You're one of the most honest men I've ever heard of." To which the guy quickly responded, "Oh, no, no, no, don't do that!" Then he leaned closer and whispered, "You see, the woman I'm with is not my wife . . . she's, uh, somebody else's wife."[4]

Interesting, isn't it? Those who often appear to be people of character are sometimes hiding a secret. Jesus has a way of penetrating the veneer. And He does that with this wayward woman by the well.

> *The woman said to Him, "Sir, I perceive that You are a prophet. Our fathers worshiped in this mountain, and you people say that in Jerusalem is the place where men ought to worship"* (vv. 19-20).

Obviously, she's uneasy. She doesn't want to talk about husbands.

She suddenly wants to talk about religious issues. "See that mountain over there? Now our people say that's where we're to worship. You people say folks are to worship in Jerusalem. Let's talk about the mountain in Samaria or the mountain in Jerusalem. Let's discuss theology, O great prophet."

Isn't that just like us? "Let's don't talk about the husband-wife thing; let's talk about mountains." Mountains and theology make for a lot more comfortable conversations than illicit relationships, right?

> *Jesus said to her, "Woman, believe Me, an hour is coming when neither in this mountain, nor in Jerusalem, shall you worship the Father. You worship that which you do not know; we worship that which we know, for salvation is from the Jews. But an hour is coming, and now is, when the true worshipers shall worship the Father in spirit and truth; for such people the Father seeks to be His worshipers. God is spirit, and those who worship Him must worship in spirit and truth. The woman said to Him, "I know that Messiah is coming (He who is called Christ); when that One comes, He will declare all things to us." Jesus said to her, "I who speak to you am He"* (vv. 21-26).

And at this crucial point in the dialogue, Jesus' disciples come back. This is a great moment I don't want us to overlook. It will take a little imagination. Here are twelve hungry disciples. They have hurried back, starving to death. And as they happen upon the scene they see Jesus nose to nose with a Samaritan woman! To put it mildly, the disciples were blown away. So they responded as we probably would have, given the same circumstances.

And at this point His disciples came, and they marveled that He had been speaking with a woman; yet no one said, "What do You seek?" or "Why do You speak with her?" So the woman left her waterpot, and went into the city, and said to the men, "Come, see a man who told me all the things that I have done; this is not the Christ, is it?" They went out of the city, and were coming to Him (vv. 27-30).

The disciples are still standing there, staring. Mouths open, stomachs growling. "How could He be talking to a woman, and of all things a *Samaritan* woman? Yuck!"

In the meanwhile the disciples were requesting Him, saying, "Rabbi, eat [Yeah, we got cheeseburgers, hamburgers, fries. What do you want? C'mon, Lord, let's eat"] (v. 31).

But He said to them, "I have food to eat that you do not know about" (v. 32).

This is one of the disciples' classic moments.

The disciples therefore were saying to one another, "No one brought Him anything to eat, did he?" (v. 33).

Airhead city! I'll tell you, there were moments when these fellas were really thick. "You didn't give Him a hamburger, did ya? Somebody already gave Jesus a cheeseburger?"

Jesus said to them, "My food is to do the will of Him who sent Me, and to accomplish His work (v. 34).

"C'mon, you guys! We're not talking about literal, physical food. We're not talking about cheeseburgers. We're talking about eternal things. Get your act together! Why, there are just a few months and then a harvest. I'll tell you, time is getting short."
And do you think the woman wasn't changed?

And from that city many of the Samaritans believed in Him because of the word of the woman who testified, "He told me all the things that I have done" (v. 39).

That, by the way, is one of the prime methods Jesus uses to change us. He forces us to face the truth, the whole truth, and nothing but the truth. Isn't it vulnerable to be in His presence? But isn't it *wonderful* to be honest when we are? Just to have someone with whom we can trust our deepest fears and longings! Someone before whom we can unveil the most intimate secrets of our lives!

> *So when the Samaritans came to Him, they were asking Him to stay with them; and He stayed there two days* (v. 40).

What He did was considered scandalous in a Jewish home, but Jesus had on His heart the eternal souls of the Samaritans. There are times tradition must bow to conviction.

> *And many more believed because of His word; and they were saying to the woman, "It is no longer because of what you said that we believe, for we have heard for ourselves and know that this One is indeed the Savior of the world"* (vv. 41-42).

She was C-H-A-N-G-E-D! What a different woman!

I want to address something you may not agree with initially, but before you throw rocks at me, just think about it. Jesus never once told her to leave that man.

Now wait a minute. Go back and check for yourself. Her living with the man wasn't Jesus' primary concern. That wasn't the major issue. He didn't rebuke her because of her immoral life. She was an *unsaved* Samaritan. Unsaved people live like that. He didn't say to her, "Clean up your act, and then you're qualified to believe." He said, "I am Messiah. And I'll tell you all the things that you've done."

In the process of coming to know Messiah it is remarkable how Messiah is able to clean up a life later on. *Then* there is power to do so—not until. Want a little tip that will help you in your witness? Don't read people a long list of rules of spirituality en route to salvation. Let the Lord do that. You present to them the Savior. You press the issue of their relationship to the Lord Jesus. Our job isn't to clean up the fish bowl, certainly not initially. It's to fish—just fish. I rather imagine that as time passed the changed woman became intensely uncomfortable with her lifestyle. You can't enjoy walking with a holy God and, at the same time, continue to enjoy living with a person out of wedlock. But before a person can be expected to walk, Christ must come and live within, giving the power that is needed.

A Blind Beggar

John, chapter 9, is an equally interesting story, completely different from the first one. This story does not have to do with a woman, but a man. Not a healthy, happy man, but a blind man—a blind beggar—blind from birth. But the outcome is very similar. Like that woman from Samaria, he, too, was changed.

And as He passed by, He saw a man blind from birth. And His disciples asked Him, saying, "Rabbi, who sinned, this man or his parents, that he should be born blind?" (John 9:1-2).

Isn't it easy to become calloused when dealing with people in need? "Case 321—here's another one, Jesus." And if you see enough of them along the road, as you do in the Middle East, your heart can easily become indifferent to beggars. By and by, you begin to see all beggars alike. Like some see all prisoners alike . . . or all harlots alike . . . or all patients alike. Ultimately, you begin to see all *humanity* alike.

And so the blind beggar became a topic of theological discussion. Not only is Jesus' answer profound, the event that followed is miraculous.

Jesus answered, "It was neither that this man sinned, nor his parents; but it was in order that the works of God might be displayed in him. We must work the works of Him who sent Me, as long as it is day; night is coming, when no man can work. While I am in the world, I am the light of the world." When He had said this, He spat on the ground, and made clay of the spittle, and applied the clay to his eyes, and said to him, "Go, wash in the pool of Siloam" (which is translated, Sent). And so he went away and washed, and came back seeing (vv. 9:3-7).

Now wait. You've probably read this story so many times your excitement is pretty dull. It's just another story . . . just another miracle.

Don't let it be! I want you to put yourself in the sandals of first-century people who have seen nothing but the same blind beggar day after miserable day, all their lives. The community knows him well. But suddenly that same man comes back from the pool, having washed the clay from his eyes, and he can see. For the first time in his entire life, he can actually see! What strikes me as remarkable are the others' reactions.

The ninth chapter of John follows the story quite closely. In verses 8 through 12 we have the neighbors' reaction; it's *astounding*. In verses 13 through 34, we have the Pharisees' reaction; it's *unbelievable*. And in verses 35 through 41 we have Jesus' response, which is so gracious, so appropriate. Let's check the neighbors' reaction first:

> The neighbors therefore, and those who previously saw him as a beggar, were saying, "Is not this the one who used to sit and beg?" Others were saying, "This is he"; still others were saying, "No, but he is like him." He kept saying, "I am the one" (vv. 8-9).

Can you believe it? The dear guy whose entire visual world has come alive, has to verify his identity to those folks! "I *am* the one. I really am the same one! I can see. Look, I can see!" He can't believe that instead of celebrating with him, the neighbors are arguing over his identity.

Now, follow their thinking here:

> Therefore they were saying to him, "How then were your eyes opened?" (v. 10).

Does that seem amazing to anybody else? No one is saying, "Bring the confetti! Somebody else bring the cream cheese, the lox, and the bagels! Let's celebrate! This guy can see!" No, they're frowning, rubbing their beards, staring intently, and looking rather suspiciously as they probe, "Tell us what happened. Exactly how did this occur?" The man responds as openly and honestly as he can.

> He answered, "The man who is called Jesus made clay, and anointed my eyes, and said to me, 'Go to Siloam, and wash'; so I went away and washed, and I received sight" (vv. 11-12).

Well, they're stumped. And in those days when you were stumped, you hauled the guy off to the religious officials. That was safe. So they brought him to the Pharisees. Now . . . hold on to yourself. This is where things get downright *unbelievable*.

> They brought to the Pharisees him who was formerly blind. Now it was a Sabbath on the day when Jesus made the clay, and opened his eyes. Again, therefore, the Pharisees also were asking him how he received his sight. And he said to them, "He applied

clay to my eyes, and I washed, and I see." Therefore some of the Pharisees were saying, "This man is not from God, because He does not keep the Sabbath." But others were saying, "How can a man who is a sinner perform such signs?" And there was a division among them (vv. 13-16).

Remember my previous chapter on Jesus' identity, where many didn't know who Jesus was? Some said He was a sinner. Some said He was a saint. Some said He was from the devil. Others said He was John the Baptizer or one of the prophets. Here is an example of that confusion. Even the Pharisees disagreed among themselves. He couldn't be from God! No way, He's a sinner. But how could a sinner do this?"

They said therefore to the blind man again, "What do you say about Him, since He opened your eyes?" And he said, "He is a prophet." The Jews therefore did not believe it of him, that he had been blind, and had received sight, until they called the parents of the very one who had received his sight (vv. 17-18).

Here was the beggar's only visible hope—his parents. But this dear couple is so intimidated, so scared of the Pharisees, that they bow to the pressure at their own son's expense.

[The Jews called the parents] *and questioned them, saying, "Is this your son, who you say was born blind? Then how does he now see?" His parents answered then, and said, "We know that this is our son, and that he was born blind; but how he now sees, we do not know; or who opened his eyes, we do not know. Ask him; he is of age, he shall speak for himself." His parents said this because they were afraid of the Jews; for the Jews had already agreed, that if any one should confess Him to be Christ, he should be put out of the synagogue. For this reason his parents said, "He is of age; ask him"* (vv. 19-23).

Astonishing! Their fear of the Pharisees is greater than their love for their own son. Frankly, that says a great deal about the intimidating power of a religious organization.

The Pharisees pounce on the man:

So a second time they called the man who had been blind, and said to him, "Give glory to God; we know that this man is a sinner." He therefore answered, "Whether He is a sinner, I do not

know; one thing I do know, that, whereas I was blind, now I see."
They said therefore to him, "What did He do to you? How did He
open your eyes?" He answered them, "I told you already, and you
did not listen; why do you want to hear it again? You do not want
to become His disciples too, do you?" (vv. 24-27).

Isn't that a great question? He's getting gutsy, isn't he? Pushing
an elbow into the side of one of the hotshots, he jabs: "You're not
getting a little interested, are you?"

I love that. The man has not only changed physically, he is already changing in his personality. The beggar is getting bold.

And they reviled him, and said, "You are His disciple; but we are
disciples of Moses. We know that God has spoken to Moses; but as
for this man, we do not know where He is from." The man an-
swered and said to them, "Well, here is an amazing thing, that
you do not know where He is from, and yet He opened my eyes. We
know that God does not hear sinners; but if anyone is God-
fearing, and does His will, He hears him. Since the beginning of
time it has never been heard that anyone opened the eyes of a per-
son born blind. If this man were not from God, He could do noth-
ing." They answered and said to him, "You were born entirely in
sins, and are you teaching us?" And they put him out (vv. 28-
34).

I never read this section of Scripture without realizing again just
how suspicious people are about our being changed by Christ. I'll
tell you, when your eyes are opened, when the blindness is removed, and especially when you begin to tell the story of your pilgrimage from blindness to faith in Christ, hang on! And don't be
surprised if you encounter the most resistance from *religious*
people. They will look at you like R2-D2 from a galaxy far, far away.
They will stare. They will really begin to wonder if you've got both
oars in the water. Religious folks are uncomfortable around authentic people whose lives have been changed by the living Christ.

So the man stumbles out of their presence. Why? They put him
out! And Jesus comes along and finds him. He always does.

Jesus heard that they had put him out; and finding him, He said,
"Do you believe in the Son of Man?" He answered and said,
"And who is He, Lord, that I may believe in Him?" (vv. 35-36).

You see, the man has physical sight, but not spiritual sight—not yet. He's not yet a believer. He just had his eyes opened. Now the Lord opens his heart and moves in.

Jesus said to him, "You have both seen Him, and He is the one who is talking with you." And he said, "Lord, I believe." And he worshiped Him (vv. 37-38).

Sometimes the Lord changes us physically. On other occasions, it is His plan to change a rebellious heart. Or an unforgiving spirit. Sometimes it's the inability to forgive; we're eaten up with the cancer—the internal acid of resentment and bitterness, and then the Lord graciously changes us. Occasionally the change takes place through people, sometimes alone. Occasionally the change takes place in a moment, sometimes it takes time—months . . . maybe years. But when it is finally complete, it sets us free. As in the case of the blind beggar, we can see. At last, we're free to see!

A Doubting Disciple

I especially like this third story. It's the briefest of the three, but perhaps the most personal for the Christian. Here is a man named Thomas who is a follower of Jesus. Before going any further, a warning is in order. We should not be too hard on him. I've spent too many hours in my ministry shooting at Thomas—and hearing others do the same. Frankly, I have matured enough over the past several years so that I see the man in a little different light having had some doubts myself, not unlike Thomas. John 20 records his response, which has been attacked for generations.

But Thomas, one of the twelve, called Didymus, was not with them when Jesus came. The other disciples therefore were saying to him, "We have seen the Lord!" But he said to them, "Unless I shall see in His hands the imprint of the nails, and put my finger into the place of the nails, and put my hand into His side, I will not believe" (John 20:24-25).

This is the same one who had earlier demonstrated a strong faith. When Jesus talked about going to see Lazarus, Thomas had suggested, "Let us also go that we may die with Him" (John 11:16). The man was committed. He was ready to go to death with his Lord. Not too many of the twelve were ready to die for Him. He's the kind of guy that when he gives himself to someone, he unloads the truck

. . . he gives with all of his heart. He sells out wholesale—lock, stock, and barrel. "Everything I have is the Lord's." The more I think about him, the more I believe Thomas was a heart-and-soul disciple.

The problem with a man or woman like that is that when they become disillusioned, the response creates a drastic swing of the pendulum. When they back off, they fall *way* back. With extreme caution they start to look at things from a safe distance. "I'm not gonna get burned again. I mean, next time it's gonna take the Rock of Gibraltar before I'll give myself." Again, I suggest, that's Thomas. "I believed once. I was ready to die for Him. But everything suddenly collapsed. I saw Him go to the cross. I watched all my dreams nailed to His hands and His feet. I saw Him die. I saw them bury Him. I've seen the tomb. Looks to me like the whole shootin' match has gone up in smoke."

Then suddenly, everybody around him started talking resurrection. Some even said they had actually *seen* the resurrected Christ. Remember, he hadn't been in the room when Jesus showed them His hands and His side (John 20:20 and 24).

While his buddies were saying, "Hey, Tom! We've seen the Lord . . . He's come back from beyond," Thomas was holding back. "Wait a minute, unless I can see what you've seen, no way am I going to believe it!" After all, they were excited because they had seen Jesus; Thomas hadn't. And I think Jesus understood the man's reluctance and reservations. If it were any other way, our Lord Jesus would have been far more severe with Thomas. Check it out for yourself. He wasn't. You'll look in vain to find a strong rebuke from Jesus. He *helps* people who struggle. Frankly, there are a lot of folks like Thomas. Not everybody finds it easy to believe.

> And after eight days again His disciples were inside, and Thomas with them. Jesus came, the doors having been shut, and stood in their midst, and said, "Peace be with you." Then He said to Thomas, "Reach here your finger, and see My hands; and reach here your hand, and put it into My side; and be not unbelieving, but believing" (vv. 26-27).

Jesus had not been present when Thomas had expressed his reluctance to believe, but He knows all about it. He said, in effect, "Thomas, you asked for this earlier. Here are My hands."

Thomas doesn't wrestle, doesn't argue. He doesn't stomp out of the room. He says, "My Lord and my God!" His doubts instantly vanish. And the disciple, like the woman at the well and the beggar on the street, is a changed man. And why not? Changing lives is Jesus' business.

Clarence Macartney writes colorful words about this scene. I have read them over and over. Take your time:

> Without any warrant for it whatsoever, Thomas has been called the Rationalist of the Apostolic Band . . . The rationalist, the ordinary skeptic, as we think of him as and as we experience him, is not looking for signs of truth in Christianity but for signs of its falsehood. He will ferret out some little seeming discrepancy of the Biblical records and magnify it into a mountain, whereas the mighty panorama of Christian history and influence fades into nothingness. . . .
>
> Thomas, it is true, asked for signs, for particular evidence, but to liken him to the rationalist, to the skeptic, in the common use of that term is to do him a great injustice and to wrest the Scriptures. The difference between the rationalist and Thomas is this: the rationalist wants to disbelieve; Thomas wanted to believe. The rationalist, of the honest type, is occasioned by study, by examination of evidence, by the pressing bounds of the natural world, making the other world seem unreal; but the doubt of Thomas was the doubt born of sorrow.
>
> This is the deepest doubt of all, the doubt born of sorrow; that is, the doubt which rises out of the experience of our lives. The great doubts are not those that are born in Germany, in the study of the critic, in the debate of religions, nor are they born in the laboratory, from the study of the laws of nature; they are not born of meditating over the rocks and the stars and the planets, of tracing out genealogies and chronologies; they are born in the library and in the laboratory of the soul; they are the dark interrogations cast by the experiences through which we pass in this strange adventure men call life. The doubt of a man who talks of the impossibility of a Virgin Birth is one thing; but let it not be confused with the doubt of a mother who has lost her first born child and wonders if God is and if her child still lives. The doubt of a man who questions the Mosaic account of the Creation of the world is one thing, but let it not be confused with the doubt of the man who sees the world in travail and sore anguish, the ceaseless invasion of hate and the eternal enmity of the evil for the good, the inhumanity of man to man, and wonders if God has forsaken His world. The doubt of Thomas was not that of a quibbler, of a cold-blooded, dilettante student; it was the doubt of a man who had lost his Lord and Master. Sorrow had filled his heart.[5]

And don't tell me you haven't had doubts like that. I can assure you, I have. And in those doubting moments when the lights are out and the valley's deep and the walls are high, thick, and cold, and tomorrow seems bleak, we also say, "He'll have to prove it to me next time." And the wonderful thing is this: He does! He comes in like a flood and shows you His hands, and He shows you His side. And He says, "Here, My child, look here, here's *proof*."

WHERE ARE YOU?

I don't know where you fit into this ninth chapter—whether you're the wayward woman, the blind beggar, the doubting disciple . . . or maybe a mixture of the three. I don't need to know. I care that *you* know where you are and that you see the application. But I know it's impossible for you to be too far gone to change. You're smart enough to figure that out. You see what this chapter has been saying, don't you? The One who changes is committed to your changing as much as He was to the woman by the well, the blind beggar in the streets, the disciple who doubted; and He will not give up. You are like soft clay in His hands; He is going to change you. It's just a matter of time.

Won't you let Him do so with less resistance? Won't you make the trip a little bit easier? Won't you relax and let Him have His way? Isn't it about time? Yes, it is. Read again the words from that grand old hymn.

Only this time . . . *mean* it.

> Have Thine own way, Lord!
> Have Thine own way!
> Thou art the Potter, I am the clay.
> Mold me and make me after will,
> While I am waiting yielded and still.

1. Project yourself *back* ten years. Do your best to recall where you were living, what you were involved in, what you were concerned about, what you struggled with, where you were in your walk with Christ. Can you do it? Now . . . ask yourself the tough question: How much have I *grown* during these past ten years? How is my life different? If you can see real strides in your knowledge, discernment, relationship with Christ, and in demonstrating the fruits of the Spirit (Galatians 5:22-23), take time to praise your Lord for His gracious leading and work in your heart. If you're discouraged by what you see, claim the truth of Philippians 3:12-14 and press on! He promises to be at work in our lives as we yield to Him (Philippians 2:13).

2. The Samaritan woman went to the village well at noon on one "ordinary" day, expecting to draw her usual day's ration of water. Instead, she came face to face with the living God. And her life was changed forever. Do you imagine that your tomorrow will be just like your yesterday . . . that nothing could lift you out of your well-worn rut? Sounds like you've stopped believing in a God with the power to bring *change*. He can make it happen! He can shatter old habits . . . blast apart old attitudes . . . wash away old resentments and hurts . . . push aside old fears and limitations and stereotypes. Yes, He can! Begin your tomorrow by meditating on Philippians 2:13 and Colossians 1:29. It's HIS energy that's at work in our lives, making the difference. Ask your Father to cleanse you, fill you with His Spirit, and use you in *any* way He sees fit. Then watch Him go to work!

3. Know a "doubting Thomas" who is struggling in his or her sorrow and perplexity with the reality of a loving God? Perhaps others have already written this individual off. Don't you do it! Take time this week to make contact with your wounded friend . . . a call or a note or a visit. Don't judge or preach. Just assure him or her of your friendship and concern, *no matter what*. Then . . . keep praying. The Lord has a way with tenderhearted Thomases.

The Holy Spirit

* * *

"I recognize the Holy Spirit as the third member of the Godhead, incessantly at work convicting, convincing, and comforting."

THE SPIRIT
WHO IS NOT
A GHOST

did an "unearthly" thing last week. In fact, I did it twice.

Thinking back over my lifetime (which is now more than five decades), I have done many adventurous things. I've even done a few crazy things; some I think would qualify as mischievous, risky, and on a few occasions, dangerous. To retain the little bit of respect I have built with my readers over the years, I am not going to reveal all of those things that I have done. But I have to tell you about this unearthly thing I did twice this past week.

By the way, I checked Webster's for *unearthly* to make sure it's the word I want. It means "nonterrestrial, not mundane . . . weird." So *unearthly* is the right word. Being an earthling, I found it to be wonderful . . . downright exciting.

I defied gravity.

Now I have to confess I didn't do it on my own—earthlings can't do that, you see. I needed help from a power outside myself, and that posed a bit of a problem because that power happens to be invisible. And that's where things got a little "eerie." How did I know it was invisible? I looked. As a matter of fact, I stared. I leaned over the fella sitting next to the window, and I watched the wings as we roared down the runway with the jets full throttle. I kept looking to see if I could see the power that would make my unearthly experience happen.

Finally, the guy sitting next to the window said to me, "Are you all right?"

"Yes," I said, as I kept staring at the wing, "I'm just checking." (I like saying things like that when you're taking off in airplanes.) And before long he was looking back and checking with me!

"What are we checking for?" he asked, as he strained his neck.

"Well," I replied, "we're looking for the stuff that holds us up." That led into a very interesting conversation, I might add.

You say, "Aw, Chuck, gimme a break. Here I was thinking you did something spooky, like *really* weird, but you just flew." You're right, that's exactly what I did. But you have to admit, even though it's now a common thing, it is still amazing. That invisible force held our plane 30,000 feet above sea level for well over two hours both going and coming. And not one of us inside the plane ever saw what did it. To borrow a line from a couple of now-famous movies, "the force was with us." Invisible, yet present.

Air is a force with incredible strength. It can snap a tree in two or demolish a landscape. Given enough velocity, air becomes a devastating wind. Energized by a hurricane or tornado, it can clear out an entire mobile home park in seconds. The power in that invisible stuff! If you contain it in a network of hoses and valves and put it under enough pressure, it can bring a massive commercial bus or truck-trailer rig to a screeching halt. It'll even stop a locomotive pulling over a hundred cars. It will break thick concrete on a driveway or a freeway if it's pushed through the right tools. It will loosen or tighten the lug nuts on your car's wheels if funneled into the right mechanism. In fact, it can lift massive amounts of weight.

The manager of a granite quarry in North Carolina once said,

> We supplied the granite for the municipal building in New York City. We can lift an acre of solid granite ten feet thick to almost any height we desire for the purpose of moving it. . . . We can do it as easily as I can lift a piece of paper.[1]

How? Air. That's all, just air.

You can't feel it. You can't see it or smell it (unless you live around Los Angeles!). You can't, except in most technical ways, measure it or weigh it. But it keeps you alive every minute. If I took air away from you who are now reading this book for five minutes, you would become brain damaged. We cannot live without it. Yet when we fly or apply our brakes or watch a mechanic work on our car, we think nothing of it. Amazing stuff, air.

Never think that because something is invisible it is therefore unimportant or weak. You may be surprised to know that the Bible talks a lot about air. The Old Testament calls it *Ruach*. The New Testament calls it *Pneuma*. We get the word *Pneumatic* from the New Testament Greek word. The English Bible, however, doesn't translate either one as *air*. Usually, it's *breath*. "God breathed into man the breath of life." Or it's called *wind.* "Like a mighty wind." Or it is translated *spirit*—as in the "spirit of man" or "the Holy Spirit."

A number of synonyms are used for Spirit—words like helper, advocate, comforter, convicter, restrainer, exhorter, and reprover. He is portrayed by symbols, too, such as a dove, fire, wind, even water. In John 7 we read of this power being called "living water."

Jesus is speaking:

> . . . *"If any man is thirsty, let him come to Me and drink. He who believes in Me, as the Scripture said, 'From his innermost being shall flow rivers of living water'"* (vv. 37-38).

And in case you wonder what He had reference to, the next verse explains:

> *But this He spoke of the Spirit.* . . .

He referred to the Spirit of God, the third member of the Trinity.

Let me paraphrase verse 38: "From the believer's inner life there will be a reservoir of enormous, immeasurable power. It will gush forth. It will pour out like a torrential river that causes rapids, waterfalls, and endless movement to the ocean." That's the idea. It's not a picture of some blasé, passive force. The Spirit of God is the dynamic of life. Like air, the Spirit may be invisible—but let us never be misled by equating invisible with impotent. This Spirit is vital to life.

We are so impressed with what we can touch and weigh and see that when it comes to something that is invisible, we pass it off. We get so used to that power that we tend to think nothing more of the force than a Monday-morning flight. Christians all around the world need the reminder that the most powerful force in life is something we can't even see . . . so powerful we are secured eternally until Christ comes, turning our destiny into reality, ushering us into eternity. I call that powerful. And until that time, He is ready to work within us and move among us in revolutionary ways, transforming our lives. No, never think that something is insignificant because it's invisible.

SOME THINGS THE HOLY SPIRIT IS NOT

There are some things the Spirit of God is not. Let me point out three or four erroneous ideas that many people have about the

Holy Spirit. In fact, when people return to their roots and attempt to explain their beliefs, they are often most confused about the doctrine of the Holy Spirit. I have often heard Him called an "it" . . . so let's start there.

The Spirit Is Not an "It," but a Distinct Personality

The Holy Spirit is a distinct person. He is a "Him," a "He." Jesus once said:

> *If you ask Me anything in My name, I will do it. If you love Me, you will keep My commandments. And I will ask the Father, and He will give you another Helper, that He may be with you forever; that is the Spirit of truth, whom the world cannot receive, because it does not behold Him or know Him, but you know Him because He abides with you, and will be in you* (John 14:14-17, emphasis mine).

What a helpful revelation! While Jesus was on the earth, the Spirit of God was *with* the people of God. But when Jesus left the earth and sent another Helper ("another of the same kind," interestingly), like Himself, the Helper came and became a part of their lives deep within. No longer near them, but *in* them. That's a mind-staggering truth. And notice He is called "He" or "Him"—never "It." Nowhere in any reliable version of Scripture is the Spirit of God referred to as "It."

The Spirit Is Not Passive, but Active and Involved

> *But I tell you the truth, it is to your advantage that I go away; for if I do not go away, the Helper shall not come to you; but if I go, I will send Him to you* (John 16:7).

What will He do? Lie around, take it easy, relax, casually kick back within us? No. Read very carefully what Jesus taught:

> *And He, when He comes, will convict the world concerning sin, and righteousness, and judgment. . . . But when He, the Spirit of truth, comes, He will guide you into all the truth; for He will not speak on His own initiative, but whatever He hears, He will speak; and He will disclose to you what is to come. He shall glorify Me; for He shall take of Mine, and shall disclose it to you* (John 16:8, 13-14).

Oftentimes we can sense that He is present. On some occasions His presence is so real, so obvious—it's almost as though we can touch Him. When He moves among a body of people, He mobilizes and empowers them. They become sensitive, motivated, spiritually alive. They are cleansed. They are purged, enthusiastic, actively excited about the right things.

Who hasn't been in meetings where His presence made the place electric? But when He is absent, it is dreadfully dead, desperately, horribly lifeless. I have witnessed both. The contrast is undeniable.

Never doubt that the Spirit of God is incessantly on the move. As with air, we cannot see Him; nevertheless, He is hard at work convicting, guiding, instructing, disclosing, and glorifying. Just a few of His activities! He's involved. He's active. We'll return to these thoughts in a moment.

The Holy Spirit Is Not Imaginary, but Real and Relevant

Let me remind you that just because you cannot see the Holy Spirit, do not assume He is not there or is not real. Just before Jesus' ascension back into heaven, He met with a group of His followers. They had questions. He had answers. He also had some crucial news regarding the Spirit who would soon come to take His place.

> *And so when they had come together, they were asking Him, saying, "Lord, is it at this time You are restoring the kingdom to Israel?" He said to them, "It is not for you to know times or epochs which the Father has fixed by His own authority; but you shall receive power when the Holy Spirit has come upon you; and you shall be My witnesses both in Jerusalem, and in all Judea and Samaria, and even to the remotest part of the earth* (Acts 1:6-8).

Familiar words to many Christians . . . packed with significance. Note especially that the Spirit is no imaginary, vague hope; that is a promise from our Savior. It is as if He were saying, "You will have His presence, and wherever you go He will be in you. He will empower you. He will be your 'dynamic' . . . a real and relevant force in My plan for your future."

The Holy Spirit Is Not a Substitute for God, but He Is Deity

This will heighten your respect for the Holy Spirit's work, if nothing else will. Christians have been known to fight for the deity of

Christ . . . and we certainly should. But what about the deity of the Spirit? Tucked away in the book of Acts is a seldom-mentioned story about a couple who paid the ultimate price for their hypocrisy. Woven into their brief biography is a statement of the Spirit's deity.

> But a certain man named Ananias, with his wife Sapphira, sold a piece of property, and kept back some of the price for himself, with his wife's full knowledge, and bringing a portion of it, he laid it at the apostles' feet. But Peter said, "Ananias, why has Satan filled your heart to lie to the Holy Spirit and to keep back some of the price of the land? While it remained unsold, did it not remain your own? And after it was sold, was it not under your control? Why is it that you have conceived this deed in your heart? You have not lied to men, but to God" (Acts 5:1-4, emphasis mine).

Connect those two parts I have underscored. When they lied "to the Holy Spirit" (v. 3), they "lied . . . to God" (v. 4).

Before going any further into this doctrinal treasure house, let me ask you to imagine what it means to have the presence of the living God within you.

Pause and ponder this, my Christian friend: The third member of the Godhead, the invisible, yet all-powerful representation of deity, is actually living inside your being. His limitless capabilities are resident within you, since He indwells you.

You think you can't handle what life throws at you?

You think you can't stand firm or, when necessary, stand alone in your life?

You think you can't handle the lure of life's temptations? Well, you certainly could not if you were all alone. You—*alone*—can't do that anymore than I can fly alone. But with the right kind of power put into operation, the very power and presence of God, you can handle it. You can do it. As a matter of fact, all the pressure will be shifted and the weight transferred from you to Him. It's a radically different way to live. And because He is God He can handle it.

I'm starting to sound a little authoritative about this awesome truth. The fact of the matter is that we know very little about how He does it—only that He is able to do it.

Reminds me of the teacher standing before a group of fifth graders. He looked over his class with a wry smile and asked, "Does anybody here understand how electricity works?" And Jimmy, one over-anxious little boy sitting toward the front of the class, lifted his hand high in the air and said, "Yes, I understand electricity." A bit surprised, his teacher looked at him and said, "All right, Jimmy, would you explain electricity to the class." Jimmy suddenly put his hands over his face and said, "Oh . . . last night I knew, but this morning I've forgotten." The teacher gave this tongue-in-cheek response, "Now this is a tragedy. The only person in all of history who ever understood electricity, and this morning he forgot it!"

I confess, I'm starting to feel a little like Jimmy. The deeper we get into this subject, the more there is to discover . . . the more profound the Spirit is! I, therefore, must come to grips with what I *can* understand God's Book to be saying about the Holy Spirit. And I must leave the rest with Him. Like electricity, I need Him, though I cannot fully explain how He works. He is extremely useful in my life—essential, in fact—yet my ability to explain each facet of His ministry is quite limited. I need Him and I rely on Him . . . but I don't pretend to know all about Him. Once I've plugged into the socket, I've about run out of knowledge. But what I don't understand, I can still enjoy!

Don't let it trouble you if you struggle with trying to define and divide meanings of words and ideas and thoughts about the Holy Spirit. Some of these things are infinite and unfathomable.

He exists in an invisible realm. He is a power and a force you will never see, though you are convinced of the force Himself. You will only see His working—the results of His enabling, His filling, His guiding. But when He, the Spirit of God, is in control, it is nothing short of awesome. And as I said earlier, when He is absent, it is dreadful. Believe me, nothing is worse than preaching a sermon without the Spirit's help. Well, maybe one thing is worse—listening to that sermon! It is the longest period of time you can endure. As a friend of mine once said, "Without the Spirit's blessing, everything is just toothpaste."

SOME REASONS THE HOLY SPIRIT IS HERE

Jesus promised the Holy Spirit would come. But why? What, precisely, can we expect from Him? For some answers, let's return to John 16.

Allow me a few moments to explain the background of the words John records here. It may help you understand why the disciples seemed so dull and unable to grasp what the Lord was saying.

First of all, the hour was late—around midnight. Jesus and His disciples were in a second-story flat in Jerusalem. There were eleven men with Him. One had been dismissed—the unfaithful Judas. In this upper room the men were reclining around a table, and there was small talk. The focus of attention finally turned to the Lord Himself. In quiet tones, He began to communicate the vital truths they were to live by after His death. When they realized how *serious* He was, they were seized with panic. Why?

Keep in mind that for over three years they'd been following the man they expected to be the ruler of the world. That meant they would be charter-member officials in the kingdom. Don't think they hadn't thought of that! And He would establish Himself as King of kings and Lord of lords. He would overthrow Rome. He would move the hypocrites in the religious world out of power as He established a new rulership marked by integrity, peace, authenticity, and righteousness. That was their dream . . . their hope. But now, out of the clear blue, He tells them He's going to *die*. In a matter of hours He would be taken under arrest and by midmorning the next day He would be nailed to a cross. By midafternoon his body would slump in death. Before dark they will have taken His body down, wrapped Him as a mummy, put Him in a tomb, and sealed it.

He—their Teacher—would be gone.

Of course they were confused! The talk of death can't help but bring panic, cause confusion, and, in addition, create an inability to grasp a set of facts.

Before you're too harsh on them, imagine the charged emotions. Their heads must have been swimming. I can assure you it isn't hard for me to imagine. Right after World War II my father had a physical breakdown—maybe some would say an emotional breakdown. Perhaps it was both. Whichever, I shall never forget the dreadful feeling when, as the youngest in a family of three children, I was called into his bedroom. I can still feel his hand sort of work its way from my elbow up to my shoulder. I still remember how he held me close as he trembled (though he wasn't an old man), exhausted from the rigors of endless work—sixteen- to eighteen-hour days, six to seven days a week, for four or five years of his life. I knew I might never see my dad again on this earth. At least, I thought I wouldn't. He gave me some information about life. He talked to me quietly and deliberately about the character he wanted me to model as I grew up without him. He told me to take care of my mother and to cooperate with my brother and sister. I shall never forget choking back the tears.

I am pleased to say he lived on. In fact, he lived many years beyond that. But at that time, if my life depended on it, when I walked out of the room that dark night, I couldn't tell you precisely what he had said or what his words meant. I had only one thing on my mind: "My daddy is gonna die!" That stabbing realization eclipsed everything else he said. It may have been important, but I missed it. I can still recall a few words he used, but that's about it. Death talk is like that.

That's what happened to those disciples. They're listening to the Messiah say: "I'm going to die, but don't worry . . . I won't leave you as orphans. I'm going to send another Helper."

They thought, "Another Helper? We want *you*. We don't want someone else."

He added, "He will be even more helpful to you than I am, because He will be everywhere at once. And He'll be within you, not just by your side."

They resisted within: "We don't want that." You know that kind of feeling . . . and that's what blocked their ability to grasp words that seem so clear to us today . . . the words John records in chapter 16.

Now centuries have passed. And we've been able to work through these verses with the help of history to guide our thoughts. In fact, we've got the verbs, prepositions, nouns, subjects, and predicates down pat. But those people merely heard these words. No one had written anything down at the time. That's why they responded like they did. "Sorrow filled their hearts," according to verse 6. The word is "grief." They were grieving over the imminent loss of their Savior, their Lord, their Friend. Even later when He was raised from the dead, they struggled to believe it. Once they convinced themselves of His death, the resurrection was almost impossible to accept. Remember Thomas in the previous chapter? He demanded to see the prints in Jesus' hands, in His feet, and in His side—the literal scars of death. These men had been convinced that He would live on and on, but now He says:

> But because I have said these things to you, sorrow has filled your heart. But I tell you the truth, it is to your advantage that I go away; for if I do not go away, the Helper shall not come to you; but if I go, I will send Him to you (John 16:6-7).

Why would it be more advantageous to them that the Helper come? Well, when the Lord Jesus was on earth, He was shackled by the body that had been formed in Mary's womb, which became visible at Bethlehem. He could be only one place at a time. But when the Spirit came, He would be everywhere at once. And within each one of them . . . and us! Isn't that remarkable? No matter where you are, He is there. And He is ready to help. You never wake Him up. He who watches over you is never interrupted when you call for assistance. Morning, noon, or the middle of the night, He's available. He'll give power. He'll guide. He'll comfort, sustain, instruct, protect, enable.

Furthermore, by having Him invisible, their faith would be strengthened. It doesn't take any faith to fly if King Kong lifts the plane up and carries it from Los Angeles and then sets it down on the runway in Dallas. That's no faith. You just wait until Kong puts you back down again. And you get out of the plane. But when you have to rely on something invisible, it gets a little shaky at times. That's why Jesus' words to Thomas apply to all generations.

Jesus said to him, "Because you have seen Me, have you believed? Blessed are they who did not see, and yet believed" (John 20:29).

SOME WORK THE HOLY SPIRIT ACCOMPLISHES

And He, when He comes, will convict the world concerning sin, and righteousness, and judgment; concerning sin, because they do not believe in Me; and concerning righteousness, because I go to the Father, and you no longer behold Me; and concerning judgment, because the ruler of this world has been judged. I have many more things to say to you, but you cannot bear them now (John 16:8-12).

In this section Jesus talks first about the Holy Spirit's ministry among non-Christians. Later He talks about His ministry among Christians.

Among Non-Christians

You may be surprised to know that the Spirit is involved in the unsaved world. He works among the unsaved at all times. As a matter of fact, in one of the letters to the Thessalonians, we read that He is actively involved restraining sin (2 Thessalonians 2:7). Do you have any idea how much evil would be on this earth if the Spirit of God were suddenly removed? His omnipresence is like a worldwide envelope of righteousness, a bubble of invisible restraint. He holds a great deal of evil in check. But when He is removed, literally all hell will break loose on this globe! Thankfully, He currently restrains sin.

Earlier we read that the same Holy Spirit "convicts the world concerning sin, righteousness, and judgment." I am comforted when I read that. It frees me from the need to moralize when I'm in a group of unsaved people. I don't have to try to convince lost people about how unrighteous they are. They already know they're unrighteous. How? The Spirit is already convincing them! I don't have to fly a big flag over my home that reads, "We're pure and holy—you're dirty and nasty." My ministry is not to convince someone else that they're really bad people. That's the Spirit's ministry. "He convicts the world of sin, because they do not believe on Me." His convicting work is much more effective than mine ever could be.

The late Merrill Tenney offers a timely word regarding the meaning of *convict*:

> "Convict" means to refute an adversary completely, to prove guilt so as to bring an acknowledgment of the truth of the charge. It implies a successful action against an opponent that results in establishing his guilt.[2]

The word is a legal term that means to pronounce a judicial verdict by which the guilt of the culprit at the bar of justice is defined and fixed! The Spirit does not merely *ACCUSE* men of sin, He brings them an inescapable sense of guilt so that they realize their shame and helplessness before God. The Holy Spirit performs an open-and-shut case of convincing.

This reminds me of that unforgettable day the prophet Nathan stood before David who had committed adultery with Bathsheba. The king was cornered when she became pregnant, so he manipulated the death of Uriah, her husband. And then he lied about it to his flock of people, the nation. He lived that lie for a year, until Nathan came and stood before him. And after a brief parable regarding taking someone else's little ewe lamb, he stared directly at David and said, "You are the man!" And David, without hesitation, responded, "I have sinned." In other words, "Guilty as charged!" That's the way it is when the Spirit works.

Many without Christ struggle with their guilt and unbelief. You'd better believe it! They try every way in the world to run away from it—through a bottle, through drugs, through travel, through activity, through education, through philosophy of some kind or another, through education, or some other means of escape. It's the inescapable guilt that haunts them.

The Spirit not only convicts the world of sin but also of righteousness. He is like the prosecuting attorney saying, "These are the facts. Here is the evidence. All these things demonstrate guilt." And they are shut up without excuse in light of facts and evidence. There is simply no way the lost can measure up to God's righteous demands. They may try, but the Spirit of God will convince them of their need.

Catalina Island lies twenty-six miles from our California shoreline. I could probably locate several folks down at Huntington Beach who can jump off the pier out into the ocean fifteen or so feet. A few could jump twenty feet. We may find a triathlete or a decathlete who can jump twenty-five feet. But we'll never find anyone who can jump all the way to Catalina. No one on earth can do that. If you want to get to Catalina, you have to take a boat.

The Spirit of God makes it clear that all have sinned and fall short of perfection. Every person who comes into the family of God has been worked on ahead of time by the Spirit. And His irresistible ministry has been, "You are guilty. You are lost. You are a sinner. You are separated from God. You are spiritually depraved. You are distant from God . . . without hope . . . lacking in righteousness. You must have Christ in order to measure up to the standard of perfection God requires."

And judgment? Jesus also taught that the Spirit would convince the world of judgment.

> *He, when He comes, will convict the world concerning judgment*
> *. . . because the ruler of this world has been judged* (vv. 8, 11).

When human sin is confronted by the righteousness of Christ, inevitable judgment is evident. And the reason it's so significant is because the ruler of this world (Satan himself) stands judged. That means that Satan was judged at the cross. And every moment that Satan exists since the cross, he stands judged. Each tick of the clock moves him closer to his doom. He's a defeated foe.

That reminds me of what happened when I taught my two boys to play chess. Bad decision on my part. Man, did they learn how to play chess! Both of them can beat me virtually every time we play. Now they *love* playing chess with me. I work hard at it—and sometimes take a long time to make a move. I'll really think it through. They go get a hamburger, eat it, come back, and about then I'll move. And what I hate is that when I finally make that move, they snicker under their breath . . . hee, hee, hee . . . I hate that laugh!

Then they'll poke some fun by asking things like, "Before you take your hands off, Dad, you wanna take that move back?"
"No!" I respond.
"Okay, then watch—(bomp . . . bomp . . . bomp . . . bomp) checkmate!"
That's the way it is with the devil. Every move Satan makes is simply one move closer to the end of the game. The prince of the world stands judged.

The point is clear: If that's true of the prince of the world, it's certainly true of the lost person. When human sin is confronted by Christ's righteousness, condemnation is self-evident. Every day the unsaved person lives is one day closer to judgment. The Spirit continues to convince the lost of inevitable judgment.

One of the reasons I'm hammering away on this is because I want to take the neurotic stress out of all who evangelize. Not the zeal or the passion, but the panic. Our responsibility is to communicate the Lord Jesus, to present the righteousness of God, to tell everybody we meet as often as we can that the Lord Jesus died for them, rose from the dead for them, offering hope beyond the grave . . . that there is forgiveness and cleansing, a relationship with God through faith in His Son, if they will only believe. It's not our job to convince them that they're lost. That's the Spirit's job! We're to tell them about the bridge of hope in Jesus Christ, inviting them to "Get on it. Get on that bridge."

Among Christians

The Spirit of truth works in believers' lives as well.

> *But when He, the Spirit of truth, comes, He will guide you into all the truth; for He will not speak on His own initiative, but whatever He hears, He will speak; and He will disclose to you what is to come. He shall glorify Me; for He shall take of Mine, and shall disclose it to you. All things that the Father has are Mine; therefore I said, that He takes of Mine, and will disclose it to you* (vv. 13-15).

The Holy Spirit not only takes the Scriptures and makes them clear (that's the ministry of illumination which I mentioned in chapter 3), but He takes circumstances in which we find ourselves and he gives us insight into them. He takes pressure and predicaments, then uses them to mature us. He guides us into all realms of the truth. He matures us. He nurtures us. He comforts us when we are fractured by fear. He tells us there's hope when we can't see the end of the tunnel. He gives us reasons to go on, though we get up in years and it looks like death is near. All of that is included in the thought, "He guides us into all the truth."

The beautiful part of all this is that He doesn't speak on His own initiative. He's not on a lark, just telling us what we would like to hear. He's taking truth from "the things of Christ," and He discloses them to us. In fact, Jesus promises "He shall glorify Me."

Let me pass along something I hope you *never* forget. If you get involved in a ministry that glorifies itself, instead of Christ, the Spirit of God is not in that ministry. If you follow a leader that is getting the glory for that ministry, instead of Christ, the Spirit of God isn't empowering his leadership. If you're a part of a Christian school or a mission organization or a Christian camping ministry in which someone other than Christ is being glorified, it is not being empowered by the Spirit of God. Mark it down: THE SPIRIT GLORIFIES CHRIST. I'll go one step further; if the Holy Spirit Himself is being emphasized and magnified, He isn't in it! *Christ* is the One who is glorified when the Spirit is at work. He does His work behind the scenes, never in the limelight. I admire that the most about His work.

We Christians love to sing a chorus:

> Spirit of the Living God
> Fall afresh on me.
> Spirit of the Living God
> Fall afresh on me.
>
> Melt me, mold me,
> Fill me, use me.
> Spirit of the Living God
> Fall afresh on me.[3]

When He does these things, when He melts us and molds us, fills us and uses us, Christ alone is exalted.

SOME WAYS THE HOLY SPIRIT IS FELT

You may have noticed how I've stayed away from "techniques" in this chapter. I've purposely not given you five ways to be filled with the Spirit . . . or six steps to the Spirit-filled life . . . or nine guarantees that the Spirit is empowering you . . . or how to be "almost perfect" in three easy steps. But I would like to apply these truths in the area of the Spirit's *melting, molding, filling,* and *using* us. I'd like to go back to my opening points in this chapter and share with you my closing thoughts. Four come to my mind.

1. *Since He is a person, we feel Him as He heals relationships.* When He does that He *melts* us. I realize that you may not have entered into the work of the Spirit in this realm. Perhaps you have big thick walls around your life, barriers of resistance, heavy fortifications that keep you distant from people. To break through those walls, a melting process is needed. Believe me, He can do that, because He wants to heal strained relationships. Maybe with your child who is now grown. Maybe with your parent. Maybe with a person who was once a very close, trusted friend. Somehow there has to be the melting work of the Spirit before such healing can happen. Ask the Spirit of God to begin melting you.

2. *Since He is active and involved, we feel Him comforting us in our sorrows and guiding us in our pursuits.* When He does that, He *molds* us. By the way, these go in order: first there's melting (as relationships are healed), and not until then can there be molding. It's nothing short of amazing how such healing clears our sights, freeing us to pursue new directions. The Spirit of God's presence is there to mold us and reshape us. By the way, it can get pretty painful. At times, you are convinced that you simply cannot go on. Yet the Spirit who shapes us is also "the Comforter" . . . He will be with you. Ask the Spirit of God to mold you.

3. *Since He is real and relevant, we feel Him giving us power and perseverance.* When He does that, He *fills* us. I often begin my day by saying something like, "Lord God, I don't know what my day holds. I don't know what's in it for You and me, but I'm Yours. I want You to guide me one step at a time. And I want Your power to mark my steps. Stop me if I'm moving in a wrong direction. Push me if I'm sluggish. Get me going again if I'm hesitant. Shake me back to my senses if I get out of line, but don't let me go my own way. Fill me today with Your peace and Your power." Because the Spirit is not imaginary, because He's real and relevant, it is remarkable how He turns that day into something else—often a marvelous series of events. Ask the Spirit of God to fill you.

4. *Since He is God, we feel Him as He controls our circumstances and transforms our lives.* When He does that, He *uses* us.

- He melts us in relationships.
- He molds us in the pursuit and the direction of His will.
- He fills us with power and perseverance to stay at it.
- He uses us as He controls our circumstances and transforms our lives.

When those things happen we become convinced we're not excess baggage. We're not models of mediocrity. We have purpose and meaning and definition—many reasons to press on. Ask the Spirit of God to use you.

Melt me. Mold me. Fill me. Use me. Will you read those words aloud? Say them slowly and with feeling: *Melt* me. *Mold* me. *Fill* me. *Use* me. Let me press the issue once again: When it comes to relationships, will you ask the Lord to melt you? When it comes to objectives and the pursuit of His will, again I ask, will you say, "Lord, mold me"? And then as the day gets long and the journey gets painful, will you beseech the Lord to fill you? "Fill me with power and perseverance." And as you face the circumstances that are upon you, can you tell the Lord you want Him to transform you? "I want You to be in control, because You're God. I sincerely want You to use me, Lord."

If you meant what you just read—if you are sincerely willing to be reshaped, refreshed, and renewed by the Spirit of God—you will begin to discover a dimension of living you've never known before.

A whole new process will start in your life. And Christ alone will be glorified. In fact, if you really mean business, you will begin living an "unearthly" life . . . nonterrestrial, not mundane.

Some might even call it weird.

1. Is the Holy Spirit "a real and relevant force" in your life? This will take a little thought. Open your notebook and take a few minutes to jot down the five biggest challenges facing you in your life these days. Name them and number them. Now . . . can you feel the weight of those daily struggles bite into your shoulders . . . that old tightness in the pit of your stomach? Let the heaviness of your list pull you down to your knees. Ask your Father to show you what it means to have the Spirit of God resident *within* you. Ask Him to shoulder the weight of these constant struggles (1 Peter 5:7). Consciously yield your challenges to the Helper's control . . . to His invisible yet limitless power (Ephesians 3:16). Don't get up from your knees until your shoulders— and your heart—feel lighter.

2. When the words of Jesus at the Last Supper finally began to sink in, the disciples were seized with panic. They could scarcely hear the vital information the Lord wanted to communicate to them. "I have so much to tell you," He said to them, "but I know you can't handle it right now" (see John 16:6, 12). It would be later, when their hearts were quieter, that the Spirit would guide them into the truth (16:13).

   Isn't that just like us? The Spirit's still, small voice is so easily drowned out by those feelings of fear, worry, dread, or panic that we experience when life's circumstances press in on us. Yet it is precisely in those moments that He has much to share with us! The next time you find pressure mounting in your life, try this: Find a restful setting where you can be alone for thirty minutes to an hour. Find a quiet booth in a coffee shop . . . go for an evening walk . . . find a room in a church . . . just get away from the noise and hassle for a while. Ask the Spirit of God to quiet your heart and speak to you while you focus on your Lord and His Word. Don't miss the opportunity to hear His voice and benefit from His counsel in the midst of your struggle and pain. He is ready to help!

3. Did you carefully consider the fourfold prayer suggested at the end of this chapter . . . MELT me, MOLD me, FILL me, USE me? On a fresh page in your notebook jot down some *specific* ideas about what each one of these aspects of the Spirit's work could imply in your life.

He is like a tree planted by streams of water,
which yields its fruit in season
and whose leaf does not wither ...

The Depravity of Humanity

"I confess that Adam's fall into sin left humanity without the hope of heaven apart from a new birth, made possible by the Savior's death and bodily resurrection."

FROM
CREATION
TO
CORRUPTION

hilosophers can be terribly confusing. What they call deep and profound we're tempted to consider dull and vague. One honest soul put it rather well: "Philosophers are people who talk about things they don't understand . . . but they make it sound like it's your fault."

Well, not always. Sometimes they are right on target. There are times philosopher types put it so succinctly that you can't improve upon it. For example there's that age-old axiom:

> Wherever there is a thing, there must have been a preceding thought . . . and where there is a thought, there must have been a thinker.

Take the place where you sit right now . . . just look around. It reflects thought. Someone had in mind that someday in the future somebody would be sitting there. Therefore, a design was planned that would make it possible for you to sit where you're sitting and for you to enjoy the surroundings in which you find yourself. The place that you enjoy (the "thing") is the seat and the room you're sitting in. And as you look around, it's obvious the design was well-planned (the "thought") by someone (the "thinker") who wanted you to be comfortable. Neither the room nor the seat "just happened."

Or let's take a walk outside. I want us to look at some cars together. If possible, let's find a new one. While you're standing there admiring the beauty of that sparkling new automobile, let's imagine

my saying to you rather quietly, "You know, there are folks who believe this car is a result of someone's design . . . but I know differently. Let me tell you what really happened":

> Many, many centuries ago, all this iron, glass, rubber, plastic,
> fabric, leather, and wires came up out of the ground. Further-
> more, each substance fashioned itself into various shapes and
> sizes . . . and holes evolved at just the right places, and the up-
> holstery began to weave itself together. After a while threads
> appeared on bolts and nuts and—amazing as it may seem—
> each bolt found nuts with matching threads. And gradually
> everything sort of screwed up tightly in place. A little later cor-
> rectly shaped glass glued itself in the right places. And you see
> these tires? They became round over the years. And they found
> themselves the right size metal wheels. And they sort of
> popped on. They also filled themselves with air somehow. And
> the thing began to roll down the street.
>
> And one day, many, many years ago—centuries, really—some
> people were walking along and they found this vehicle sitting
> under a tree. And one of them looked at it and thought, "How
> amazing. I think we should call it '*automobile*.'" But there's
> more! These little automobiles have an amazing way of multi-
> plying themselves year after year . . . even changing ever so
> slightly to meet the demands of the public. Actually, that pro-
> cess is called "automutations."

I have a sneaking suspicion that, having heard all that, you would
want to remove yourself from my presence. You probably would call
my wife and ask if I've been feeling well lately.

Let's get serious! I would be a first-class lunatic if I believed that
automobiles evolved. The auto is in the category of a thing, and it
reflects thought. And for there to have been thought given to the
design of the automobile, there must have been a thinker . . . a de-
signer.

Now, multiply that design process an infinite number of times,
and you find yourself in touch with the universe, which God said
He made. In fact, He was bold enough to say in the first sentence of
the Bible that He *created* the heavens and the earth. Only ten words
appear in the opening sentence of our Bible (actually only seven
words in the Hebrew Bible), and yet that sentence has become a
watershed of controversy. Why? Because people far more brilliant
than we have come up with the theory that the world really wasn't
created; it has evolved, as has mankind . . . and then they're off into
the meanderings of scientific imaginations expressed in sophisticated gobbledygook.

To complicate things, many people believe the theories so firmly that when they read Genesis 1:1, they respond with words like, "The verse may be characterized as a veritable treasure house of myths" and "The statement is a joke, an absolute impossibility."

Why? Why would people with bright minds . . . why would competent and intelligent men and women embrace the theories of man rather than the statement of God when it comes to the creation of a world and the origin of mankind? After all, they are people of research and scholarship and facts. They'll tell you they don't believe in blind chance. But when they come to our universe and the people who fill it, it's just too much. They cannot bring themselves to believe in divine creation. Why?

Perhaps it's just too simple for the sophisticated. Obviously, it requires a belief in a thinker, a supreme being greater than they. And, to them, that's a leap in the dark, a thought too risky to embrace. But it's at that very point that I find those who deny creation so illogical. *They* are the ones guilty of making a leap in the dark when they embrace the theories of evolution. The existence of our world and mankind defies all mathematical calculations of chance!

This was driven home to me many years ago when I came across an illustration from a noted scientist. As I recall, he was a former president of the New York Academy of Sciences. It went something like this: "Let's say I have ten pennies and I mark each one with a number (one to ten), then place all ten in your pocket. I would ask you to give your pocket a good shake so that the pennies are no longer in any order in your pocket. What chance would I have to reach in and pull out penny number one? One in ten. Let's say I put the penny back . . . then I reach again into your pocket and draw out penny number two. My chance of doing that would be one in a hundred. Putting the penny back, if I were to reach in and draw out penny number three, my chances would jump to one in a thousand. If I were able to continue doing the same, in successive order, right up through number nine, do you know what my chance would be by the time I got to the number ten and pulled it out of your pocket? *One in ten billion*. If I pulled that off you would say, 'The game is fixed!' My answer: 'You're right . . . and so is creation.'"

How different from the theories of man! Read this "explanation" very carefully. Try not to smile.

> By and large, cosmologists have become accustomed to the idea that the Universe began with an initial singularity of infinite density and infinitesimally small volume. This idea is strongly supported by the singularity theorems which Penrose and Hawking produced in the 1960s. But now, in an about-face

that has come from a consideration of quantum mechanical effects on the origin of the Universe, Hawking and colleagues suggest that the Universe had a non-singular beginning followed by a period of very rapid expansion (which goes under the name of inflation) and then a transition to the conventional development described by the hot big-bang model. A longstanding problem of cosmology, to explain the origin of the density fluctuations that are needed to account for the galaxies, is solved along the way by quantum fluctuations.[1]

I am not trying to be cute or clever. That is an actual quotation from a highly respected scholar who has bought into a humanistic answer to how the universe began.

A FRESH LOOK AT OUR ROOTS

My interest is not in defending creation. My interest is in simply declaring the creation of man. Reading what Scripture records about those earliest hours of time—returning to that epochal moment when God, having made all the other things in their kind, made mankind—I find answers that make good sense.

If you have a Bible handy, open it to Genesis 1. You will see the same words repeated again and again. First, take a look at the passage:

Then God said, "Let the earth sprout vegetation, plants yielding seed, and fruit trees bearing fruit after their kind, with seed in them, on the earth"; and it was so. And the earth brought forth vegetation, plants yielding seed after their kind, and trees bearing fruit, with seed in them, after their kind; and God saw that it was good. And there was evening and there was morning, a third day.

Then God said, "Let there be lights in the expanse of the heavens to separate the day from the night, and let them be for signs, and for seasons, and for days and years; and let them be for lights in the expanse of the heavens to give light on the earth"; and it was so. And God made the two great lights, the greater light to govern the day, and the lesser light to govern the night; He made the stars also. And God placed them in the expanse of the heavens to give light on the earth, and to govern the day and the night, and to separate the light from the darkness; and God saw that it was good. And there was evening and there was morning, a fourth day.

Then God said, "Let the waters teem with swarms of living creatures, and let birds fly above the earth in the open expanse of the heavens." And God created the great sea monsters, and every living creature that moves, with which the waters swarmed after their kind, and every winged bird after its kind; and God saw that it was good. And God blessed them, saying, "Be fruitful and multiply, and fill the waters in the seas, and let birds multiply on the earth." And there was evening and there was morning, a fifth day.

Then God said, "Let the earth bring forth living creatures after their kind: cattle and creeping things and beasts of the earth after their kind"; and it was so. And God made the beasts of the earth after their kind, and the cattle after their kind, and everything that creeps on the ground after its kind; and God saw that it was good (vv. 11-25).

Did you notice the oft-repeated words (v. 11) "after their kind . . ." (v. 12); again, "after their kind . . ." (v. 21); "after their kind . . ." (v. 24); and even three times in one verse, "after their kind, after its kind . . ." (v. 25). Meaning what? When God created living things He maintained precise distinctions. Distinct species. These vast categories of created things and beings are spelled out in quick order in Genesis 1. And each one has a uniqueness about it, each is according to its "kind." The fowls of the air . . . the fish of the sea . . . the beasts of the field. Each one was created according to its "kind."

There is a most significant statement made in 1 Corinthians 15 which underscores the same idea:

All flesh is not the same flesh, but there is one flesh of men, and another flesh of beasts, and another flesh of birds, and another of fish (v. 39).

God made each with a different physical texture, a different internal makeup. You can't ignore those distinctions and lump them all together and maintain the correct biblical position on creation.

Now 1 Corinthians 15:45:

So also it is written, "The first man, Adam, became a living soul." The last Adam became a life-giving spirit.

How terribly important! Look again at those words, "The first man." This is a translation of the Greek terms *Ho Protos Anthropos*. A paraphrase might read, "the first in the category of mankind" was Adam, the first created human being. Adam's "kind" was a first. Nothing before him fell into the category of his species. In Adam we find a fully developed adult human being, equipped with intelligence and godlike capabilities from the very beginning: intelligence, emotions, will. No other living thing or living being was like *Anthropos*. No animal or fowl or fish or plant could know God or love and respond to God or obey God . . . or utilize the earth's resources in ways consistent with God's creative purposes. In other words, *Ho Protos Anthropos* was (and still is) altogether unique.

Look at Genesis 1:26.

> *Then God said, "Let Us make man in Our image, according to Our likeness; and let them rule over the fish of the sea and over the birds of the sky and over the cattle and over all the earth, and over every creeping thing that creeps on the earth."*

I find it very interesting, as I reflect on the philosophical axiom I quoted earlier, that the statement works in *reverse* order here in the creation account. First is the thinker—"And God said." Then comes the *thought*:

> *Then God said, "Let Us make man in Our image, according to Our likeness. . . ."*

And the *thing*? Verse 27 tells us. "God created man."

When it came to the first in the category of mankind, the pattern God followed was "in Our image." In other words, "The man will be unlike anything I have created. No other created being has a mind to know Me. No other created being has a heart to love Me. No other created being has a will to obey Me. Therefore, no other creation has an eternal destiny like this created being has. We'll make him distinct. Only humans will have *imago Dei*, the image of God, stamped on them." What a privileged position!

HOW IT ALL STARTED . . . HISTORICALLY

Creation and Instruction

Let me reiterate a couple of observations about our creation that remain true to the present moment. *First*, I observe that mankind is *unique*. We are unique because this species is the only species created in God's image, after God's likeness. *Second*, I notice that the "mankind species" is *superior*. No other creature was told to rule over anything. Verse 26, however, states, "Let mankind rule." The Hebrew verb is vivid: "to trample down, to dominate, to master, to prevail over." Strong words. This creature (and none other) is destined by God to dominate the world in which he finds himself. It isn't wrong to explore our world or to travel into space; it's wrong *not* to. Even though we may lose some lives in the risk of our research, we are to press forward. We are to probe into our universe. It isn't wrong to use (though not abuse) the resources of this world; it's wrong *not* to. God gave us the command to do so. It isn't wrong to take charge of the creatures that live on this world—not to abuse them, but to control them. God gave *Anthropos* that superior position.

Listen to Genesis 1:28:

> And God blessed them; and God said to them, "Be fruitful and multiply, and fill the earth, and subdue it; and rule over the fish of the sea and over the birds of the sky, and over every living thing that moves on the earth."

Now here is man, receiving instruction—he is told to reproduce, and he is told to rule. In fact, he is also told to work . . . to keep the garden beautiful.

> Then the Lord God took the man and put him into the garden of Eden to cultivate it and keep it (Genesis 2:15).

Work isn't a curse. We need to remember that work was created in a context of absolute innocence.

"But I thought work was a curse," you answer. No, it is the anxiety of dealing with people that's the curse. The sweat that comes to our brows because of the wrongdoing of others and our own selves, *that's* the curse. But work was originally established in a context of innocence. The earliest occupation was landscaping—the work of horticulture. It was to maintain and cultivate the garden.

And man was given one negative command, only one. It had to do with the tree in the garden called "the tree of the knowledge of good and evil." That tree is mentioned in Genesis 2:17:

> But from the tree of the knowledge of good and evil you shall not eat, for in the day that you eat from it you shall surely die.

Interesting how those last four words appear in the Hebrew: "Dying, you will die." Dying spiritually (the moment you eat from the tree), you will begin to die physically. Would Adam and Eve have lived forever had they not taken of the tree? Yes, indeed. And because they took of the tree of the knowledge of good and evil, they introduced death to this world of ours—not only death but also all that precedes it by way of sickness and disease. The issue of this tree was extremely significant . . . representing a nonnegotiable command . . . plain, clear, and simple: "Don't eat of the tree of the knowledge of good and evil." There was no way Adam could have misunderstood.

Temptation and Corruption

The original story of innocence and beauty becomes a study in selfishness and tragedy beyond the warning. Genesis 3 is familiar to all Bible students—especially as it relates to the temptation in the Garden, which culminates at verse 6.

> *When the woman saw that the tree was good for food, and that it was a delight to the eyes, and that the tree was desirable to make one wise, she took from its fruit and ate; and she gave also to her husband with her, and he ate.*

Notice the words, "she took from its fruit and ate . . . and . . . her husband with her . . . ate." That's where all our troubles began. And the root word for all our troubles? Depravity.

Up until then nothing but innocence was flowing through the bloodstream of mankind. There was an enviable, uninterrupted communion with the living God, mankind's Creator. There was the blessing and delight of walks with God, the joy of His presence, the unguarded relationship, the familiar friendship. There was an absence of rebellion, selfishness, defensiveness, and embarrassment. There was . . . but no longer!

At that awful moment the original couple yielded to temptation, depravity entered and contaminated the human bloodstream. Depravity intercepted innocence and ruined it, leaving mankind alienated from God. Instead of the mind being clear and full of the knowledge of God, it became clouded. And instead of possessing that once-strong love for God, man became resentful of God, an emotional wreck . . . fragile and weak. And the will, once obedient, became rebellious.

The disease continues! Instead of adoring God, we fight with Him. Instead of believing what He says, we reject His truth. Instead of wanting to do what He would have us do, we delight in doing what *we* want to do. And to make matters even worse, instead of facing it, we cover it up. It all goes back to the original scene.

Let me show you. Verse 7 begins with the word "Then." When? Immediately after they had eaten from the forbidden tree.

> *Then the eyes of both of them were opened, and they knew that they were naked. . . .*

Up until then they did not even know they were naked! Adam and Eve did not realize that they were in each other's presence without clothing. They lived in perfect and unpretentious innocence. They enjoyed the delights and intimacies of marriage. They enjoyed an innocent nakedness in the presence of one another—not only physically but also emotionally. They were totally comfortable, totally at ease, totally secure. But no longer!

Immediately after eating from the fruit they became (get this) self-conscious for the first time. They knew they were naked. And realizing their nakedness, they did the most natural, human thing one can do—they covered up. Verse 7 continues:

> *. . . they sewed fig leaves together and made themselves loin coverings.*

But their hiding isn't over, it's just begun.

> *And they heard the sound of the Lord God walking in the garden in the cool of the day, and the man and his wife hid themselves from the presence of the Lord God among the trees of the garden (v. 8).*

I'm fascinated by that word picture. As at other times, the Creator-God is coming down the trail to meet with His creation. But how things have changed! He doesn't find man and woman. Why? Because—

> *. . . the man and his wife hid themselves from the presence of the Lord God among the trees of the garden (v. 8).*

As a result of becoming self-conscious, there was an immediate cover-up, personally. And then there was a hiding from the Creator, relationally. It still goes on today. The scene is different, but the principles are the same.

> *Then the Lord God called to the man, and said to him, "Where are you?" (v. 9).*

I don't know why, but people have the strange idea that God really didn't know where Adam and Eve were. Sort of like He was stumbling around in a quandary, calling "A-a-a-a-d-a-a-am! Where a-a-a-re you, Eve? Come on, tell Me!"
No! He knew exactly where they were. He is God! His question implies, "Why are you where you are? What are you doing there? You've never hidden from Me." Embarrassed, Adam reluctantly responds:

> . . . "I heard the sound of Thee in the garden, and I was afraid because I was naked; so I hid myself" (v. 10).

Two brand new statements appear in Adam's confession: "I was afraid . . . I was naked." God answers, "Who told you that you were naked?"
That question seems so strange to us today, because we've never entertained such innocence. Let me ask you rather bluntly, are you aware when you're naked? *I hope to shout.* We know about every button that's missing, every hole in our pants or shirt, every zipper that won't stay zipped. Every time we're in public we can't think of anything else but the ripped pants or the hole in the shirt or the broken zipper. Why? *Because we are self-conscious creatures.* Why, the slightest hint of nakedness brings shame and embarrassment.
My wife and I were invited to minister together in Colorado Springs not long ago. Busily engaged in getting our seat selection and baggage tags at the airport in Los Angeles, we were both bending, lifting, stooping, and maneuvering our way through the process. On my final stoop-and-lift movement, I felt the seat of my trousers r-r-r-rip. Not just a tiny rip, either.
Well! All my other clothing for the trip was now sliding out of sight on the conveyer belt, heading toward our plane. I didn't have time to return home to change . . . I was on my own. I did all the things you have to do to keep a secret like that. I kept jerking my coattail down in the back . . . or backing up and standing near a wall. I even carried my briefcase *behind* me when I got on and off the plane. You're gonna laugh, but when we got to our destination, there were three flights of stairs we had to walk up to get to our room . . . and they were busy with people in front of us and *behind* us. Never before have I walked up stairs sideways . . . but I managed. By then, of course, the r-r-rip was really a r-r-r-r-rip!
I have Adam to thank for my embarrassment. It's all part of the depravity package. Like Adam, "I knew that I was naked . . . so I hid myself." But, unlike Adam, I wasn't found out.

God's question was pointed: "Who told you were naked?" And before Adam could answer:

> . . . *"Have you eaten from the tree of which I commanded you not to eat?"* (v. 11).

Trouble, serious trouble, has entered the home of Adam and Eve. And it would *never* leave. Created in pristine innocence and flawless beauty, they now find themselves distant from the One who made them. Because at this moment depravity, the presence of sin, has invaded and polluted their lives.

God confronts them, which results in one of those unforgettable dialogues in Scripture. God speaks first with Adam, then Eve, and finally the serpent. He says to Adam: "Did you eat from the tree?"

> *And the man said, "The woman whom Thou gavest to be with me, she gave me from the tree, and I ate"* (v. 12).

Notice how he preceded the confession with an alibi, a veiled statement of blame. That's also very common. Rather than, "Yes, guilty as charged," Adam says, "Now God, if it hadn't been for the woman *You* gave me, I probably would still be pure. But because of what *You* did and *she* did, well, I ate." God doesn't argue. He faces Eve next, who must have been shaking in her apron:

> . . . *And the woman said, "The serpent deceived me, and I ate"* (v. 13).

We will do anything on earth to keep from saying, "I am responsible, no one else." Fact is, we *love* substitutes.

That came to my mind when I found an interesting ad in a newspaper. Can't even remember which newspaper. It was called "Rent-A-Jogger," offering something like "Rent me for $1.95 and I will jog for you at least one mile each day (weather permitting) for the next year." A customer gets a suitably framed certificate, attesting to the world that "your jogger is securing for you the benefits of a healthful glow, extraordinary stamina, an exciting muscle tone, and power-filled sense of total well-being."

"Rent-A-Jogger" was the idea of some forty-five-year-old stockbroker who is also the guy who runs for the customer. Believe it or not, within several days after the ads appeared, 322 people had sent him $1.95, which more than paid for the ads!

When it comes to wrong, we'd like to "rent a sinner." We'll do anything to keep from saying, "I have sinned." We'll cover up. We'll hide. We'll rationalize. We'll point to somebody else. We'll find a scapegoat and blame him or her. We'll do anything but say, "I have sinned."

They finally said it. And the curse that fell way back then has left us in a desperate state of affairs. Yes, the right word is "desperate." The desperation has grown into full-blown depravity.

WHERE IT ALL LED . . . THEOLOGICALLY

Webster says *depraved* means, "marked by corruption or evil, perverted, crooked." It's important that you understand this is an internal disease; you can't detect it from the outside. Most folks don't "look" depraved. Most of us do a masterful job of covering up. But never doubt that underneath, deep down inside, there is this disease that eats away at us and pollutes our thoughts and our words (intellect), our relationships (emotions), and our actions (will).

One theologian describes depravity this way:

> This doctrine has suffered from many misconceptions, for the average person would define total depravity by saying that it means that man is as bad as he can be. However, if we adopt that as an acceptable definition, immediately our theology is brought into question because we know men who are not as bad as they can be. We know many men who are good men, kind men, generous men, moral men, men who contribute much in the home and in the community. Rather, the doctrine of depravity says that man is as bad *off* as he can be. There is a vast difference between being as *bad* as he can be and being as bad *off* as he can be.
>
> The doctrine of depravity has to do, not with man's estimation of man, but rather with God's estimation of man. We are the heirs of generations of the teaching of evolution which sees man in an ever-ascending spiral, rising higher and higher from the depth from which he has sprung, until finally he will reach the stars. So widely accepted is that concept that we have come somehow to feel that there is so much good in the worst of us that man is not so bad off after all. When we measure men by man, we can always find someone who is lower than we are on the moral or ethical scale, and the comparison gives us a feeling of self-satisfaction. But the Scriptures do not measure men by man; they measure men by God who has created them. The creature is measured by the Creator and is found to be wanting.[2]

Someone said it best when he suggested "If depravity were blue, we'd be blue all over." Cut us anywhere and we'll bleed blue. Cut into our minds and you'll find blue thoughts. Cut into our vision and there are blue images full of greed and lust. Cut into our hearts and there are blue emotions of hatred, revenge, and blame. Cut into our wills and you'll find deep blue decisions and responses.

The tragedy is we don't *look* blue! We look good, almost white at times. We look clean. We're among "the beautiful people" of the twentieth century. I think we look physically better than our world has ever looked. But there's something deep within that is depraved. It's called our nature. That's why we *can't* clean up our act. That's why we can't handle our own lust. That's why we can't say no to certain temptations. That's why we fight with each other and fight with God—realizing that we shouldn't. And yet we can't seem to stop. We can't seem to keep our promises. If we are going to have control over all this it must come from *outside* ourselves!

Cain couldn't stop either. Cain, you remember, was Adam and Eve's firstborn. Abel was Cain's younger brother. Cain kept the fields; Abel kept the sheep. And there was a growing conflict between the two of them because of a requirement from God. Cain was rejected; Abel was accepted. The hate in Cain's heart simmered and stewed. Then one day it boiled over.

> Now Cain said to his brother Abel, "Let's go out to the field." And while they were in the field, Cain attacked his brother Abel and killed him (Genesis 4:8, NIV).

Why? Because mentally, his mind was depraved. Emotionally, he was insanely jealous. Volitionally, he was defiant. Spiritually, he was dead. Physically, he carried his hatred to the extreme. Cain took a knife and slit the throat of his brother, as he had often seen Abel kill the sheep. He murdered his own brother in a cold-blooded act of rage . . . and he wasn't even remorseful about it.

I don't know if you watched the television docu-drama sometime back called *Into Thin Air*. It was the true account of a young Canadian collegian who decided to go to school in the United States. He drove the family Volkswagen van toward Colorado to begin his schooling. The family was a little concerned about the condition of the car and warned him that he might have some trouble. The young man seemed unconcerned about the problem as he kissed his family good-bye and sped off to school.

He vanished "into thin air." The parents became more than worried, because as time passed it was obvious that wrong had occurred. Ultimately, they were forced to believe their son must have been killed. Indeed he was. He had been murdered by two brutal men.

The murderers were finally caught. There is a gripping scene toward the end of this drama where one of the guilty murderers sits in the office of the FBI investigator. He's answering questions rather calmly during this interrogation. When he gets to the actual killing that he and his partner committed, it is incredible how cool his remarks seem.

He repeats a statement, "And so we killed him." There is a photographic flashback to the scene in the back of the van where the boy is face down on the floorboard, bound and gagged. Then you see the men as they drag the boy out into the snow. Back to the FBI room— "And so we killed him." Flashback: One man has a knife and stabs, stabs, stabs, stabs that knife into the chest of the boy. In the FBI room— "And so we killed him." Flashback: The scene is now on the slope of a snow-covered hill as they drag him to a rapid-moving stream and a waterfall where they dump his bloody body into the water. A crimson color fills the whole stream and his body bobs face down in the icy water. In the interrogation room— "And so we killed him . . . we killed him."

The common response when listening or watching such a program is to think, "What a terrible man!" and to imagine, "How much better I am." NO—wrong assumption. Before you resist that thought, remember you, too, are depraved. In the heart of every one of us is the same murderous nature. We may not stab with a hunting knife, but we stab with our vile tongues. We stab with our thoughts. We stab with our looks. We stab with our actions. We kill. We murder. We deceive. We deny. We reject. We kick. We batter. And all the while we ignore our depravity as we cluck our tongues at a man who says, "So we killed him."

It's only a difference of degrees. Except for the grace of God . . . I could have confessed to the same thing. And so could you.

Why? Genesis 5:1, 3:

> This is the book of the generations of Adam. In the day when God created man, He made him *in the likeness of God*. . . . When Adam had lived one hundred and thirty years, he became the father of a son *in his own likeness*, according to his image, and named him Seth (emphasis mine).

Look! Verse 1: ". . . in the likeness of God," that's when God made Adam. A little later, ". . . in his own likeness," that's when Adam and Eve had a child. When Eve gave birth, it was in Adam's likeness, not

God's. Why? Because depravity had flooded humanity and polluted the innocence. Sin intercepted the pass and it will *never* give the ball back—never! Not on this earth. The real tragedy is that the disease has spread to all mankind. It is not limited to the Old Testament. It is not limited to the family of Adam and Eve:

> *What then? Are we better than they? Not at all; for we have already charged that both Jews and Greeks are all under sin; as it is written,*
>
> *"THERE IS NONE RIGHTEOUS, NOT EVEN ONE;*
> *THERE IS NONE WHO UNDERSTANDS,*
> *THERE IS NONE WHO SEEKS FOR GOD;*
> *ALL HAVE TURNED ASIDE, TOGETHER THEY HAVE*
>   *BECOME USELESS;*
> *THERE IS NONE WHO DOES GOOD,*
> *THERE IS NOT EVEN ONE.*
> *THEIR THROAT IS AN OPEN GRAVE,*
> *WITH THEIR TONGUES THEY KEEP DECEIVING,*
> *THE POISON OF ASPS IS UNDER THEIR LIPS;*
> *WHOSE MOUTH IS FULL OF CURSING AND*
>   *BITTERNESS;*
> *THEIR FEET ARE SWIFT TO SHED BLOOD,*
> *DESTRUCTION AND MISERY ARE IN THEIR PATHS,*
> *AND THE PATH OF PEACE HAVE THEY NOT KNOWN.*
> *THERE IS NO FEAR OF GOD BEFORE THEIR EYES."*
> (Romans 3:9-18).

I can imagine a cartoon that might appear in some business magazine, showing a tired business man late one evening—tie pulled loose after a busy day—watching a business report. Only this time things are much more realistic. Imagine his startled look as he hears:

"Closing averages in the human scene were mixed today:
- Brotherly Love—down a couple of points.
- Self-interest—up a half.
- Vanity showed no movement.
- Guarded Optimism—slipped a point in the sluggish trading.

Over all, really nothing changed."

The guy would probably blink in amazement, but he would have no reason to be that surprised. After all, he is a student of humanity. He knows in his heart that "really nothing changed." Depravity is monotonously predictable.

*Therefore, just as through one man sin entered into the world,
and death through sin, and so death spread to all men, because
all sinned—* (Romans 5:12).

Think of it this way: There is a king named Sin; there is a queen
named Death. Both of them rule over mankind . . . "so death spread
to all men, because all sinned."

WHAT IT ALL MEANS . . . PERSONALLY

Now here's our problem. We suffer from the very same disease as
did Adam, Eve, Cain—you name 'em. This Book called the Bible
may be old, but it isn't out of date. It may tell us our story in ancient
terms, but its message is still true, still relevant. We've got the disease, the same root problem—*depravity.*

And that root problem yields fruit—*sinfulness*—sinful thoughts,
sinful words, sinful actions. There is nobody on earth who can help
us! We're not unlike an egg named Humpty Dumpty:

> Humpty Dumpty sat on a wall.
> Humpty Dumpty had a great fall.
> All the king's horses and all the king's men
> Couldn't put Humpty together again.

I was thinking about that not long ago (to give you some idea of
the depth of my thoughts) and decided to go down to the library
and do some study on Humpty Dumpty.

I will never forget the librarian's face when I asked, "Have you
anything in the research stacks on Humpty Dumpty?" She just
stared at me. So I thought I'd put it another way, "How about something on the etymology of Humpty?" That didn't help either.

Even though she couldn't help me, I managed to find some interesting things. I found that the little rhyme was never connected with
an egg, not originally. That was added later. I discovered that
Humpty Dumpty was perhaps originated by a rather creative
teacher in the colonial days of our United States when children sat
on hard oak benches and learned their ABCs. My reason for
suggesting this is based on what I found in the New England
Primer. In the Primer is this quaint couplet, not unlike Humpty
Dumpty, that reads,

In Adam's fall
We sinned all.
Xerxes the Great did die,
And so must you and I.

It was used to teach children the letters "A" and "X." Who knows but what some teacher thought of a rhyme that would teach even more letters, for after all, "King Sin" and "Queen Death" still reigned in the seventeenth and eighteenth centuries.

We need help. We need somebody to put us together again. Romans 5:17 announces there *is* Someone!

For if, by the trespass of the one man, death reigned through that one man, how much more will those who receive God's abundant provision of grace and of the gift of righteousness reign in life through the one man, Jesus Christ (NIV).

Isn't that good news? There is Someone to whom we can turn. You won't find anybody on earth who qualifies as a sinless sacrifice. Being such a sacrifice requires perfection. That's why He was virgin born. God intercepted the birth process and placed in Mary's womb the embryo perfectly designed to provide the sinless sacrifice . . . the Lamb of God who would take away the sin of the world. After living a perfect life, He went to the cross where he satisfied—once for all— the righteous demands of a holy God against sin.

Even though "we sinned all," thanks to Adam . . . even though "Xerxes the Great did die, and so must you and I," Christ is our hope. He came to our rescue. He saw us in our depravity, He heard our confession of need, He gave us the hope of forgiveness.

So let me close with my own revised edition of Humpty Dumpty.

Jesus Christ came to our wall;
Jesus Christ died for our fall.
He slew Queen Death.
He crushed King Sin.
Through grace He put us together again.

The best part of all? "He put us together again." He picked up the pieces. He unscrambled the egg. To change the terms of the philosopher; wherever there is sin, there must have been a preceding sinner. And wherever there is a sinner, there must be a Savior.

And there is.

1. Have you thought of work—your daily tasks—as a curse? A dread? Applying what you've learned about the power of God's Holy Spirit within you, ask the Lord to give you a new vision—a new attitude toward the "garden" He has given you to tend. If difficult on-the-job relationships with other people have contributed to your work anxieties, ask a friend to join you in praying specifically for the individuals and situations that produce the most tension. Don't depend on your own strength!

2. Children have no difficulty at all accepting the truths of biblical creation. It's *adults* who are bothered by all the phony intellectual baggage that accompanies this vital subject. Take the first opportunity you find to talk to a young child about the wonder of God's creation as revealed in Genesis. If possible, highlight the discussion by a walk outside to observe things such as flowers, leaves, trees, and so on. Take time to carefully note the child's observations and questions. The questions can be tough—like, why did God make flies? But you'll never have a better opportunity to gain a fresh, unspoiled perspective on God's marvelous handiwork. Pray with the child to thank God for all that He has made.

3. In the days of their innocence, Adam and Eve seemed to have a special time of day set aside to walk and talk with their God. When they didn't show up one day both they and God knew something was terribly wrong. Do you have a daily appointment with God—a special time reserved for just the two of you . . . a time when you give yourself to reading His Word and listening for His footsteps . . . for His voice? You've probably heard preachers and teachers suggest a *regular, daily* time with the Lord again and again. What will it take for you to begin? Ask someone to "hold you accountable" to spend time alone with the Lord each day—even if for only five or ten minutes. Ask your friend to check on you once a week for three or four weeks. If you have no idea how to start a consistent time with God, check at a Christian bookstore for the little booklet *Seven Minutes With God*, published by Inter-Varsity Press.

EXPOSING
THE DARK SIDE

like good news. Therefore, I prefer to emphasize the happy, bright, colorful side of life. But my problem with that emphasis is this: That is only *half* the message of Christianity. When we stop to think about it, we really cannot appreciate the bright and beautiful side of life until we know how dark and dismal the backdrop is. So, to be true to my calling and to be complete in this presentation of biblical doctrine, it is necessary to expose, along with the bright side of life, the dark side.

It was back in 1886 that Robert Louis Stevenson wrote a classic story that exposed everybody's life. He called it *Dr. Jekyll and Mr. Hyde*. Although a little older, Stevenson was a contemporary of Mark Twain, the American storyteller. And perhaps it was from that story that Twain came up with the statement so familiar to all of us: "Everybody is a moon; and has a dark side which he never shows to anybody."[1]

No one ever said it better than Jesus when He spoke so sternly against the hypocrisy of the Pharisees and scribes.

> *Woe to you, scribes and Pharisees, hypocrites! For you are like white-washed tombs which on the outside appear beautiful, but inside they are full of dead men's bones and all uncleanness. Even so you too outwardly appear righteous to men, but inwardly you are full of hypocrisy and lawlessness* (Matthew 23:27-28).

Lest you live under the delusion that the "dark side" was a problem only former generations struggled with, just think about your

life over the past several days. Think inwardly rather than out-
wardly. More than likely you behaved yourself rather well externally
. . . but not from within! Call to mind the impulses, the drives, the
secrets, the motives behind the actions you lived out. Perhaps a few
of them did surface, but most of your dark side remained hidden to
the public. French essayist Michel de Montaigne put it this way:

> There is no man so good, who, were he to submit all his
> thoughts and actions to the laws, would not deserve hanging
> ten times in his life.[2]

DEPRAVITY DEFINED AND EXPLAINED

My opening statements in this chapter have to do with our most
ancient and all-pervasive disease. It's helpful to remember that the
deadliest killer of humanity is not heart disease or cancer . . . it is
depravity. Every one of us has it. Every one of us suffers from the
consequences of it. And to make matters even worse, we pass it on
to each new generation. As we learned in chapter 11, it has "spread
to all men."

One of the most sweeping, broad-brush statements in all of Scripture on the depravity of humanity is found in Genesis 6:5:

> *Then the Lord saw that the wickedness of man was great on the
> earth, and that every intent of the thoughts of his heart was only
> evil continually.*

Are you as gripped as I am when I read three words in that verse?
Look at them again: "every," "only," "continually." The scene described in this verse is an inescapable, universal cesspool in the
inner person of all humanity—a hidden source of pollution that lies
at the root of wrong. Even from childhood this is true.

A number of years ago the Minnesota Crime Commission released this statement:

> Every baby starts life as a little savage. He is completely selfish
> and self-centered. He wants what he wants when he wants it—
> his bottle, his mother's attention, his playmates' toy, his uncle's
> watch. Deny him these once, and he seethes with rage and ag-
> gressiveness, which would be murderous were he not so help-
> less. He is, in fact, dirty. He has no morals, no knowledge, no
> skills. This means that all children—not just certain children—
> are born delinquent. If permitted to continue in the self-

centered world of his infancy, given free reign to his impulsive actions to satisfy his wants, every child would grow up a criminal—a thief, a killer, or a rapist.[3]

Now that's reality. And if it's your tendency as a positive thinker to ignore it, it still won't go away. If it's your tendency as a parent to ignore it, that root of depravity will come back to haunt you in your home. A permissive, think-only-about-the-bright-side-of-life philosophy will be eaten alive by problems of depravity as your child grows up without restraints and without controls. Not even a kind and professional Dr. Jekyll could remove the savage-like Mr. Hyde from his own life. Face it, the dark side is here to stay.

Psalm 51 is another section of Scripture worth examining as we come to terms with depravity. It is the psalm David wrote following Nathan's confrontation with him after the adultery-murder-hypocrisy scandal.

Be gracious to me, O God, according to Thy lovingkindness; according to the greatness of Thy compassion blot out my transgressions. Wash me thoroughly from my iniquity, and cleanse me from my sin. For I know my transgressions, and my sin is ever before me. Against Thee, Thee only, I have sinned, and done what is evil in Thy sight, so that Thou art justified when Thou dost speak, and blameless when Thou dost judge. Behold, I was brought forth in iniquity, and in sin my mother conceived me (Psalm 51:1-5).

He begins with a plea for grace, which shouldn't surprise us. The only way David could expect to survive would be by the grace of God. That's the reason *any* of us survive! What is grace? How would you define it? Probably, the most popular two-word definition is "unmerited favor." To amplify that a bit: Grace is what God does for mankind, which we do not deserve, which we cannot earn, and which we will never be able to repay. Awash in our sinfulness, helpless to change on our own, polluted to the core with no possibility of cleaning ourselves up, we cry out for grace. It is our only hope.

That's why David's prayer begins, "Be gracious." He doesn't deserve God's favor. He's fallen into sin. His life is a mess. So he asks that God would be gracious according to His lovingkindness.

Following his unguarded, open confession, David addresses the nucleus of his problem. He was "brought forth in iniquity" because his mother conceived him "in sin." He doesn't mean that the act of conception was sinful. The Amplified Bible handles the meaning quite well:

Behold, I was brought forth in [a state of] iniquity; my mother was sinful who conceived me [and I, too, am sinful].

"I have come from sinful parents, and therefore I have had the same disease passed on to me . . . so please be gracious to me, O God." That's the idea.

Lest we feel a little smug, thinking that David was all alone in the struggle against sin, let's return to the Jekyll-and-Hyde reminder . . . we've *all* got the disease. Depravity affects all of us. Because Adam fell, we, too, fell. Theologian Dwight Pentecost addresses the issue of Adam's fall. Read his words carefully:

> One of the most important questions which you can face is the question, "How far did Adam fall?" A number of different answers have been given to that question.
>
> The liberal says that Adam fell upward, so that Adam's lot was better after the fall than before the fall because something was added to the personality of Adam of which he had been deprived previously. Consequently, Adam was a fuller and more complete person after the fall than he was before the fall. There are those who say that when Adam fell, he fell over the cliff, but that when he was going over the cliff he grabbed something on the top of the cliff and held on. He fell downward, but he held on before he slipped over the brink, and if he exerts enough will and enough strength he can pull himself back up over the brink and stand on solid ground again. Those who have that concept are trying to lift themselves by their own bootstraps and work their way into heaven.
>
> Then, there is the teaching that says that when Adam fell, he slipped over the brink but he landed on a ledge part way down and that the ledge is the church and the church will lift him up and put him on solid ground again.
>
> But the Word of God says that when Adam fell he fell all the way. He became depraved, totally depraved, unable to do anything to please God. He is under sin, dead, under judgment, under Satan's control; he is lost.[3]

HUMANITY SURVEYED AND EXPOSED

One of the wonderful things about the Bible, which only adds to its credibility, is that it tells us the truth, the whole truth, and nothing but the truth regarding its characters. I often say it doesn't airbrush the pen portraits. When it paints its heroes, it paints them warts and all. The scars are not hidden. And about the time you're tempted to elevate certain men and women in Scripture to a pedestal of worship, God brings them down to size. Each one is completely, totally, and thoroughly H-U-M-A-N. They are all as James refers to Elijah: "... a man with a nature like ours ..." (James 5:17).

Three Old Testament Characters

Noah

I'd like to introduce the first man, who appears in Genesis, chapter 6. What a wonderful man he was! We need to be reminded of the times in which he lived. We just read about that awful scene in Genesis 6:5 as it described Noah's surroundings. The Lord said that He was grieved that He had even made man. And so before judging humanity with the flood, He surveyed the world, looking for one who would qualify as a righteous man. And He found one, only one, who found favor in His sight. His name was Noah.

These are the records of the generations of Noah. Noah was a righteous man, blameless in his time; Noah walked with God (6:9).

This verse says three things about Noah: He was righteous, blameless, and he walked with God. That's quite a résumé! Here is a good man, surrounded by gross wickedness ... a flower growing out of a cesspool. He was so good, God appointed him to build the ark and to save his family from death. And that's exactly what Noah did. He worked on it consistently for 120 years. And while he worked, he preached. And as he preached, he warned. And when he finished the ark, he got his family inside, though nobody else was interested, and the flood came. They alone were saved from destruction. It's one of those stories we never tire of hearing. And Noah comes out, of course, smelling like a rose. Public hero number one!

Chapter 9 brings us to the end of the flood and presents Noah and his family to a new earth.

Here stands a man who has been walking with God for all these years. What a model of courage and determination! But as soon as we're about to fall on our knees to worship him ... we find he has feet of clay. Yes, even Noah. Unlike the moon, he is forced to show his dark side.

> *Then Noah began farming and planted a vineyard. And he drank of the wine and became drunk, and uncovered himself inside his tent. And Ham, the father of Canaan, saw the nakedness of his father, and told his two brothers outside* (9:20-22).

I don't pretend to know all that his uncovering himself implies. It was, no doubt, sexually perverse, because his sons were ashamed to be in his presence in his naked condition. On top of that, the man was drunk.

It seems amazing that a good man—so good he was picked above all other men—would get himself drunk in his tent and blatantly uncover himself. So wicked was Noah's disobedience that his sons were not only shamed by it, but cursed because of it. As in the case of Adam and Eve, a divine curse followed disobedience . . . it is like an instant replay. It's shocking if you forget that even in Noah there was a depraved nature.

Every now and then a once-great man or godly woman will fall. So great will be the fall that their defection will make headline attention in Christian and secular publications alike. Even though we know the doctrine of depravity, we're still stunned.

In one sense it is only natural to be surprised since we trusted the person to live obediently. In another sense we really have no reason to be shocked. Depravity affects us all—and even the so-called heroes of our life occasionally drop through the cracks. Before you become too disillusioned, remember Noah. Not even he was immune. Sometimes there is drunkenness, and sometimes there is sexual perversity. And when the truth comes out, our heroes die a painful death in our minds.

Learn a major lesson from this study: *No one on earth deserves your worship.* You tread on very thin ice when you enshrine any human individual—no matter how mightily he or she is being used of God.

Is it okay to have heroes? Sure it is. And it is certainly appropriate to respect them. But our respect should never come anywhere close to man-worship. When it does, and then your hero suddenly shows his weakness, you are going to be terribly disillusioned. It may not be as scandalous as it was with Noah, but they will fall in some way. They will show intemperance, or anger, or impatience, or even a lack of courtesy. If you get to know them well enough, you'll discover they're just people who have to put their britches on one leg at a time. Just like everyone else.

Try to remember that every person on earth is still a depraved human being. Some are being used by God, but in no way are they free from the disease. Example: Noah . . . a good man who distinguished himself in bad times . . . but was still imperfect.

Moses

The second man worth our consideration appears first on the pages of Scripture in Exodus, chapter 2. His name is Moses. I like Moses. So do you. Who wouldn't like Moses? He comes from an extremely humble origin. He very graciously handles his early successes. Hebrews 11 says that he refused to be called the son of Pharaoh's daughter. And finally, though he was well-educated, mighty in words and deeds, and considered by many to be the Pharaoh-elect, he was a man who decided to serve the Lord, rather than himself. And after a lengthy period of preparation he was used to lead the people through the wilderness. You probably know his story.

No other man in Scripture talked with God face to face. When Moses came down from the mountain, his face literally glowed with the Shekinah glory of Jehovah, having been in the presence of God. He was there when the finger of God drilled the Torah into stone. He came down from the mountain and presented the first copies of the written Word of God to the people of God. He oversaw the building of the tabernacle. He led a whole nation through the trackless deserts of the Sinai. He stayed faithfully by their side, though they often came at him with verbal guns blazing.

Now you'd think the man could virtually walk on water, but he couldn't. This same man, Moses, had a record of murder in his life. It occurred during his mid-life years.

> *Now it came about in those days, when Moses had grown up, that he went out to his brethren and looked on their hard labors; and he saw an Egyptian beating a Hebrew, one of his brethren. So he looked this way and that, and when he saw there was no one around, he struck down the Egyptian and hid him in the sand* (Exodus 2:11-12).

Is that amazing? Well, not really . . . not if you believe in the depravity of humanity. In an unguarded moment, a moment of rash decision, Moses acted in the flesh as he killed an Egyptian. Yes, in a rage of anger he murdered him. And then tried to hide the evidence. Why? Because he knew he had done wrong.

Forty years later (aged eighty) he's out in the wilderness. He thinks he's going to be leading sheep for the rest of his life. And God steps on the scene and says, "You're the one I have chosen to lead My people out of Egypt." Now here is an eighty-year-old man with murder on his record. He knows that he has failed the Lord, and yet he hears God graciously coming back saying, "You are going to be My spokesman." You would think he would have learned enough to

say right away, "Wherever You lead me, I will go." Does he do that?
No.

Don't call Moses' response (recorded in Exodus 3:11-4:17) *humility*. It's stubbornness. It's willful resistance.

Moses also battled with a temper—a short fuse. It may have gotten a little longer the older he got, but he never fully conquered it. But those of us who are impatient can't afford to be too critical of Moses. We know what it is to fight a bad temper. We try many ways to keep the fuse wet. When it gets dry it tends to make everything explode. Moses is a man who had that problem. Why? Because he was depraved. He was a good man. He was a leader. He was God's spokesman. But He still had a depraved nature. A Mr. Hyde nature lived inside his Dr. Jekyll skin. You see him on display in these lines from Number 20:

> *And there was no water for the congregation; and they assembled themselves against Moses and Aaron. The people thus contended with Moses and spoke, saying, "If only we had perished when our brothers perished before the Lord! Why then have you brought the Lord's assembly into this wilderness, for us and our beasts to die here? And why have you made us come up from Egypt, to bring us in to this wretched place? It is not a place of grain or figs or vines or pomegranates, nor is there water to drink." Then Moses and Aaron came in from the presence of the assembly to the doorway of the tent of meeting, and fell on their faces. Then the glory of the Lord appeared to them; and the Lord spoke to Moses, saying, "Take the rod; and you and your brother Aaron assemble the congregation and speak to the rock before their eyes, that it may yield its water. You shall thus bring forth water for them out of the rock and let the congregation and their beasts drink." So Moses took the rod from before the Lord, just as He had commanded him; and Moses and Aaron gathered the assembly before the rock. And he said to them, "Listen now, you rebels; shall we bring forth water for you out of this rock? Then Moses lifted up his hand and struck the rock twice with his rod; and water came forth abundantly, and the congregation and their beasts drank. But the Lord said to Moses and Aaron, "Because you have not believed Me, to treat Me as holy in the sight of the sons of Israel, therefore you shall not bring this assembly into the land which I have given them" (vv. 2-12).*

What a story! Many people see only judgment here. I see grace. Did you catch those words? ". . . and water came forth abundantly. . . ." If you had been God, would *you* have brought water out of the rock? No way. But grace brings water even when there's disobedience. Why would Moses, this good man, strike the rock, when God has just said, "Speak to it"? I'm going to repeat it until it sinks in: *Because he was depraved.* Color Moses blue. He had a dark side he didn't want anybody to see, but on this occasion it was on display.

Before you get too pious and judgmental with Moses, just think about the rods and rocks in your life. Call to mind a few of the times you knew what was best and you did what was worst . . . when you realized in your heart that patience pays off, yet you acted impatiently. Want to know why you did it? Because *you're* depraved. Because you too have a dark side. Maybe it's a temper. Maybe it's greed. Or gossip. Or lust. Or overeating or drugs and booze. It could be envy, jealousy, or a dozen other things I could name. We all have them and they are often our besetting sins. Depravity reveals itself in numerous ways . . . all of them dark.

David

Having looked at Noah and Moses, let's consider perhaps the most popular character in the Old Testament, the man after God's heart, King David. My favorite piece of sculpture is a work by Michelangelo, the statue of David—white marble, standing at the end of a long corridor in Florence, Italy. As you study the statue, you stand in awe, not only of an artist's ability with a mallet and chisel but of God's marvelous plan in taking a teenager from a flock of sheep owned by his father and bringing him to lead His people. A beautiful summary of his story appears in Psalm 78.

> *He also chose David His servant, and took him from the sheepfolds; from the care of the ewes with suckling lambs He brought him, to shepherd Jacob His people, and Israel His inheritance. So he shepherded them according to the integrity of his heart, and guided them with his skillful hands* (vv. 70-72).

But the earliest reference to David is found in 1 Samuel 13 as Samuel speaks to Saul—who has forfeited the right to rule the people.

> *And Samuel said to Saul, "You have acted foolishly; you have not kept the commandment of the Lord your God, which He commanded you, for now the Lord would have established your kingdom over Israel forever. But now your kingdom shall not endure.*

The Lord has sought out for Himself <u>a man after His heart</u> . . .
(vv. 13-14a, emphasis mine).

You could write in the margin of your Bible, "Reference to David." A man after the very heart of God. And David stays faithful to God for well over a dozen years while jealous Saul hunts him down.

Finally, David is given the throne of Israel. He takes a nation that's bottomed-out spiritually, militarily, and economically. He expands its boundaries from 6,000 to 60,000 square miles. He establishes trade routes with the world. He equips them with a respectable military fighting force. David literally puts the nation on the map. He gives Israel a flag that flies higher than it had ever flown before. What a leader. What a hero. What a man of battle. What a courageous, faithful man of God . . . "a man after His own heart."

If you're looking for somebody to respect as a leader in biblical days, you don't have to go much further than David. David proves himself to be a man who continues to walk with God as he leads the nation correctly and courageously.

Until you get to 2 Samuel, chapter 11.

Until you come to one particular evening.

As king, he should have been in battle with his troops. Instead he was at ease in the palace. And that was how he happened to take a fateful walk on his roof.

> *Now when evening came David arose from his bed and walked around on the roof of the king's house, and from the roof he saw a woman bathing; and the woman was very beautiful in appearance. So David sent and inquired about the woman. And one said, "Is this not Bathsheba, the daughter of Eliam, the wife of Uriah the Hittite?" And David sent messengers and took her, and when she came to him, he lay with her; and when she had purified herself from her uncleanness, she returned to her house. And the woman conceived; and she sent and told David, and said, "I am pregnant"* (vv. 2-5).

You know the rest of the tragic story. Not only had our hero been involved with another woman outside wedlock (he certainly didn't need another woman), he had now found himself in a place of intense compromise and pressure. The thought of abortion was never in their mind—certainly not. But she was pregnant with his child. In a state of panic, David realized he had to do something about her husband Uriah. He tried to mask the story. Brought the man back from battle. Hoped that he would sleep with his wife. But Uriah, more faithful to the cause of Israel than David was, refused. And finally, the king instructed Joab to put Uriah into the heat of the battle. When that happened, of course, Uriah was killed. Joab sent a messenger back, knowing the heart of his leader, and among other things, he said, "You be sure and tell King David that Uriah was killed." The deceptive plot thickened.

I ask you, how could a man as godly as David fall as far as he did with Bathsheba? How could he be responsible for murdering a man on the battlefield? How could he live the life of a hypocrite for almost a year? How could David do that? He's our hero! He's that faithful shepherd! He's the giant killer!

The answer is going to sound terribly familiar—he is depraved. He has a nature that will never improve. He has lust, just like every man and every woman reading these words right now. And he yielded to it. As lust played its sweet song, the king of Israel danced to the music. He was responsible, just as you and I are every time we yield. Like Noah and Moses, David's lapse into sin left him vulnerable to its consequences. When depravity wins a victory, many get hurt . . . not just the one who is most responsible. Never forget that!

Most of us have been down the pike far enough to know that we cannot trust our sinful nature. Heed this word of counsel: *Don't get yourself in a situation where your nature takes charge.* If you are weakened by lust when you are with the opposite sex, you have to keep yourself out of those tempting situations where you will yield. If you play around the fire, it is only a matter of time. It won't be "if" but "when." And make no mistake about it, it will be your fault because you played the fool. And I can assure you, others will be burned in the same fire.

It is terribly important, especially in the area of personal morality, that we keep a safe distance when there is the temptation to be involved in illicit activity. I hope you never forget this warning. We are living in a day when moral purity and marital infidelity are being rationalized and compromised. More and more people— more and more *Christians*—are convincing themselves it's okay to fudge a little.

If you're sleeping with somebody who is not your mate, you're in sin. You're displeasing God. If you're walking away from God in an area of sexual activity, it is hurting your testimony and hurting the ministry of Jesus Christ. Face the music and get back in step! Claim the grace that's coming to you through Christ. Say, as David finally said ". . . I have sinned," and turn around. Do it now!

And may I add? If you are in ministry and doing that, clean up your life or get out of the ministry. Do everyone else in ministry a favor, if you refuse to repent . . . just step out of the ministry and say, "I have sinned. I have forfeited the right to lead a flock. I've compromised. I've ruined my personal testimony, but I refuse to ruin the testimony of the Church." Better still, return to the Lord and claim His forgiveness. Christ is coming back for His Bride, the Church, expecting her to be pure, "having no spot or wrinkle or any such thing; but that she should be holy and blameless" (Ephesians 5:27).

Two New Testament Characters

Before we wrap up this chapter, let's glance at a couple of New Testament heroes.

Peter

One of those heroes must surely be Peter! Remember his greatest moment with his fellow disciples and his Lord?

> *Now when Jesus came into the district of Caesarea Philippi, He began asking His disciples, saying, "Who do people say that the Son of Man is?" And they said, "Some say John the Baptist; some Elijah; and others, Jeremiah, or one of the prophets." He said to them, "But who do you say that I am?" And Simon Peter answered and said, "Thou art the Christ, the Son of the living God"* (Matthew 16:13-16).

What a grand statement of faith! Good for you, Peter! With boldness and uncompromising assurance, the man spoke the truth. His theology? Impeccable. His faith? Impressive. I think Jesus wanted to applaud him. He did, in effect, when He told him that flesh and blood hadn't revealed that to him. Peter's answer came from the very portals of heaven. "God revealed that to you, Peter." It was his moment.

A little later on, Peter is again with his Lord. And the Lord is telling him about the future.

> *And Jesus said to them, "You will all fall away, because it is written, 'I will strike down the shepherd, and the sheep shall be scattered.' But after I have been raised, I will go before you to Galilee." But Peter said to Him, "Even though all may fall away, yet I will not"* (Mark 14:27-29).

Now Peter meant well. I've said things like that, haven't you? In a moment of great emotional gush, Peter made sweeping promises to his Lord. Reminds me of the standard New Year's resolution:

Journal Entry: January 1—I'll meet with You every
                   day of this new year, Lord.

January 4—Lord, I've missed the last
two days, but I'm back.

Let's not be too critical of Peter. The man meant it with all his heart.

> . . . *"Even though all may fall away, yet I will not." And Jesus said to him, "Truly I say to you, that you yourself this very night, before a cock crows twice, shall three times deny Me"* (Mark 14:29, 30).

And that's exactly what happened. The fact is, he later denied his Lord, openly and unashamedly. How can it be that this sincere disciple who made such a right-on statement of faith could drift so far, so fast?

In the same chapter of Mark's Gospel, we find the same man masking his identity:

> . . . *he* [Peter] *began to curse and swear, "I do not know this man* [Jesus] *you are talking about!"* (v. 71).

Peter's "Mr. Hyde" was on display. A darkness so horrible we don't even want to imagine it. Peter, however, could never forget it. And then we read:

> *And immediately a cock crowed a second time. And Peter remembered how Jesus had made the remark to him, "Before a cock crows twice, you will deny Me three times." And he began to weep* (v. 72).

I don't think there is any weeping as bitter as the weeping brought on by spiritual failure. It's downright terrible! I'm thinking of a minister friend of mine who has failed the Lord through sexual compromise. He has stepped away from leadership and ministry. His flock is still in shock. At this very moment he is going through the time of weeping, like Peter. He knows he has forfeited the right to lead. And now that he has repented and come clean, he realizes the heinous condition of his soul during that period of time when he was compromising. I met with him to encourage him. Several times he broke into audible sobs. Like Peter, he was weeping in anguish before God. He is now seeking God's will for his future.

Why did Peter do that? Why did my friend do that? I repeat, at the risk of sounding like a broken record, you and I are prone to wander, prone to leave the God we love *because of the depravity of humanity.*

Paul

Can it be that a man as fine as Paul would be included? Romans, chapter 7, I think, is the finest explanation of humanity's depraved nature found anywhere in the Scriptures. We've looked at Noah and Moses and David. In the New Testament we're looking at Peter and Paul. If I had time, I could also include Mary—Peter, Paul, and Mary (couldn't resist it). But we'll stop with Paul.

Listen to the personal testimony of a great man of God, the theologian par excellence, the missionary, the apostle, the founder of churches, the man who forged out the finer points of our theology, who wrote more of the New Testament than any other writer. Read Paul's admission slowly and thoughtfully:

> *I do not understand what I do. For what I want to do I do not do, but what I hate I do. And if I do what I do not want to do, I agree that the law is good. As it is, it is no longer I myself who do it, but it is sin living in me. I know that nothing good lives in me, that is, in my sinful nature. For I have the desire to do what is good, but I cannot carry it out. For what I do is not the good I want to do; no, the evil I do not want to do—this I keep on doing. Now if I do what I do not want to do, it is no longer I who do it, but it is sin living in me that does it.*
>
> *So I find this law at work: When I want to do good, evil is right there with me. For in my inner being I delight in God's law; but I see another law at work in the members of my body, waging war against the law of my mind and making me a prisoner of the law of sin at work within my members. What a wretched man I am! Who will rescue me from this body of death?* (Romans 7:15-24, NIV).

I hardly need to amplify. Paul's testimony is everyone's testimony. That's why we sin. That's why the ark builder got drunk and why a leader lost his temper and why a king committed adultery and why a disciple denied his Lord. Even though we wish to do good, evil is present in us . . . all of us. John R.W. Stott said it best:

> We human beings have both a unique dignity as creatures made in God's image and a unique depravity as sinners under his judgment. The former gives us hope; the latter places a limit on our expectations. Our Christian critique of the secular mind is that it tends to be either too naively optimistic or too negatively pessimistic in its estimates of the human condition, whereas the Christian mind, firmly rooted in biblical realism,

both celebrates the glory and deplores the shame of our human being. We can behave like God in whose image we are made, only to descend to the level of the beasts. We are able to think, choose, create, love, and worship, but also to refuse to think, to choose evil, to destroy, to hate, and to worship ourselves. We build churches and drop bombs. We develop intensive care units for the critically ill and use the same technology to torture political enemies who presume to disagree with us. This is 'man,' a strange bewildering paradox, dust of earth and breath of God, shame and glory.[4]

THE ONE GREAT EXCEPTION

Jesus Christ is the exception—no shame in Him, only glory. No dark side, only light. No blue, only spotless white.

The Scripture says three things of Christ. He *knew* no sin; He *had* no sin; He *did* no sin. No sin nature. Born without sin. Lived without sinfulness. Knowing no sin, having no sin, doing no sin, He qualified as the Lamb of God who took away the power of sin and the dread of death. Therefore, when we confess our sins, He hears us and cleanses us. What a relief! We confess "Guilty as charged." He answers, "Heard and forgiven!"

> And this is the message we have heard from Him and announce to you, that God is light, and in Him there is no darkness at all. If we say that we have fellowship with Him and yet walk in the darkness, we lie and do not practice the truth; but if we walk in the light as He Himself is in the light, we have fellowship with one another, and the blood of Jesus His Son cleanses us from all sin. If we say that we have no sin, we are deceiving ourselves, and the truth is not in us. If we confess our sins, He is faithful and righteous to forgive us our sins and to cleanse us from all unrighteousness (1 John 1:5-9).

TWO OPTIONS—CHOOSE ONE

When we boil chapters 11 and 12 down to basics, we really have two options. *First, we can choose to live as victims* of our depravity . . . for "evil is present in me," as Paul wrote. Or *second, we can choose to live as victors* through the power of Jesus Christ. The last thing I desire to do is to leave in your mind the impression that you must spend your years as a helpless, pitiful victim of depravity.

Each one of these people we've studied made a deliberate decision to sin. They weren't duped. It came as no sudden surprise.
They played into the hand of the old nature, and they carried out
exactly what the old nature performs . . . disobedience. They *chose*
to live as victims, at least at that moment.

Let me encourage you to live as a victor through the power of
Jesus Christ. Start by coming to the cross, by faith. Ask Christ to
come into your life. Then as you face evil, as you come across it, as it
rears its head in temptation, claim the power of God that Christ offers, now that He's living within you.

You can say, "Lord, right now, at this moment, I am weak. You're
strong. By Your strength I'm stepping away from this evil, and Your
power is going to give me the grace to get through it victoriously.
Take charge right now." And walk away. Stand firm!

Remember the old gospel song "Just As I Am"? It is used at the
close of every Billy Graham Crusade. While attending the crusade
at Anaheim Stadium in 1985, I listened to that song night after
night as thousands of people poured onto the playing field to turn
their lives over to Jesus Christ. Some were lost; some were saved.
But all sought help with the same problem—their sin. Only the
Lamb of God can solve that problem.

> Just as I am, without one plea,
> But that Thy blood was shed for me,
> And that Thou bidd'st me come to Thee,
> O Lamb of God, I come! I come!
>
> Just as I am and waiting not
> To rid my soul of one dark blot,
> To Thee whose blood can cleanse each spot.
> O Lamb of God, I come! I come!
>
> Just as I am, Thou wilt receive,
> Wilt welcome, pardon, cleanse, receive;
> Because Thy promise I believe,
> O Lamb of God, I come! I come![5]

Mr. Hyde has a greater bark than a bite. Trust me . . . no, trust
God's Word. The Lord Jesus will help you face reality. He will see
you through. Come to the Lamb of God. Hear again His promise of
forgiveness.

> Forgive us, Lord . . . for the things we have done that make us
> feel uncomfortable in Thy presence. All the front that we polish
> so carefully for men to see does not deceive Thee. For Thou

knowest every thought that has left its shadow on our memory. Thou hast marked every motive that curdled something sweet within us.

We acknowledge—with bitterness and true repentance—that cross and selfish thoughts have entered our minds; we acknowledge that we have permitted our minds to wander through unclean and forbidden ways; we have toyed with that which we knew was not for us; we have desired that which we should not have.

We acknowledge that often we have deceived ourselves where our plain duty lay.

We confess before Thee that our ears are often deaf to the whisper of Thy call, our eyes often blind to the signs of Thy guidance.

Make us willing to be changed, even though it requires surgery of the soul and the therapy of discipline.

Make our hearts warm and soft, that we may receive now the blessing of Thy forgiveness, the benediction of Thy "Depart in peace . . . and sin no more." Amen.[6]

—Peter Marshall

1. A problem we all have at one time or another is allowing unconfessed sin to build up in our lives—cutting us off from fellowship with our Lord and generally making us miserable. What specific things happened in David's life when he refused to confess his sin (Psalm 32:3-4)? What happens in your life when you have held onto certain sins, resisting the Holy Spirit's voice? What did David find to rejoice about after he "came clean" before the Lord? Think of at least one practical way you might remind yourself to "keep short accounts with God"—that is, coming to Him in confession *immediately* after you become aware of sin in your life.

2. If you have not done so already, memorize what has become one of the most frequently quoted and beloved promises in all of the Bible, 1 John 1:9.

3. Identify the "danger areas" in your life—those tendencies or weaknesses that carry the greatest hazard of plunging you into sin. Carefully evaluate what activities, situations, or associations during the course of an average week bring you closest to those areas of "thin ice." (In David's case, a particular *place* on his rooftop at a particular *time* in the evening gave him a particular *view* that led him into disaster. The *situation* of idle time also seemed to be a dangerous one for the king.) Identifying these dangers is a very important step. Many need to avoid proximity to alcoholic beverages and the availability of habit-forming drugs. For others of us it's airport newsstands. Or certain situations with co-workers of the opposite sex. Or the strong urge to overeat. It is also very important to get prayer support from your spouse or a close friend. Having someone "check up on you" from time to time in these highly sensitive, highly dangerous areas can literally mean the difference between victory and defeat. We need each other! Let's call for help.

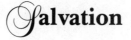alvation

"I believe the offer of salvation is God's love-gift to all. Those who accept it by faith, apart from works, become new creatures in Christ."

"MR. SMITH,
MEET YOUR SUBSTITUTE"

hen Peter Marshall preached,
people listened. Even if they didn't believe what he said. Even when
they said they were not interested. The man refused to be ignored.

Who can fully explain it? There was something about his win-
some, contagious style that made it impossible for people not to listen. Even when he became the chaplain of the United States Senate
and prayed more than he preached, his prayers became legendary.
Ask those who were fortunate enough to have heard him. They'll
tell you that everywhere Marshall preached, crowds gathered. Even
if it were raining or snowing outside, the main floor and balconies
would be full, packed with people, with many others who could not
find a seat were willing to stand and listen as he spoke the truth of
the living God.

Peter Marshall was Scottish, but his popularity went deeper than
his Scottish brogue. And it certainly was more than just a charming
personality or his well-timed humor that would win a hearing. The
man had a way with men as well as with women. He was admired by
both. A man's man and yet such a sensitive touch. At times one
would swear he was more a poet than a preacher. He wasn't extem-
poraneous. To the surprise of many, Marshall *read* his sermons, considered a no-no by most professors of homiletics. But I suppose if one
could read like Peter Marshall, who really cared if he broke that rule?

A contemporary of Marshall's said it best with this terse analysis:

> What Peter Marshall says, you never forget. . . . But it isn't *how*
> he says it, so much as *what* he says, you never forget. . . . He has

a gift for word pictures, for little dramas and folksy incidents; he takes you out on the road to Galilee and makes you think you belong there, and he brings you back sharply to Main Street. He never preaches over your head.[1]

Perhaps that, more than any other single ingredient, was the secret of the man's success. He certainly had the ability to go much deeper, but he purposely restrained himself. He was always cognizant of his audience. Since he was from an impoverished background, he understood the common man and woman. So he spoke in plain terms, colorful to be sure, and dramatic at times; but people never had trouble connecting with what Peter Marshall was saying.

Listen to a part of one of his sermons:

> Our country is full of Joneses, and they all have problems of one kind or another. "All God's chillun' got trouble these days."
>
> The Church has always contended that God can solve these problems through the individual's personal fellowship with a living Lord.
>
> Let's put the question bluntly, as bluntly as Mr. Jones would put it.
>
> Can you and I really have communion with Christ as we would with earthly friends?
>
> Can we know personally the same Jesus whose words are recorded in the New Testament, Who walked the dusty trails of Galilee two thousand years ago?
>
> I don't mean can we treasure His words
>   or try to follow His example
>   or imagine Him.
>
> I mean, is He really alive?
>   Can we actually meet Him,
>   commune with Him,
>   ask His help for our everyday affairs?
>
> The Gospel writers say "yes."
>   A host of men and women down the ages say "yes."
>   And the church says "yes."[2]

Appropriately, he entitled that sermon "Mr. Jones, Meet the Master." I have hitchhiked on the man's idea by choosing a similar title for this chapter: "Mr. Smith, Meet Your Substitute." I figure that Mr. Jones has been picked on long enough. We need to give Jones a break. So, Mr. Smith, this is for you . . . as well as for your wife . . .

and the Johnsons, the Franklins, the Clarks, the Parkers, or whatever your name may be. Because I'm writing to the common man and woman today who happens to find himself or herself in the same precarious predicament.

The predicament is called sin. And that's why you need a substitute.

FOUR MAJOR ISSUES

Let's talk about that "why" issue.

The sixth book in the New Testament is the book of Romans. In the third chapter of that book (which is actually a letter originally written to some people who lived in Rome, Italy, in the first century), you may be surprised to hear that *your* biography is included. It doesn't actually include your name or your place of residence, but it does tell the story of your personal life. The stuff it mentions isn't very attractive, I should warn you, but it is the truth. And so, Mr. Smith, this is your life. I mentioned it earlier, but it bears repeating.

Our Condition: Totally Depraved

What then? Are we better than they? Not at all; for we have already charged that both Jews and Greeks are all under sin; as it is written,

"THERE IS NONE RIGHTEOUS, NOT EVEN ONE;
THERE IS NONE WHO UNDERSTANDS,
THERE IS NONE WHO SEEKS FOR GOD;
ALL HAVE TURNED ASIDE, TOGETHER THEY HAVE
*   BECOME USELESS;*
THERE IS NONE WHO DOES GOOD,
THERE IS NOT EVEN ONE.
THEIR THROAT IS AN OPEN GRAVE,
WITH THEIR TONGUES THEY KEEP DECEIVING,
THE POISON OF ASPS IS UNDER THEIR LIPS;
WHOSE MOUTH IS FULL OF CURSING AND BITTERNESS;
THEIR FEET ARE SWIFT TO SHED BLOOD,
DESTRUCTION AND MISERY ARE IN THEIR PATHS,
AND THE PATH OF PEACE HAVE THEY NOT KNOWN.
THERE IS NO FEAR OF GOD BEFORE THEIR EYES."

Now we know that whatever the Law says, it speaks to those who are under the Law, that every mouth may be closed, and all the world may become accountable to God; because by the works of the Law no flesh will be justified in His sight; for through the Law comes the knowledge of sin. . . . For all have sinned and fall short of the glory of God (Romans 3:9-20, 23).

Honestly, now, does that sound like your life? Is that a fairly apt description of the inner you . . . down inside where nobody else can look? I think so. How do I know? Because it describes me, too. To borrow from my earlier comment, you and I are "blue all over." Even when we try to hide it, even when we put on our sophisticated best, it comes out when we least expect it.

Maybe you heard about the large commercial jet that was flying from Chicago to Los Angeles. About a half hour after takeoff, the passengers on board heard a voice over the loud speaker. "Good morning, ladies and gentlemen. This is a recording. You have the privilege of being on the first wholly electronically controlled jet. This plane took off electronically. It will soon be flying at 30,000 feet electronically. It will ultimately land electronically in Los Angeles. This plane has no pilot or copilot and no flight engineer because they are no longer needed. But do not worry, nothing can possibly go wrong, go wrong, go wrong, go wrong, go wrong, go wrong. . . ."

God's Character: Infinitely Holy

Next, my friend Smith, I should mention something that will only add insult to injury. God is righteous, perfect, and infinitely holy. That's His standard. It is sometimes called "glory" in the New Testament. We looked earlier at Romans 3:23. Let me paraphrase it:

For all have sinned [that's our condition] *and fall short of the perfection, holiness, righteousness, and glory* [that's His standard] *of God.*

Unlike all humanity, God operates from a different level of expectation. His existence is in the realm of absolute perfection. He requires the same from others. Whoever hopes to relate to Him must be as righteous as He is righteous. How different from us! To relate to me you don't have to be perfect. In fact, if you act like you are, I get very uncomfortable. "Just be what you are," we say. But God is not like that. God doesn't shrug, wink, and say, "Ah, that's okay."

Let me put it another way. God's triangle is perfect. And in order for you and me to fellowship with Him, our triangles must be congruent. The sides and the angles must match. So must the space within. Perfection requires matching perfection.

Ah, there's the rub! We have sinned and fallen short of the perfection of God. No one qualifies as perfect. Don't misunderstand, there are times that our goodness is astounding. We take great strides, we produce great achievments. We may even surprise ourselves with periodic times of goodness, gentleness, and compassion. But "perfect"? Never. Or "infinitely holy"? How about "pure"? No, only God is those things. Romans 3:21 calls God's perfection, holiness, and purity ". . . the righteousness of God which is being manifested in the Law and the Prophets." Compared to *that* standard, all humans come up short.

J. B. Phillips, in his paraphrase, puts it like this:

> . . . *indeed it is the straight edge of the Law that shows us how crooked we are.*

Isn't that the truth? He is perfect and spotless white. Not a taint of gray. Not a hint of blue. And along comes our blue rectangle, trying to work its way into that perfect, holy, and pure triangle. And the two just won't match! There is no way, Mr. Smith, that we can match His righteousness.

Our Need: A Substitute

Here we are, sinners by birth, sinners by nature, sinners by choice, trying to reach and attain a relationship with the holy God who made us. And we "fall short." We can't make it because we're spiritually crippled. In fact, the New Testament teaches that we're "dead in trespasses and sin."

What do we need? Let me put it plain and simple, Mr. Smith; we need help outside ourselves.

We need some way to become clean within so that we can relate to a God who is perfect. Scripture says, ". . . God is light, and in Him there is no darkness at all" (1 John 1:5). If we hope to know God and walk with God and relate to God, we must be able to stand the scrutiny of that kind of light. But our light is out. We're all dark and He is all light. In his immortal hymn, Charles Wesley envisioned us in a dark dungeon, chained and helpless—

> Long my imprisoned spirit lay
> Fast bound in sin and nature's night. . . .[3]

We can't get out of the dungeon, not even if we try. Our own sin holds us in bondage. We need someone to rescue us from the hole. We need an advocate in the courtroom of justice. We need someone who will present our case. We need someone to be our substitute. So God provided the Savior.

God's Provision: A Savior

> . . . and are justified freely by his grace through the redemption that came by Christ Jesus. God presented him as a sacrifice of atonement, through faith in his blood. He did this to demonstrate his justice, because in his forbearance he had left the sins committed beforehand unpunished—he did it to demonstrate his justice at the present time, so as to be just and the one who justifies those who have faith in Jesus (Romans 3:24-26, NIV).

Is that great news? Mr. Smith, you have just been introduced to your substitute. He is Christ, the sinless and perfect Son of God. He is the One who accomplished your rescue. It occurred on a cross. It was effective because He was the only One who could qualify as our substitute before God. Sin requires a penalty—death—in order for God's righteous demands to be satisfied. The ransom must be paid. And Christ fills that role to perfection. You and I need to be washed. We need to be made sparkling clean. And God can't give up on His plan, for He hates sin. Being perfect He cannot relate to sinful things. He couldn't even if He tried, because His nature is repelled by sin. Sin calls for judgment. And that is why the cross is so significant. It became the place of judgment. It was there the price was paid in full.

In verse 24 of Romans 3, the term *justified* appears. Let's work with that word a few moments. It does not simply mean "just as if I'd never sinned." That doesn't go far enough! Neither does it mean that God makes me righteous so that I never sin again. It means to be "declared righteous." Justification is God's merciful act, whereby He declares righteous the believing sinner while he is still in his sinning state. He sees us in our need, wallowing around in the swamp of our sin. He sees us looking to Jesus Christ and trusting Him completely by faith, to cleanse us from our sin. And though we come to Him with all of our needs and in all of our darkness, God says to us, "Declared righteous! Forgiven! Pardoned!" Wesley caught the significance of all this as he completed that same stanza:

> Thine eye diffused a quick'ning ray,
> I woke, the dungeon flamed with light;
> My chains fell off, my heart was free;
> I rose, went forth and followed Thee.[4]

I like the way Billy Graham imagines all this in a courtroom scene:

Picture a courtroom. God the Judge is seated in the judge's seat, robed in splendor. You are arraigned before Him. He looks at you in terms of His own righteous nature as it is expressed in the moral law. He speaks to you:

GOD: John (or) Mary, have you loved Me with all your heart?

JOHN/MARY: No, Your Honor.

GOD: Have you loved others as you have loved yourself?

JOHN/MARY: No, Your Honor.

GOD: Do you believe you are a sinner and that Jesus Christ died for your sins?

JOHN/MARY: Yes, Your Honor.

GOD: Then your penalty has been paid by Jesus Christ on the cross and you are pardoned. . . . Because Christ is righteous, and you believe in Christ, I now declare you legally righteous. . . .

Can you imagine what a newspaperman would do with this event?

SINNER PARDONED—
GOES TO LIVE WITH JUDGE

It was a tense scene when John and Mary stood before the Judge and had the list of charges against them read. However, the Judge transferred all of the guilt to Jesus Christ, who died on a cross for John and Mary.

After John and Mary were pardoned the Judge invited them to come to live with Him forever.

The reporter on a story like that would never be able to understand the irony of such a scene, unless he had been introduced to the Judge beforehand and knew His character.

Pardon and Christ's righteousness come to us only when we totally trust ourselves to Jesus as our Lord and Savior. When we do this, God welcomes us into His intimate favor. Clothed in Christ's righteousness we can now enjoy God's fellowship.[5]

All of that is included in what it means to be "justified." I come to Him in all my need. I am hopelessly lost, spiritually dead. And I present myself to Christ just as I am. I have nothing to give that would earn my way in. If I could I would, but I can't. So the only way I can present myself to Him in my lost condition is by faith. Coming in my need, expressing faith in His Son who died for me, I understand that God sees me coming by faith and admitting my sinfulness. At that epochal moment, He declares me righteous.

On occasion I think of the cross as a sponge . . . a "spiritual sponge" that has taken the sins of mankind—past, present, and future—and absorbed them all. At one awful moment, Christ bore our sins, thus satisfying the righteous demands of the Father, completely and instantaneously clearing up my debt. My sin is forgiven. My enslavement is broken. I am set free from sin's power over me once and for all. Redemption, another significant word in verse 24, also occurs. I am set at liberty, so as never to come back to the slave market of sin—never again in bondage to it. And remember, the rescue occurred because of what *Christ* did—not because of what I did!

I love the way Romans 3:28 reads:

> *For we maintain that a man is justified by faith apart from works of the Law.*

I remember hearing a seasoned Bible teacher say, "Man is incurably addicted to doing something for his own salvation." What a waste! Scripture teaches that salvation is a by-faith, not-by-works transaction.

In Romans 4:4-5, this is made ever so clear:

> *Now to the one who works, his wage is not reckoned as a favor, but as what is due. But to the one who does not work, but believes in Him who justifies the ungodly, his faith is reckoned as righteousness.*

Just think of your paycheck, Mr. Smith. When your boss or someone from your boss's office brings you your paycheck, you take it. You take it, I might add, without a great deal of gratitude. You don't drop to your knees and say, "Oh, thank you—thank you so very much for this gift." You probably grab the check and don't give much thought to saying thanks. Why? Because you *earned* it. You worked *hard* for it. Now, if your boss attaches a bonus of a thousand bucks (and maybe even adds, "Though you're dropping in your efficiency, I want you to know I love you), wouldn't that be great? Great? That would be a miracle! There's a lot of difference between a wage and a gift.

God looks at us in all of our need and He sees nothing worth commending. Not only are we dropping in our spiritual efficiency, we have no light, no holiness. We're moving in the opposite direction, despising Him, living in a dungeon of sin, habitually carrying out the lifestyle of our sinful nature. Realizing our need, we accept his miraculous, eternal bonus—the gift of His Son. And in grace, our dungeon "flamed with light." You and I didn't even deserve the light, yet He gave it to us as an unmerited gift. Look again at verse 5:

> *But to the one who does not work, but believes in Him who justifies the ungodly, his faith is reckoned as righteousness.*

I love that verse! Because there's no way you and I can get any credit. We're bound in a dungeon, lost in ourselves. We don't even know where to find the light. Even when we try, we are like the line out of the country-western song, we "look for love in all the wrong places."

Reminds me of the story I read this past week about a drunk down on all fours late one night under a streetlight. He was groping around on the ground, feeling the cement, peering intently at the little cracks. And a friend drives up and says, "Sam, what are you doing there?" Sam answers, "I lost my wallet." So the friend gets out of his car, walks over, gets down on his hands and knees with him, and they both start looking. Neither one can find it. Finally the friend says to the drunk buddy:

"Are you sure you lost the wallet here?"
"Of course not! I dropped it a half a block over there."
"Then why are we looking here?"
"Because there's no *streetlight* over there."

Mr. Smith, I'm going to level with you. I know you fairly well, even though we've never met. You read these words about the *gift* of eternal life and you simply cannot fathom them, so you won't take them. I mean, you've got your pride so you will reject them. I can even imagine your reluctance: "Too good to be true, Chuck. Sounds great. Looks good in a book. And it's definitely an intriguing idea. Who wouldn't want to tell people that? But if I get into heaven, I'll earn it on my own."

Well, let me give you just a little logic to wrestle with. If you plan to work your way in, how much work is enough work to guarantee that you have made it? And if it's something you work for, why does God say in His Book that it's for "the one who does *not* work, but believes . . ."? Let me spell it out:

God's Character:	infinitely holy
Our Condition:	totally depraved
Our Need:	a Substitute
God's Provision:	a Savior

When God provided the Savior, He said to each one of us, "Here is my Gift to you." How often, when folks hear that, they shake their heads and mumble, "I can't believe it."

In 2 Corinthians 5:20, we find these words:

> *Therefore, we are ambassadors for Christ, as though God were entreating through us; we beg you on behalf of Christ, be reconciled to God.*

That's the message of this chapter in a nutshell. I beg you . . . be reconciled to God. Watch that barrier crumble, the one between you and God, as you step across by faith. Look at the next verse.

> *He made Him who knew no sin to be sin on our behalf, that we might become the righteousness of God in Him.*

Now, let me identify the pronouns:

> *He* [God, the Father] *made Him* [God, the Son] *who knew no sin to be sin on our behalf* [that happened at the cross], *that we* [the sinner] *might become the righteousness of God in Him* [Christ].

Let's boil it down:

God:	the righteous
Christ:	the sacrifice
We:	the sinner
Christ:	the life

How? The cross.

But how can the sinner in the black hole of his need ever know God in the spotless white of all of His righteousness? Verse 20 tell us. By coming to know Him who knew no sin, the one who became sin on our behalf. Put your pride in your pocket, Mr. Smith. You need a substitute. You need a defense attorney . . . an eternal advocate. And in Christ—and Christ alone—you've got one.

THREE CRUCIAL QUESTIONS

Seems to me there are three crucial questions we must answer. Each has a two-word answer.

Question	*Answer*
1. Is there any hope for lost sinners?	Yes, Christ.
2. Isn't there any work for a seeker to do?	No, believe.
3. Is there any way for the saved to lose the gift?	No, never!

Now let me spell that out.

First question: Is there any hope for lost sinners? Yes, Christ. Not Christ and the church. Not Christ and good works. Not Christ and sincerity. Not Christ and giving up your sins. Not Christ and trying real hard. Not Christ and baptism, Christ and christening, Christ and morality, or Christ and a good family. No! Christ (period). Otherwise, it's works. He died for our sins and was placed in the grave as proof of His death. He rose from the dead bodily, miraculously, in proof of His life beyond. If you believe that He died and rose for you, you have eternal life. It's a gift.

Second question: Isn't there any work for a seeker to do? Don't I have to add to it? Answer: No (period). Believe!

One of my favorite illustrations of the importance of believing and not working is to consider a nice meal you and I enjoy together. You invite me over. I come to your home. We have planned this for quite some time, and you've worked hard in the kitchen. You have prepared my favorite meal. You are thrilled because you have a great recipe. And I'm happy because it's going to be a delightful evening with you. I knock on your door. I walk in and can smell the meal (ahh!) all the way to the front door. I'm starved. We sit down together at the table, and you serve this delicious meal. We dine and dialogue together. What a thoroughly enjoyable evening!

Then, as I get up to leave, I reach into my pocket and say, "Now, what do I owe you?" You're *shocked*! That's an insult. You knew what I needed, and out of love for me, you fixed it and served it. Why, a major part of being a good host is that you pick up the tab. For me to suggest that I'll pay for it is like a slap in the face. You don't even want me to help with the dishes. Love motivated your giving me this great meal. It is your gift to me. To ask to pay for it repels your love.

Do you realize that there are men and women all around the world who are reaching in their pockets this very day saying, "Okay, God . . . how much do I owe You?"

I have communicated this same message for years, but I will never forget the time I had a lady come to the platform after a meeting to see me. She had dissolved in tears. She said, "Here's my Bible. Would you sign your autograph in the back, just your autograph? And then," she added, "would you put underneath it in quotes 'Salvation is a *gift*'"?

"You see," she explained, "my background is religious and all my life I've worked so hard. All my friends are from that same religion and they are all still working so hard. Now—for the first time in my life, I realize that God is really offering me a gift. The thing I have noticed about all of us, all these years, is that not one of us has ever been secure. We've never known that salvation was ours *forever*—because we worked so hard for it. Our plan was to keep working so we could keep it in us."

She had been reaching into her purse all these years, trying to pay God for His gift. Was it free? No, not really. It cost Christ His life at the cross many centuries ago.

Third question: Is there any way to lose the gift? No, never! Now stop and think before you disagree. Stay with biblical logic, not human reasoning. If you work for it, then you can certainly lose it. And that would mean it is not a gift; it's what you've earned. We really confuse things when we try to turn a gift into a wage. Furthermore, just as no one can say how much work is enough to earn it, no one can ever say how little work is enough to lose it.

Salvation is simply a gift. It's simple, but it wasn't easy. It's free, but it wasn't cheap. It's yours, but it isn't automatic. You must receive it. When you do, it is yours forever.

Two Possible Responses

We're back to basics, Mr. Smith. When you return to the roots of salvation, you can either believe and accept this gift, or you can refuse and reject it. And you can go right on living, by the way. You won't suddenly get struck by lightning if you reject Christ. I've noticed that God doesn't immediately start doing bad things to people who refuse His Son. He doesn't make you look foolish. He won't suddenly cut your legs off at the knees. He doesn't scar your face or make you lose your job. He doesn't keep your car from starting because you reject the message. He doesn't kill your closest friend or cause your mate to leave you as a judgment because you didn't believe. That's not the way God operates.

He simply waits.

And that fakes people out. That makes some folks think that if He really meant it, then He'd zap them for refusing to take His gift. No. Not necessarily. Those who think like that don't understand God. He holds out His grace and He makes it available even if we choose to reject it.

One Final Reminder

But I must remind you of something: You don't have forever. With no intention of manipulating you, you need to remember that death is certain. I wish I had kept track of the funeral services I have conducted in the last ten years on behalf of those who died before the age of fifty. Without trying to sound dramatic, I think it would shock you to know how many die before they turn fifty. And I'm sure some of them thought, "I've got a long time to go."

Listen, sin is terminal. And Mr. Smith, you've got that disease. It leads to death. It may not even be a year before you are gone . . . and you will have thought you had plenty of time.

I'm sure Peter Marshall thought he had a long, long time. May I return to his life? He was appointed to the Senate chaplaincy in early January 1947 . . . a specimen of good health. Yet it was a shade beyond two years that this forty-seven-year-old man was seized with a heart attack and died. He was as eloquent and creative as ever right up to the last . . . but within a matter of hours, his voice was hushed forever. Only the printed page speaks for Marshall today.

A sermon of his that one can never forget is what he called "The Tap on the Shoulder."

> . . . if you were walking down the street, and someone came up behind you and tapped you on the shoulder . . . what would you do? Naturally, you would turn around. Well, that is exactly what happens in the spiritual world. A man walks on through life—with the external call ringing in his ears, but with no response stirring in his heart, and then suddenly, without any warning, the Spirit taps him on the shoulder. The tap on the shoulder is the almighty power of God acting without help or hindrance . . . so as to produce a new creature, and to lead him into the particular work which God has for him.[6]

We're only a little over halfway through this book, but you may have already felt God's tap on your shoulder. If so, respond. Stop reading. Close the book, bow your head, and tell the Lord you have felt His tap—and you want to accept His gift of eternal life. Thank Him for giving you His Son, Jesus Christ.

If you have done that, Mr. Smith . . . you have just met your Substitute.

1. I can vividly recall conversations with individuals who resisted the idea that they needed a Savior. Instead, they pointed out to me all the good things they had been "doing," feeling that it would "balance out on the scales" when they stood before God. How might you respond to that line of reasoning? To what Scriptures might you direct such an individual? What illustrations could you use to help him or her get a grasp on the central truth of this chapter?

2. Become familiar with a simple gospel presentation that clearly illustrates how we cannot reach God through our own efforts. Booklets such as *Steps to Peace with God* (Billy Graham) and *The Four Spiritual Laws* (Campus Crusade for Christ) and *The Bridge to Life* (NavPress) are good examples. Choose one and buy several copies of it—keeping one handy in your wallet, pocket, or purse. You might meet a Mr. Smith or Miss Smith this week who needs to meet the Substitute.

3. I've quoted a bit from Romans 3 and 4 in this chapter. Carve out some time this week to get a feel for this liberating portion of Scripture. Read Romans 3-5, preferably in two different translations of Scripture, if you have them. (Reading these verses in either The Living Bible or the J. B. Phillips paraphrase is an added treat.) Ask the Lord to give you fresh insight as you trace this all important faith-root.

THE REMEDY
FOR OUR DISEASE

*S*omething historic happened off the coast of South China, on a high hill overlooking the harbor of Macao.

Portuguese settlers, many centuries ago, spent ten years building a massive cathedral on that hill. It seemed imperishable to passers-by. Many thought it would stand forever. But the awesome velocity of the winds from a typhoon literally reduced the thing to ruins. Everything except the front wall was leveled. The sheer wall, looking like one side of a massive fortress, stood alone against a deep blue sky. High on top of that wall stands a huge bronze cross, challenging the elements . . . almost as if to say to the winds: "You may tear down the other part of this cathedral, but you will not destroy my cross!"

In 1825 Sir John Bowring was in a terrible storm in that same harbor off the South China coast. Suffering shipwreck, he had no idea where to find land. Though it was in the light of day, the threatening skies and great swells blocked his ability to keep his bearings. If you've ever been in a storm at sea, you understand how easily one can lose perspective. Hanging onto the wreckage of his ship in the angry sea, sure to die, he caught sight of the bronze cross atop the old cathedral wall. The near-death rescue that followed was so dramatic, John Bowring was led to write several lines of poetry, expressing his gratitude to God for saving his life. Someone later put music to those words, and for over a hundred and fifty years God's people have sung Bowring's message, most of them knowing nothing of its origin:

In the cross of Christ I glory,
Tow'ring o'er the wrecks of time;
All the light of sacred story
Gathers round its head sublime.

When the sun of bliss is beaming
Light and love upon my way,
From the cross the radiance streaming
Adds more luster to the day.[1]

That which led to Bowring's rescue from the sea has led to our rescue from sin—the cross. But we need to understand that it isn't the cross itself that we honor. I know we refer to giving honor to the cross, and we are to lift up the message of the cross. But it isn't the literal cross we are to exalt. It isn't those original cross beams, those rugged, blood-soaked pieces of timber that stood on Golgotha centuries ago, that we honor. It is not the actual wood and nails. It is not its shape or it's location. It is the One who hung on it whom we honor. It is what the cross represents and the rescue it provides.

It was there our Substitute took our place. It was there the price for our sins was paid in full. It was the agony suffered on that cross that made the remedy for our disease effective.

No wonder so many of our Christian songs and hymns revolve around the subject of the cross. "Lift High the Cross." "At Calvary." "Am I a Soldier of the Cross?" "Down at the Cross Where My Savior Died." "The Old Rugged Cross." "When I Survey the Wondrous Cross." "Beneath the Cross of Jesus." "At the Cross." "Were You There When They Crucified My Lord?" "I Saw One Hanging on a Tree" . . . and so many more, all familiar hymns the church has sung for centuries.

But again, remember the cross is merely the symbol of what we honor. You may remember that in the Old Testament era there was a time that God told the wilderness people of Israel to look upon a bronze serpent if they suffered from snake bite. He promised them relief if they would only look at that metallic snake that Moses had made and lifted up high on a standard for all to see. Those who refused to look died from the poisonous venom. Once the bronze carving served its purpose, once all those people were delivered from death, the Israelites were to discard the piece of bronze.

But if you ever make a study of that bronze serpent, you'd be surprised to discover that rather than discarding it, they dragged it around the wilderness and on into the days of the kings and the prophets. In fact, it became a fetish. They burned incense to it. Nothing wrong with the bronze serpent, and certainly nothing wrong with the idea, but it had served its purpose, and they wouldn't give it up. Finally, King Hezekiah was led of God to break it into pieces.

He removed the high places and broke down the sacred pillars and cut down the Asherah. He also broke in pieces the bronze serpent that Moses had made, for until those days the sons of Israel burned incense to it; and it was called Nehushtan (2 Kings 18:4).

In the Hebrew tongue, Nehushtan means "a piece of brass." And that's all it was . . . nothing more than a piece of metal.

This may hit you pretty close to home, but the cross itself is a piece of wood . . . nothing more than that. Once it has served its purpose, the cross *itself* loses its significance. But the Savior who died on that cross lives on. And the redemption He provided continues to be significant and effective. He is our glory. He is the object of our adoration. So keep in mind, when we sing about the cross or when we speak of holding high the cross, that it is what that cross represents, the place where we gain our *spiritual* freedom. It was there our Substitute died in our place, providing the remedy for our spiritual disease.

A PREDICTION OF THE SUBSTITUTE

Since we are living in a day when animal sacrifices are not performed, it's necessary that we familiarize ourselves with what that meant. Chances are good that most people have never even seen such a thing . . . though in biblical times such sacrifices were observed on a daily basis.

Even though the idea of offering up sacrifices seems strange to us, it was as common to people in the early days as the courtroom scene is to us today. You can hardly read a newspaper without reading of some courtroom scene. It's a daily affair—like "Perry Mason" reruns.

The sacrifices in ancient days were also daily affairs. Blood flowed freely out of places of worship. Deep-red bloodstains marked altars of stone and wood. For centuries sheep could be heard gagging and dying as priests slit their throats and poured the blood over an altar. You see, in those days they had priests in places of worship, just as we have attorneys in courtrooms today. In those days they followed the laws of Moses, just as we today obey the laws of the state and of our federal government.

But that which tied people together with the living God was blood sacrifice. Because it was so important, I want to familiarize you with some things that perhaps you haven't thought of before—and certainly things you've never seen before.

In the Old Testament there are two great predictions of Jesus' death on the cross—lengthy predictions. One is in Psalm 22 and the other one is in Isaiah 53. Psalm 22 emphasizes His person. Isaiah 53 emphasizes His work. Psalm 22 helps us hear the agony of Christ on the cross. Isaiah 53 causes us to appreciate the completed work of Christ which was predicted by the prophet. Isaiah's words describe our condition as well as the solution to our dilemma.

Our Condition

> *Who has believed our message and to whom has the arm of the Lord been revealed? He grew up before him like a tender shoot, and like a root out of dry ground. He had no beauty or majesty to attract us to him, nothing in his appearance that we should desire him* (Isaiah 53:1-2, NIV).

What does all this mean? Among other things, there was nothing in Jesus' physique that was attractive. There was nothing in His person, as far as appearance was concerned. that caused Him to stand out from any one else in His day. He looked like any other adult Jew. You would not have been attracted to Him had you lived in His day. There was no visible aura around Him or halo above Him. When He walked across the sandy path He got dirty like everyone else. When He slept He slept like everyone else. When He arose in the morning, I would imagine His hair was mussed just like everyone else's. He had all of the marks of humanity just like we have. The difference was that He was perfect within. In nature, He was not only man, He was God. But you couldn't tell it from the outside. That's what the prophet means when He says, "His appearance was not such that we would be attracted to Him." With the next stroke of his pen, Isaiah goes much deeper and addresses the sacrifice He paid.

> *He was despised and forsaken of men, a man of sorrows, and acquainted with grief; and like one from whom men hide their face, He was despised, and we did not esteem Him* (v. 3).

The Amplified Bible says, ". . . we did not appreciate His worth."

There was no one in His day who realized the value of His person or the worth of His life. Oh, there were a few who believed and there were some who acknowledged that He certainly did the work of God. And there were some who believed He, in fact, was God. But most didn't have a true appreciation for Him that today, centuries later, many have. I've heard it said that in order for a person to be fully appreciated, to be seen as great, that individual needs to die and be removed from the earth for many, many years. Only then will some realize the person's greatness. So it is with many of our presidents and heroes, and so it is with Christ. Isaiah predicts, "We did not esteem Him."

The Solution to Our Dilemma

So much for His person . . . now notice His work.

> *Surely our griefs He Himself bore, and our sorrows He carried; yet we ourselves esteemed Him stricken, smitten of God, and afflicted (v. 4).*

Notice, it was *our* griefs and it was *our* sorrows that He bore on *our* behalf. Not His. The burden of the cross was that he took the weight of that which was not His and carried it to the full. That explains our need for the Substitute. And people's response to Him? No respect! Our depravity blinds us. Therefore, we do not value His worth as the Bearer of our sins. Read on—

> *But He was pierced through for our transgressions, He was crushed for our iniquities; the chastening for our well-being fell upon Him, and by His scourging we are healed (v. 5).*

Peter picks up that same thought in his first letter:

> *For you have been called for this purpose, since Christ also suffered for you, leaving you an example for you to follow in His steps, who committed no sin, nor was any deceit found in His mouth; and while being reviled, He did not revile in return; while suffering, He uttered no threats, but kept entrusting Himself to Him who judges righteously; and He Himself bore our sins in His body on the cross, that we might die to sin and live to righteousness; for by His wounds you were healed (1 Peter 2:21-24).*

Literally, the word "wounds" is singular. "For by His stripe, by His welt, His bruise. . . ." In other words, Peter pictures our Savior hanging on the cross as one massive welt, one awful bruise. He ought to know; he was there. The memory must have been a terrible one.

I will never forget an experience I had in elementary school when I was living in Houston. I was in the fifth grade at the time. Sitting in front of me was a classmate whose home life was nothing short of horrible. I'll never forget coming to school one day and seeing maroon-colored stains on the back of his shirt as he sat in front of me. I called his name and said, "You have something on your shirt." He didn't want to talk to me about it. When we went outside for recess and I mentioned it again, he grabbed me and said, "Come here, I wanna show you something." So we went into the boys' room and he lifted his shirt. I had never seen such bruises and welts in my life. He told me he had been beaten by his father that morning. I found out later that his dad was an alcoholic. And it wasn't uncommon for the boy to be battered by his dad. My stomach turned as I looked across his back. I couldn't stand what I saw. It was like one massive bruise, so sore he could hardly bear anything to touch it. Just the slight weight of his shirt on his back was painful. Now when I read, "by His stripe (by His welt, by His bruise) we are healed," I always think of that boy's back.

But remember, this wasn't simply Jesus' back—this was his body. That's why Isaiah describes Him as being pierced through, crushed, chastened, and scourged. Why? Why did that happen? The answer is in verse 6:

> All of us like sheep have gone astray, each of us has turned to his own way; but the Lord has caused the iniquity of us all to fall on Him.

We need to be careful not to overdo the physical agony of the cross to the exclusion of the spiritual impact. Actually, the physical pain was not the worst part. It was the awful separation that occurred between the Son and the Father when "all our sin was laid on Him." For the first and only time, in all of time, the Father and the Son were separated, because God the Father could not look upon sin as all of it fell on Him. He turned away from His Son, causing the Lord Jesus to scream, "*Eli, Eli, lama sabachthani*—My God, My God, why hast Thou forsaken Me?" (Matthew 27:46). At that moment the Lord Jesus felt the crushing weight of all mankind's iniquity.

An Explanation of the Sacrifice

Why was it necessary for that terrible moment to occur?

The explanation of His sacrificial death takes us back into the handbook of worship that the Jews used for centuries—the book of Leviticus, chapter 4. From this chapter I want to show you four stages that occurred when someone came to offer a sacrifice before God. Once we see this, Christ's sacrifice will become much clearer.

In ancient days, when a sinner found himself or herself in sin, broken in fellowship with God, it was essential that there be an animal sacrifice. Sometimes the sacrifice was with a goat, sometimes with a bull, sometimes with a heifer, or a sheep, or a dove, or even a pigeon. The details of such sacrifices are spelled out in this ancient book of worship used by the Jews and carried out by the priests—the Levites.

We find the process spelled out in four stages. *The first stage: The sinner brings an animal without defect to the altar.*

> *Then the Lord spoke to Moses, saying, "Speak to the sons of Israel, saying, 'If a person sins unintentionally in any of the things which the Lord has commanded not to be done, and commits any of them, if the anointed priest who sins so as to bring guilt on the people, then let him offer to the Lord a bull without defect as a sin offering for the sin he has committed'"* (Leviticus 4:1-3).

The plan was designed to be uncomplicated. As soon as one realized that sin had come into his life, intentional or unintentional, that individual knew that the sin had caused a separation from fellowship with God. To clear that up, an animal had to be brought to an altar. Not any animal, but an animal that was without defect. The animal would become a "sin offering."

The second stage: The sinner lays his hand on the animal.

> *And he shall bring the bull to the doorway of the tent of meeting before the Lord, and he shall lay his hand on the head of the bull . . .* (v. 4a).

According to Leviticus 4, this is the job of the priest who, in this case, is the sinner. He lays his hand upon the head of the animal. Why did he do that? The act symbolized the transfer of guilt from himself to the animal. I cannot explain how such a transfer could occur, only that that was what God required. So the animal is brought and hands are laid on the animal.

The third stage: The animal is to be killed.

> *But if he cannot afford a lamb, then he shall bring to the Lord his guilt offering for that in which he has sinned, two turtledoves or two young pigeons, one for a sin offering and the other for a burnt offering. And he shall bring them to the priest, who shall offer first that which is for the sin offering and shall nip its head at the front of its neck, but he shall not sever it. He shall also sprinkle some of the blood of the sin offering on the side of the altar, while the rest of the blood shall be drained out at the base of the altar: it is a sin offering* (Leviticus 5:7-9).

Have you ever read anything like that before in your life? "Just 'nip' the neck so there is a sprinkling of the blood."

Every detail was so clearly defined. They were even instructed on *how* to offer the sacrifice.

Why the emphasis on blood, you wonder? Let me show you the key verse in the book of Leviticus.

> *For the life of the flesh is in the blood, and I have given it to you on the altar to make atonement for your souls; for it is the blood by reason of the life that makes atonement* (17:11).

Look at the word "atonement." It's mentioned twice in this single verse. If you divide it into syllables, you come up with at-one-ment. God devised this plan: By the shedding of blood, two will be brought together as one. The blood of the animal will bring at-one-ment between humanity and God. The Hebrew term is *Chah-phar*. (Just think of the word "cover.") The blood would cover sin.

This might be a good time for you to turn to the glossary of terms at the back of the book and check the word "atonement" as well as "redemption." It was blood that bridged the gap.

Now back to Leviticus, chapter 4. We have seen the animal brought by the sinner. We have watched the hands of the priest being placed on the head of the animal. Next, the animal is slain at the altar.

The fourth stage: The blood is poured or sprinkled as God required.

> *Then the anointed priest is to take some of the blood of the bull and bring it to the tent of meeting, and the priest shall dip his finger in the blood, and sprinkle some of the blood seven times before the Lord, in front of the veil of the sanctuary. The priest shall also put some of the blood on the horns of the altar of fra-*

grant incense which is before the Lord, in the tent of meeting; and all the blood of the bull he shall pour out at the base of the altar of burnt offering which is at the doorway of the tent of meeting (Leviticus 4:5-7).

God required His priests to handle the blood ever so carefully . . . precisely according to His instructions. The details aren't important to us right now, but the significance of it is.

Since the earliest days, as these Jews connected at-one-ment with their Lord, there was a constant emphasis on blood and sacrifices. Sheep were slain at Passover by the thousands. The blood literally ran out of the city of Jerusalem. Priests were ceaselessly dealing with blood sacrifices. Day in and day out. *God required it.* That is why we must resist the modern tendency to remove the blood from our theology and our hymnody. Without blood, there is no remedy for sin.

But think of the treadmill of the ancient priestly task. Those of us who minister today know how, at times, some of our work can become a little monotonous. People on the outside usually don't think of it that way. But there are a few tiring and even repetitive assignments connected with the tasks of ministry. But nothing nearly *that* monotonous!

Just try to imagine killing the animals and pouring out the blood, killing more animals and pouring out more blood. Day after wearisome day . . . year after predictable year. Moffatt speaks of "the Levitical drudges"—because of the constant emphasis on the repetition of blood sacrifices.

But do you realize that these sacrifices never permanently took away sins? Never! The people found momentary relief from their guilt. They found temporary forgiveness. They went on their way rejoicing, which lasted for a while . . . but they'd soon be back with another animal.

And the focus? Sin. Sin. SIN! That's what caused Luther, when he finally turned the corner and realized the emptiness of his sin-repeating religion, to believe the good news concerning Christ. Prior to that it wasn't uncommon for the monk to be heard in his cell repeating, "Oh, my sin, my sin, my sin, my sin, my sin." The weight of that sin filled his thoughts. There was an awful desperation in his prayers, though he did everything he could to make it work.

Do you have any idea how many religious people still live like that today? They have the same frame of reference. They live their lives with no more hope than those who brought animal after animal and pail of blood after pail of blood, altar sacrifice after altar sacrifice after altar sacrifice. And yet those Old Testament sacrifices never took away sins, not permanently . . . not until Christ.

When Christ died on that cross and once for all poured out His blood, He cried out, "*Tetelestai!*" IT IS FINISHED! The Greek term has as its root, *Telos*, "complete, end." "It's over. It's done. It's complete!" The sacrifice of the Lamb of God was once for all. We will never have to offer another sacrifice. It's not needed. His death on the cross finished the task.

Now that isn't my idea, it is what Hebrews, chapter 10, tells us.

> *For the Law, since it has only a shadow of the good things to come and not the very form of things, can never by the same sacrifices year by year, which they offer continually, make perfect those who draw near. Otherwise, would they not have ceased to be offered, because the worshipers, having once been cleansed, would no longer have had consciousness of sins?* (vv. 1-2).

Had the ancient priests' sacrifices been permanently effective, they would have walked away smiling, "Praise God. That's it. I'm through with all the animals, through with the altar, through with all the blood sacrifices." But that never could be said.

> *But in those sacrifices there is a reminder of sins year by year. For it is impossible for the blood of bulls and goats to take away sins* (vv. 3-4).

The writer continues the thought:

> *By this will we have been sanctified through the offering of the body of Jesus Christ once for all. And every priest stands daily ministering and offering time after time the same sacrifices, which can never take away sins; but He, having offered one sacrifice for sins for all time, sat down at the right hand of God* (vv. 10-12).

Christ never again has to die! After His one-time sacrificial death, the Father said, "I am satisfied." The cross payment satisfied the Father's demands against sin. How do we know He's satisfied? He raised His Son from the grave. He brought Him back from death. The resurrection was God's "Amen" to Christ's, "It is finished." The theological word here is *propitiation*. (That's another good word to look up in the glossary.) What a mighty, liberating thought! The

Father is completely satisfied. The cross absorbed all our sin and all the Father's wrath.

A practical message in all of this is that if God is satisfied with the death of His Son, and if I am in Christ, He is satisfied with me!

I don't have to live under the demanding enslavement of working, begging, pleading, fearing, bargaining, or paying penance to find favor with my God. In Christ, the Christian is as safe and secure as the Son before the Father. As one man once said:

> Nearer, nearer,
> Nearer, I cannot be,
> For in the person of His Son,
> I am as near as He.

A DECLARATION OF THE SAVIOR

The declaration of the Savior is found in the final verse of 2 Corinthians 5, which we looked at toward the end of the previous chapter.

He made Him who knew no sin to be sin on our behalf, that we might become the righteousness of God in Him (v. 21).

Remember the laying of hands on the animal? God the Father, as it were, placed His hands on His Son and said, "The sins of all mankind are transferred to You. At this moment You bear those sins." And He did. He did it on our behalf. That's the wonderful part of this message. He who knew no sin was made sin on our behalf. Christ, the spotless Lamb, took all our sin and guilt at the cross and cleared our debt. Why? "That we might become the righteousness of God in Him." I call that great news. Thankfully, it is all done. The work of salvation is finished work. It is provided for me as a sinner if I will simply come to Christ.

It is as if the Savior looks each one of us in the eyes and says, "I've paid your debt in full at the cross. If you come to Me, I will give you perfect righteousness."

My friend, Cliff Barrows, the song leader of the Billy Graham Crusade ministry, has ministered to many of us for years. We love him and his wife dearly. It is easy to forget that Cliff is also a husband and faithful father. Something once occurred in Cliff's home life that illustrates what I've been trying to say in this chapter. Evangelist Billy Graham relates the story this way:

My friend and associate, Cliff Barrows, told me this story about bearing punishment. He recalled the time when he took the punishment for his children when they had disobeyed.

"They had done something I had forbidden them to do. I told them if they did the same thing again I would have to discipline them. When I returned from work and found that they hadn't minded me, the heart went out of me. I just couldn't discipline them."

Any loving father can understand Cliff's dilemma. Most of us have been in the same position. He continued with the story: "Bobby and Bettie Ruth were very small. I called them into my room, took off my belt and my shirt, and with a bare back, knelt down at the bed. I made them both strap me with the belt ten times each. You should have heard the crying! From them, I mean! They didn't want to do it. But I told them the penalty had to be paid and so through their sobs and tears they did what I told them."

Cliff smiled when he remembered the incident. "I must admit I wasn't much of a hero. It hurt. I haven't offered to do that again, but I never had to spank them again, either, because they got the point. We kissed each other when it was over and prayed together."

In that infinite way that staggers our hearts and minds, we know that Christ paid the penalty for our sins, past, present, and future.

That is why He died on the cross.[2]

And that is why, after his historic rescue off the South China coast, Sir John Bowring could write, "In the Cross of Christ I Glory."

1. Read, contemplate, and *personalize* Isaiah 53 in a good paraphrase, such as The Living Bible. Can you visualize the Lord Jesus being crushed and weighed down by *your* sins? Find an "alone place" . . . an unhurried moment . . . and thank Him for dying for you so that you can experience daily "newness of life" (Romans 6:4).

2. Imagine the kind of letter you might write to someone who had risked his or her own life to plunge into a swollen river and rescue you from drowning. Have you ever taken time to thank the Lord Jesus for literally laying down His life so that you could experience salvation and eternal life? Knock the rust off of your pen once again, open up your notebook, and write a letter of heartfelt gratitude and praise to your Savior for what He did for *you*.

3. Are there any "symbols" in your home—perhaps a cross, a figurine, a family Bible, or an artist's conception of Jesus that might draw away the adoration, attention, and honor that belongs to the Lord alone? Make a careful evaluation and deal decisively with that which could potentially become a stumbling block to you.

The Return of Christ

"I anticipate my Lord's promised return, which could occur at any moment."

HIS COMING IS SURE...
ARE YOU?

he return of Jesus Christ
never fails to create mixed emotions. For those who are ready for it,
there is always a sense of comfort and anticipation. A feeling not unlike the Delta Airlines motto—"We're ready when you are." For
those who are not ready for it (or do not believe in it), there is a mixture of responses. Some are irritated. Some are intimidated. A few
are afraid, maybe a little panicked. Most simply refuse to think
about it. But no one can remain neutral on the subject.

These thoughts remind me of the true story of what happened to
a friend of mine many years ago before he became a Christian. He
was hitchhiking his way across the United States. Around dusk one
evening, when it looked like rain, he was hoping for a car to pull
over before the showers began to fall. Sure enough, a car swerved
over to his side of the road, the door flew open, and he heard the
driver say, "Hop in." So my friend hopped in, slammed the door
and they took off just as the rain started to fall.

Although daylight was rapidly fading, my friend could just make
out the words on a small poster that had been stuck to the
dashboard—

WARNING, IN THE EVENT OF CHRIST'S RETURN
THIS DRIVER WILL DISAPPEAR;
THIS CAR WILL SELF-DESTRUCT

Then in bold, red letters, four final words:

YOU BETTER GIT READY

Years later as he was relating the story to me, I asked him how he felt that eerie evening when he read those words. Smiling, he said, "Well, as a matter of fact, it was spooky! I didn't know whether to write my will, to pray, or to jump. But I remember doing two things. First, I kept my door unlocked (as if that were going to help); and second, I engaged the driver in nonstop conversation. I figured he wouldn't suddenly disappear if we kept on talking together."

Isn't it funny how superstitious people can be about future things? And isn't it amazing what decisions people make, thinking that "somehow things will just work out" if they stay close to the right people? It calls to mind the lady who wanted to marry four different men in her lifetime. She said each one would help her with the four things she needed most. First, she wanted to marry a banker. Second, a movie star. Next, a clergyman. And finally, a funeral director. When asked why, she answered, "One for the money, two for the show, three to get ready, and four to go!"

Back to my original story. The driver of the car considered Christ's coming a solid comfort, but the rider viewed it as something spooky . . . a fearful thought. Again, it is almost impossible to remain neutral regarding this future event.

EXTREMES THAT BLOCK OUR BALANCE

Fanatical Intensity

Some Christians drop straight off the deep end when prophetic subjects come up. They almost "go nuts" over the subject. When that happens, they seem to lose their practical equilibrium. Such fanatical intensity invariably drives others away as these well-meaning folks overreact to the teaching of prophecy.

Some of the telltale signs? They begin to read prophecy into most newspaper articles, current events, and certainly each major disaster or calamity. They are often surprised that you don't see it as clearly as they do. What's worse, their neurotic intensity creates within them a lack of interest in the here and now. Nothing—absolutely nothing—is more important to them than the then and there.

Often, they tend to live rather sheltered and/or irresponsible lives. Some don't mind increasing their indebtedness. After all, their soon departure from Planet Earth provides the perfect escape from financial responsibility! They don't worry too much about today's assignments, either, because they are so caught up in the tomorrow of God's plan.

The ultimate extremists would be those who set specific dates, then quit their jobs and mooch off others as they wait for the Lord's return.

Many years ago I found a big tract stuck under the windshield wiper on my car. I remember it well. It was one of those four-page, tiny-print jobs. Almost needed a magnifying glass to read the stuff. I can't recall how many dozens of points there were that this person (who happened to be a member of a religious cult) tried to communicate. But his logic was strange and the verses he quoted were twisted and wrenched from their context.

What caught my eye was the date that was set . . . January 31, 1974! Some kind of comet with a blazing tail of fire would bring a "baptism of fire" that would cause a wave of insanity and suicide throughout the earth shortly before Christ returned . . . and we wouldn't be able to escape it if we remained in the United States. We in America needed to be prepared by moving to Canada or Mexico or Puerto Rico or even Hawaii. (It's always safer in Hawaii, it seems.) Everything was sure to end January 31, 1974. Well, on February 1, 1974, I wrote to the address that appeared on the bottom of the tract. I asked a few pointed questions, but I never got an answer. Maybe they were all in Hawaii by then.

Frankly, I call that sort of stuff "prophecy gone to seed." Too much prophetic intensity gets dangerously close to personal insanity.

No matter how much we may love the Lord Jesus Christ and believe in His Word, we need to remember that there is still a life to be lived and responsibilities to be faced. And to cop out because Christ is coming is not only poor practicality, it's abominable theology. Never once in Scripture is irresponsibility excused on the basis of one's confidence in Christ's return. Anticipation is one thing. Blind fanaticism is quite another.

Theological Ignorance

The other extreme to the far left is theological ignorance. Maybe "personal indifference" would be another way of putting it. The former problem is one of being over-involved and super-intense. But the indifferent individual sees no reason at all to be alert. In fact, he seriously questions that there will even be such a thing as a Second Coming. A person like that has no interest in evangelism (I have never seen an exception), because there is an absence of urgency. He understands neither God's overall world program nor specifically the imminent (at-any-moment) return of Christ.

There's something about Christ's soon return that stirs up our urgency and keeps us involved. God planned it that way. Anticipating the Savior activates our involvement in today's needs.

C. S. Lewis writes:

> Hope is one of the theological virtues. This means that a continual looking forward to the eternal world is not (as some modern people think) a form of escapism or wishful thinking, but one of the things a Christian is meant to do. It does not mean that we are to leave the present world as it is. If you read history, you will find that the Christians who did most for the present world were just those who thought most of the next. . . . It is since Christians have largely ceased to think of the other world that they have become so ineffective in this. Aim at heaven and you will get earth "thrown in": aim at earth and you will get neither.[1]

Needed Balance

Let's be neither insane nor indifferent about His return. What we need is a balance. We need to be informed and aware, thinking it could occur at any moment, but carrying out our lives as responsibly as if His return would not be for another two or three generations.

In other chapters we have examined Peter's words. Let's look again, this time at his second letter. In this section he writes as an eyewitness of the Lord Jesus. He is building to a climax: the return of the Lord.

> *For we did not follow cleverly devised tales when we made known to you the power and coming of our Lord Jesus Christ, but we were eyewitnesses of His majesty. For when He received honor and glory from God the Father, such an utterance as this was made to Him by the Majestic Glory, "This is My beloved Son with whom I am well-pleased"—and we ourselves heard this utterance made from heaven when we were with Him on the holy mountain. And so we have the prophetic word made more sure, to which you do well to pay attention as to a lamp shining in a dark place,*

until the day dawns and the morning star arises in your hearts
(2 Peter 1:16-19).

Is that a relevant word? You bet! "I have seen Him. I have heard the
voice from heaven. I have listened to His teachings with my own
ears and we have a more sure word. You'd do well to listen up."

Next, glance at chapter 3, verses 3 and 4. He writes perhaps to
skeptical ears as he says:

> *Know this first of all, that in the last days mockers will come with
> their mocking, following after their own lusts, and saying,
> "Where is the promise of His coming? For ever since the fathers
> fell asleep, all continues just as it was from the beginning of crea-
> tion."*

Does that sound like something you heard in your science classes?
Did they teach you that in your undergraduate or graduate studies?
Probably so. It's called the theory of uniformitarianism. Since the
beginning of time to this present day there has been the unfolding,
the evolving, of an *uninterrupted* flow of events in history.

"Wrong," says Peter. "They are wrong. They systematically overlook something that intercepted time—the deluge, the universal
flood."

> *For when they maintain this, it escapes their notice that by the
> word of God the heavens existed long ago and the earth was
> formed out of water and by water, through which the world at that
> time was destroyed, being flooded with water* (vv. 5-6).

"They overlook a very important fact," says Peter. "They forget that
this earth, as it was created by God and as history was unfolding,
was destroyed. They ignore the fact that in the middle of the movement of time, God stepped in and brought a flood. And it caught
the attention of everyone on this earth—this deluge." To this day
most scholars overlook (or, in some cases explain away) the possibility of a universal flood.

Suddenly, Peter jumps to the future.

> *But the present heavens and earth by His word are being reserved
> for fire, . . .* (v. 7a).

Before, it was destroyed by water. Someday in the future it will be
destroyed by fire.

. . . kept for the day of judgment and destruction of ungodly men. But do not let this one fact escape your notice, beloved, that with the Lord one day is as a thousand years, and a thousand years as one day. The Lord is not slow about His promise, as some count slowness, but is patient toward you, not wishing for any to perish but for all to come to repentance (vv. 7b-9).

The Lord is going to return. We need to "git ready." He doesn't wish for any to perish. I call that clear, specific, and reliable information. When it comes to balance, that says it well. Let's not mistake our Lord's current patience for permanent absence. He *is* coming back.

PREDICTIONS THAT AFFIRM OUR ASSURANCE

Before looking at other verses of Scripture, let me take you on a brief safari. To begin with, here are some facts about prophecy that will surprise most people:

- One out of every 30 verses in the Bible mentions the subject of Christ's return or the end of time.
- Of the 216 chapters in the New Testament, there are well over 300 references to the return of Jesus Christ.
- Only 4 of the 27 New Testament books fail to mention Christ's return.
- That means one-twentieth of the entire New Testament is dedicated to the subject of our Lord's return.
- In the Old Testament, such well-known and reliable men of God as Job, Moses, David, Isaiah, Jeremiah, Daniel, and most of the minor prophets, fixed at least part of their attention on the Lord's return.
- Christ spoke of His return often, especially after He had revealed His death. He never did so in vague or uncertain terms.
- Those who lived on following His teaching, who established the churches and wrote the Scriptures in the first century frequently mentioned His return in their preaching and in their writings.

After those apostles left the earth that message of Christ's return did not die. On the contrary, it found its way into the Nicene Creed, into the Athanasian Creed, and into the thirty-nine Articles of the

Church of England, the fourth of which says, "He ascended into heaven and there sitteth until He returns to judge all men at the last day." The Augsburg Confession deals with it somewhat at length. The familiar Apostle's Creed, repeated at many churches in their liturgy of worship, includes the statement, "from thence He shall come to judge the quick and the dead."

I remember repeating those words as a little boy in a church where our family worshiped. I wondered who "the quick" would be at that time. I understood "the dead." I didn't grasp that *quick* is the Old English term for "living." "He will come to judge the living and the dead."

The Bible teaches it. The Lord Jesus stood upon its truths. The apostles declared it and wrote about it. The creeds include it and affirm it. Quite obviously, His return has not been considered an insignificant issue through the centuries. But the strange thing is that many Christians in this generation either ignore it or are somehow confused by it. Too bad. It is a marvelous truth that only gains significance as we move closer to death.

A few days ago I had a part in the burial of a twenty-one-year-old man who died in an automobile accident. It was a heartrending service. I thought of Christ's return as I looked at the casket. The thought gave me reassuring hope. Only a few days later, one of our long-time church "saints," a godly, one-hundred-year-old woman, passed into the Lord's presence. And when I heard that news, immediately thoughts of Jesus' return flashed through my mind:

> *For the Lord Himself will descend from heaven with a shout, with the voice of the archangel, and with the trumpet of God; and the dead in Christ shall rise first. Then we who are alive and remain shall be caught up together with them in the clouds to meet the Lord in the air, and thus we shall always be with the Lord* (1 Thessalonians 4:16-17).

Whether young or old, those who pass into eternity have the same truth to claim . . . and so do those of us who remain. It is something you can cling to when it seems as though all hell has broken loose in your life. When the events of your days seem out of control, having neither rhyme nor reason. Deep within you are reminded that the end has not yet come. When He comes it will all make sense.

Let's take a moment to look briefly at several verses of Scripture that underscore His soon coming.

Matthew 24 is a great place to start. Jesus is speaking:

> *Therefore be on the alert, for you do not know which day your Lord is coming. But be sure of this, that if the head of the house had known at what time of the night the thief was coming, he would have been on the alert and would not have allowed his house to be broken into. For this reason you be ready too; for the Son of Man is coming at an hour when you do not think He will* (vv. 42-44).

> *But when the Son of Man comes in His glory, and all the angels with Him, then He will sit on His glorious throne* (25:31).

Notice the words "when" and "will"—not "if," but "when" . . . not "may," but "will." There was no question in Jesus' mind.

From Matthew 25, turn to Mark, chapter 8.

> *For whoever wishes to save his life shall lose it; and whoever loses his life for My sake and the gospel's shall save it. For what does it profit a man to gain the whole world, and forfeit his soul? For what shall a man give in exchange for his soul? For whoever is ashamed of Me and My words in this adulterous and sinful generation, the Son of Man will also be ashamed of him when He comes in the glory of His Father with the holy angels"* (vv. 35-38).

This kind of teaching must have stunned the disciples. They had anticipated the establishment of Jesus' earthly kingdom then and there. They expected it to be in motion before the end of their generation, when Jesus would be ruling as King of kings and Lord of lords. They envisioned themselves as charter members in His kingdom band. With great delight they would witness the overthrow of Rome and Israel's numerous enemies. What a hope!

But then one dark night in a second-story flat, along some street in the city of Jerusalem, Jesus ate His last meal with them. There, he unfolded the startling truth that His death was only hours away. They must have wanted to stop their ears from hearing Him say, "I'm going to leave you. I'm going back to My Father."

Looking into the eyes of those disillusioned men who must have felt a bit orphaned, Jesus said:

> *Let not your heart be troubled; believe in God, believe also in Me. In My Father's house are many dwelling places; if it were not so, I would have told you; for I go to prepare a place for you* (John 14:1-2).

It is very important that you understand heaven, our eternal destiny, is an *actual place*. It isn't a misty dream or a floating fantasy. Don't let any of the mystical religions confuse you. Heaven is reality. Literal real estate which He is preparing for His own. Jesus says so in the next statement.

> And if I go and prepare a place for you, I will come again, and receive you to Myself; that where I am, there you may be also (v. 3).

The body of every believer that now resides in a casket, every believer torn apart by ravenous beasts, or by the elements of the sea, or by warfare, or awful murder will be received by Christ at His return. Regardless of the condition of that body, the Lord Jesus says, "I *will* come again, and I *will* receive you unto Myself." That's a direct promise from His lips. Most of those men who heard His words that evening died horrible deaths. More than one of them were sawn in two. Some were torn apart by wild beasts. Yet their Lord said, in effect, "I will come again, and I'll receive you unto Myself. The condition of your body doesn't concern Me. This promise stands firm."

Shortly thereafter Jesus went to the cross. When He died He was placed in a tomb. Three days later, He emerged in bodily form from the tomb, victorious over death. He is the only one thus far who has ever been resurrected—the only one to come back to this earth in a glorified condition. So He has overcome death. In light of that, it shouldn't surprise us that He is able to bring us from the grave when He returns.

Forty days after His resurrection He stood on a mountain with His followers. While there, just before He ascended to heaven, the same subject was brought up again—His return.

> And so when they had come together, they were asking Him, saying, "Lord, is it at this time You are restoring the kingdom to Israel?" He said to them, "It is not for you to know times or epochs which the Father has fixed by His own authority; but you shall receive power when the Holy Spirit has come upon you, and you shall be My witnesses both in Jerusalem, and in all Judea and Samaria, and even to the remotest part of the earth." And after He had said these things, He was lifted up while they were looking on, and a cloud received Him out of their sight (Acts 1:6-9).

Wow! Can you *imagine* that moment? As they watched, Jesus was lifted up out of sight. We think we're pretty hot stuff because we can put people in a rocket and send them into an orbit around the earth a few times, then bring them back. Yet with no physical assistance, with nothing around Him or near Him, He was lifted up from the earth—whoosh!—and went directly through the clouds back to heaven. His followers did just what you and I would have done— they stood with mouths open, gazing intently into the skies.

> *And as they were gazing intently into the sky while He was departing, behold, two men in white clothing stood beside them; and they also said, "Men of Galilee, . . . (v. 10-11a).*

I want to write the following words to people who are preoccupied with Christ's return, spending most of their time looking up, as if they had nothing else to do—

> *. . . "Men of Galilee, why do you stand looking into the sky? This Jesus, who has been taken up from you into heaven, will come in just the same way as you have watched Him go into heaven."*

He is coming back. Looking up won't bring Him any sooner. We're never told simply to stand around gazing up to heaven. In fact, we're told *not* to do that. We aren't even commanded to do a lot of talking about it. There's a bigger job to be done than sitting around discussing the details of His return!

In the last book of the Bible, Revelation, Jesus is being quoted by John who writes these last words:

> *I, Jesus, have sent My angel to testify to you these things for the churches. I am the root and the offspring of David, the bright morning star. . . . He who testifies to these things says, "Yes, I am coming quickly." Amen. Come, Lord Jesus (22:16, 20).*

SCRIPTURES THAT DESCRIBE OUR DESTINY

So much for a general overview. There are two passages that are worth turning back to and getting a little closer focus on. First Corinthians 15:50-58 is the first and 1 Thessalonians 4:13-18 is the second. Both of these scriptures describe our destiny. The Corinthian passage emphasizes the *changes* that will come over us when Christ returns for His own. The Thessalonian passage emphasizes the *order of events* that will occur in the future.

First Corinthians 15:50-58

After developing a thorough statement on resurrection, the apostle Paul presents a transition in verse 50.

Now I say this, brethren, that flesh and blood cannot inherit the kingdom of God; nor does the perishable inherit the imperishable.

Understand what he means. He is talking to those of us who are earthlings, people who have been earthbound all our lives. We are people in the process of dying. How many of us in our fifties can remember our younger days when we were in our twenties? We felt differently and we certainly looked differently. Now there are physical signs on our bodies that mark us as aging people. We all have loved ones in their seventies and eighties, maybe even their nineties, who certainly reveal "perishable" mortality. In order for these bodies of ours to last throughout eternity in what is here called "the kingdom of God," *there must be a change* so that our bodies are made ageless. There must be some kind of molecular reconstruction within us that prepares us for eternity. Our bodies must be changed into a glorified state. All these changes will equip our bodies to last eternally. Since our future will be a bodily existence in heaven, we must undergo bodily changes. Remember now, our eternal existence is not simply spirit existence, but bodily existence. So Paul emphasizes our future changes in the next three verses:

Behold, I tell you a mystery; we shall not all sleep, but we shall all be changed, in a moment, in the twinkling of an eye, at the last trumpet; for the trumpet will sound, and the dead will be raised imperishable, and we shall be changed. For this perishable must put on the imperishable, and this mortal must put on immortality (vv. 51-53, emphasis mine).

Paul calls this revelation "a mystery." In our day, a *mystery* suggests something that is complicated, like a riddle, hard to unravel and difficult to solve . . . complex. But a mystery in Paul's day (*Musterion*) was not something that was complex, but something that was more like our word "secret." It's like he was writing, "Listen, I want to tell you a secret." There's a difference. Once someone tells you a secret, it isn't complicated. All you need is the information.

Here's the thought: "Behold, I want to reveal something that has been a secret up to now . . . something you will find mentioned nowhere else in God's revelation prior to this revelation." What is that secret? Namely this: There will be a generation alive at the time Christ comes back . . . and those living believers, at the time Christ returns, will be instantly changed and taken back to be with Him forever. Not only will the dead be raised and changed, but those believers who are alive will also be changed.

> But when this perishable will have put on the imperishable, and this mortal will have put on immortality, then will come about the saying that is written, "Death is swallowed up in victory. O death, where is your victory? O death, where is your sting?" (vv. 54-55).

Paul didn't get that from Shakespeare; Shakespeare got that from Paul! Death will have won its final victory. When we are taken up, the grim reaper will hang up his scythe. Finally, at long last, Death will bite the dust. Up to now it may seem he is king. Death visits every home. He steps into the life of every person who has ever lived. No matter how great or how cruel, how good or how bad, death comes. And as he is often pictured, the grim reaper cuts everyone down to size. Euripedes the poet was right, "Death is the debt we all must pay." But the marvelous good news is that when our final change at Christ's coming occurs, death will never again have charge of us. At that glorious moment we shall begin a timeless, ageless existence. For the next few moments, meditate on the closing words in this chapter.

> The sting of death is sin, and the power of sin is the law; but thanks be to God, who gives us the victory through our Lord Jesus Christ. Therefore, my beloved brethren, be steadfast, immovable, always abounding in the work of the Lord, knowing that your toil is not in vain in the Lord (1 Corinthians 15:56-58).

How often I quote these words to myself!

First Thessalonians 4:13-18

Remember now, we have nothing to worry about regarding the condition of the body when death occurs. *We shall be changed.* The One who made our bodies from nothing will have no difficulty making us again, even from little bits and pieces if necessary. He'll be able to put us all together.

Let me point out four observations from this passage.

1. *We are to be informed.*

But we do not want you to be uninformed, brethren, about those who are asleep . . . (v. 13a).

As I have said all along, ignorance is not bliss. The Lord doesn't smile on us when, as we think about the future, we say, "Well, actually, nobody can know for sure. We just hope things work out all right." That's an ignorant and incorrect response. He *wants* us to be informed and knowledgeable. We are to know what's in front of us—at least the broad brush strokes of His plan. Knowing the future gives us confidence in the present.

2. *We are not to grieve as those without hope.*

But we do not want you to be uninformed, brethren, about those who are asleep, that you may not grieve, as do the rest who have no hope (v. 13).

Death brings sorrow. Sorrow brings tears. Tears are part of the grieving process. God never tells us, "Don't cry. Don't grieve." He says we are not to grieve *as those who have no hope.* I am saddened when I see parents, well-meaning though they may be, who correct their children for crying because a loved one dies. Crying is the most natural response when we lose someone or something important to us. We have every reason to grieve and to be sad, but our grief is not as the hopeless when they grieve. You see, we have an answer beyond the grave. They do not. It is this hope that ultimately brings comfort.

3. *We are to face death without fear.*

For if we believe that Jesus died and rose again, even so God will bring with Him those who have fallen asleep in Jesus (1 Thessalonians 4:14).

Now the reason Christ's own resurrection is so important is because we can anticipate rising as He did. Had He not come back from beyond, we couldn't expect to either. I often think of the followers of some guru. They die. They look next to them in the grave and—there's their guru! Their great spiritual leader. He's still there. If he didn't get out himself, then I ask you how is he going to get *them* out? But no one will ever see a dead Jesus. Why? He has been raised. He has gone beyond the grave. His tomb is empty. Because He died and rose again He is able to give us an answer to sin, death, and the grave. If we believe in Him, then we are ready to be taken with Him. He will bring us along with all those who have fallen asleep in Jesus. Because He lives, all fear is gone!

4. *We're to know the order of events.*

> *For this we say to you by the word of the Lord, that we who are alive, and remain until the coming of the Lord, shall not precede those who have fallen asleep. For the Lord Himself will descend from heaven with a shout, with the voice of the archangel, and with the trumpet of God; and the dead in Christ shall rise first. Then we who are alive and remain shall be caught up together with them in the clouds to meet the Lord in the air, and thus we shall always be with the Lord* (vv. 15-17).

Here is the overall order of events: "The Lord Himself will descend from heaven." That's *first.* I like the way Phillips renders it:

> One word of command, one shout from the Archangel, one blast from the trumpet of God. . . .

Imagine the scene! Perhaps all those things will come simultaneously . . . in one great voice, one grand sound. I smile as I write these words. They never fail to excite me!

Next, "the dead in Christ shall rise first."

Then, "we who are alive and remain shall be caught up together with them. . . ."

With whom? The dead who have been changed, who have been raised ahead of us.

Finally, we—

> . . . *shall be caught up together with them in the clouds to meet the Lord in the air, and thus we shall always be with the Lord* (v. 17b).

It is my personal conviction that our Lord Jesus will come for us in the sky—in the clouds. Following that reunion in the air, there will occur on this earth a time of awful judgment, a time of unrestrained pain and great tribulation, following which our Savior will return to this earth and establish the fulfillment of His millennial promises to Israel, a literal one-thousand-year reign over this earth as He serves as King of kings and Lord of lords. My personal belief is that the return of the Lord Jesus for His own, as described in Thessalonians and in Corinthians, is *prior* to that awful time of tribulation on the earth and *prior* to His establishment of a literal kingdom on earth over which He reigns as King.

This pegs me as a pretribulational premillenialist! But don't let all that make you nervous. I still have great fellowship with those in other camps. Not everybody does, however. I heard about a guy who was so premillennial he wouldn't even eat Post Toasties!

Now the most important thing for you to understand is that *He is coming again*. And, secondly, that *it is a comfort to you* because you have believed in Him. Be sure that the one you believe in has conquered death, otherwise he won't get you into heaven. Hell awaits you. The only way to get beyond the grave and into the Lord's presence is to place your trust on One who has gone before you and has paved the way.

ACTIONS THAT REVEAL OUR READINESS

I think there are at least three ways we reveal our readiness.

First, we continue to walk by faith. Rather than walking by sight and shaping our lives on the basis of the visible, we walk by faith.

Second, we continue to live in peace. We view the present and our future not with panic but with peace. We don't live worried, hassled lives.

And *third*, we rely on hope. The hope that gets me through the tests on this earth is the same hope that will get me through the grave at death, because the One in whom I have believed has gone before me. He is preparing a place for me. He is the embodiment of my hope. Because He lives, we shall live also. The secret of escape from the prison of this body and the pain of this planet is knowing the One who can guarantee our getting beyond the grave.

A recent "Alfred Hitchcock" TV episode showed the flip-side to this sure and certain hope. As you might expect, the point was made in a rather chilling way.

There was this rather wicked, two-faced woman who murdered an individual. And though she had often done wrong on previous occasions and had always gotten away with it, the court found her guilty in this case and the judge sentenced her to life in prison. Even though she screamed in the judge's face and announced that she would escape from any prison they put her into, they sent her away.

She took that infamous bus ride to the prison. En route, she noticed something that became part of her escape plan. She saw an old man, an inmate, covering up a grave outside the prison walls. She realized the only way to get out of the prison was to know someone who had the key to the gate. The only one who did was the old man who assisted in the burial of those who died within the walls. Actually, he built the caskets as well as placed the remains in each casket. His job included rolling the casket on an old cart to the grave-site outside the wall and then lowering it into the hole and covering it up with dirt.

The old man was going blind. He needed cataract surgery, but he had no money to pay for it. She told him that it would be worth his while if he would help her escape.

"No ma'am, I can't do that."

"Oh, yes you can," she insisted. "I have all the money you need outside these walls to pay for your cataract surgery. And if you hope to have that operation, then you help me out of this place."

He reluctantly agreed.

Here was the plan: The next time she heard the toll of the bell, which signaled the death of an inmate, she would slip down to his workroom where he made the caskets. She was to locate the casket in which the old man had placed the corpse and then (if you can imagine!) secretly slide herself into that same casket and pull the top down tightly. Early the next morning the old man would roll her, along with the corpse in the casket, out to the place of burial, drop it into the hole, and dump the dirt on it. The next day he was to come back, uncover the grave, pry the top loose, and set her free. Perfect plan. Almost.

Late one night she heard the deep toll of the bell . . . someone had died. This was her moment! She secretly slid off her cot, made her way down an eerie hallway, and, looking into the dimly lit room, she saw the casket. Without hesitation, she lifted the lid and in the darkness slipped into the box and, after squeezing in beside the corpse, she pulled the lid down tightly.

Within a matter of hours she could feel the wheels rolling as they were making their way to the gravesite. She smiled as the casket was placed in the hole. She began to hear the clumps of dirt as they hit the top of the casket. Before long, she was sealed beneath the earth—still smiling.

Silence followed. She could hardly contain her excitement. Time began to drag. The next day came and passed into the night without the old man showing up. By now she has broken into a cold sweat. "Where was he? What could possibly have gone wrong? Why hadn't he shown up?"

In a moment of panic she lights a match and glances at the corpse next to her. You guessed it—*it is the old man himself* who had died!

Slowly, the camera lifts from the gravesite, and all you can hear is the hollow, wailing cry of the woman who will never get out of the grave.

I thought of the proverb, "There is a way that seems right unto a man, but the end thereof are the ways of death." She thought she could escape death's jaws, but the one in whom she had placed her hopes was, himself, a victim of the very thing she dreaded most. She trusted in the wrong man.

One day Jesus Christ will come for us. His coming is sure, and He will keep His promise. Since He has conquered death, He will get us beyond those jaws as well.

If you are ready, the thought of His coming is a comfort. If not, it's a dread. The secret of escape is being sure you know the One who can get us out of the grave. His coming is sure . . . are you?

1. The moviemakers and booksellers of the world throw around lines like "non-stop excitement" or, "incredible action" or, "gripping narrative." Well, maybe. But compared to 1 Thessalonians 4:13-18, their stuff is about as exciting as reading the telephone book or watching reruns of "Mr. Roger's Neighborhood." Talk about high drama! Take a walk outside, weather permitting, with your New Testament in hand. Read again this startling glimpse into the future—*your* future. Let your eyes sweep the skies. Feel the thunder and joy and awe. Remind yourself that this experience could happen at any moment—even before you return from your walk . . . or draw your next breath. Let your Lord know that you are watching for His return.

2. It's good to contemplate our Lord's sudden descent from heaven . . . and yet Scripture urges us to do more than stand around staring at the sky. The last words of the Thessalonian passage above urge us to "*comfort* one another with these words." The Greek term Paul uses here for "comfort" is translated as "encourage" in 1 Thessalonians 3:2. It's from the Greek terms *Para*, meaning "beside, alongside," and *Kaleo* "to call." *Called alongside*. In one of my earlier books I noted that this implies more than a shallow sympathy card with rhyming words and gold-glitter greeting. It is eternally more than a "slap on the back" or a quick "cheer up" bit of advice. Paul was writing to a group of people who were enduring intense pressure and persecution for their faith. And he's saying, "Listen, come alongside one another and *encourage* each other with this thought—Jesus is coming back! We'll meet Him—together—in the clouds!" Watch for an opportunity in the coming days to come alongside a struggling fellow believer with the encouragement contained in this passage. When it arrives, comfort!

3. Memorize 1 John 3:2-3. Verse 3 says: "Everyone who has this hope fixed on Him purifies himself, just as He is pure." What does it mean, in a very practical way, for you to live with your hope *fixed* on Him? What impact should the knowledge of His imminent return have on the way you live? Why is this so? Write about these thoughts in your notebook.

UNTIL HE RETURNS...
WHAT?

his is a book on doctrine . . .
the major doctrines taught in the Bible. As I have written or implied
all along, it isn't a theoretical, exhaustive textbook but more of a
practical guide to help people focus on and think through their
faith. This approach allows me the wobble room I need to deal with
sideline issues that relate to a doctrine, though they do not necessarily fall into a major doctrinal category.

Looking back, for example, we have not only thought about the
doctrine of the Bible, but also the importance of discernment as we
study the Bible and the value of handling the Bible with accuracy.
Furthermore, we not only thought through Jesus' virgin birth and
incarnation, but we took the time to see how He impacts and
changes lives. To me, those practical issues are too significant to
leave unsaid. Each doctrine has a practical side we dare not overlook.

All this brings me to chapter 16. In the previous chapter you just
read, we investigated the scriptural evidence of Christ's return . . .
not in great detail, but sufficiently to realize that He is indeed coming back. As I mentioned in chapter 15, we cannot ignore the fact
that, while His return is sure, He may not return in this generation—or even the next. So what do we do in the meantime? That
question may not be a major doctrine but it certainly is a major
issue. The late Francis Schaeffer asked the right question, "How
Should We Then Live?" What ought to occupy our time? What do
we do between now and when He returns?

There once lived a farmer named William Miller. It was back in the nineteenth century. Miller began a religion. One of the marks of his religion was an intense belief in Christ's return. He was notorious for setting dates. He and his followers (known as the Millerites) often met for camp meetings. During one of these meetings, a date was set for the Lord's return. The Millerites decided to pull together and rally around the prediction regardless of public reaction.

The date was announced: Jesus would return between March 21, 1842, and March 21, 1843. During that year they were to ready themselves for Christ's arrival. He was sure to return! To make a year-long story short, He didn't. Disappointment swept through the Millerite ranks, though Miller himself was undaunted. He had simply "miscalculated." So he sharpened his pencil, refigured the details, and set another date. This time Jesus would *definitely* return. The announcement was made on August 12, 1844: He would come between October 20 and October 22, 1844. "Get ready for the end of the world."

As time drew very near, a sign was displayed on a Philadelphia store window:

THIS SHOP WILL BE CLOSED IN HONOR OF THE KING OF KINGS WHO WILL APPEAR ABOUT THE TWENTIETH OF OCTOBER. GET READY, FRIENDS, TO CROWN HIM LORD OF ALL.

A group of about two hundred Millerites sold or gave away their possessions (I've often wondered why they sold their things if they were sure the world was going to end) and prepared their wardrobe for the soon-coming King. They gathered and waited in white robes for His coming. And waited. And waited. And waited. October 20 came and went. So did the 21st and the 22nd, and, of course, the 23rd . . .; Five years later, William Miller died. I think the wisest statement that was ever made by the Millerites was put on his tombstone. It reads, "At the appointed time the end shall be." Finally, they demonstrated good theology! Not on March 21, 1842, or on October 20, 1844. Not on July 7, 1909, or on November 25, 1947, nor even the first day of the year 2000, but *at the appointed time* the end shall be.

It may not be when you think it's going to be. It may not even be as soon as you think it will be. Chances are good it will be sooner than many anticipate. But, again I repeat, no one can say when. To put it bluntly, date-setters are out to lunch. Always have been . . . always will be! No one knows for sure. But there are a couple of things we *do* know. We can be sure of both.

Historically

We are sure that Christ will return. As we saw in the previous chapter, that fact is well-documented. Look at Matthew, chapter 24, for example . . .

> *Heaven and earth will pass away, but My words shall not pass away. But of that day and hour no one knows, not even the angels of heaven, nor the Son, but the Father alone. For the coming of the Son of Man will be just like the days of Noah. For as in those days which were before the flood they were eating and drinking, they were marrying and giving in marriage* (vv. 35-38a).

The picture Jesus is painting is a normal lifestyle. Before the flood in Noah's day, some people were working, others were sleeping. Some were being born, while others were marrying. People were dying. It was a normal, everyday lifestyle.

> *. . . until the day that Noah entered the ark, and they did not understand until the flood came and took them all away, so shall the coming of the Son of Man be. Then there shall be two men in the field; one will be taken, and one will be left. Two women will be grinding at the mill; one will be taken, and one will be left. Therefore be on the alert, for you do not know which day your Lord is coming* (vv. 38b-42).

Now the point here is rather obvious. We do not know the exact time, but we are absolutely sure of the fact. He *is* coming again. It will occur when life on earth is rolling along.

Now before we consider the second thing we know for sure, let's listen to the words of a reputable student of prophecy:

> A short time ago, I took occasion to go through the New Testament to mark each reference to the coming of the Lord Jesus Christ and to observe the use made of that teaching about His coming. I was struck anew with the fact that almost without exception, when the coming of Christ is mentioned in the New Testament, it is followed by an exhortation to godliness and holy living. While the study of prophecy will give us proof of the authority of the Word of God, will reveal the purpose of God and the power of God, and will give us the peace and assurance of God, we have missed the whole purpose of the study of prophecy if it does not conform us to the Lord Jesus Christ in our daily living.[1]

You see, God never intended the truth of His Son's return simply to stir up our curiosity or to give us the big-time tingles. God has given us the truth concerning His Son's return to prompt holy living. We study the prophetic word so we can keep our act cleaned up, so that we will be ready at any moment and will not be embarrassed to meet Him face to face. You may remember that on the heels of that great New Testament chapter on resurrection and Jesus' return, 1 Corinthians 15, the final verse exhorts us to stay at the tasks of responsible living.

> *Therefore, my dear brothers, stand firm. Let nothing move you. Always give yourselves fully to the work of the Lord, because you know that your labor in the Lord is not in vain* (v. 58, NIV).

Prophetically

We also know this: Nothing stands in the way of Christ's return. That is why I have repeatedly used the term *imminent* . . . Jesus' coming could occur at any moment. In other words, there is no future event in God's timetable that must take place before Christ comes in the clouds for His own. Nothing! Candidly, I find that rather exciting. Since we know for sure He's coming, yet we don't know for sure when . . . any day or any hour could be the one!

H. L. Turner was right, over a hundred years ago, when he wrote:

> It may be at morn, when the day is awaking,
> When sunlight through darkness and shadow is breaking,
> That Jesus will come in the fullness of glory,
> To receive from the world His own.
>
> O joy! O delight! should we go without dying,
> No sickness, no sadness, no dread and no crying,
> Caught up through the clouds with our Lord into glory,
> When Jesus receives His own.[2]

My maternal grandfather, whom I loved dearly, used to say that he looked forward to dying because he wanted to go through the whole process as a Christian. Rather than bypassing death, he wanted to go through it. He wanted to know in a conscious manner, the joy of life beyond the grave. He wanted to experience his body's bursting out of the ground, glorified and fitted for eternity, brought immediately into the Lord's presence. As I recall, he used to say that those who were going to be taken up while they are alive are only getting part of the blessing. But those who go through the whole death process "are going to get their money's worth!" In fact, they get preferential treatment. As we saw earlier, we will not precede those who have fallen asleep. They will be raised first, and then we will be brought up with them, glorified, to meet the Lord in the air.

Well, dear, old L. O. Lundy got his wish. He has died and his body awaits the Savior's arrival. Any day now he's going to get his "money's worth."

What if He doesn't return in this generation? What if that little family you're beginning to raise grows up and you grow old, still waiting for the Lord's return? What if you become a grandparent or a great-grandparent in the distant years of the future, and He still hasn't come back? How are we to conduct ourselves? What does the Bible teach about life during the interlude?

BUT ... IN THE MEANTIME

There are four words I want you to remember. You might even want to commit them to memory. These four words represent God's "marching orders" for us—our in-the-meantime standard operating procedure:

- Occupy
- Purify
- Watch
- Worship

If someone asks you, "What are we supposed to do before Christ comes? What is our involvement? Our commitment?" These four words will provide an answer. They are not only wise words of practical counsel, all four are taught in the Scripture. Let's examine each one in greater detail.

Occupy

Dr. Luke records a parable Jesus taught in which He addressed the importance of life continuing on until the Lord returns. Take the time to read the entire account.

> *And while they were listening to these things, He went on to tell a parable, because He was near Jerusalem, and they supposed that the kingdom of God was going to appear immediately. He said therefore, "A certain nobleman went to a distant country to*

receive a kingdom for himself, and then return. And he called ten of his slaves, and gave them ten minas, and said to them, "Do business with this until I come back." But his citizens hated him, and sent a delegation after him, saying, "We do not want this man to reign over us." And it came about that when he returned, after receiving the kingdom, he ordered that these slaves, to whom he had given the money, be called to him in order that he might know what business they had done. And the first appeared, saying, "Master, your mina has made ten minas more." And he said to him, "Well done, good slave, because you have been faithful in a very little thing, be in authority over ten cities." And the second came, saying, "Your mina, master, has made five minas." And he said to him also, "And you are to be over five cities." And another came, saying, "Master, behold your mina, which I kept put away in a handkerchief; for I was afraid of you, because you are an exacting man; you take up what you did not lay down, and reap what you did not sow." He said to him, "By your own words I will judge you, you worthless slave. Did you know that I am an exacting man, taking up what I did not lay down, and reaping what I did not sow? Then why did you not put the money in the bank, and having come, I would have collected it with interest?" And he said to the bystanders, "Take the mina away from him, and give it to the one who has the ten minas." And they said to him, "Master, he has ten minas already." "I tell you, that to everyone who has shall more be given, but from the one who does not have, even what he does have shall be taken away. But these enemies of mine, who did not want me to reign over them, bring them here, and slay them in my presence" (Luke 19:11-27).

A "mina" was a lot of money, in fact about a hundred day's wages (nearly twenty dollars in those days). The nobleman gave his slaves ten of those coins as he instructed all of them to "do business" while he was away.

You may wish to circle the words "do business." More than one version of Scripture renders the same command "occupy." "Do business," however, is a good way of saying it. The point is clear. It was the nobleman's desire that his servants not sit back, doing nothing—letting his money collect dust—until he returned. But they failed to do as He had commanded.

Finally, he returned. Immediately the nobleman was interested in their activity while he had been away. The report was anything but pleasing. Except for the first one who had multiplied his investment tenfold and the second one fivefold, the slaves had failed to "occupy" during his absence.

The lessons from this story are numerous, but it is noteworthy that the nobleman (Jesus) smiled upon the wise use of money during the interlude. He was pleased with the investments of those who made much of the goods of this earth. That's a part of doing business. To put it in different words, we "occupy" when we live responsibly, work diligently, plan wisely, think realistically, invest carefully. In neither the Old nor New Testament is laziness smiled upon, especially laziness that is rationalized because one believes in the soon-coming of Christ. Our Lord frowns on the lack of discipline and diligence. He smiles on a well-ordered private life. He is pleased with the wise use of our time and the proper handling of our possessions. Some excuse irresponsibility by giving it a spiritual-sounding title, like "walking by faith" or "trusting the Lord." Let's not tempt the Lord with such rationalization.

There once lived a group of Christians who bought into that mentality. They thought that since they knew Christ was coming and since their teacher, the apostle Paul himself, had assured them that the Lord was coming soon, why work? Why even concern themselves with the mundane details of everyday life? They'd just spend their days awaiting His coming. And until He arrived they would live off of others. If others chose to work, fine; but they would be the ones who "lived by faith." Once Paul heard of that, he jumped on it like a hen on a June bug:

Now we command you, brethren, in the name of our Lord Jesus Christ, that you keep aloof from every brother who leads an unruly life and not according to the tradition which you received from us. For you yourselves know how you ought to follow our example, because we did not act in an undisciplined manner among you, nor did we eat anyone's bread without paying for it, but with labor and hardship we kept working night and day so that we might not be a burden to any of you; not because we do not have the right to this, but in order to offer ourselves as a model for you, that you might follow our example. For even when we were with you, we used to give you this order: If anyone will not work, neither let him eat. For we hear that some among you are leading an undisciplined life, doing no work at all, but acting like busybodies (2 Thessalonians 3:6-12).

Honestly, doesn't a part of that sound like your dad's counsel? I can just hear my father's voice in those words! Especially, "If anyone will not work, neither let him eat." But this is more than a father's advice ... these are words from the authoritative Scripture. Those who have a right to eat are those who work. Even though we believe strongly in Christ's soon return, and even though we claim to be walking by faith, if we plan to eat while waiting, working is God's plan for us.

Then this final admonition:

> But as for you, brethren, do not grow weary of doing good. And if anyone does not obey our instruction in this letter, take special note of that man and do not associate with him, so that he may be put to shame (vv. 13-14).

I call that straight talk—hard talk.

Every once in a while we meet up with some dear soul with eyes at half-mast, who wants to sit on a hill, strum a guitar, eat birdseed, and sing Christian folk tunes. His (or her) idea of the faith-life is just gathering dew and watching the weeds and daisies grow up all around. This Scripture strikes at the heart of such thinking. God has limited patience with people who irresponsibly hide behind "faith" as they leave it to others to pay their bills.

And to make matters worse, they say the reason they're doing that is because they *really* love the Lord Jesus. No, more often than not the reason they do that is because they are lazy. For them, the soon-coming of Christ is a wonderful cop-out. The next time one of them attempts to quote verses to support their rationalization, I suggest you counter with 2 Thessalonians 3:10— "If anyone will not work, neither let him eat." There are still a few Christians who think manual labor is president of Mexico.

So much for "occupy." Get a job. Work hard. Think realistically. Plan ahead. Reorder your private world. Get your act together. Live responsibly. Invest carefully.

Our Lord expects nothing less.

Purify

There is a second word to remember while we're in the process of preparing for his coming, *purify*. I find biblical support for this in Titus 2:11-14:

> For the grace of God has appeared, bringing salvation to all men, instructing us to deny ungodliness and worldly desires and to live sensibly, righteously and godly in the present age, looking for the blessed hope and the appearing of the glory of our great God and Savior, Christ Jesus; who gave Himself for us, that He might redeem us from every lawless deed and purify for Himself a people for His own possession, zealous for good deeds.

Let me interject a telltale sign of heresy: a ministry that emphasizes the Lord's return but does not, with equal gusto, emphasize a godly life. Mark it down. Whoever highlights the coming of Christ is also responsible to teach the importance of a pure life. Why not? They mesh together, like teeth in gears. If indeed He is coming again, there is one thing we want to have in place—personal purity.

I wouldn't have much confidence in a person who prides himself in being a good surgeon who at the same time doesn't worry too much about sterile instruments. Wonder how many patients he would have if he said, "To tell you the truth, I've got a new plan in surgery. We do all of our surgery in the back room here at the clinic. I just push this stuff out of the way, then you crawl up on the table, and I'll give you a shot. You've got nothing to worry about."

One thing about practicing good medicine is that you cooperate with the rules of sterilization. You can't be too careful about cleanliness and sterility. And if anyone is going to talk about the coming of the Lord Jesus, then be sure that the same person balances all that talk with an emphasis on purity of life.

The apostle John agrees wholeheartedly with the apostle Paul's words to Titus:

> *See how great a love the Father has bestowed upon us, that we should be called children of God; and such we are. For this reason the world does not know us, because it did not know Him. Beloved, now we are children of God, and it has not appeared as yet what we shall be. We know that, when He appears, we shall be like Him, because we shall see Him just as He is. And every one who has this hope fixed on Him purifies himself, just as He is pure* (1 John 3:1-3).

Why, of course!

We have been to enough splendid, unforgettable weddings to realize that the object of attention is the beautiful bride, dressed in white. The excitement of the entire ceremony occurs when the center aisle doors are opened and the organist begins to play full crescendo, as the bride, with her proud (and often frightened) father are making their way down to the altar.

Finally, she stands there in all her purity. Although I have officiated at hundreds of wedding ceremonies, I will never get over the thrill of that moment! Did you know that our Lord often calls His church His bride? Like a bride of beauty and purity in no other color than white, all Christians represent that they are pure "spiritual" virgins awaiting the joys and intimacies of heavenly marriage with their Groom. What an analogy! John's words seem so appropriate: "Everyone who has this hope . . . purifies himself."

But how? How can we maintain such a commitment to purity? We learn to live by short accounts. We refuse to let the filth of our life stack up. We don't ignore even the little things that have broken our fellowship with God or with others. We are to live, in the words of the New Testament, with "a conscience void of offense." That's how we can dress in white for His coming, as a bride prepares for her groom. Perhaps all of that is included in our judging ourselves so that we may not be judged.

Watch

Let's look next at the word *watch*. In the Gospel by Mark, chapter 13, the word *watch* is implied in the commands "Keep on the alert!" and "Stay on the alert!" and "Be on the alert!" Observe those three commands in these seven verses:

> *Heaven and earth will pass away, but My words will not pass away. But of that day or hour no one knows, not even the angels in heaven, nor the Son, but the Father alone. Take heed, keep on the alert; for you do not know when the appointed time is. It is like a man, away on a journey, who upon leaving his house and putting his slaves in charge, assigning to each one his task, also commanded the doorkeeper to stay on the alert. Therefore, be on the alert—for you do not know when the master of the house is coming, whether in the evening, at midnight, at cockcrowing, or in the morning—lest he come suddenly and find you asleep. And what I say to you I say to all, "Be on the alert!"* (vv. 31-37 emphasis mine).

In light of the urgency in Jesus' words, I find it nothing short of remarkable how many days we live without a single conscious thought flashing through our minds regarding Christ's return . . . not even a passing thought. Isn't it amazing? I've noticed that those who become increasingly more sensitive to spiritual things fix more and more of their attention on His coming. And they don't need the reminder from others.

We have all had the same experience of someone's telling us that he's going to come see us on a particular day. He doesn't state a time, but he tells you it'll be sometime during that day. As time wears on through that day, the more often we look. We check the street out front so often that we get the drapes dirty! We're looking. We're watching. We keep waiting until night falls. We turn the front porch light on. We make sure the door is unlocked. We check it four more times to make sure! Why? Because we're anxiously anticipating our friend's coming. We watch every set of headlights that comes around the corner. We stay alert. We are thinking about it. That's what our Lord has in mind here.

I'll be honest with you. Maintaining a balance in all this is tough to do. When I teach on prophetic subjects, I feel a little bit like a parent who warns a child against a stranger. Hoping to guard people from fanaticism, I might go too far and talk them out of being full of anticipation. Parents who teach children to be careful about strangers have to be careful not to overdo it. Because a child can begin to live so suspiciously that everyone is in question—no one can be trusted. It's easy for a child to "overlearn" such warnings.

So while I warn you against the extreme of foolish fanaticism, let me quickly add that God honors watching, having a heart that pumps faster, when we think of His Son's return. In fact, do you know that there's a reward promised? There's an actual crown that will be given for people who live lives full of anticipation of His coming.

> *I have fought the good fight, I have finished the course, I have kept the faith; in the future there is laid up for me the crown of righteousness, which the Lord, the righteous Judge, will award to me on that day; and not only to me, but also to all who have loved His appearing* (2 Timothy 4:7-8).

The "crown of righteousness" is reserved for all who live their lives anticipating the Savior's return. He honors us for living with a watchful eye. By the way, it's a whole lot easier to keep our lives pure when we realize His coming is near. There's a lot of built-in motivation when we think that His return will usher in the "Judgment Seat of Christ." That is why Jesus exhorts us:

> *Be dressed in readiness, and keep your lamps alight. . . . And be sure of this, that if the head of the house had known at what hour the thief was coming, he would not have allowed his house to be broken into. You too, be ready; for the Son of Man is coming at an hour that you do not expect* (Luke 12:35, 39-40).

Worship

In all my years of attending church services and hearing the Bible taught, I cannot remember hearing much said about the importance of worship as we await Christ's coming. But it is clearly an emphasis in Scripture, just as important as occupying, purifying, and watching. I'll write only a little about worship here since I plan to address the subject at length in chapter 22.

The biblical basis for my comments on worship is found in 1 Corinthians 11:23-26.

> *For I received from the Lord that which I also delivered to you, that the Lord Jesus in the night in which He was betrayed took bread; and when He had given thanks, He broke it, and said, "This is My body, which is for you; do this in remembrance of Me." In the same way He took the cup also, after supper, saying, "This cup is the new covenant in My blood; do this, as often as you drink it, in remembrance of Me." For as often as you eat this bread and drink the cup, you proclaim the Lord's death until He comes.*

How long are Christians to participate in worship? How long are we to gather around the Lord's Table and hold in our hands the elements that symbolize our Savior's body and blood? He tells us in the last three words—"until He comes." Every time we worship around the Lord's Table, it is another reminder that He's coming. One of these times will be our last time to observe it on earth. It's kind of exciting, isn't it? It will be our last spiritual meal on earth together. But until then, we are to worship the Lord Christ. Every meal at His table is another reminder that His coming is nearer. We worship Him with great anticipation.

HOW TO STAY ALERT AND READY
∎

There's no reason to get complicated about this matter of in-the-meantime living. A couple of thoughts seem worth emphasizing.

The first is: *Remember Jesus promised it would occur someday* (and He tells the truth!). Keep that in mind. When you read the paper, think of His coming. And remember His promise to return as you see events transpiring that relate to the nation Israel or relate to calamities in our times or those signs and tragedies He predicted would be telltale signs of His arrival. Each of these events—while not directly connected to Christ's return—collectively assure us that we are certainly living in the last days. Call it to mind when you hear of such events, when you lose a loved one, or when something of value is cut out from under you. Hope in the future takes the sting out of the present. Life won't be so hard if we learn to live in the conscious hope of His soon return.

Here's a second tip: *Realize the promise could occur today* (and that will be the moment of truth). Let me make a suggestion. Let me help you form a new habit for getting out of bed in the morning. Just as soon as your tootsies hit the floor, even before you lift yourself up to your feet headed for the day, look out the window. As you look, repeat these two lines:

"Good morning, Lord."
"Will I see you today?"

I've started doing that and it is amazing how often I have seen Him in my morning or in the face of a child, in a circumstance that I would otherwise have missed Him, in a response from an individual, in an interruption, in a telephone conversation. One of these days, sooner than many of us think, we'll see Him in death. And who knows? One of those days in which we've said those two sentences will be the day He'll come. How great to be able to say, "Why, hello, Lord . . . I've been looking for You."

When former President Eisenhower was vacationing in Denver a number of years ago, his attention was called to an open letter in a local newspaper, which told how six-year-old Paul Haley, dying of incurable cancer, had expressed a wish to see the President of the United States. Spontaneously, in one of those gracious gestures remembered long after a man's most carefully prepared speeches are forgotten, the President decided to grant the boy's request.

So one Sunday morning in August, a big limousine pulled up outside the Haley home and out stepped the President. He walked up to the door and knocked.

Mr. Donald Haley opened the door, wearing blue jeans, an old shirt, and a day's growth of beard. Behind him was his little son, Paul. Their amazement at finding President Eisenhower on their doorstep can be imagined.

"Paul," said the President to the little boy, "I understand you want to see me. Glad to see you." Then he shook hands with the six-year-old, and took him out to see the presidential limousine, shook hands again and left.

The Haleys and their neighbors, and a lot of other people, will probably talk about this kind and thoughtful deed of a busy President for a long time to come. Only one person was not entirely happy about it—that was Mr. Haley. He can never forget how he was dressed when he opened the door. "Those jeans, the old shirt, the unshaven face—what a way to meet the President of the United States," he said.[3]

I can tell you a situation that could be a lot more embarrassing than that. One day there will be a shout, a voice, a trumpet blast, and we won't even have *time* to change clothes. Instantly, we'll be swept into His glorious, eternal presence.

But . . . until He comes, what? Remember the watchwords: occupy, purify, watch, and worship. If you're engaged in those four things, you won't have to get ready, you'll *be* ready! No need to set a date or quit your job or dress in white. Just live every day is if this were the one.

"At the appointed time, the end shall be." One of these days will be "the appointed time." You are ready, aren't you?

Root Issues

1. Write the four "watchwords" I suggested in the front of your Bible or—better still—at the beginning page of each new month if you use a date book or calendar. OCCUPY, PURIFY, WATCH, WORSHIP. To cement these concepts in your mind, explain to someone else the life-impact of each of these words.

2. Why do we usually wait until New Year's Eve—or perhaps after a near brush with death—to soberly weigh the investments of our time, money, and abilities? The truth is, we could find ourselves face to face with our Master *at any moment*. And we should be ready to give an accounting of our activities on His behalf. Consider again the searching truths of the Lord's parable in Luke 19:11-27. Does the story suggest anything to you about the manner in which you are living your life? Ask the Spirit of God to underline areas where you need to seek change.

3. Do you find the thought of Christ's return a *dread* rather than a *joy* to contemplate? If you do, talk about your feelings with your pastor or a close Christian friend.

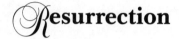esurrection

🌳 🌳 🌳

"I am convinced that all who have died will be brought back from beyond—believers to everlasting communion with God and unbelievers to everlasting separation from God."

VISITING
THE *REAL*
TWILIGHT ZONE

he crisp voice of the late Rod
Serling is still familiar to many of us. Those well-enunciated words.
That inimitable style. And always such a creative script to carry the
audience from the world of the seen to the unseen, out of the realm
of the now into another dimension called "The Twilight Zone."

Serling, the original host of that television series, was a master at
grabbing our attention. And those haunting strains of music . . .
only four notes, but oh, so captivating! The series is enjoying a renewal of interest these days, which is understandable.

"The Twilight Zone" programs never fail to take us into another
world where the bizarre appears as real . . . where the things we fear
become the very things someone else faces. Interestingly, it isn't uncommon for the stories to deal with death and life outside the here
and now. One of the reasons for that, perhaps, is that most people
are fascinated by that subject. And the fascination is growing. There
is even a name for the subject—*Thanatology*, from the Greek
Thanatos, meaning "death." Thanatology is the study of death.

Thanatologist Edwin Shneidman, for example, found that the
first time he taught a course on death at Harvard, two hundred
undergraduates from Harvard and Radcliffe showed up in a classroom that could seat only twenty. Since then, colleges everywhere
have been offering courses, seminars, and dialogues on death and
dying. Topics like grief, immortality, suicide, euthanasia, and out-
of-body experiences are extremely popular on both high school

and university campuses. There seems to be a renewed interest, certainly in the 1970s and 1980s, in the after-life phenomena, especially in visions. Even the medical profession, once suspicious of such things, is now sitting up and taking notice.

J. Kerby Anderson, a research associate with Probe Ministries and lecturer on college campuses, finds his classes packed out. He has revealed in his book, *Life, Death, and Beyond*, "Students are signing up in order to try to register for my course later in the year." Yes, there is a growing interest in the *real* twilight zone.

DEATH: ITS INEVITABILITY AND EFFECT

You and I are going to die. There is no escaping it. Who hasn't heard of the two inescapable facts: death and taxes. I like the comment one wag made: "Maybe death and taxes are inevitable, but death doesn't get worse every time Congress meets."[1]

Arnold Toynbee, the philosopher and historian, insightfully wrote:

> Man alone . . . has foreknowledge of his coming death . . . and, possessing this foreknowledge, has a chance, if he chooses to take it, of pondering over the strangeness of his destiny. . . . [He] has at least a possibility of coping with it, since he is endowed with the capacity to think about it in advance and . . . to face it and to deal with it in some way that is worthy of human dignity.[2]

For the next few pages I want us to do those things that Toynbee suggests. I want us to think about it in advance. I want us to face it head on. That means that rather than denying it, we shall come to terms with it. Death is sure . . . and just because we will no longer be seen on earth is no reason to believe that we'll stop existing. On the contrary, that which is invisible may be just as real as that which is seen and heard. Maybe more so! We thought about that at length in chapter 10 as we considered the analogy between air and the Holy Spirit.

Sometimes death is sudden. Sometimes it is long and drawn out. Occasionally, it's beautiful, sweet, and peaceful. At other times it is wrenching and hideous, bloody and ugly. Sometimes it comes too early, which we call "premature." On other occasions it seems the cold fingers of death linger too long as some dear soul beyond the age of a hundred endures in pain and sadness, loneliness, and even loss of mind. But it comes . . . there's no getting around it.

What Does Scripture Teach?

Scripture speaks often and clearly about death. Here are just a few samples from God's Word:

You will have to work hard and sweat to make the soil produce anything, until you go back to the soil from which you were formed. You were made from soil, and you will become soil again (Genesis 3:19, GNB).

Who can live and never die? How can man keep himself from the grave? (Psalm 89:48, GNB).

Seventy years are given us! And some may even live to eighty. But even the best of these years are often emptiness and pain; soon they disappear, and we are gone (Psalm 90:10, TLB).

There is a right time for everything: A time to be born, a time to die; a time to plant; a time to harvest (Ecclesiastes 3:1-2, TLB).

The person who sins will die (Ezekiel 18:20).

Sin came into the world through one man, and his sin brought death with it. As a result, death has spread to the whole human race because everyone has sinned (Romans 5:12, GNB).

For just as all people die because of their union with Adam, in the same way all will be raised to life because of their union with Christ (1 Corinthians 15:22, GNB).

Everyone must die once, and after that be judged by God (Hebrews 9:27, GNB).

How do you know what will happen even tomorrow? What, after all, is your life? It is like a puff of smoke visible for a little while and then dissolving into thin air (James 4:14, Phillips).

And I saw a great white throne and the one who sat upon it, from whose face the earth and sky fled away, but they found no place to hide. I saw the dead, great and small, standing before God; and The Books were opened, including the Book of Life. And the dead were judged according to the things written in The Books, each according to the deeds he had done (Revelation 20:11-12, TLB).

From Genesis to Revelation the death knell sounds. The Bible is replete with reminders that we must die. There is one appointment we all must keep—our appointment with death. We haven't kept it yet, but we will.

An old legend tells of a merchant in Bagdad who one day sent his servant to the market. Before very long the servant came back, white and trembling, and in great agitation said to his master: "Down in the market place I was jostled by a woman in the crowd, and when I turned around I saw it was Death that jostled me. She looked at me and made a threatening gesture. Master, please lend me your horse, for I must hasten away to avoid her. I will ride to Samarra and there I will hide, and Death will not find me."

The merchant lent him his horse and the servant galloped away in great haste. Later the merchant went down to the market place and saw Death standing in the crowd. He went over to her and asked, "Why did you frighten my servant this morning? Why did you make a threatening gesture?"

"That was not a threatening gesture," Death said. "It was only a start of surprise. I was astonished to see him in Bagdad, for I have an appointment with him tonight in Samarra."[3]

Yes, all of us have our own appointment in Samarra. Though we may try, the appointment will not be canceled.

But what happens at death? What happens when we keep that appointment? What exactly occurs when life departs from the body?

RESURRECTION: PROMISES AND PROCEDURE

I'd like us to turn to the *real* twilight zone and see our future— 2 Corinthians, chapter 5.

For Christians

First, let me address you who are Christians. I want to write to you who know that you have eternal life with Jesus Christ. It will help you to think in terms of categories. I want you to think about that which is seen (your body, your outer person) and that which is unseen (your inner person, your soul, your spirit). Think in those categories as we read this analogy of a house which has been torn down. It's a picture of the earthly body when it dies.

For we know that if the earthly tent which is our house is torn down, we have a building from God, a house not made with hands, eternal in the heavens. For indeed in this house we groan, longing to be clothed with our dwelling from heaven; inasmuch as we, having put it on, shall not be found naked. For indeed while we are in this tent, we groan, being burdened, because we do not want to be unclothed, but to be clothed, in order that what is mortal may be swallowed up by life. Now He who prepared us for this very purpose is God, who gave to us the Spirit as a pledge. Therefore, being always of good courage, and knowing that while we are at home in the body we are absent from the Lord—for we walk by faith, not by sight—we are of good courage, I say, and prefer rather to be absent from the body and to be at home with the Lord (2 Corinthians 5:1-8).

Return for a moment to verse 1. God promises us that there will be some kind of bodily existence, some kind of "eternal house not made with hands" that will be with us throughout eternity. And the point of this passage is that as long as we are living in this earthly body, He postpones giving us our glorified body, called in this passage our "building from God . . . eternal in the heavens." In the waiting period—during our earthly holding pattern—we "groan" (v. 2).

Prior to speaking on this subject recently, I talked with a friend of mine who told me of his daughter who, though not old in years, is now struggling with a tragic disease. I spoke earlier with another friend whose sister has been in a cross-cultural mission ministry for forty-five years. She recently returned to the United States. During an extensive physical examination, the physician found cancer in her abdomen. Two up-to-date illustrations that our bodies "groan." The illustrations could be multiplied by the hundreds every day. You or I may be next!

You discover through the frown of your physician that the X-ray doesn't look good. You are told that the prognosis is bleak. And you're surprised because you're still so young . . . you didn't expect to be carrying in your body the marks of disease and death. But you do, and you are. The body longs to be changed. And as long as we are present in this groaning body, we are absent from our Lord. That's a major point of these verses: "at home in the body . . . absent from the Lord" (v. 6).

In one word, death means *separation*. When death occurs, the inner part of us is separated from the outer . . . the soul and spirit depart from the body. That is the simplest description of death— the soul and spirit are instantaneously removed from the physical body. Our "outer shell"—that part of us that pumps blood and breathes, our anatomy comprised of muscle and bone, tendons and organs—that part of us dies and immediately begins to decay. But the inner part of us, the personality, the soul-spirit, the people we really are, the real, albeit invisible, part of us is taken to the presence of the Lord. Did you notice how Paul put it in verse 8?

We are of good courage, I say, and prefer rather to be absent from the body and to be at home with the Lord.

Now this is good news. We who know the Lord Jesus carry about within ourselves a soul and a spirit. It was that part of us which He invaded at the moment we were born from above—when we became Christians. He has taken up residence there, having given us a new nature. He has become a part of our inner being. And even though our outer shell hurts and groans and is dying, our inner person is maturing, awaiting its home with the Lord. That connection occurs the moment we die.

We read elsewhere in the New Testament:

Therefore we do not lose heart, but though our outer man is decaying, yet our inner man is being renewed day by day. For momentary, light affliction is producing for us an eternal weight of glory far beyond all comparison, while we look not at the things which are seen, but at the things which are not seen; for the things which are seen are temporal, but the things which are not seen are eternal (2 Corinthians 4:16-18).

Keep in mind that death always means separation . . . an instant separation of the soul and spirit from the body. The body (whether cremated or embalmed and placed in a casket or a crypt, or whether it is destroyed in some tragic death) remains on earth as the soul and spirit depart to be with the Lord. So then . . . what happens to the body?

Job, that venerable, old saint, once wrote:

For I know that my redeemer liveth, and that he shall stand at the latter day upon the earth: and though after my skin worms destroy this body, yet in my flesh shall I see God (Job 19:25-26, KJV).

He then said, "My eyes will see Him." In other words, at some time in the future, we will be in face-to-face touch with each other.

What did Job have in mind? He envisioned the next phase of the *real* "Twilight Zone"—the *resurrection* of the earthly body.

Two verses need to be read together at this point, 2 Corinthians 4:14 and 1 Thessalonians 4:16-17. The former states the promise; the latter, the procedure (which we examined in chapter 15).

> *Knowing that He who raised the Lord Jesus will raise us also with Jesus and will present us with you . . .*
>
> *For the Lord Himself will descend from heaven with a shout, with the voice of the archangel, and with the trumpet of God; and the dead in Christ shall rise first. Then we who are alive and remain shall be caught up together with them in the clouds to meet the Lord in the air, and thus we shall always be with the Lord.*

What helpful insight these two passages provide! Here's the way the after-life procedure will occur. When death takes place, the soul and spirit depart immediately into the presence of the Lord. There is no soul sleep. Neither is there reincarnation nor reentry of any kind. Remember Hebrews 9:27? "It is appointed unto man to die once"—to die ONCE. The soul and spirit, having gone instantly into the presence of the Lord, will await the resurrection of the body. When the body is resurrected, the soul and spirit will be joined to that glorified body (which will no longer "groan," or age, or suffer any of its former earthly limitations). It will be fitted for eternity. And in this glorified state, we will spend eternity with our God.

What an encouragement to hang onto! We will have no more tears, no more death, no more sadness, no more crying, no more disease, no more temptations, no more deformity or retardation or struggle with Satan, no more oppression of any kind. No more paralysis or crippling diseases. None of that! All those things are passed away as eternity dawns. I can hardly imagine how this information must thrill those who are physically or mentally handicapped, living with all their limitations. In a context of perfect peace, physically and personally, all Christians will enjoy the presence of our Lord forever and ever and ever.

That is why the psalmist could declare with such assurance:

> *Precious in the sight of the Lord is the death of His godly ones* (Psalm 116:15).

Every believer in Jesus Christ who goes home to be with the Lord has this unshakable and marvelous future in front of him or her. Every death is a reminder that the fight against pain has ended.

Every burial is a reminder that life is merely a temporary abode for this body. Never, ever doubt it: This body will be raised and will be changed. The more I think about it, the more outstanding this doctrine becomes. What a future God has planned for those who love Him and live lives pleasing to Him! The old gospel song says it well, "O that will be glory for me!"

For Non-Christians

But there is also bad news. The bad news does not relate to those who know the Lord, only to those who do not. Non-Christians face a future that makes this present earthly existence, by comparison, seem like a rose garden.

To grasp the impact of the contrast, we must force ourselves to think in another category. We've considered the future of the believer who dies. The body is placed in the grave awaiting the resurrection when it will be joined with the soul-spirit. And that wonderful union will be in a glorified, peaceful state forever with the Lord. But what about the nonbeliever? Let's allow Scripture to speak, rather than human opinion.

The New Testament is not silent about the destiny of the unbeliever. You may be surprised to know that the Bible says much more about hell than it does about heaven. It is possible to develop a rather clear and concise theology of hell; though when we come to the subject of heaven, much of it is left to one's imaginative, interpretive, creative thoughts. But there's no guesswork when it comes to the destiny of the damned.

> But when the Son of Man comes in His glory, and all the angels with Him, then He will sit on His glorious throne. And all the nations will be gathered before Him; and He will separate them from one another, as the shepherd separates the sheep from the goats. . . . Then He will also say to those on His left, "Depart from Me, accursed ones, into the eternal fire which has been prepared for the devil and his angels" (Matthew 25:31-32, 41).

That is a most interesting statement. Tragic, yes . . . but interesting. The place that was originally prepared for the devil and his demonic host will one day also include those "accursed ones" who lived their lives apart from faith in Christ Jesus.

You will observe the reference in Matthew 25:41 to "eternal fire." It means just what it says. Even the universalist John Robinson, who wrote the book *But This I Can't Believe*, had to admit that it is futile to attempt to prove Christ taught no belief in hell or eternal punishment.

DESTINY: HELL OR HEAVEN

When the unbelieving person dies, the body (as with the believer) begins to decay. It is either cremated or placed in a grave, or perhaps in death it was blown apart—whatever. However, the soul and spirit of the unsaved, rather than going into paradise—the place of God's presence—go to Gehenna, called Hades in the New Testament or, more often, "hell." It is a place of temporary, conscious pain. I say temporary because it too awaits final resurrection of the body.

Now before I go any further, let me say that many who hear such a thing become fearful and respond quickly by thinking, "I need to get more religious. I need to go to church more. I need to start carrying a Bible. I need to start doing a lot of good works. I have to deal with this guilt that I'm living with. So maybe if I get religion, I'll escape this eternity that frightens me."

If we were to turn back a couple of chapters, we would meet up with the most religious people who ever lived, the scribes and Pharisees. For all who think religion is going to help, read again what Jesus said to these religious people who were living in hypocrisy, mouthing mere words about their faith:

> *You serpents, you brood of vipers, how shall you escape the sentence of hell?* (Matthew 23:33).

Religion doesn't relieve anyone from the future of hell. Neither does going to church, studying the Bible, being baptized, being christened, paying your bills, living a good life, obeying the law, or contributing great sums of money to the church or some other good cause. None of that will ingratiate anyone before a holy God who requires perfect righteousness, not human goodness. You read that correctly; He requires *perfect* righteousness. And not even religious people can provide that kind of righteousness. Righteousness that equips us for eternal life comes only through the Lord Jesus Christ.

Christ spoke of another response in Mark, chapter 9. Many people will excuse themselves by saying, "I'm only human. I can't help it if I've got these eyes that lust . . . I've got these hands that commit wrong . . . I have these feet that take me to ungodly places.

I walk in darkness, not in light, but I'm a helpless victim of my own humanity. What did Jesus say about all that?

And if your hand causes you to stumble, cut it off; it is better for you to enter life crippled, than having your two hands, to go into hell, into the unquenchable fire.

And if your foot causes you to stumble, cut it off; it is better for you to enter life lame, than having your two feet, to be cast into hell.

And if your eye causes you to stumble, cast it out; it is better for you to enter the kingdom of God with one eye, than having two eyes, to be cast into hell (Mark 9:43, 45, 47).

There are times you take the Bible literally; there are also times you understand that it is using symbolism or accommodating terminology, as here. Jesus isn't saying that we're to enter life with no hands, no feet, and no eyes. His terms are severe and super-extreme to communicate His point. He is saying it is foolish for us to hide behind the lame excuse of a hand or an eye or a foot that disobeys. You prepare yourself by preparing your heart. You prepare yourself by placing your whole self at the disposal of Jesus Christ who cleanses hands, eyes, heart, feet, the whole life. But it's worth noting that He refers not once, not twice, but three times in a row to hell, which is a place ". . . where the worm does not die, and the fire is not quenched" (v. 48).

Look further at John, chapter 5. Jesus is speaking again.

Truly, truly, I say unto you, an hour is coming and now is, when the dead shall hear the voice of the Son of God; and those who hear shall live. For just as the Father has life in Himself, even so He gave to the Son also to have life in Himself; and He gave Him authority to execute judgment, because He is the Son of Man. Do not marvel at this; for an hour is coming, in which all who are in the tombs shall hear His voice, and shall come forth; those who did the good deeds to a resurrection of life, those who committed the evil deeds to a resurrection of Judgment (John 5:25-29).

There is no getting around it. Unless you wish to do an enormous amount of semantic footwork, or you have an airtight scheme of cutting out certain Scriptures that makes you feel uncomfortable, you're left with some pretty damaging evidence. And I would suggest that we not joke any longer about hell. Many other things may be, but hell is not a laughing matter . . . though many laugh to nullify hell's significance.

The following quotation may seem a little blunt, but the author has an excellent point. Don't let his abrupt approach dull the edge of that point.

> It is not unlikely that within the last twenty-four hours you've heard someone say, "What the hell are you doing?" Or, "I sure as hell will." Or, "Who in the hell do you think you are?"
>
> That word *hell* has become a conversational byword in our day. Good friends dare to say playfully to one another, "Go to hell." They surely don't mean, "Go to the place of punishment for the wicked after death," though that is how the dictionary defines the word *hell*.
>
> But why use the word *hell*? Why not instead, "What the jail are you doing?" Or, "I sure as school will." And why not say, "Oh, go to Chicago"? Simply because *jail*, *school*, and *Chicago*, even for the enemies of each, have no real sting. They have only the flavor of vanilla at a time when chocolate or peppermint is needed.
>
> When it comes right down to it, in the English language, *hell* is the strongest expletive available that carries the idea of ultimate deprivation, devastation, fear, torment, punishment, suffering, and loss. Whether or not the user of the term *hell* believes in an actual, literal hell is of little or no consequence. There is an inbuilt, inarticulated, yet understood bite in the very word itself.
>
> So if hell really is the place for eternal punishment of the wicked after death, how come it's used so lightly millions and millions of times each day? Why is there such an apparent lack of seriousness about the word? Why is a word so heavy with meaning used so indifferently? Why do people pretend the place doesn't exist?
>
> When is the last time you heard a serious sermon on the subject or read an article of note dealing with judgment and eternal punishment? Even the evangelical crowd has, by and large, avoided the topic—opting for a more "positive" approach. Hell has come on hard times.
>
> Deep below the surface of things, a proliferating erosion concerning the seriousness of hell, brought on by a complex web of modern ideas about hell, has stripped this weighty word of most of its awesomely solemn content.[4]

Truth is not always comforting and easy to hear. But I would not be a true servant of God or a loyal ambassador of His will if I failed to tell you the truth about hell. Furthermore, you would be ill-informed regarding your future if all you chose to read in the Bible were only those passages regarding heaven. It is true that there is a certain destiny for the saved. It is called "Paradise" or "at home with the Lord," "God's presence" or "heaven." It is also true that there is a certain destiny for the lost. It is called "Hades" or "hell" or "the lake of fire."

I suggest we stop using any of those terms lightly. We should reserve the word "hell" for its singular purpose—the destiny of the lost. It is the most hideous scene the mind can imagine, though it isn't imaginary. It is the worst possible place ever prepared for anyone's existence.

The ultimate scene is in the final five verses of Revelation, chapter 20. You owe it to yourself to take a look. You may not like what you see, but when you read Revelation 20:11-15, you'll be reading the truth. Let's understand where we are before we attempt to imagine this awful scene. Perhaps a little review will help.

When the *believer* dies, the body goes into the grave; the soul and spirit go immediately to be with the Lord Jesus awaiting the body's resurrection, when they're joined together to be forever with the Lord in eternal bliss. When the *unbeliever* dies, the body goes to the grave, while the soul and the spirit of that body go into Hades or hell where it is kept in conscious torment (which we shall study in the next chapter). Those souls in hell are awaiting the resurrection of the body, which will occur immediately before the last judgment. That particular judgment is the judgment for the lost—the scene portrayed in Revelation 20.

> *And I saw a great white throne and Him who sat upon it, from whose presence earth and heaven fled away, and no place was found for them* (v. 11).

We're looking at a scene that will occur somewhere in space. There is no longer any earth. It's been burned up. There is no longer the atmospheric heavens as we know of them. This incredible scene is not some imaginary twilight zone, but the ultimate *real* twilight zone.

> *And I saw the dead, the great and the small, standing before the throne, and books were opened; and another book was opened, which is the book of life; and the dead were judged from the things*

which were written in the books, according to their deeds. And the sea gave up the dead which were in it, and death and Hades gave up the dead which were in them; and they were judged, every one of them according to their deeds. And death and Hades were thrown into the lake of fire. This is the second death, the lake of fire (vv. 12-14).

Technically, the ultimate abode of the lost is not hell. Hell itself is only a temporary location of the damned. The eternal abode of the lost is the lake of fire, the destiny of all who die without faith in the Lord Jesus Christ.

And if anyone's name was not found written in the book of life, he was thrown into the lake of fire (v. 15).

PREPARATION: RESPONSE AND RESULT

With no desire to play on your emotions or manipulate some response from you, I must communicate the truth for all who read this book. There are two very important facts that everyone must face. The *first*: The only time to prepare for then is NOW. The *second*: There is no chance of change after death. I've not been writing of some playful, imaginary, and entertaining scene. I've been dealing with truth and reality painful to read and, I can assure you, unpleasant to write. I do not care what you were told as you were being raised, or what you have been taught later on by whomever. According to an intelligent and careful study of the Scripture, I can assure you on the authority of the Word of God, this is the truth. You must prepare for it now since there is no chance of changing things after you die.

What is the issue? I turn, finally, to the letter of 1 John to answer that question. John explains the issue in simple terms. It is relatively simple to read and easy to grasp, but the question is: Will you believe it?

The one who believes in the Son of God has the witness in himself; the one who does not believe God has made Him a liar, because he has not believed in the witness that God has borne concerning His Son. And the witness is this, that God has given us eternal life, and this life is in His Son. He who has the Son has the life; he who does not have the Son of God does not have the life. These things I have written to you who believe in the name of the Son of God, in order that you may know that you have eternal life (1 John 5:10-13).

Don't misunderstand. *Everybody* has eternal life because everyone has an eternal soul. The issue is not "Do I have eternal life?" It is, rather, "Where will I spend my eternal life?" If the most exciting moment of your life is *behind* you, you're lost. If the most exciting moment of your life is still *in front* of you, you're saved.

Three men were the closest of friends. They enjoyed the out of doors and often hunted and fished together. On this occasion they found themselves around a fire in Northern India drinking coffee and watching the distant light of early dawn. Several weeks before this trip, the oldest of the three men had become a Christian. He had not yet had the opportunity to share the excitement of his new destiny with the others.

As they sat around the fire they began talking about their various adventures. One of the younger men suggested they each answer the same question—What's the most exciting experience in all your life?—by sharing some intriguing story.

The first man to answer told of the tiger hunt he'd been on . . . about how they had to stalk the beast for more than two days. The final six hours were the most thrilling when he found himself face to face with that big cat. Just as the hungry animal leaped, he fired. The cat lay dead . . . but he thought he was going to die of fright.

The second hunter told of an experience in Alaska, north of the Aleutian Islands, involving an enormous bear. He said it all happened so fast that it wasn't until the whole experience was over that he realized how close to death he had been. He had to squeeze off three final rounds before that huge beast finally dropped virtually at his feet. He reminded them that the furry, skinned bear was now a rug covering the floor in his den.

Finally, the oldest man spoke. "My most exciting experience? It hasn't happened yet. But it will occur only seconds after I die." This led into an opportunity to talk with his closest friends about Christ. They listened with rapt attention as he described the thrilling anticipation he never knew before. Death was no longer a fearful thing on the distant horizon . . . but rather an entrance into the most awesome delight the mind can imagine.

The crisp voice of Rod Serling is no longer heard. He's dead. And every time I hear the haunting melody of *The Twilight Zone*, I wonder where Rod Serling is today. I really wonder.

1. Contemplate once again the searching words of Moses' prayer in Psalm 90. Pause at verse 10. If you knew for sure that you would pass from this earth at the age of seventy, how many years of life would you have left? Sobering? Time is a very limited resource, isn't it? Pull out your calculator and take it a step further. How many *days* would that leave you in your life's hourglass . . . how many *hours*? Keying off Moses' words in verse 12, what does it mean to *you*—to your priorities—to present to God "a heart of wisdom"?

2. What incident within the last year reminded you of Paul's assertion in 2 Corinthians 4:16 that "our outward man is decaying," or temporary? Are you living in the reality of the *second* half of that verse? What does the specific phrase "day by day" suggest to you?

3. If you'd like to pass along some of these thoughts about heaven, hell, and our eternal destiny in a concise, "transferable" form, you might want to consider buying several copies of my booklet *DESTINY: Choosing to Change the Course of Your Life* (Multnomah Press, 1982) at a Christian bookstore. Give them to those who are considering the issues of knowing Christ. Explain why you want them to read it. After several days get back in touch with them.

AN
INTERVIEW
WITH ONE
FROM BEYOND

s late as the 1960s, Americans were known as a death-denying culture. Our opinions were traditional. Our views were antiquated. Worst of all, our lips were sealed.

When loved ones were told that their disease was terminal, only the closest stayed near until the end. It was virtually unheard of to bring the dying home. They remained isolated in hospitals and "rest homes." And when death came, isolation turned to awkward silence. Few words were said as we buried the dead while the world rushed on.

This inability to face such grim realities was not overlooked by everyone, however. A ground swell of concern refused to remain still much longer.

By April of 1970, a few brave souls broke the silence barrier. In a rare and long overdue article on death in America, a national news magazine lamented the fact that we are guilty of denying this reality. Their words penetrated. They became like the ever-enlarging hole in the dike as more and more information began to flow from the media. It was only eight years later that the same publication titled its cover "Living with Dying," heralding a newfound interest in the study of death . . . a subject no longer shrouded in mute mystery.

WHAT BROKE THE BARRIER?

Anyone my age or older would want to know what broke the barrier. What caused us to come out of the closet? What helped us to stop denying? Surely it was more than a magazine article. At least four causes have contributed to the change.

1. *The Medical Profession.* Within the past two decades the medical profession has focused increased interest on death and dying. Books, research, seminars, and journal reports (especially out-of-body experiences—OBE—and euthanasia) have begun to flow from competent physicians. These professionals have become more candid regarding their struggles with the issues as well as more willing to dialogue with other professionals and research scientists.

2. *The Educational World.* As I mentioned in my last chapter, educational curricula have begun to include courses on death and dying. Medical schools, distinguished universities, community colleges, and high schools alike are addressing the subject. Some go so far as to take field trips to mortuaries, or interview those who have had OBE.

3. *The Media.* No one can overlook the evergrowing number of films, plays, radio talk shows, and news stories that now emphasize death-related issues. Within the last two years there have been numerous television programs focusing attention on subjects once considered unmentionable.

4. *Public Interest.* Patients who were once given up as dead are now kept alive through new techniques and equipment. Questions are now being asked by the public that weren't even thought of three decades ago:

- Who should be allowed to "pull the plug"?
- Why can't my loved one die at home?
- What are the telltale signals of potential suicide?
- When is it acceptable to end one's own life of pain?
- How can we say that "afterlife visions" aren't reliable?

It is the last question that introduces the subject of this chapter. But first, perhaps it would help to make a few observations about death-bed phenomena and afterlife visions.

SEVERAL COMMON DEATH-AND-DYING EVENTS

A physician, Dr. Marshall Goldberg, has interviewed many patients resuscitated from cardiac arrest. Since it takes three or four minutes for the brain to die after the heart ceases to function, some patients (interviewed before a rapidly developing amnesia effaces the memory) have related some remarkable visions, feelings, sounds, and related OBE. A few of the more recurrent descriptions include:

- Surprisingly peaceful surroundings
- An almost sound-proof, pain-deadening "curtain" that descends
- "Flashbacks," in which one's entire life passes in review—one person referred to it as "an autobiographical slide show"
- Bright light, warm feelings, buzzing and ringing sounds[1]

If this subject fascinates you, there are a couple of books I could recommend which are reliable works: *Life After Life* by Raymond Moody, Jr., M.D., and *Life, Death, and Beyond* by J. Kerby Anderson. I'd like to quote from both of these sources before we turn to the Scriptures for even deeper insight:

Dr. Moody writes:

Despite the wide variation in the circumstances surrounding close calls with death and in the types of persons undergoing them, it remains true that there is a striking similarity among the accounts of the experiences themselves. In fact, the similarities among various reports are so great that one can easily pick out about fifteen separate elements which recur again and again in the mass of narratives that I have collected. On the basis of these points of likeness, let me now reconstruct a brief, theoretically "ideal" or "complete" experience which embodies all of the common elements, in the order in which it is typical for them to occur.

A man is dying and, as he reaches the point of greatest physical distress, he hears himself pronounced dead by his doctor. He begins to hear an uncomfortable noise, a loud ringing or buzzing, and at the same time feels himself moving very rapidly through a long, dark tunnel. After this, he suddenly finds himself outside his own physical body, but still in the immediate physical environment, and he sees his own body from a distance, as though he is a spectator. He watches the resuscitation attempt from this unusual vantage point and is in a state of emotional upheaval.

After a while, he collects himself and becomes more accustomed to his odd condition. He notices he still has a "body," but one of a very different nature and with very different powers from the physical body he has left behind. Soon other things begin to happen. Others come to meet and to help him. He glimpses the spirits of relatives and friends who have already died, and a loving, warm spirit of a kind he has never encountered before—a being of light—appears before him. This being asks him a question, nonverbally, to make him evaluate his life and helps him along by showing him a panoramic, instantaneous playback of the major events of his life. At some point he finds himself approaching some sort of barrier or border, apparently representing the limit between earthly life and the next life. Yet he finds that he must go back to the earth, that the time for his death has not yet come. At this point he resists, for by now he is taken up with his experiences in the afterlife and does not want to return. He is overwhelmed by intense feelings of joy, love, and peace. Despite his attitude, though, he somehow reunites with his physical body and lives.

Later he tries to tell others, but he has trouble doing so. In the first place, he can find no human words adequate to describe these unearthly episodes. He also finds that others scoff, so he stops telling other people. Still, the experience affects his life profoundly, especially his views about death and its relationship to life.[2]

And one more comment from J. Kerby Anderson:

Those who have been involved in research on out-of-body experiences [OBE] have noted a very interesting phenomenon. Even when a person is having an OBE, he is still in contact with his body. He is attached to his body by means of a "cord." On one of his out-of-body excursions, Robert Monroe describes looking for the cord that connected his physical body with his Second Body.

I turned to look for the "cord" but it was not visible to me; either it was too dark or not there. Then I reached around my head to see if I could feel it coming out the front, top, or back of my head. As I reached the back of my head, my hands brushed against something and I felt behind me with both hands. Whatever it was extended out from a spot in my back directly between my shoulder blades. . . . I reached outward, and it formed into a "cord," if you can call a two-inch-thick cable a "cord."

Such a phenomenon is not limited to out-of-body experiences. It has also been reported by those at a deathbed.[3]

Because of the increasing number of similar reports, it is to the point where one wonders if there might be something to all these OBE accounts. I am not ready to say that all of these things actually occur, but, quite frankly, I am unable to ignore how much in agreement they are. It's the similarity of them that I find so intriguing.

BIBLICAL HOPE FOR CHRISTIANS TO CLAIM

I am grateful that we aren't limited to opinions of observers and feelings of people on deathbeds. The Scripture addresses the subject often and freely. These scriptural passages provide us with great peace when the chilling winds of death blow near us. Each one gives the Christian hope and comfort. Here are several pertinent passages:

Now He who prepared us for this very purpose is God, who gave to us the Spirit as a pledge. Therefore, being always of good courage, and knowing that while we are at home in the body we are absent from the Lord—for we walk by faith, not by sight—we are of good courage, I say, and prefer rather to be absent from the body and to be at home with the Lord (2 Corinthians 5:6-8).

Precious in the sight of the Lord is the death of His saints (Psalm 116:15).

Now I say this, brethren, that flesh and blood cannot inherit the kingdom of God; nor does the perishable inherit the imperishable. Behold, I tell you a mystery; we shall not all sleep, but we shall all be changed, in a moment, in the twinkling of an eye, at the last trumpet; for the trumpet will sound, and the dead will be raised imperishable, and we shall be changed. For this perishable must put on the imperishable, and this mortal must put on immortality. But when this perishable will have put on the imperishable, and this mortal will have put on immortality, then will come about the saying that is written, "Death is swallowed up in victory. O death, where is your victory? O death, where is your sting?" The sting of death is sin, and the power of sin is the law; but thanks be to God, who gives us the victory through our Lord Jesus Christ. Therefore, my beloved brethren, be steadfast, immovable, always abounding in the work of the Lord, knowing that your toil is not in vain in the Lord (1 Corinthians 15:50-58).

But we do not want you to be uninformed, brethren, about those who are asleep, that you may not grieve, as do the rest who have no hope. For if we believe that Jesus died and rose again, even so God will bring with Him those who have fallen asleep in Jesus. For this we say to you by the word of the Lord, that we who are alive, and remain until the coming of the Lord, shall not precede those who have fallen asleep. For the Lord Himself will descend from heaven with a shout, with the voice of the archangel, and with the trumpet of God, and the dead in Christ shall rise first. Then we who are alive and remain shall be caught up together with them in the clouds to meet the Lord in the air, and thus we shall always be with the Lord. Therefore comfort one another with these words (1 Thessalonians 4:13-18).

And I heard a loud voice from the throne, saying, "Behold, the tabernacle of God is among men, and He shall dwell among them, and they shall be His people, and God Himself shall be among them, and He shall wipe away every tear from their eyes; and there shall no longer be any death; there shall no longer be any mourning, or crying, or pain; the first things have passed away" (Revelation 21:3-4).

And there shall no longer be any night; and they shall not have need of the light of a lamp nor the light of the sun, because the Lord God shall illumine them; and they shall reign forever and ever (Revelation 22:5).

Remember this: Every time you attend a funeral or memorial service, you are merely viewing the physical remains of the deceased individual. You are seeing only the body, which is decaying, decomposing. You are not viewing the person—only the outer "shell." Regardless of how we refer to the remains— slumbering, at rest, at peace—or how "natural" he or she may look, we are looking at that which is going to be changed and glorified, renewed so that the body can endure eternity. As we learned in the previous chapter, the soul-spirit, that invisible part of the Christian, has been taken to be in the presence of the Lord. What you are seeing before you is the external "suit of clothes"; or as 2 Corinthians 5 calls it, you're seeing "the house" which is now destroyed. The funeral service provides us a time to give God thanks for the memory of the person and for the fact that that body will be raised some day in the future.

One of my favorite lines that I often state once the funeral party gathers at the grave site is related to that future day when the dead will be raised. I will usually say, "Whether you realize it or not, at this very moment you are standing on resurrection ground." (I've actually seen people look down, then step aside two or three feet!)

There will be a time when the graves will be opened and the bodies will be removed in a glorified state to be forever with the Lord Jesus. Plain and simple, the Christian has no reason to fear death since the future is so full of hope and happiness. Even though we cannot turn to any Scripture that states that a believer was interviewed after death, we know these things are true.

ULTIMATE REALITIES FOR NON-CHRISTIANS TO FACE

There is, however, an extremely vivid account where an *unbeliever* is interviewed. Don't misunderstand, we're not going to read of another fascinating OBE, but a startling narrative of the afterlife related by the ultimate authority on the subject—the Son of God Himself.

A number of commentators refer to Luke 16:19-31 as a parable. I'm not so sure. By naming two of the key characters in the account, I believe that Jesus gives us ample reason to interpret these verses as an actual historical event. A true story of two men . . . and their eternal destinies.

Luke sets the stage:

> *Now there was a certain rich man, and he habitually dressed in purple and fine linen, gaily living in splendor every day. And a certain poor man named Lazarus was laid at his gate, covered with sores, and longing to be fed with the crumbs which were falling from the rich man's table; besides, even the dogs were coming and licking his sores* (Luke 16:19-21).

It is a pathetic scene. First there is a rich man who, as we shall see, is eternally lost. Then there is a poor man who is eternally saved. They live in two different worlds in their earthly lives. But there is a remarkable change of events at death. Death, the greatest of all levelers, reduces everything to the lowest common denominator. Look at the way Jesus describes the reversal of roles:

> *Now it came about that the poor man died and he was carried away by the angels to Abraham's bosom; and the rich man also died and was buried* (v. 22).

When Lazarus, the believer, died, his body was probably tossed in the local dump, the refuse pile. Chances are good he didn't even receive a decent burial. But his soul and spirit were taken immediately into the presence of the Lord, called here "Abraham's bosom."

When we read, "The rich man also died and was buried," we can be sure his burial was one of great pomp and elaborate ceremony. So much for his body. It is his eternal soul that interests us. We find him "in Hades" as we continue to read Jesus' words:

> And in Hades he lifted up his eyes, being in torment, and saw Abraham far away, and Lazarus in his bosom (v. 23).

In the verses that follow, we will not read of some paranormal experience reported by a man who saw lights and heard buzzing. This, I believe, is an event, not a vision. It becomes an interview, as it were.

Notice several things that occur. First, there is *agony*. There is literal pain. He is in torment. And somehow he catches a glimpse of those who are at peace. Second, he is *fully conscious*. Third, he not only has his *senses*, he has his *memory*. Neither is obliterated by death.

> And he cried out and said, "Father Abraham, have mercy on me, and send Lazarus, that he may dip the tip of his finger in water and cool off my tongue, for I am in agony in this flame" (v. 24).

The scene becomes increasingly bleak. Scripture pulls no punches. Earlier it mentioned "torment." Now it's "agony." Observe that the man could reason. He could also visualize his surroundings. He had feeling. He could hear. He could taste. It was as if he still had a tongue.

Abraham (who seems to speak for the Lord) answers the man's request in verse 25:

> . . . Child, remember that during your life you received your good things, and likewise Lazarus bad things; but now he is being comforted here, and you are in agony.

Now for those who joke about hell and say, "Well, we'll be there for a while and somebody will just pray us out," take a good look at the next verse:

> And besides all this, between us and you there is a great chasm fixed, in order that those who wish to come over from here to you may not be able, and that none may cross over from there to us (v. 26).

The "fixed chasm" suggests a perpetual situation. In other words, it is impossible to change destinies or to escape one's location after death. Even if others wish for you to be released, they cannot come to your rescue. Realizing this, the man begins to bargain—

> *And he said, "Then I beg you, Father, that you send him to my father's house . . . " (v. 27).*

Now this is where the account becomes extremely moving. The man in torment remembers his family at home. His concern for them is enormous, and understandably so.

> *. . . for I have five brothers—that he may warn them, lest they also come to this place of torment (v. 28).*

Let me interrupt the story long enough to ask a question. Is it your feeling that the lost who are dead care about the lost who are alive? If you're uncertain about your answer, read verse 28 again. Since he was unable to escape, his number-one concern was that someone might go to his brothers and communicate the truth about hell to those who are still living. Don't miss the urgency, ". . . that he may warn them." Talk about a missionary message! Talk about evangelistic zeal! If it exists nowhere else, an evangelistic passion exists in hell. "Oh, that someone could go to my brothers . . . if only someone could rise from the dead and appear to my five brothers who are living like I lived, denying what I denied."

This certainly silences the superficial comments we hear from some who joke, "Aw . . . I'll just be in hell with all my buddies." All it takes is a few verses from this account to realize there's no companionship there. On the contrary, there is an awful, gnawing, inescapable loneliness.

In response to the man's request, Abraham says to him, ". . . They have Moses and the Prophets." Meaning what? They have the Scripture, the very Word of God. They have God's voice in God's Book. In other words, "Let them who are alive hear the truth of Scripture." Applying it to our day, "They have ample opportunity to hear the truth. Let them pick up the Bible and read it for themselves. Let them hear the preachers. Let them hear the broadcasts. Let them hear the gospel as it is contained in God's Word."

He pleads with greater intensity:

> *But he said, "No, Father Abraham, but if someone goes to them from the dead, they will repent!" (v. 30).*

"Father Abraham," he reasons, "I know they've got God's Word. But it would make a greater impact if someone were to go to them from the dead. They'd repent. They'd believe. That's all it would take."

I find the following response nothing short of remarkable:

> But he said to him, "If they do not listen to Moses and the Prophets, neither will they be persuaded if someone rises from the dead" (v. 31).

You talk about the power of the Scripture! If you could bring someone back from beyond—someone who has been in hell—to tell people what the future holds, it would not be as effective as Holy Scripture! The most invincible, convincing power on earth is the Word of God as the Holy Spirit uses the truth to convince the lost.

We have sufficient truth available to us in our Bibles to do the job. It is all that is needed to convince the person without Christ that they are missing what life is about. Even if we could do something miraculous, like bring someone back from beyond, it would not have as great an impact as simply presenting the Scriptures.

> . . . They have Moses and the Prophets . . . (v. 29).

> . . . If they do not listen to Moses and the Prophets, neither will they be persuaded if someone rises from the dead (v. 31).

If I were asked to put the message of this entire chapter into one sentence, it would not contain more than twenty-one words: *Those who ignore the Word of God in life will not be ignored by the God of the Word in eternity.*

MAJOR QUESTIONS WORTH ANSWERING

If I were sitting where you're sitting, having read what you have just read, I believe I would have four or five questions hanging in my head. I have an idea what they might be. So, before we leave this section on resurrection, let's consider several significant concerns.

1. *How can a loving God send people to hell?* The way that question is worded bothers me. Even though it is commonly asked that way, I don't like the way it sounds, because I don't like what it implies. So if you'll allow me to analyze the question before I answer it, I think it will help.

The question seems to imply that God is indulgent and a bit impotent . . . and that mankind is being taken advantage of, handled cruelly, and treated unfairly—with very little feeling on God's part. Almost like God is taking delight in watching people squirm, saying, "Get out of My sight," as He pushes people into hell against their wills. So if that is what is meant by the question, then that needs to be dealt with first. Suffice it to say, that is *not* what Scripture teaches.

But if it's an honest question, where you wrestle with God's loving character and hell's awful consequences, then I would begin by saying that God has established the ground rules. That's His sovereign right. As the Creator of life, His divine rule states that those who believe in His Son will have eternal life with Him. Those who do not believe in His Son will not have eternal life with Him. The believers will have the blessedness of heaven. Those who reject the message must face the punishment of that rejection.

And lest you think God is calloused and unconcerned over that scene, you'll need to return to 2 Peter 3:9, which states:

> *The Lord is not slow about His promise, as some count slowness, but is patient toward you, not wishing for any to perish but for all to come to repentance.*

Never forget that verse! When someone presents to you the idea that God cruelly and gleefully dances about heaven as the last people are dumped against their will into hell, remind them of Peter's words. With patience and grace He offers the gift of eternal life and heaven to all who will accept it. Those who refuse the gift He offers must suffer the consequences, having made their own decision about eternity.

2. *What about those who have never heard?* Or, *What about those who sincerely follow their own beliefs and their own religion?* We must always be careful about stepping into the role of God. Only He knows the destiny of people. People you and I may think are in the family may not be . . . and vice versa.

God alone knows the heart. He alone is the One who makes the final determination. Not all who call Him Lord will enter into the kingdom. And conversely, not all who think they are lost are actually lost. Some have genuinely come to know Christ and live under the misguided assumption that they've lost their salvation.

But to answer the question, we need to read again the words of Romans 10 in order to determine the basis of salvation.

That if you confess with your mouth Jesus as Lord, and believe in your heart that God raised Him from the dead, you shall be saved; for with the heart man believes, resulting in righteousness, and with the mouth he confesses, resulting in salvation. For the Scripture says, "WHOEVER BELIEVES IN HIM WILL NOT BE DISAPPOINTED." For there is no distinction between Jew and Greek; for the same Lord is Lord of all, abounding in riches for all who call upon Him; for "WHOEVER WILL CALL UPON THE NAME OF THE LORD WILL BE SAVED." How then shall they call upon Him in whom they have not believed? And how shall they believe in Him whom they have not heard? And how shall they hear without a preacher? And how shall they preach unless they are sent? Just as it is written, "HOW BEAUTIFUL ARE THE FEET OF THOSE WHO BRING GLAD TIDINGS OF GOOD THINGS!"

However, they did not all heed the glad tidings; for Isaiah says, "LORD, WHO HAS BELIEVED OUR REPORT?" So faith comes from hearing, and hearing by the word of Christ (vv. 9-17).

The only way to have eternal life with God is through faith in the Lord Jesus Christ. God has wonderful ways of getting our attention. He uses natural phenomena. He uses general revelation. He uses circumstance, blessing, and suffering. He uses people. He uses written material. He uses human beings who make the message known. He will use tragedies and calamities, the loss of a loved one, a crippling disease, bankruptcy, divorce, and a hundred other situations. The marvel of His plan is that He has an endless number of ways of reaching the lost. As they are reached, as the Holy Spirit uses the truth of Scripture to convince them, they will believe.

While I'm on this subject, let me add there will always be some who will not have as much divine input as others. Because that is true, I believe there will be degrees of eternal punishment. Before you pick up stones to stone me, look closely at these words of Jesus:

And that slave who knew his master's will and did not get ready or act in accord with his will, shall receive many lashes, but the one who did not know it, and committed deeds worthy of a flogging, will receive but few. And from everyone who has been given much shall much be required; and to whom they entrusted much, of him they will ask all the more (Luke 12:47-48).

Let's understand that no one without Christ spends eternity in heaven. But the *specifics* of how God handles those who are without Christ because they heard so little might very well be answered by this idea of degrees of punishment. But we do know for sure that heaven will not be their home.

3. *What about deathbed repentance?* This is another gnawing question. I hear about people who turn to the Lord their last day on earth . . . maybe even their last hour. They have spent their entire life apart from faith in the Lord Jesus and now, dying, they express strong and confident faith in the Lord. Is that valid?

Once again remember, no one on earth can determine with absolute certainty the eternal destiny of another individual, since God alone knows the heart. But who is to say no one can become a Christian at the end of his or her life? Remember one of the thieves on the cross? He had lived the life of a criminal, a thief. He had lived his entire life without Christ. But in his final breath he makes a statement regarding eternity, and Christ acknowledges it.

> *And one of the criminals who were hanged there was hurling abuse at Him, saying, "Are You not the Christ? Save Yourself and us!" But the other answered, and rebuking him said, "Do you not even fear God, since you are under the same sentence of condemnation? And we indeed justly, for we are receiving what we deserve for our deeds; but this man has done nothing wrong." And he was saying, "Jesus, remember me when You come in Your kingdom!" And He said to him, "Truly I say to you, today you shall be with Me in Paradise"* (Luke 23:39-43).

There is no doubt in my mind that that thief will spend eternity in heaven.

By the way, we need to be careful about expecting people to say the exact words we want to hear so we can say in return, "Now you're a Christian." Be careful about giving them *the* prayer that they must recite or giving them *the* words that they must repeat. Who can say for sure what language the heart speaks when one "believes in his heart"? I don't think that I've ever heard anyone I have led to the Lord say, "Jesus, remember me when You come in Your kingdom." But in this case that was sufficient. The Lord read the language of his heart. Only He can do that. Yes, deathbed repentance can be sincere and effective.

4. *What about the death of babies?* This question is extremely important to those who have lost an infant at birth or a little child who

never reached an age of spiritual comprehension. It's my understanding that small children who die before reaching a primary level of maturity (when they are able to reason with the basic issues of salvation and faith in the Lord Jesus) go immediately into the presence of the Lord.

No passage of Scripture is any clearer on this subject than 2 Samuel 12:23, where David says of his infant who has just died, "... I shall go to him, but he will not return to me." Somehow, in God's wonderful plan, He has reserved in heaven a place for the precious infants and little people whose lives ended prematurely on this earth. David states the truth as he testifies to the inability of his baby to return to earth. But when David himself dies, he will see his child as he enters the presence of the Lord. By the way, the erroneous teaching regarding reincarnation is nullified by David's remark "He will not return to me"—which brings me to my final question.

5. *Is reincarnation valid?* If you can believe it, I have heard some say that Jesus' words in John 3—"You must be born again"—provide a basis for belief in reincarnation. I've also heard Hebrews 12 quoted as biblical justification: "We are surrounded by a great cloud of witnesses." Proponents of reincarnation say, "See, people have come back, and they now 'surround' us." Quite probably, if there were reincarnation, I think Scripture would clearly refer to several deaths that the same soul passes through. But there is no such occurrence in Scripture. The Bible consistently refers to the death of an individual in the singular. Furthermore, Hebrews 9:27 says, "It is appointed for men to die ONCE and after this comes judgment" (emphasis mine). Job's words are also worth noting:

> The eye of him who sees me will behold me no more; Thine eyes will be on me, but I will not be (Job 7:8-10).

And don't forget that "great chasm fixed," which we read about earlier. Luke 16:26 seals the door shut:

> And besides all this, between us and you there is a great chasm fixed, in order that those who wish to come over from here to you may not be able, and that none may cross over from there to us.

When death occurs, a fixed destiny has been determined. The teaching of Scripture denies the possibility of reincarnation.

Now I have one final question for you, which only you can answer.

WHERE ARE *YOU*
GOING TO SPEND ETERNITY?
■

Only you can answer that. Read the question once again. I plead with you, do not go on to chapter 19 until you have come to terms with this all-important question.

Our country may have been a death-denying culture as recently as the 1960s. What concerns me a great deal more than that is that the majority are still a Christ-rejecting people . . . especially so in these closing years of the twentieth century. But since when do thinking people like you take their cues from the majority? You have certainly read far enough in this book to know what it means to become a Christian. I ask you directly, have you become one?

To be a death-denying individual is not nearly as tragic as being a Christ-rejecting individual. One simply means you'd rather not talk about it, which is fine. The other means you refuse to *believe* it, which could be final. Before you decide to die like that, better remember the "certain rich man" Jesus talked about. While he was alive, he didn't believe either.

He does now.

1. While the content of this crucial chapter is still fresh in your memory, write down your personal response to what you have encountered. What are your feelings? What did you learn—or relearn? How do you think the Lord might lead you to respond to what you've read?

2. Besides the sobering glimpse into the afterlife provided by Luke 16:19-31, there are some serious matters to consider about *this* life. Do you, for instance, have any "Lazaruses" living near your "front gate"? Near your community? Have you seen the faces of the poor looking at you from the "gate" of your television . . . or magazines in your home? What is the danger of habitually closing your eyes and ears to the desperate needs of the poor? Consider some of the following scriptures and ask the Lord how He might lead you to respond: Matthew 25:31-46; Psalm 82:3-4; Proverbs 14:31; Proverbs 21:13.

3. Luke 16:29-31 offers startling evidence of the Scripture's power to impact lives. Take a close look at these verses and compare them to the ringing words found in Hebrews 4:12. In what ways could you incorporate this powerful force for God into your daily contacts, correspondence, and conversations?

The Body of Christ

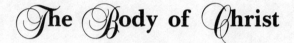

"I know the Lord is continuing to enlarge His family, the universal Body of Christ, over which He rules as Head."

GOD'S
BODY-BUILDING
PROGRAM

typical American family was
driving home from church one Sunday. Dad was fussing about the
sermon being too long and sort of boring. Mom said she thought
the organist played too loudly during the second hymn they sang.
Sis, who was a music major in college, said she thought the soloist
sang about a half note off key during most of her song. Grandma
said she couldn't hear very well—since they were sitting toward the
back. As they pulled in the driveway, little Willie, who had listened
to all of this, started to fuss about the woman who sat in front of him
with that big hat. Then he paused, nudged his dad, and said, "But,
Dad, you gotta admit, it was a pretty good show for a nickel."

Ouch!

To more people than we would dare admit, attending church is a
lot like watching a show. The better the entertainment, the more
they enjoy coming. But the less they like what they see and hear, the
more they grumble and complain. Let the "show" get really bad,
and there's no way most people are going to see it through. Yet,
we've got to admit that the "price of admission" is still pretty hard to
beat. Compared to what the public is willing to pay for live theater
or a professional ball game, it's still "a pretty good show for a nickel."

All of this is true, of course, until you get serious about this business of "the church." Things change when you do. You feel less like
seeking entertainment. You feel less freedom to fuss and complain.
You feel more like investing your time, your treasure . . . your very
life.

As a matter of fact, it isn't long before you realize that this is one of the few involvements you mess around with that has eternal dimensions on earth. And when you *really* get hooked, you discover there is not one other single involvement more important than the Lord's whole-world outreach.

When you stop and think about it, God is involved in only two worldwide construction projects. The first is called *evangelism*, where He stretches His big arms around the world to reach and to win the lost to Himself. He uses all different kinds of people and many different methods, but in every case His objective is to offer the good news of His Son, Jesus Christ, to those who have yet to respond. The scope of God's world program is limitless; it reaches across the street, across the States, and across the seas.

The second worldwide program God is involved in is *the Church*. I think of the Church as God's Body-building program. Do you know the materials He uses for building the Church? That's easy to figure out, isn't it? He uses those He recruits in evangelism. So these two programs work in sync with each other. The lost are found as they respond positively to the good news of Christ. Then they begin to be built up in Christ and become personally involved in God's world program. The Church's mission is a never-ending project, drawing its manpower (should I say person power?) and its funding from those who have caught the vision.

You need to understand that I am not writing about some local church *per se* or some denomination. I don't have any geographical location in mind either. Or color of skin or nationality or culture or language. I'm referring to the universal Church when I mention the Body. I must admit, the more I study God's plan and program for the Body, the more I believe in it, the more I admire what He has done and is doing, and the more I want to be involved.

When I meet folks who bad-mouth the Church or see little significance in its existence, I pity that individual rather than feel offended. I realize he or she simply doesn't understand. It's a little like attending a symphony with someone who has no understanding of or appreciation for classical music. The whole event seems a waste of time and energy when, in actuality, the problem lies within his or her own mind.

Before I go any further, I should come up front and say that my desire in this chapter is to elevate your appreciation for the Body of Christ, if by chance it's been sagging a little lately. In case you've gotten burned or had the edge of its significance dulled or you've begun to question the necessity of your involvement in His projects,

I want to come back to some basics and help you gain both a fresh perspective and a new appreciation.

It is no secret that I am a "satisfied customer" when it comes to the Body. I am involved in it up to my ears. I'm not ashamed to confess that I think of it in the daytime, dream of it at night, and pour all of my creative energies into its mission and message. Because of my wholehearted belief, I seek to "sell the product" everywhere I go.

Ah, but be careful! Once this passion gets hold of you, you'll be addicted. Not only that, you'll realize that you haven't the time to be absorbed in the petty stuff so many superficial "churchy" folks focus on.

I notice that people who look upon the Church as "a pretty good show for a nickel" spend a lot of time thinking about the clothing people wear and what kind of car they drive or how they look or the color of their skin or the mess they've made of their former lives—horizontal issues, petty matters, small-picture stuff. Now *that's* a waste of time and energy! The longer I live and the better I understand the big picture, the less I even notice those petty things . . . the less I care about horizontal hassles. That's not the Church, that's man-made religion, designed to consume our energies and keep our vision out of focus.

Well, if that's not the Church, then what is?

A BRIEF HISTORICAL SURVEY

Let's learn a little history together. Rather than listing numerous dates and dozens of people, I'll make this quick 'n easy. Ready?

The Church in the first century—in its most pristine condition—was the object of God's attention and affection. It was purified by persecution, which caused its influence to spread like a flaming wheatfield in Nebraska. Its contagious momentum impacted every little nook and cranny of the known world. People all across the Roman Empire, much to the embarrassment of its emperor, began to buy into it. And before long there were pockets of believers in villages, towns, and cities, none of them with ornate cathedrals you understand, but all of them with a heart for God. Their leaders walked with Jesus and taught His truth. Most of them ran the race until martyrdom. Many of their followers were handed the mantle and became the new leaders of the Church. They, too, were martyred.

This fervent, often bloody chapter of history continued into the second, third, and fourth centuries. But during the latter part of that era, something strange happened in the Body. Church became a formal thing. Christianity ultimately became an "official religion." It took upon itself the marks of an organization. Its leaders increased their roles of authority. Their authority finally shifted to unquestioned power, and soon there emerged *the* voice of *the* Church. Worshipers, kept ignorant of the Word of God, became increasingly more manipulated and intimidated.

Predictably, the Church lost its way as its divine power was replaced with human authority. Zeal and excitement drained away. The shadow of the Dark Ages edged across the religious landscape. The Church's authoritative guide—the Bible—was chained to the pulpit, with its message now hidden in the secret language of the clergy. Great edifices were built that pushed people away from the up-front leaders, holding them at bay. The common people remained in the dark—stone ignorant of the Scripture. It is hard to imagine the darkness of those decades. There were exceptions, but for the most part, God's truth was silenced. The Church, like a bloated whale, lay awkward, enormous, *lifeless* atop the swells and waves of historic events. Its leaders existed in their private world—inaccessible and unaccountable.

That condition could endure only so long. By the fourteenth, fifteenth, and into the sixteenth century, a growing band of straight-thinking, tough-minded men emerged from obscurity. These "reformers" courageously stood against the uncontested power bloc of the official Church and had the audacity to bring back the authority of Holy Scripture. As they broke with tradition, they spoke for God. Vital doctrines were rethought, restated, and reintroduced to the common people so that they could understand them and apply them to their lives. As you would expect, many of those reformers became martyrs . . . but their vision caught on. The fiery movement had gained too much momentum to be stopped. To the frowning dismay of the prelates of the Church, these "protestants" became such a sizable body of people, they could no longer be swept aside and ignored. A spiritual revival flamed across Europe and into England, igniting the Great Awakening that ultimately spanned the Atlantic to America.

The rest is familiar history. God's Body-building program was again on the move. No power was strong enough to shut it down.

We have the Reformation to thank for the development of two major doctrines—*soteriology* (the doctrine of salvation) and *ecclesiology* (the doctrine of the Church). The two are inseparable, as we shall learn in the balance of this chapter. I agree with theologian Lewis Sperry Chafer who said, "Next to salvation truth, it is vitally important for the believer to know the Bible doctrine of the Church."

Some Essentials About the Church

Down through the centuries, God's program has been like a massive crescendo mark on a musical score. From the Church's beginning point on the day of Pentecost when the Spirit of God came (Acts 2), right up to the present day, it is ever expanding, ever enlarging. To represent its future growth we could add an extended dotted line, because the Church, Christ's universal Body, will continue to enlarge. The Church is larger today than it was yesterday. It will be larger tomorrow than it is today, because God is forever reaching people with the good news of Christ and bringing them into His Body.

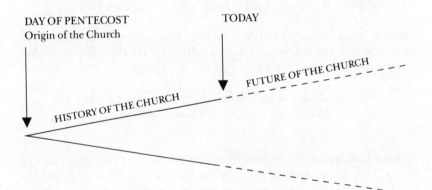

DAY OF PENTECOST
Origin of the Church

TODAY

FUTURE OF THE CHURCH

HISTORY OF THE CHURCH

Prediction

Not only was the doctrine of the Church developed late in history, even the mention of the term "church" appears late in Scripture . . . never once in the Old Testament and not until Christ is well underway in His ministry. Jesus mentions the Church toward the end of a dialogue between Himself and His disciples. Matthew records the conversation in the sixteenth chapter:

> *Now when Jesus came into the district of Caesarea Philippi, He begun asking His disciples, saying, "Who do people say that the Son of Man is?" And they said, "Some say John the Baptist; some, Elijah; and others, Jeremiah, or one of the prophets." He said to them, "But who do you say that I am?"* (vv. 13-15).

Jesus is asking that question to the whole group—the "you" is plural in verse 15. Now the reason I mention the plural "you" is because the whole group doesn't answer . . . Peter alone answers the question. We take a lot of shots at Peter, and he is often criticized for his weaknesses and failures; but the man stands tall at this moment. His answer is right on target!

> *And Simon Peter answered and said, "Thou art the Christ, the Son of the living God"* (v. 16).

Jesus offers a threefold response: first a blessing, then a promise, and finally a prediction.

> *. . . Blessed are you, Simon Barjona, because flesh and blood did not reveal this to you, but My Father who is in heaven* (v. 17).

"You've been talking with My Father, Peter—good for you! That came right from heaven. What insight!" That's the idea here. He continues:

> *And I also say to you that you are Peter, and upon this rock I will build My church; and the gates of Hades shall not overpower it* (v. 18).

Now look carefully at Jesus' promise, "I say to you that you are *Petros*." My, that must have been wonderful for Peter to hear! We can't appreciate it, because we don't speak that language. Actually, Jesus gave him a nickname. All of his life Peter had been known as *Simon*, which, if you pressed it to the limit, would mean "vacillating one, shifting, moody, changing." But *Petros* meant "Rock." In effect, Christ says, "Good job, Rock. That's the way to go. That's the right answer. Peter, you're like a rock."

Then, drawing on that nickname, Jesus makes some promises: "And upon this *Petra* . . ." *Petra* is not quite the same word as *Petros*. Some have taught that this means Jesus built His Church on Peter. No, had that been the case, He would have said, ". . . upon this *Petros*—on you, Peter," but He didn't. Jesus built His Church on the rocklike truth Peter had just uttered. Matthew caught the signifi-cance by recording *Petra* ". . . Upon this rocklike truth." And what is this truth? "You are the Messiah, the Anointed One, the Son of the Living God"—the very truth Peter had uttered when answering Jesus' opening question. And then Jesus predicted:

> . . . *and upon this* [truth] *I will build My church; and the gates of Hades shall not overpower it* (v. 18).

Stay with me for a minute while we snap on a telephoto lens and focus in closely on this crucial prediction: "I will build My church."

Note first to whom the Church belongs—Jesus. "I will build *MY* church." It is not pressing the issue out of bounds to emphasize that the Church is not the work of some pastor or priest or body of elders or some other governing hierarchy. It is Jesus who builds it. The Church is solely His. He doesn't have to clear His decisions with Rome or London or Wheaton or New York or Minneapolis. The Church is *not* owned by some denomination. Or group of clergy-men. Or some official religious organization. Or the Pope himself.

To use today's terms, Christ is our Boss, our final authority. If I used a first-century term, Christ is our Lord, *Kurios*, and we are His servants; our *Despotes*, and we are His subjects. That has never changed, though in the passing of centuries all sorts of philosophies and governments have dictated a different plan than that. The Church was and is His genius . . . He originated it. He alone is its Master.

Let's zero in even closer. "I will *BUILD*." The dictionary says to *build* means "to form by uniting materials by gradual means into a composite whole, to construct." Another definition, "to develop by a definite process." That is going on right now in Christ's Body. Al-ways has been since the first century. His Body-building program will never stop until Christ comes for His own. He's the Groom and He will come for His bride.

Sounds a little humorous to say it this way, but the bride is getting heavier every year, waiting for the Groom to come. She's enlarging her size. Every day she's getting bigger and bigger, waiting for His arrival. And the Groom will someday come and say to the bride, "You're mine. Come on home with Me." Until then He remains in the building process. And the building is made up of all nations, all cultures, all creeds, all languages, all colors. In fact, the Church in the First World is fast becoming the minority as His Body is being built up to an even greater degree in the Second and Third World countries.

Earlier we learned a little history, now let's learn a little Greek. This word *Church* is translated from the Greek *Ekklesia*, which comes from two words. The first is *ek,* a prefix particle meaning "out from among." The second is *Klesia*, a derivative from the verb *Kaleo*, "to call." Combining the two, *Ekklesia* means "to call out from among." To render Jesus' prediction literally, "I will build My called-out ones."

What a wonderful thought! Since the beginning of the Church, our Lord has been reaching down into the ranks of humanity, selecting, choosing, calling out, drawing people to Himself. These people are men, women, boys, girls, teenagers, older folks, all different sizes with all different personalities, from all different nations and tribes. He continues to "call them out" from the full spectrum of humanity, from busy urban centers to distant jungles. And He places them . . . where? He places each one of them in His Body. Because each one comes the same way, each one enjoys the same benefits.

Remember the little chorus:

> I'm so glad I'm a part of the family of God
> I've been washed in the fountain, cleansed by His blood!
> Joint heirs with Jesus as we travel this sod.
> I'm so glad I'm a part of the family of God.[1]

Every one of us who is in the Family of God can sing that because we've all come the same way. That means the Body is exclusive— and I mean that in the right sense. The only way you become a member of this Body is to place your total trust in Jesus Christ. This Body is comprised of only believers in Christ. If you're a believer, you're in.

How permanent is it? Is it going to face the threat of extinction as time passes? We're back to the same scripture for our answer. Christ said, "The gates of Hades shall not overpower it." In other words, if all the wicked forces were unleashed from the open gates of Hell itself, the Church would not be hindered in its growth. Nothing could ever destroy the Church. It's a permanent building process that will never be crippled by some outside force, never be rendered obsolete, and never be stopped by any power, person, or plan. Period.

Definition

Explanations are essential for clarification. There is nothing like a definition to pinpoint the meaning of terms. I suggest this definition for Church: *The ever-enlarging body of born-again believers who comprise the universal Body of Christ over whom He reigns as Lord.* I believe that covers all the essential bases. The Church is ever-enlarging, it is universal in scope, it is continually in process, it is exclusive in membership, and it is impervious to destruction.

Let me ask you: Can you think of anything more worthy of your time and treasure?

Not too many weeks ago, I had a moving conversation with an engineer who had recently decided to change his whole career in midstream. I'll bet you can guess why. He had gotten excited about God's world program. His decision was prompted by his local church. We had met at a conference where he shared his vision with me. He had made quite a decision regarding his future as he stepped away from the familiar into another realm.

"Why are you doing this?" I asked him.

"Well, Chuck," he said, "I'll be honest. I finally faced the fact that everything I was designing and building was some day going to wind up under a layer of dirt or ashes. Every project I was involved in had a termination point, while God's project is eternal. When that thought grabbed me, my whole mentality turned around."

Obviously, God does not lead everyone that way. He led the engineer that way when he got a fresh perspective of the Church. When people begin to realize that Church isn't just "a pretty good show for a nickel," but rather a passion for living with eternal dimensions, it revolutionizes their whole frame of reference. Their world suddenly enlarges from this tiny speck of time and circumstances to a worldwide, invincible project over which Christ serves as Lord.

RAPID GROWTH OF THE EARLY CHURCH

Let's observe how rapidly the Body expanded in its earliest years of existence. As the Holy Spirit came on the day of Pentecost, He ignited a small body of people with enthusiasm and holy zeal. They poured out into the streets of Jerusalem and fearlessly declared their faith. "Petros" became their spokesman, and the immediate results were nothing short of phenomenal!

> So then, those who had received his word were baptized; and there were added that day about three thousand souls (Acts 2:41).

Think of it! Three thousand brand new believers. There they stood in the streets of Jerusalem. I love the thought of this!

They had no church building.

They had no pastor.

They had no "church constitution" (which is probably the reason they got along so well).

They had no board members . . . no handbook . . . no promise of what the future held for them.

Then what *did* they have? They had Christ! They had the unhindered, boundless joy of Christ's presence in their inner beings.

They also had each other. The ties of love held them closely together.

And what did they *do*?

And they were continually devoting themselves to the apostles' teaching and to fellowship, to the breaking of bread and to prayer (v. 42).

They involved themselves in those four objectives—teaching, fellowship, the ordinances, and prayer. To this day those same four objectives are still the essentials of a church—teaching, fellowship, the ordinances (baptism, communion), and prayer.

Immediately this body of believers began to grow. The momentum grew as well.

And at the hands of the apostles many signs and wonders were taking place among the people; and they were all with one accord in Solomon's portico. But none of the rest dared to associate with them; however, the people held them in high esteem. And all the more believers in the Lord, multitudes of men and women, were constantly added to their number (Acts 5:12-14).

Observe that the Lord kept His Word—He was building the Body. That building process continued, in spite of hardship.

And the word of God kept on spreading; and the number of the disciples continued to increase greatly in Jerusalem, and a great many of the priests were becoming obedient to the faith (Acts 6:7).

Look at that breakthrough. All these months the priests must have been wondering and thinking, "What's with these folks? Who are they? Why are they so happy, so confident, so closely connected to each other, so unintimidated?" Unable to ignore the movement, the priests became curious and began to listen. And then they got involved. And then, of all things, these formal, religious leaders tore away their masks of religion and committed their lives to the Lord Jesus Christ. Talk about revival!

Finally, because of persecution, the growth of the Body extended beyond Jerusalem:

> So then those who were scattered because of the persecution that arose in connection with Stephen made their way to Phoenicia and Cyprus and Antioch, speaking the word to no one except to Jews alone. But there were some of them, men of Cyprus and Cyrene, who came to Antioch and began speaking to the Greeks also, preaching the Lord Jesus. And the hand of the Lord was with them, and a large number who believed turned to the Lord. And the news about them reached the ears of the church at Jerusalem, and they sent Barnabas off to Antioch. Then when he had come and witnessed the grace of God, he rejoiced and began to encourage them all with resolute heart to remain true to the Lord, for he was a good man, and full of the Holy Spirit and of faith. And considerable numbers were brought to the Lord (Acts 11:19-24).

We've seen televised pictures of volcanoes that have erupted, causing molten lava to pour over the lip of the crater and run down the crevices and on into the valley and villages below. Wherever the lava flows, it leaves its mark. I think of that when I think of those early years of the Church. The heat of persecution drove the Christians into new regions, leading to further growth.

Just as Christ had predicted, the "gates of Hades" did not overpower the Church. On the contrary, "considerable" numbers were "brought to the Lord." But the growth didn't stop there. It continued on into Greece and European regions. Lives were changed drastically as Christ's message penetrated and permeated. We see this clearly when we read of the events that transpired in Ephesus, a metropolitan center in western Turkey.

> And this became known to all, both Jews and Greeks, who lived in Ephesus; and fear fell upon them all and the name of the Lord Jesus was being magnified. Many also of those who had believed kept coming, confessing and disclosing their practices. And many of those who practiced magic brought their books together and began burning them in the sight of all; and they counted up the price of them and found it fifty thousand pieces of silver. So the word of the Lord was growing mightily and prevailing (Acts 19:17-20).

What a remarkable account! How can it be that pagan people could be changed so completely? Surely it involved more than simply "joining a church." Indeed! These changes occurred because Christ had invaded their lives. Let me explain.

CHANGES THAT OCCUR WHEN WE BELIEVE

When you trusted Christ Jesus as your Savior, many things happened to you. Two are crucial enough to mention.

1. Something happened *within* you. According to 2 Corinthians 5:17, you became an entirely new creation within.

> *Therefore if any man is in Christ, he is a new creature; the old things passed away; behold, new things have come.*

You gained new motivation, new interests. Your mind was no longer blinded to the truth of Scripture and held in bondage to fleshly lust. Your interests began to shift from yourself to others . . . from the things of the flesh to the things of God.

And a new group of people appeared on the horizon of your life . . . other Christians. You began to be more vulnerable, more open, more willing to confess the wrongs of your life. Your desire to hide from God changed to wanting to spend time with God. Why? You had become a new creature within.

2. Something happened *to* you. You were automatically and instantaneously placed into the family of God. You didn't necessarily feel any different. You didn't hear angelic choirs. You didn't see flashing lights or falling stars. But something happened to you the moment you believed. You became instantly related to God's forever family. And this new family relationship opened to you an entirely new realm you never before realized was in existence.

Those same two things happened to people in biblical times. They became new creatures. They joined God's family. And those two factors never change!

VITAL SIGNS OF A HEALTHY CHURCH

Sometimes people ask, "Do I have to join a church to become a Christian?" My answer is, "No, but God always joins you to the Church." No, you don't have to join some local church in order to become a Christian. He wants you to be connected with a local church, ultimately, but that's a separate issue from becoming a Christian. But you automatically become a member of the universal Body, His Church, when you believe. No problem there. But if we do encounter problems regarding the Church, it will be when we cast our lot with a *local* church. It need not be an unhappy experience, but it often is. Why? Because the vital signs of health and wholeness are missing.

I remember when my mother died early in 1971, my father called me on the phone. He spoke very briefly and quietly as he told me that he thought my mom was dead.

"Sis is on her way," he said. "Can you come?"

Of course I jumped into my car, and by the time I got there they had already covered my mother with a blanket as she lay lifeless on the sofa. She had died a very quick, painless death by heart attack.

As I arrived I said to my father and sister, "Have you called the doctor?"

"Well, no, we haven't," they replied. "We didn't really know what to do."

I grabbed the phone immediately and called her physician. He said, "Now, Charles, there are some vital signs you need to look for. Let's make absolutely certain—while the paramedics are on their way—that she is, in fact, dead." So he gave me four or five signs to check. We did exactly as he instructed us. They removed all doubt. The vital signs were missing. When the paramedics arrived, we stepped back and watched as they went through the same basic procedures. It was clear to all of us that she was gone.

When we think about a healthy body, the vital signs are important. I want to mention six vital signs of a healthy church. I find each one either mentioned or implied in 1 Corinthians 12.

First, *the presence of unity and harmony.*

> *For even as the body is one and yet has many members, and all the members of the body, though they are many, are one body, so also is Christ* (v. 12).

The first time I read that verse, it seemed like a tongue twister. Yet the longer I meditated on it, the clearer it became. It helps to change the word "member" to "organ," like the organs of the body. Let me do that for you, and you'll see how much clearer it reads:

> *For even as the body is one and yet has many organs, and all the organs of the body, though they are many, are one body, so also is Christ's Body.*

That's the idea here. The point I want you to see is the unity and harmony of the Body. Though the Church is comprised of many members, there is still only one Body. Such unity is also emphasized in John 17:20-23 as well as Ephesians 4:1-6, which you should stop and read.

Second, another sign of good health is *the absence of favoritism, status, and prejudice.*

> *For by one spirit we were all baptized into one body, whether Jews or Greeks, whether slaves or free, and we were all made to drink of one Spirit* (v. 13).

In the first-century Roman world, the equality found in the Church was much more significant than it is today. In that day there were definite castes (still familiar to the people of India, but not as much to the people of America). In those days there was nobility and there was slavery. There was the slave owner and the slave— nothing more than a human "tool" in the hands of his owner.

In another letter from Paul, these similar words appear:

> *For you are all sons of God through faith in Christ Jesus. For all of you who were baptized into Christ have clothed yourselves with Christ. There is neither Jew nor Greek, there is neither slave nor free man, there is neither male nor female; for you are all one in Christ Jesus* (Galatians 3:26-28).

In a healthy Church one of the vital signs is an absence of favoritism, prejudice, and status. In any other earthly organization, when you draw together a number of human beings, you're going to have prejudice, emphasis on status, and a display of favoritism. But not in the Body of Christ! This is one place that has no room for "preferred customers" or second-class citizens.

A third vital sign is *an emphasis on individual dignity and mutual variety.* We find this vital sign in verses 14-20. I love this passage. There's a little humor in it, so don't miss it. Think of the human body as you read these words.

> *For the body is not one member, but many. If the foot should say, "Because I am not a hand, I am not a part of the body," it is not for this reason any the less a part of the body* (vv. 14-15).

Feet can't go on strike. Because they are part of the body, the feet stay connected. It gets even more imaginative.

And if the ear should say, "Because I am not an eye, I am not a part of the body," it is not for this reason any the less a part of the body (v. 16).

And now he carries the analogy to the ultimate extreme!

If the whole body were an eye, where would the hearing be? If the whole were hearing, where would the sense of smell be? (v. 17).

Try to picture an "eye-body"—one massive six-foot eye! How useless, how unattractive. You couldn't hug it or kiss it. You wouldn't have anything to kiss with, unless you "batted each other" when you got up close. You'd get dirt in your eye all the time as you rolled around the house. You couldn't move around. Think of trying to drive a car or getting into bed. The same could be said for an "ear-body." Bill Cosby could do wonders with verse 17, couldn't he?

By now you are smiling . . . and that's what you're supposed to do! The point is so ridiculous that it's humorous. We make six-foot eyeballs out of people. We make five-foot-nine-inch ears out of certain people. We make them our stars, celebrities, big time pedestal types. But they're just eyes and ears. They're just noses. They're just lips. No one person in the Body is the whole Body. Let's stop making idols out of people in the Body! Sure, we need heroes, people we admire and love and respect. But we don't need six-foot eyeballs.

But now God has placed the members, each one of them, in the body, just as He desired. And if they were all one member, where would the body be? But now there are many members, but one body (vv. 18-20).

Let's imagine this. You have just entered into God's family. God is speaking—

"Welcome to the Family of God. I'm just passing out assignments. You . . . you'll be a nose. And that fella next to you . . . I'll make him a foot. Shorty over there, I'm going to make you something special. You'll be the big toe—part of the foot inside a sock inside a shoe. How does that sound?"

"Oh, rats!" Shorty replies. "Really had my heart set on being an eye. Hey, the foot already has enough parts. It doesn't need me."

Ever had a problem with some part of your foot? Maybe a tiny corn on your baby toe? A small callous? I know a lady who can hardly walk because of a minute growth on her foot. It needs attention, and the longer she waits, the more painful it becomes.

Sometimes it hurts so much she has to sit down and lift her foot to get some relief. Even though a small growth on her smallest toe is the only problem, her whole body aches.

Ever tried to walk with a tiny pebble in your shoe? You can't stand it, so you take off your shoe and pull that baby outta there and find that it's really nothing but a speck of sand . . . but it felt like a boulder!

> *But now God has placed the members, each one of them, in the body, just as He desired. And if they were all one member, where would the body be? But now there are many members, but one body* (v. 18-20).

Let's never forget this third vital sign: *an emphasis on individual dignity and mutual variety.*

Now we're ready for the fourth vital sign: *a de-emphasis on independence and self-sufficiency.* Listen to this, self- sufficient, strong and natural leaders! Pay attention, all entrepreneurs! Hear ye, hear ye, independent-minded Lone Rangers!

> *And the eye cannot say to the hand, "I have no need of you"; or again the head to the feet, "I have no need of you." On the contrary, it is much truer that the members of the body which seem to be weaker are necessary; and those members of the body, which we deem less honorable, on these we bestow more abundant honor, and our unseemly members come to have more abundant seemliness . . .* (vv. 21-25a).

Our younger daughter Colleen has a chronic problem with her pancreas. The tiny duct that secretes fluid is too tight to function properly. Every once in awhile something will get lodged in that duct—perhaps a very small stone—and her whole body goes into an incredible spasm of pain. She's immobilized. You wouldn't think a pancreas would cause that big a deal. It's hard to believe that something that small could affect her whole body, but that's the way God made the body. No organ is completely independent and unrelated.

So it is in the Body of Christ. There's a little member of the Body down in there somewhere. And the happiness or sadness of the whole Family of God rests on the functioning of that little, tiny part of the Body. Interdependence cannot be ignored among the Body members.

This brings us to the fifth vital sign: *the support of others, whether they are hurting or being honored.*

. . . that there should be no division in the body, but that the members should have the same care for one another. And if one member suffers, all the members suffer with it; if one member is honored, all the members rejoice with it (vv. 25b-26).

Isn't that great? Talk about a healthy Church! Someone is hurting . . . you feel the sting of pain. Someone can't keep up; you slow down and encourage him or her. You are promoted and honored, others applaud and cheer. They rejoice as you rejoice. Is that the way it works? I hope so. What one member feels, all the others feel. That's the way it is to be in a healthy Body.

Sixth and last: *exaltation of Christ as Head and supreme authority.*

Now you are Christ's body, and individually members of it (v. 27).

Let us never forget that the Body has one Head, only one. The Head, remember, is Christ. He—alone—is Lord.

CONTAGIOUS DISEASES THAT CRIPPLE THE CHURCH

Staying with the same analogy of the human body, there are some diseases that can spread infection throughout the Body. The mind can become swollen with pride. The heart can grow cold and indifferent because of sin. The digestive system can get clogged by sterile theory and unapplied theology, so the Body can't digest what needs to be turned into energy or eliminate what needs to be released. When that occurs we start to fight among ourselves or we lose our equilibrium and find ourselves unable to stay balanced.

Let me get even more specific: The Body can have eyes that feed on lust and greed, tongues that wag, and ears that listen to gossip. (I don't know of any disease that's hurting the Body worse these days than a wagging, unrestrained tongue.) It can have knees that seldom bend to the Lordship of Christ; hands that applaud the works of man more than the work of God; minds that are closed to new ideas; emotions that are either out of control or under rigid wraps; muscles that are not exercised—mental muscles that have stopped being stretched, financial muscles that have stopped releasing with generosity, faith muscles that have become soft and flabby.

Where are you in that physical analysis of the Church? What's your temperature? How's your health? Is it possible that your condition is more serious than you may suspect? A Christian physician challenges our thinking with his penetrating words.

> Sometimes a dreaded thing occurs in the body—a mutiny— resulting in a tumor. . . .
>
> A tumor is called benign if its effect is fairly localized and it stays within membrane boundaries. But the most traumatizing condition in the body occurs when disloyal cells defy inhibition. They multiply without any checks on growth, spreading rapidly throughout the body, choking out normal cells. White cells, armed against foreign invaders, will not attack the body's own mutinous cells. Physicians fear no other malfunction more deeply: it is called cancer. For still mysterious reasons, these cells—and they may be cells from the brain, liver, kidney, bone, blood, skin, or other tissues—grow wild, out of control. Each is a healthy, functioning cell, but disloyal, no longer acting in regard for the rest of the body.
>
> Even the white cells, the dependable palace guard, can destroy the body through rebellion. Sometimes they recklessly reproduce, clogging the bloodstream, overloading the lymph system, strangling the body's normal functions—such is leukemia.
>
> Because I am a surgeon and not a prophet, I tremble to make the analogy between cancer in the physical body and mutiny in the spiritual body of Christ. But I must. In His warnings to the church, Jesus Christ showed no concern about the shocks and bruises His Body would meet from external forces. "The gates of hell shall not prevail against my church," He said flatly (Matthew 16:18). He moved easily, unthreatened, among sinners and criminals. But He cried out against the kind of disloyalty that comes from within.[2]

Few doctrines are more important than this one. Because the Church is under constant attack, we need to be good students of the subject. Because we are fellow members of the Body, we need to apply ourselves to mutual harmony. And because disease can diminish the effectiveness of the Body, we must maintain habits of health and a consistent program of exercise in harmony with God's Body-building program.

Furthermore, a regular checkup by the Great Physician is a must. Not once a year but at least once a week. And be prepared for the cost of that visit.

If you're looking to get it done for a nickel, you're in for a real surprise.

1. Every local church body—if it is alive and animated by the Spirit of God—has a "cutting edge". . . . areas of the local community or world community where its impact for the Lord Jesus Christ is being felt and is making a difference. Where is your church's cutting edge? Are you part of the "action" . . . in the front lines of ministry? Through faithful, informed prayer? In a strategic support ministry? As you pray about your role in the King's Army, consider investing some focused conversation time on these issues with someone in your church's leadership.

2. Let the words of 1 Corinthians 15:58 sift down into the deepest part of your being as you draw encouragement and motivation for service from this marvelous promise.

3. Generations of popular "Wild West" novelists have created the image of the self-sufficient frontiersman . . . the squint-eyed, close-lipped, saddle-hardened, raw-boned fella who needs no one, trusts no one, and leans on no one (except maybe his horse). This mythology has penetrated every facet of American life . . . including the Church. How does this go-it-alone mentality stack up against the truths expressed in 1 Corinthians 12? Read through that crucial chapter once again asking the Holy Spirit to help you examine your own attitudes. Record your response in your notebook. This would be a good time to express in writing your commitment to the Church.

THREE CHEERS
FOR THE CHURCH

ou remember Alexander, don't you? Well, maybe not. I introduced him to many of my readers a few years ago. Some of you may have forgotten. The little book that contained a slice out of his day was called *Alexander and the Terrible, Horrible, No Good, Very Bad Day*. This kid is my kind of guy. The stuff he goes through is so typical, you'd swear you've been inside his skin.

I'm glad to say that the lady who wrote his biography (I think it was his mother, Judith Viorst) has continued to write. She's written a book about herself called *How I Became Forty . . . and Other Atrocities*. Great little book!

Then she wrote *If I Were in Charge of the World and Other Worries*, which is pretty close to something that Alexander might have written. So think about that little five- or six-year-old fellow when you read the next few lines:

> If I were in charge of the world
> I'd cancel oatmeal,
> Monday mornings,
> Allergy shots.

> If I were in charge of the world
> There'd be brighter night lights,
> Healthier hamsters, and
> Basketball baskets forty-eight inches lower.

> If I were in charge of the world
> You wouldn't have lonely.

You wouldn't have clean.
You wouldn't have bedtimes.
Or "Don't punch your sister."
You wouldn't even have sisters.

If I were in charge of the world
A chocolate sundae with whipped cream and nuts
    would be a vegetable.
All 007 movies would be G.
And a person who sometimes forgot to brush,
And sometimes forgot to flush,
Would still be allowed to be
In charge of the world.[1]

Like I said, he's my kind of guy. Actually, I've been thinking about that line for a long time: "If I were in charge of the world . . ." If that were ever true, what would I do?

If God allowed me to be in charge for just twenty-four hours, I'd do *one* thing . . . *I'd change people's opinion about the church*. I would remove all prejudice about the church. I would erase all church scars and heal all church splits, all church bruises, and all hurts that came from church gossip. I would remove all those horrible offenses. And in place of all that? I would have everybody see only the value of the church. If all I had was twenty-four hours, that's what I'd do if I were in charge of the world.

But since I'm not, I will ask you to do the next best thing: I will ask you to take charge of your thoughts. And for the next few pages I challenge you to allow no negative thoughts about the church to enter your mind, only positive ones. (No fair cheating, now.) I'll do that with you. And let's see what a marvelous thing God has done in giving us churches.

FOR A FEW MINUTES, REMEMBER SOME CHURCHES

Let's go back to our childhood. Let's go way back. Let's go all the way back to when we first heard the hymns and we first listened to sermons and we first formed our impressions about church. And while we do that, let's allow the letter to the Philippians to guide us in our mental journey.

Days of Childhood

Some of us have very pleasant memories. A few, unfortunately, are not so pleasant. But since we're committed to staying on the sunny side of the street for a few pages, we may need to think of the kind of church we would have wanted to have as a child if we can't think of one that was real. For some, it was an urban church located in a busy city. And there were cars buzzing by outside and horns honking because of busy intersections. And there were multiple buildings and wide hallways and stained glass windows. Maybe when you were a little child, you were in a big, Gothic style church. Others were raised in a suburban church—the distant city just visible on the skyline. Perhaps your home was within walking distance. For many of us, it was a country church with a steeple, located in a rural part of the state where we lived—like the one William Pitts wrote of years ago:

> There's a church in the valley by the wildwood,
> No lovelier place in the dale;
> No spot is so dear to my childhood
> As the little brown church in the vale.
>
> Oh, come to the church in the wildwood,
> Oh, come to the church in the dale.
> No spot is so dear to my childhood
> As the little brown church in the vale.[2]

That was my church: little country town, little country church. But what a place! To this day I cherish healthy memories about that little house of worship.

> *Paul and Timothy, bond-servants of Christ Jesus, to all the saints in Christ Jesus who are in Philippi, including the overseers and deacons: I thank my God in all my remembrance of you, always offering prayer with joy in my every prayer for you all, in view of your participation in the gospel from the first day until now* (Philippians 1:1-5).

A statement in verse 3 should be linked with a thought in verse 5: "I thank my God in all my remembrance . . . in view of your partnership in the gospel from the first day . . ."

Think about your "first church." You were just a little girl . . . you were just a little guy. It was probably there where you first received formal instruction and learned to respect the authority of Scripture. You learned to sit still (longer than you wanted to) and to pay attention to something you didn't fully understand. You remember those early days when you listened to the hymns, when you formed your earliest religious impressions. It was there you discovered that there was a man of God who opened God's Book and believed it with all his heart. You probably sang your first solo there. Saw your first wedding . . . and funeral . . . and baptism. Joined your first choir or ensemble. It was there you discovered that you had leadership skills. It was there you learned the hard way that when God speaks it's best to listen . . . and not only listen, but also to obey.

It was there you gave yourself to that first group of people. They became a part of your life. You saw them every week, and you laughed with them, you wept with them, you celebrated with them, and you grieved with them. Just a little pocket of people. And because of them, the seasons had new meaning. Easter, Thanksgiving, and Christmas took on new color— even the new year gained purpose and significance. You thank God upon every remembrance of those people who were partners with you in the gospel. You and I have the church to thank for all those rich childhood memories.

Times of Crisis

Now let's travel a little deeper into the time tunnel and recall times of crisis in our past.

> *For it is only right for me to feel this way about you all, because I have you in my heart, since both in my imprisonment and in the defense and confirmation of the gospel, you all are partakers of grace with me. For God is my witness, how I long for you all with the affection of Christ Jesus* (vv. 7-8).

Observe his reference to imprisonment. Let's let that represent our trials, our life crises. Think about that. You may have lost your mom or your dad . . . a brother or a sister. And as helpful as the hospital staff or the physician tried to be, no one could minister to you like the people of the church. No one put their arms around you and said "I understand" like they did.

Some of you can recall stumbling out of the physician's office, having heard the news about the disease that could (and probably *would!*) take your life. It most likely was not a neighbor or some coworker at the office who entered into your crisis and said, "I understand"; it was someone at your church.

When your mate said, "It's over . . . I'm leaving," and then walked out, who helped you cope? In all of the embarrassment, the rejection, the anger, and the disillusionment, you probably didn't receive comfort from someone at the local bar or your bridge club. Chances are good that there was somebody from your church who said, "I've got a scar like that. And while you're hurting, I want you to know that I hurt with you. Even though you feel pushed out of society and shoved aside like a second-class bum, I understand your pain. And I stand in defense of you. In fact I love you."

Remember when grief struck you at the deepest level? Remember when your loved one was put in a casket? Maybe the banker could tell you where you could find a loan to get you through that hard time. Or maybe the insurance man helped you by bringing the check. Perhaps an attorney gave you sound advice. But who was there when the flowers wilted? Chances are good, the person who spoke well of your departed loved one was the pastor of a church. The people who surrounded you and gave you hope to go on were church people. They understood your world, they brought light to your darkness. That's the way God designed the church.

Remember disillusionment as a youth? (Just spend a moment thinking about that! I've never met anybody who wanted to be a teenager again.) Crisis after crisis. And remember the youth pastor who believed in you when you didn't even believe in yourself? Remember the Sunday school teacher who said she (or he) loved you, *regardless?*

Remember not knowing exactly what you should do in your career, and some pastor spoke directly from the Scripture, cutting a clear path of purpose through your dense fog of confusion?

Remember the tape of some sermon you played over and over and over again? What if there had never been a church? What if there had never been a cassette recording of some pastor who ministered to you? Remember, it wasn't from some law office or from some doctor's waiting room or even from some funeral home that your help came. Quite likely, your help to go on came from the church.

MOMENTS OF CELEBRATION
—■—

While we're traveling memory's lane, let's not miss the flowers!

> *And this I pray, that your love may abound still more and more in real knowledge and all discernment, so that you may approve the things that are excellent, in order to be sincere and blameless until the day of Christ; having been filled with the fruit of righteousness which comes through Jesus Christ, to the glory and praise of God* (vv. 9-11).

Where did you find your mate? More than likely you (like I) found her or him in a church. Where were you married? If you weren't married in a church, you probably wish you could have been. Who gave you the best counsel? Probably a pastor. Who was there to dedicate your first baby? Who said, "Marriage gets a little cold. And we've got a conference designed to help add a little spark to it . . ."? Who ministered to you when you really got scared about how to rear your family? Who said, "We affirm the family. We stand with you all the way through it, even at this time when your daughter has run away. We're here. We're not leaving"? Who was most effective in convincing her not to get an abortion? Who rejoiced with you when she turned back to the Lord?

Celebration times. Times of praise. Times when we are

> . . . filled with the fruit of righteousness which comes through Jesus Christ, to the glory and praise of God (v. 11).

How about when you made a decision to serve the Lord Jesus in your future career? How about when you celebrated a graduation out of school, and maybe even out of seminary? Who was there to say, "We're with you, we applaud your achievement—and if God leads you overseas, we won't forget you"? Perhaps the church held you closer than your own family. Perhaps the church contributed more to your income than any family member has ever contributed, because the church believed in you.

When a pastor or a music minister or an associate pastor defects from the faith, the tragedy will make the headlines. How often a church split will scandalize a neighborhood . . . or a brother or sister become offensive and say an ugly thing to you, or about you. And that weighs on your mind so heavily it possesses your thinking when someone brings up the subject of church. I know many people today who say, "Don't bother me with church. I've had it up to here." I understand. But I am saddened to meet people so jaded, because I realize how much they lose. There will come a day when those same bitter people will need the church. What a marvelous thing is the local family of God!

Let me go a step further. As helpful and beneficial as most parachurch ministries are, they are all dependent upon the church to exist. When you're in college and Inter-Varsity, Campus Crusade or some other campus ministry has really guided you and encouraged you, it is worth singing praises to God. But when you graduate, you need a church. The church, alone, has staying power.

It is in the church, week after week, where we learn faithfulness. It is in the church that we first learn to give and to tithe. It was the first place I gave out of my allowance. I remember squeezing my allowance in my hot little hand until I thought the buffalo would roar. But my mom and dad convinced me, "Son, this is where part of your money goes." It is in the church that we first learn generosity. I didn't give it to a friend. I didn't give it to a family member. Or a school. I gave it to God's work. It is in the church that discipleship is carried out. It is in the church that accountability is modeled. It is in the church that marriage is upheld and singleness is dignified without your being hustled. It is in the church of Jesus Christ that we find the doctrinal roots that establish us in our faith.

When the plan to reach out onto some foreign soil is determined, the church is there to make it happen. When an evangelistic series is promoted in the community, it is the church that does so. When the project is over, when the crusade team members have all gone home, *the church stays*. It takes the new converts and nurtures them into their own walk. Three cheers for the church! In spite of all her weaknesses and human flaws, it is still the most significant rallying point for Christians on this earth today. It will continue to be so until Jesus Christ returns.

WHY THE CHURCH IS SO SIGNIFICANT

Let me show you why the church is significant in the world and in the community.

In the World

> Now I want you to know, brethren, that my circumstances have turned out for the greater progress of the gospel, so that my imprisonment in the cause of Christ has become well-known throughout the whole praetorian guard and to everyone else, and that most of the brethren, trusting in the Lord because of my imprisonment, have far more courage to speak the word of God without fear (vv. 12-14).

I understand that Paul means this personally. But allow me to broaden the application and apply it to the church. Why is the church significant to the world? Because the church represents penetrating light and undiluted salt in a lost, confused, insipid society. Interestingly, when a church remains neutral on a moral issue that affects the community, the public will criticize that church. The public will state that it has let the community down. In the public arena, the Church of Jesus Christ is *expected* to stand for righteousness. Even the uncommitted, the nonchurch crowd know in their hearts that a church that is weak regarding sin has lost its way.

I remember reading about the late president Calvin Coolidge, who returned home from attending church early one Sunday afternoon. He was asked by his wife what the minister spoke on.

"Sin," Coolidge replied.

Wanting to know more, she pressed him for some words of explanation. And being a man of few words with his wife, he responded, "I think he was against it."

When the pulpit denounces sin, people are influenced to stand against it. When the pulpit speaks on moral issues, people learn to penetrate the fog of compromise and gain courage to stand alone. For many, many years in our nation the church gave our nation its conscience. As its pulpits stood, its people stood.

"You are the salt of the earth," said Jesus. "You are the light on a hill. Don't put a bushel basket over it." Let the light shine. Let the salt bite. That's your role, Christian! The world expects it from us, even though it doesn't agree. In Paul's day "the whole praetorian guard" became aware of Christ! Even though many will not enter the doors of a local church (though they are invited), they expect us to stand for the truth as we see it in the Scripture. To do less is to diminish our distinctive and to lose our integrity.

In the Community

Are you ready for a surprise? What I am about to write will make a few of my readers swallow hard. Some of you who look with a squint-eye at other ministries, criticizing them because they don't agree with you, are going to be shocked by these next four verses:

> Some, to be sure, are preaching Christ out of selfish ambition, rather than from pure motives, thinking to cause me distress in my imprisonment. What then? Only that in every way, whether in pretense or in truth, Christ is proclaimed; and in this I rejoice, yes, and I will rejoice (vv. 15-18).

Why is the church significant in the community? For at least two reasons. First of all, because churches provide the availability of variety. And second, because churches offer a singularity of message. Here's what this passage is saying. There will be churches of all different kinds. Think of the windshield wiper on your car. Churches will go from one extreme to another. Churches that are worth attending and supporting have the same pivot point, the Lord Jesus Christ. Christ is exalted. Christ is declared. Christ is central. But some will go at it from one direction, while others will go at it from another. A different style of worship. Another approach, emphasis, and methodology. And even a difference in *motive* (according to what Paul wrote).

J. B. Phillips paraphrases these verses:

> *I know that some are preaching Christ out of jealousy, in order to annoy me, but some are preaching him in good faith. These latter are preaching out of their love for me. For they know that God has set me here in prison to defend our right to preach the gospel. The motive of the former is questionable—they preach in a partisan spirit, hoping to make my chains even more galling than they would otherwise be. But what does it matter? However they may look at it, the fact remains that Christ is being preached, whether sincerely or not, and that fact makes me very happy* (vv. 15-18).

I have a strong word to all who are given to public criticism of other ministries. Watch yourself! Rather than being discerning, you may have become too narrow and rigid! Learn from Paul. Even ministries that may employ a few deceptive motives, even churches that you choose not to attend, Paul said, in effect, "I rejoice that at least Christ is proclaimed."

Let's face it, if everybody attended where you attend, the community couldn't fit in. We must learn to give God praise that there is a variety of ministries. We gain nothing by promoting the idea that we have *the* corner on the truth, and that our pastor is the only one who has *the* answers for life. No, no, a thousand times, no! God may be using this man with his style for this ministry and that man with another approach for that ministry . . . each one exalting and presenting Christ to different types of people.

My advice? Don't waste your time criticizing other ministries. Just attend the one that you prefer and give God praise that Christ is exalted. You may be thinking, "Sounds pretty liberal to me." Well, it sounds biblical to me. If Philippians 1:15-20 isn't teaching that, then, frankly, I'm at a loss to know what it means. In our zeal it is very easy to think we've got the *only* church with the *only* answers for the entire community. We don't.

As a pastor, I am relieved and grateful that I am not the only fish in the pond. What an awesome responsibility that would be! Furthermore, that's *Christ's* role, since He is the Head of the Church. I look back on some of the things I have said, and I realize now I gave wrong counsel—or weak, at best. On occasion I listen to some of the cassette taped sermons I once preached (which is always a tough assignment!), and I no more agree today with what I said back then than the man in the moon! After a few years I see it in a little different light and my words come back to haunt me. I'm so grateful not everybody believed my stuff way back then any more than they do now!

And while I'm confessing, I might as well admit, I'm thankful that even when I preached with the wrong motive (as I have on a few occasions, much to my shame), God honored His message at that time and rebuked me later. You see, in many communities there is a variety of churches available, but, praise God, if you listen attentively, you're going to hear Christ preached. Stop exalting one church as though it were *the only* place to attend! It is not. We would do well to remember that Christ is to be exalted . . . not some church.

Since the late 1970s God has allowed my wife and me to serve together in a radio ministry, "Insight for Living." She directs the operation of this outreach (with the help of almost one hundred and fifty others) as I supply the voice and the messages. To our continual surprise, the Lord has given growth and caused His name to be increasingly more exalted through these broadcasts. Occasionally, I have wondered why. Perhaps one of the reasons is that we have no interest whatsoever in either promoting ourselves or in criticizing others. God's hand is on *many* ministries and He is using *many* ministers to get the job done. They differ from us in style, often in content, and perhaps in objective or even motive. But those who are proclaiming Christ cause us to rejoice. After all, they are able to reach certain folks we would never reach.

The same could be said of the church I pastor. There are many churches in southern California. They range in variety from the super-conservative to the loosey-goosey extreme. But the interesting fact is this: People attend every one of them. They choose to go there because they are ministered to and because they are comfortable with the style, the approach, the objectives. For every place where Christ is proclaimed and exalted, I sincerely rejoice. Thank God, I'm not the jealous or the competitive type. If God raised up those ministries, who am I to tear them down? That would not only be disobedient, it would be a waste of precious time and energy.

For the Christian

The church is significant not only to the world and in the community but to the Christian as well.

> *But I am hard pressed from both directions, having the desire to depart and be with Christ, for that is very much better; yet to remain on in the flesh is more necessary for your sake. And convinced of this, I know that I shall remain and continue with you all for your progress and joy in the faith, so that your proud confidence in me may abound in Christ Jesus through my coming to you again. Only conduct yourselves in a manner worthy of the gospel of Christ; so that whether I come and see you or remain absent, I may hear of you that you are standing firm in one spirit, with one mind striving together for the faith of the gospel; in no way alarmed by your opponents—which is a sign of destruction for them, but of salvation for you, and that too, from God. For to you it has been granted for Christ's sake, not only to believe in Him, but also to suffer for His sake, experiencing the same conflict which you saw in me, and now hear to be in me* (vv. 23-30).

This passage tells us something that the Masonic Lodge or the bowling team will never tell us. It says something the school board or the city council will never tell us. The church alone tells the Christian to:

> . . . *conduct yourselves in a manner worthy of the gospel of Christ*. . . .

You won't hear that from any other organization! No one will push hard against your breastbone and say, "Shape up your life. Get with it. You say you're a Christian? Walk like it. You've done wrong? Confess it and come back to God."

No one else does that. Only the church.

I'll add more—only those who continue faithfully in the attendance of church services will hear reproof and exhortation and encouragement and rebuke that will help keep their lives in line. In fact, I recently came up with a list of four specific benefits of church attendance:

- Accountability
- Consistency
- Unity
- Stability

I won't take the time to develop each one, but they are interwoven through these verses.

What I have observed is that Christians who lose faith in a local church and walk away, saying, "No thanks, I don't need it," have struggles, without exception, in one or more of these four areas—sometimes all four. They lose (or *wish* to lose) accountability. They lack consistency in their walk. They cultivate an independent spirit, rather than an interdependence of love and concern. And when pressure strikes, they lack stability. Why? The answer isn't that complicated: There's no family around.

My counsel is predictable—before you think that you really don't need a church, run down that list one more time. The consequences are inescapable. Especially if you have available to you a small group of caring, loving folks with whom you are free to interact, share the details of your life, and enter into theirs as well.

I might also add that apart from the church, there is no place to observe the sacred ordinances . . . something I dare not overlook in this book on doctrine.

Two Ordinances Unique to the Church

In this wonderful body called the Church, God has given two very unique sacraments or celebrations. In no other organization will you find such things. One is called the Lord's Supper (your church may call it Communion, the Eucharist, or simply the Table). The other is baptism. The Lord's Supper is a memorial of remembrance, and baptism is a celebration of reflection. With no desire to offend anyone, I sometimes think of them as sacred pantomimes. They are sermons without words . . . full of symbolic significance. The Lord's Supper is saying, "He died for me." The baptismal celebration is saying, "He lives in me."

Both require only a few words of explanation. Both are for believers only. Both are rich in symbolism, yet beautiful in simplicity. And both make bold statements to the world regarding the Christian faith.

Neither, however, is essential for salvation. By that I mean that they are *because of* salvation, not a means to it. Yet neither is to be treated lightly or viewed as if they are of little importance.

The Lord's Supper

Have you stopped lately to think about the Lord's Supper? What a simple ceremony—and so strange in the eyes of the world! A little bit of pastry and a swallow of liquid—how strange. In places all around the world there are little pieces of pastry and there are little cups of wine or juice. Regardless of the exact substance, or the amount, it is what each represents that is so extremely important—the bread representing our Savior's body and the cup representing His blood, both given for us at the Cross. Both, taken in His remembrance, cause us to recall that He died for us.

I've often stated publicly that one of the most memorable communion times I can remember takes me back to the early 1960s when I was with a large group of Christian collegians up on the northern California coastline, not far from Santa Cruz. It was a church-sponsored outing. We were sitting on a windswept, chilly beach. We had sung a few songs around sunset. All we had to serve were chips and cola. Yet it was marvelous! I have never before or since served chips and cola at the Lord's Supper, but the elements were insignificant. Our Lord's presence was there in the sunset over the Pacific, in the pounding of the surf, in the faces of those young believers, in the tears that fell, in the testimonies that were spoken. And we worshiped our God as we met at that open place, sand between our toes, swimming suits on, towels wrapped around us as we shivered around the fire and passed the chips and cola among us. We did it all "in remembrance of Me."

The biblical basis for the Lord's Supper takes us back to the last meal Jesus had with His disciples before He was crucified. Matthew records the event in the simplest of terms.

> *And while they were eating, Jesus took some bread, and after a blessing, He broke it and gave it to the disciples, and said, "Take, eat; this is My body." And He took a cup and gave thanks, and gave it to them, saying, "Drink from it, all of you; for this is My blood of the covenant, which is to be shed on behalf of many for forgiveness of sins. But I say to you, I will not drink of this fruit of the vine from now on until that day when I drink it new with you in My Father's kingdom." And after singing a hymn, they went out to the Mount of Olives* (Matthew 26:26-30).

The apostle Paul draws upon that scene when he later writes these words in the Corinthian letter:

> *For I received from the Lord that which I also delivered to you, that the Lord Jesus in the night in which He was betrayed took bread; and when He had given thanks, He broke it, and said, "This is My body, which is for you; do this in remembrance of Me"* (1 Corinthians 11:23-24).

Obviously, participation is not optional; on the contrary, it is a command, "Do this. . . !" Don't look upon the Lord's Supper simply as an available, optional part of your worship. We are assigned by God to do it continually. In fact, the command is a present imperative, "Keep on doing this in remembrance of Me."

Some observe the Supper every time they meet. Some observe it every other week. Some "keep on doing this" once a month. It would seem inappropriate to observe it less frequently than once a month since we are to "keep on doing this."

The instruction continues:

> *In the same way He took the cup also, after supper, saying, "This cup is the new covenant in My blood; do this, as often as you drink it, in remembrance of Me." For as often as you eat this bread and drink the cup, you proclaim the Lord's death until He comes* (vv. 25-26).

We'll be eating together at this simple table in our churches until our Savior returns. It will be regularly observed by believers in rugged churches with thatched roofs as well as in beautiful cathedrals with high ceilings and ornate walls lined by stained glass . . . in brand new places of worship only a week or two old, as well as in places centuries old, they'll still be observing the Lord's Supper. That's the church's ordinance.

The place is not significant, but the condition of the heart is. Before we ever eat the bread or drink from that cup, each Christian asks within himself, "Is there anything between my Father and me? Is my heart clean?" A strong warning is attached to the instruction:

> *Therefore whoever eats the bread or drinks the cup of the Lord in an unworthy manner, shall be guilty of the body and the blood of the Lord. But let a man examine himself, and so let him eat of the bread and drink of the cup. For he who eats and drinks, eats and drinks judgment to himself, if he does not judge the body rightly. For this reason many among you are weak and sick, and a number sleep* (vv. 27-30).

The Corinthians turned the Lord's Supper into a carnal event. Instead of an atmosphere of worship and humble confession, they made light of the event by eating too much, drinking too much, and showing favoritism to the cliques in the church. A circus atmosphere ruined what was designed to be the most memorable moments of worship a church family can enter into together. We must learn from their carnal display of disobedience. Each believer must examine his or her own heart before participating in the eating and drinking of the elements of the communion table.

Water Baptism

Through the centuries, Christians have also declared their commitment to Christ by submitting themselves to water baptism, a public act of deep significance. Even though Romans 6 has reference to Spirit baptism, the word picture is appropriate for water baptism.

> *Or do you not know that all of us who have been baptized into Christ Jesus have been baptized into His death?* (Romans 6:3).

In the first century the term *baptism* meant "identification." In fact, it was a fuller's term—the dry cleaner of ancient days. When he took a white garment and dipped it into a scarlet dye, he was said to have "baptized" the garment. The white garment's identity was changed to scarlet. *Baptizo* was the term used when he "changed its identity." That's the word used here, transliterated "baptized."

> *Or do you not know that all of us who have been baptized into Christ Jesus have been baptized into His death? Therefore we have been buried with Him through baptism into death, in order that as Christ was raised from the dead through the glory of the Father, so we too might walk in newness of life* (vv. 3-4).

Did you know that in the ordinance of baptism, the water is a picture of death? Have you ever been told that when a person goes under the water or has the water sprinkled over him or her that the water is a picture of their identification with the death of Christ? It is true. And as the water runs off, or as the person is brought up out of the water, it is symbolic of the resurrection of Christ out of death. The person being baptized is "acting out" his or her death to sin and subsequent newness of walk in Jesus Christ. This act of obedience isn't simply a take-it-or-leave-it issue. No. While it isn't essential for salvation, it is certainly expected of the believer. As with the Lord's Supper, it is a picture of our being united with Christ Jesus in the likeness of His death and His resurrection.

In my travels outside the United States, I have discovered that baptism is the most significant point of change in the eyes of the public. Internationally, the world believes that the one being baptized is indeed a Christian when he or she steps into the baptismal waters—a public testimony of faith in Christ. That act is a public declaration, saying, "I belong to Jesus Christ. I identify with His death for me. And by being raised from the water, I identify with a new kind of life that I could never live on my own, but by His power I will be able to experience. I've been born again. And that's why I want to display what has happened to me already in my life."

I appreciate the words that Philip Henry, father of Matthew Henry, wrote for his children. It became their baptismal statement:

> I take God to be my chief end and highest good.
> I take God the Son to my prince and Savior.
> I take God the Holy Spirit to be my sanctifier,
>   teacher, guide, and comforter.
> I take the Word of God to be my rule in all my actions
>   and the people of God to be my people
>   under all conditions.
> I do hereby dedicate and devote to the Lord all I am,
>   all I have,
>   and all I can do.
> And this I do deliberately, freely, and forever.

LONG LIVE GOD'S PEOPLE!

When we began this chapter, I asked you to take charge of your thoughts. I'd like you to do that again as I close the chapter. I urge you to ask yourself several hard questions: Where do I really stand regarding the work of a local church? Is my participation halfhearted or wholehearted? Does my walk reflect its purity? Does my giving reflect generosity? Dig deeper. Probe your own heart. Have I taken the ordinances seriously as He has planned them to be taken? Have I prayed for the church's mission and ministry? Do I support it in active service, not simply in passive presence? Perhaps you have been overly critical of other ministries and too exclusive regarding your own. Maybe you have stopped attending any local church. Now is the time to deal with those things. Please do.

As you align yourself with the church, you join a body of people who have played a vital role in the shaping of history. They have often been maligned and misunderstood. They have occasionally been fanatical and unbalanced, at times ignored and at other times admired and quoted. But they have usually been sincere. Whatever, the church is God's project. It will not fail. Long live the church!

The following piece, though not original with me, sums up my convictions exactly:

God has always had a people, a people who believe by faith, who trust and obey His Word, a people whose God is the Lord.

Many a foolish conqueror has made the mistake of thinking that because he had forced the Church of Jesus Christ out of sight, He had stilled its voice and snuffed out its life.

But God has always had a people; He has always had a people who believe; that believe His Word, a people whose God is the Lord.

The powerful current of a rushing river is not diminished because it is forced to flow underground. The purest water is the stream that bursts crystal clear into the sunlight after it has forced its way through solid rock.

There have been charlatans, like Simon the magician, who sought to barter on the open market that power which cannot be bought or sold. But, God has always had a people . . . men who could not be bought, and women who were beyond purchase. God has always had a people—people who believe by faith!

There have been times of affluence and prosperity when the Church's message has been diluted into oblivion by those who sought to make it socially attractive, neatly organized, and financially profitable.

It has been gold-plated, draped in purple, and encrusted with jewels. It has been misrepresented, ridiculed, lauded, and scorned.

These followers of Jesus Christ have been, according to the whim of the times, elevated as sacred leaders, and martyred as heretics. Yet, through it all there marches on that powerful army of the meek—God's chosen people who cannot be bought, flattered, murdered, or stilled! On through the ages they march!

God has always had a people—the Church, God's Church triumphant! God has always had a people, followers of Jesus—chosen people. A people who believe by faith, who trust and believe His Word, a people whose God is the Lord. God has always—*always*—had a people![3]

1. When you hear that someone within your local church body is hurting because of a disappointment or loss, is your first thought—"What can I do to show my love and the love of Christ to that person?" or is it, "Well, someone else will surely do something—I don't even know him or her that well." Let Romans 12:9-15, 1 John 4:7-12 and Philippians 2:4 guide you as you seek to become a wider, deeper channel for the love of our Lord within His body.

2. Are you helping your children learn faithfulness to the Lord and to His people through *giving* . . . perhaps by encouraging them to set aside a portion of their allowance for the Lord's work? How about considering a special "family project," perhaps selecting a missionary, "adopting" a Third World child, or assisting a struggling family in your community? Let the children feel the excitement and see the results as they learn to express the love of Christ through giving of their own means.

3. Have you ever felt "unprepared" for a time at the Lord's Supper? You felt, perhaps, like you had to do a quick "heart search" for unconfessed sin in your life. Or a "hurry-up" meditation on what the body and blood of our Lord really means to you in a personal way. While there is nothing wrong with either of these actions, you may find the time at the table to be a much more meaningful worship experience if you begin your heart preparation on *Saturday*. Before you slip between the covers that night, take a few minutes to ponder the familiar words of 1 Corinthians 11:21-31 . . . or perhaps one of the "confession" psalms such as Psalm 32 or 51 . . . or one of the Gospel accounts of that meal in the Upper Room or those dark hours on the cross. Ask your Lord to meet with you in a new way as you come to that simple meal.

The Family of God

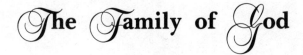

"I am grateful to be a part of a local church which exists to proclaim God's truth, to administer the ordinances, to stimulate growth toward maturity, and to bring glory to God."

ENCOURAGEMENT
SERVED
FAMILY STYLE

id you ever get a song on your mind? Sure, it happens to all of us. I've had one on my mind for several days . . . ever since I returned from a weekend conference I spent with several hundred of our church folks at a Christian conference center in the mountains. It's not one of the great hymns of the Church, but rather a very familiar folk song we sang during a fun time we spent together:

> O give me a home where the buffalo roam,
> Where the deer and the antelope play,
> Where seldom is heard a discouraging word,
> And the skies are not cloudy all day.
>
> Home, home on the range . . .

While turning that tune over in my mind all the way back from Forest Home, I began to think about that third line, "Where seldom is heard a discouraging word . . ." I asked myself: Who wouldn't like to be in a home like that? Unfortunately, we usually think of it as existing as a fantasy in some imaginary "Home On the Range." It's probably too ideal to be true. I thought, what we need is a place like that in the city . . . not on some idealistic blue-sky range far away. I also thought about the need for such a setting in the church today.

So I wrote another set of words that could be sung to the same tune.

> O give me a church where folks in the lurch
> Are encouraged, then healed from above;
> Where seldom is heard a discouraging word,
> And the truth is modeled in love.

Ever been in one like that? If you find one, I can guarantee the place will be packed to the rafters Sunday after Sunday. That kind of Body will draw folks in like a magnet. Why? Because we live in a world where the theme of life seems to be putting people down, finding their faults, and discouraging them.

ENCOURAGEMENT DEFINED AND EXPLAINED

I checked with Webster and found that the verb *discourage* means "to deprive of courage, to dishearten, to hinder, to deter." And, in contrast, the same source defines *encourage* as "to inspire with courage, to give spirit or hope; hearten, to spur on, stimulate, to give help."

When I analyze the English word *encouragement*, my thoughts turn to the word *enthusiasm*. The Greek term *Entheos* is the root. It means "to put God (theos) into (en) something or someone." Since that is true, then *encourage* would mean "to put courage into someone." You may be surprised to discover who needs it . . . sometimes the most unexpected people you could imagine need it.

While I was hurrying to get away for the conference at Forest Home, I whipped through the mail at home and found my copy of *Sports Illustrated*. I shoved it into my briefcase since I knew there would be some time to relax on Saturday afternoon up in the mountains. Sure enough, I was able to curl up in a corner with a cup of coffee and browse through the new issue . . . one of my favorite pastimes. While reading it, I came across a gripping story of a relatively unknown athlete—a young man named Brian Hiemer.

> Nebraska football players will wear the numeral 94 on their helmets this season in tribute to senior Brian Hiemer, 21, who died after shooting himself in the head on August 13, the day he was to report for fall practice. Hiemer's death shocked an entire state. "Nobody wanted to believe what happened," says Bill Morgan, owner of the A and B Cafe in Shelby, Nebraska . . . Hiemer's hometown. "Everyone wants to know why."

The article continues:

> An all-state kicker and tight end as well as a yearbook editor and prom king, Hiemer had a storybook high school career. At Nebraska he was dubbed the Comeback Kid. When he was cut after his freshman season, he persuaded head coach Tom Osborne to give him another chance, he then rose rapidly from 10th on the Cornhusker depth charts to first string. . . .

After describing his great season last year, it ends:

Hiemer had returned to the family's 320-acre farm from the university on Friday evening, August 9. Over the weekend, he mowed the lawn and walked the fields with his father. On Tuesday, however, Loyola Hiemer noticed that her son was unusually restless and quiet. That afternoon, while his father was in the north fields and his mother was in the house, Hiemer walked behind a wooden shed and sat down with a .22 caliber rifle, one bullet in the weapon. He was found about 4 p.m. by his father. Walking near the shed last week, Willard Hiemer said, "You look for something, a warning. Maybe there was a reason, but Brian didn't tell us."

. . . Kriss King, a classmate who dated him last spring, says that Hiemer, with an eye on a pro career, was trying unsuccessfully to put on extra weight. . . . King and Gregg Reeves, a defensive end, both say that Hiemer was worried about a future life on the farm. "He didn't think that with just him and his dad it was economically feasible," says Reeves. . . .

Nebraska is now preparing for the season opener against Florida State this Saturday, September 7, but the team has already suffered its biggest loss of the season. Hiemer is gone, and no one understands the reason. Huey says, "Whatever it was, it will rest with Brian."[1]

Frankly, that could be your son . . . or mine.

It could be your roommate, or maybe your neighbor. Could be your own mom or dad. Could be the person who sits right next to you in church on Sunday. Who would have ever imagined?

I don't mean to be dramatic about it, but this business of discouragement is real. It hits like a silent plague and cripples us within. I cannot emphasize enough the importance of those words:

Give me a church where folks in the lurch
Are encouraged, then healed from above;
Where seldom is heard a discouraging word,
And the truth is modeled in love.

That isn't some dreamy idea that comes out of a theoretical mind. That comes straight out of the Scriptures. Did you know that we are actually *commanded* by our God to encourage one another? He expects us to serve it to one another "family style."

Believe me, if we in God's family fail to do it, it is doubtful we'll find it anywhere else.

BIBLICAL BASIS FOR ENCOURAGEMENT

The scripture I want us to look at first is Hebrews 10. All the way through this letter the spotlight has been upon Jesus Christ, the Superior One. He has opened for us a new and living way to the Father. We don't have to go through a system of works. We don't have to go through some other person who will represent our cause. We don't have to earn our way into the presence of God and hope that He will lend an ear and hear our requests. No, not that. Finally, the climax:

> *Since therefore, brethren, we have confidence to enter the holy place by the blood of Jesus, by a new and living way which He inaugurated for us through the veil, that is, His flesh, and since we have a great priest over the house of God*... (Hebrews 10:19-21).

His point is this: Since we have confidence to enter the Lord's presence and since we have Christ as our "great Priest," let us execute the following three commands, each of which is introduced by "Let us . . . "

> *Let us draw near with a sincere heart in full assurance of faith, having our hearts sprinkled clean from an evil conscience and our bodies washed with pure water* (v. 22).

This is symbolic language. It means: Let us come into the presence of our God clean and pure. Let's have no lingering sin hanging heavily over us like an anchor as we attempt to storm the throne with our needs. Let us draw near!

The next command:

> *Let us hold fast the confession of our hope without wavering, for He who promised is faithful* (v. 23).

This second command is a strong one, written before the ink is dry on the first. "Let us draw near." Amen! "Let us hold fast." Amen! But also:

> *And let us consider how to stimulate one another to love and good deeds* (v. 24).

Did you ever know that was in the Bible? Let us give attention to *how* we might stimulate our brothers and sisters in the family of God. It isn't just a suggestion, an off-the-cuff, casual idea like, "Oh, by the way, . . . it might be good, while you're holding fast to the faith, to toss in a little encouragement."

But he's not through with the thought. It is completed in the next verse:

Not forsaking our own assembling together, as is the habit of some, but encouraging one another; and all the more, as you see the day drawing near (v. 25).

It is impossible to stimulate someone else to love and good deeds if we are not around them. We cannot be an encouragement if we live our lives in secret caves, pushing people away from us. People out of touch don't encourage others. Encouragement is a face-to-face thing. So, in effect, he says:

Let us not neglect our church meetings, as some people do, but encourage and warn each other, especially now that the day of his coming back again is drawing near (v. 25, TLB)

I see a couple of thoughts woven through these lines.

1. *Encouragement is not the responsibility of a gifted few, but the responsibility of all in the family of God.* Obviously, the official role of a pastor is the responsibility of a few. And the role of an elder is another responsibility for a few. Maybe an officer or a teacher is the responsibility of a few people in a church. But I don't find this passage addressed to any specific, gifted individual, rather to all in the family. That means *you.*

2. *Encouragement is not something that is needed less in the Body, but more.* You'll notice that the writer refers to this being needed "all the more as you see the day [of Christ's return] drawing near." Do you know why? We looked at the reason earlier in this book. It is mentioned in 2 Timothy 3:1.

This know also, that in the last days perilous times shall come (KJV).

Interesting word that Paul uses, translated "perilous" in the King James Bible. "Troublesome" is the paraphrase that some will use. It is also like our English term *savage.* "In the last days, savage times will come." These are the days in which we live.

Now why do I emphasize that? Because that's the reason we need encouragement all the more. Like early American pioneers who braved the new frontiers, when we walk out of the loving fellowship of God's family, we move into "savage territory." In that realm we are threatened and we can be easily intimidated. In light of that fact, God's people need to turn on the encouragement! The family of God is not a place for verbal put-downs, sarcastic jabs, critical comments, and harsh judgment. We get enough of that from the world. This is a place we need to assemble for the purpose of being encouraged . . . a place we are free to be ourselves.

One New Testament scholar does a fine job of tracing the meaning of encouragement through the New Testament. He points out how it was used in extra-biblical literature for exhorting troops who were about to go into battle.

> Euripides . . . describing the plans for battle says: "So they did hail them, *cheering* them to fight." Xenophon, uses it of urging the soldiers to embark upon the ships and set out on an adventurous voyage . . . Polybius uses it of . . . Demetrius rallying his men and addressing the ranks before they embarked upon battle . . . And the word he uses of embarking upon battle is *Diakinduneuein*, which means to accept the risk of battle.

> Again and again we find that *Parakalein* is the word of the rallying-call; it is the word used of the speeches of leaders and of soldiers who urge each other on. It is the word used of words which send fearful and timorous and hesitant soldiers and sailors courageously into battle. A *Parakletos* is therefore an *Encourager*, one who puts courage into the faint-hearted, one who nerves the feeble arm for fight, one who makes a very ordinary man cope gallantly with a perilous and a dangerous situation . . .

> . . . The word *Parakalein* is the word for exhorting [others] to noble deeds and high thoughts; it is especially the word of courage before battle. Life is always calling us into battle and the one who makes us able to stand up to the opposing forces, to cope with life and to conquer life is the *Parakletos*, the Holy Spirit, who is none other than the presence and power of the risen Christ.[2]

Parakalein—that's the word that is most often translated "encourage" in our Bibles. We find it again in Hebrews 10:25.

> *Not forsaking our own assembling together, as is the habit of some, but encouraging one another . . .*

Celeste Holm, the film star of yesteryear, was quoted on one occasion as saying, "We live by encouragement, and we die without it—slowly, sadly, angrily."

Why would I address this issue in a book on doctrine? Because I have observed how easy it is for Christians to become attracted to theological truths to the exclusion of close relationships with each other. We need both/and, not either/or. The place of strong spiritual instruction is also to be a place of deep, personal compassion. The same Scriptures that encourage our growing in knowledge also exhort us to grow in love, tolerance, grace, and acceptance. Those passages that urge keen thinking and clear discernment are well balanced by other passages that affirm our understanding and, yes, our encouraging one another.

Blind songwriter, Ken Medema, seldom fails to put his finger on a tender nerve. His lack of eyesight has sensitized his insight, giving him that sixth sense we who see often miss. I love his song "If This Is Not a Place," which says everything that I am trying to communicate, only so much better.

> If this is not a place where tears are understood,
> Then where shall I go to cry?
> And if this is not a place where my spirit can take wings,
> Then where shall I go to fly?

> I don't need another place for tryin' to impress you
> With just how good and virtuous I am, no, no, no
> I don't need another place for always bein' on top of things
> Everybody knows that it's a sham, it's a sham.
> I don't need another place for always wearin' smiles
> Even when it's not the way I feel.
> I don't need another place to mouth the same old platitudes ·
> Everybody knows that it's not real.

> So if this is not a place where my questions can be asked,
> Then where shall I go to seek?
> And if this is not a place where my heart cry can be heard,
> Where, tell me where, shall I go to speak?

> So if this is not a place where tears are understood,
> Where shall I go, where shall I go to fly?[3]

ENCOURAGEMENT: HOW TO DO IT

For the next few pages, I want us to limit our thoughts on encouragement to the *tongue*. I want us to see, as if for the very first time, how much weight is carried by the words we utter and the tone we use. To keep it simple, let's stay in the Book of Proverbs, the wisdom book. Think of these words as God's counsel to all of us in His family, for indeed they are.

Proverbs 10:11-13a

> *The mouth of the righteous is a fountain of life, but the mouth of the wicked conceals violence. Hatred stirs up strife, but love covers all transgressions* (vv. 11-12).

We cannot deny that the tongue is an instrument of forgiveness. It has the ability to conceal violence and cover transgressions. Continuing on:

On the lips of the discerning, wisdom is found (v. 13a).

There is a transfer of wisdom from one life to another through the vehicle of the tongue.

What power! A fountain of life. An instrument of forgiveness. A concealment of violence. A source and/or transfer of wisdom.

Proverbs 10:19-21a

When there are many words, transgression is unavoidable, but he who restrains his lips is wise (v. 19).

I'm glad God included those words in His Book. It is easy to think that all we need to do when we're together is talk, talk, talk. Sometimes well-chosen words, though brief, are much more eloquent than a paragraph of information dumped from someone's mouth to another's ears. Proverbs 10:19 extols rationing our words.

He continues:

. . . The tongue of the righteous is as choice silver. . . . The lips of the righteous feed many. . . . (vv. 20-21).

The tongue, with words as valuable as choice silver, brings treasured nourishment to hungry hearts.

Proverbs 12:17-18

He who speaks truth tells what is right, but a false witness, deceit. There is one who speaks rashly like the thrusts of a sword, but the tongue of the wise brings healing.

I don't know if you have been the recipient of healing from someone's tongue, but I certainly have. Perhaps you can recall being hurt so deeply the wound refused to heal. No scab would form within. And about the time it started to heal, it got ripped off again. You bleed. You're uncomfortable. You may be humiliated, perhaps frightened by the savage world around you. And someone in God's forever family cares enough to look deep into your eyes and say just the right thing at just the right time. What happens? "The tongue of the wise brings healing."

I can't emphasize enough the importance of the ways moms and dads talk with their children. As a matter of fact, I was really caught off guard when I first found this next proverb. You talk about a reproof from God, I got it! And I have never forgotten it.

Proverbs 18:21

Death and life are in the power of the tongue, and those who love it will eat its fruit.

In recent years I have come to know and have grown to love and respect Gordon MacDonald, president of Inter-Varsity Christian Fellowship. I now consider Gordon one of my friends. The man has written one of the finest books on parenting ever published. It is entitled *The Effective Father*. I have read and reread sections of this book so much, they are now ripped and ragged. I always stop at this illustration, since it describes a scene so typical, so painful in lives today.

A forty-two-year-old man has allowed me to look into the inner recesses of his life and see what makes him what he is today: a man who is frantically working himself into exhaustion; one who spends every dime he makes for impressive artifacts of luxury and success; a volatile human being whose temper explodes at the slightest hint of disagreement or criticism. As we talk I ask Tom to tell me about his childhood.

At one impressionable point in boyhood, when my friend was apparently displeasing his father with the way he was doing a chore, his father said to him, "Tom, you will always be a bum. You're not going to amount to a thing; you're a bum!" Tom goes on to tell me that whenever he and his father had angry moments, the same prediction would be repeated until it burned its way into the boy's spirit so deeply that, like shrapnel embedded in flesh, the words could never be removed. Thirty years later, Tom still suffers from his father's verbal malpractice. They drive him day and night from a subconscious source to attempt to prove that his father was wrong. Ironically, even though Tom's father is dead, the habit patterns of Tom's inner life still maintain fever pitch to convince a dead father and a slightly unsure Tom that he is not a bum. Let anyone suggests to Tom that he is doing something wrong or that he is deficient in some aspect of his life, and hostility, defensiveness, and furious energy are unleashed to guard against what he senses is a resurrection of the old accusations from a thoughtless father who verbally set a wrong pace.[4]

Moms and dads, pastors and teachers, counselors and coaches, your tongue possesses the power of life and death. Let us never think our words will be overlooked and easily erased. You and I can remember a statement from a teacher who, in a moment of haste, said something that pierced our hearts and ripped its way in, leaving a scar. It will never be fully forgotten.

We can't change yesterday, but, my, the possibilities that await us tomorrow! Maybe your son or your daughter is now grown or almost grown. Don't wait another day . . . start now! *It is never too late to start doing what is right.*

I have discovered that an encouraging church family is such because its homes are that. Let me ask you: Is *yours* an encouraging home? If I were to drop by as an invisible guest and listen in on conversations, would I hear sarcasm, put-downs, and caustic comments? Or would I hear, "Good job! I notice you're growing up. What a delight you are to our family. How pleased I am to see that you have begun to master such-and-such skill"? Or, "I know you've failed, and I understand. I've been there. It'll be better tomorrow. Let me work with you. Let me help you."

"Death and life are in the power of the tongue." Think of it this way: *Death words* destroy, hurt, create hateful and humiliating feelings. *Life words* build and increase strength of character. They lift spirits. They center on the truth, therefore they set the person free who would otherwise be in bondage.

Would you like a brief definition for encouragement? In two words, it is a *courage transfusion*. Every time we encourage someone, we give them a transfusion of courage.

That could create a problem. In order for courage to be transferred, the one doing the transferring has to have sufficient inner strength and must be secure enough, confident enough, resourceful enough to provide a surplus to someone else. That explains why unforgiving, fighting, critical people are not encouragers. Only those who are excited about life can transfer courage. People who are down on themselves, uncertain regarding their own self-image, can't do that.

A CLASSIC EXAMPLE OF AN ENCOURAGER

If you are like me, you appreciate seeing biblical principles illustrated in the lives of biblical characters. I've chosen one of our favorites—David.

While still a teenager he killed the giant Goliath, a story familiar to most people. But what followed is not as well known. That heroic act shocked the king whose name was Saul. He didn't even know who young David was when the event occurred. But once that deed was done, *everybody* in Israel became familiar with the young giant killer. Eventually, he joined the king's staff.

Within a few hours the people of Israel composed a simple song: "Saul has slain his thousands, David his ten-thousands!"

Everybody (but one) sang that tune . . . everybody (but one) applauded the accomplishment. Saul hated that song, because *he* wanted the people's applause. He was too insecure to see someone else promoted above him in popularity. What happened? Exactly what you would expect. Saul began to watch him. His intense jealousy increased his suspicion. And before long the paranoia turned to hate, then to rage, and finally to thoughts of murder. Saul took a spear and literally tried to kill him. David was forced to run for his life. For over a dozen years(!) David lived as a fugitive, hiding from Saul.

Ironically, in the meantime, Saul's son Jonathan developed a close relationship with David. It was a deep relationship of love— genuine love. "He loved him," says 1 Samuel 18:3, "as he loved himself." Unlike his father, Jonathan had a strong self-image, hence he was able to give himself to David. They became "soul mates." They understood each other. Their lives fit together like teeth in gears. They didn't have to explain themselves. They were completely at home in each other's presence. They loved each other deeply.

But all the while Saul's intensity increased. Finally, David is driven into the wilderness like a wild animal, not knowing where to turn. His fear is reaching maximum proportions. Disillusioned, confused, and hunted, David is near the breaking point. At that moment, Jonathan arrived on the scene with a "courage transfusion."

> *Now David became aware that Saul had come out to seek his life while David was in the wilderness of Ziph at Horesh* (1 Samuel 23:15).

Before reading any further, take a moment to identify with David in the wilderness. Every sunset added to his panic. Each new dawn introduced another day of running, watching, escaping, hiding. With relentless determination, Saul and his army pursued him. Next verse:

> *And Jonathan, Saul's son, arose and went to David at Horesh, and encouraged him in God* (v. 16).

The Hebrew term for *encouraged* conveys the idea of putting strength into someone's hand, arms, or body, so they can resist a pressure or an attack. Not waiting for an invitation, Jonathan arose and sought out David. To do what? To pass along fresh courage and new strength. Why? Because he loved him.

There are times you'll have to swim upstream to bring encouragement. Usually, it is unnecessary to wait for an invitation. Let me pass along a simple little formula about encouragement. It isn't original with me. "Words that encourage are inspired by love and directed toward fear." The source of that statement is a fine book entitled *Encouragement: The Key to Caring.*

> It is a mistake to think of encouragement as a set of specific words or phrases. Encouragement depends less on which words we use than the motivation behind them. Words that encourage are inspired by love and directed toward fear. These two conditions must be met for words to encourage.[5]

Let's look at the two conditions. Condition one: Words that encourage are inspired by love, not by fear; that is, the words spoken must never function as a "layer" for the speaker. Condition two: Words that encourage are aimed not at another's "layers" with the intent of rearranging them, but rather at another's hidden fear with the intent of reducing it. Read those thoughts again, slowly. It's extremely important that you grasp both conditions. I'll explain it further in a moment.

That is what makes Jonathan's time with David so significant. He really loved him. His presence and words conveyed the feelings, "I love you, David. I believe in you." And when he came to David, David didn't hide the truth and say, "Hey, I'm not afraid. I'll take on Saul and his army. Why in the world are you here?" He didn't fake it and try to act strong. David was scared. And in the presence of his friend, he didn't hide it. Nor did Jonathan hide his motivation. "David, I love you too much to leave you alone." David's response must have been, "Jonathan, how I need you right now! Thank you for coming."

Let me show you in a few words what I'm trying to say by referring to the four levels of encouragement in the chart on the next page. For a few moments think in terms of "layers" and "core." Unfortunately, most of us build layers around ourselves. Most of us give off an air of being on top of things. We're winning. We've got life by the tail. We can handle it. And so we give superficial comments to people, and we respond superficially in return, from layer to layer, and that doesn't bring encouragement.

LEVELS OF ENCOURAGEMENT

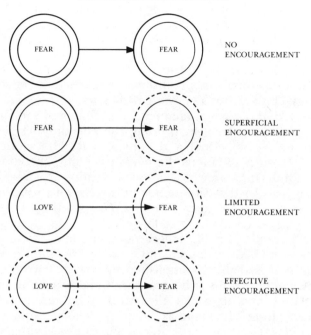

(See Crabb and Allender, Encouragement, pp. 72-73)

I can just hear the fellow who's had a coaching background. He's a tough guy, and he's got a son who weighs 101 pounds, who is hoping to be a running back for a high school football team that's full of 200-pound-plus football players. And the little kid is scared out of his mind . . . but he can't tell his daddy he's scared. Every morning his daddy says to him, "Suck it up, Bucko." And junior says, "Right, Dad." As he walks out of the house for school to catch the bus, the kid is scared to death. He's thinking about facing the team that afternoon in practice. But he can't admit his fear to his dad because his dad doesn't leave room for that. We're talking layer-to-layer relationship, which brings *no* encouragement. Look at the chart. This relationship is illustrated at the top level.

There's another level. It's a level of fear inside one individual, but somehow that same person can penetrate beneath the layer of another person and reach the true fear within. That's what we might call "superficial encouragement." Behind a shield of success and false security, we can come across with right words, even quoting verses and telling someone we'll pray for them in their fear or in their need. But that, at best, brings only *superficial* encouragement.

It does not last. By the way, a meaningful relationship is not developed between those two people even though right words were spoken—even scriptural words.

There's a third level, where the person doing the encouraging really does love the other individual, but somehow can't bring himself to say it. So in another guise he or she will communicate to the fear of this individual, and that brings *limited* encouragement. And it lasts a little longer, but it's never permanent.

The best kind of encouragement (represented at the bottom of the chart) is when the person doing the encouraging genuinely loves the other individual and expresses it. That's our friend Jonathan. In such situations the person needing encouragement honestly admits his fear, which causes a meaningful connection between the two. In that situation, soul meets with soul. And the deepest level of needs begin to be met. *That* is our goal . . . *effective* encouragement served family style!

When "layered" Christians meet together and everyone remains hidden beneath invisible masks and protected behind untouchable walls, nothing is really accomplished by way of encouragement. Everyone maneuvers his or her way through the maze of unspoken feelings, unwilling to admit the truth. What an unsatisfying, strained encounter! It's about as satisfying as kissing someone with a pane of glass between you . . . or taking a shower with a raincoat on. But it goes on in churches year after year.

Is it ever possible for me to encourage myself?

Yes, as a matter of fact, I think that the more we operate on this fourth level, the more we are able to give ourselves a transfusion of courage when necessary. I do not believe, however, that we ever reach the place where we never need some kind of encouragement from someone else. If we did, we wouldn't have the command in Hebrews 10:25 to "encourage one another, and all the more as we see the day approaching." But there are times we must encourage ourselves. When you travel a little further into David's biography, you see that he came to a place where everything, it seemed, had broken loose in his life. Not only was he exhausted from battle, the enemy had ransacked his home and kidnaped his wife and children. Even his men entertained thoughts of mutiny. Jonathan wasn't around to give his friend a "courage transfusion." David was all alone. We read that ". . . David strengthened himself in the Lord his God" (1 Samuel 30:6b).

I have discovered that when I haven't anyone near me upon whom I can call, when I'm all alone, I find the Book of Psalms my most consistent source of encouragement. When I turn to the psalms, it is amazing how much courage is poured into my soul. Often, it is as if God were speaking directly to my immediate needs. Have you made the same discovery?

Another source of personal encouragement is the hymnbook. I happen to love the hymns, especially the grand old hymns, many of which I've committed to memory. I will often pray through a song or a hymn. And somehow in the rhythm, the meter, the profoundly personal message of that music, I find my heart lifted up . . . another "courage transfusion" occurs.

THREE CRUCIAL QUESTIONS REGARDING ENCOURAGEMENT

Let's wrap up our thoughts with three crucial questions.

1. *Who should I attempt to encourage?* Ideally, everyone I meet; but realistically, those with whom I have established a close relationship. By the way, don't think that is automatic. You know with whom I am closest? My wife and my four children. You know who are often *last* to get encouragement from me (I confess with some embarrassment)? My wife and my four children. Yet I cannot overstate the value of "courage transfusions" among family members.

I challenge you to recall the last time you deliberately gave encouragement to your mate. There wasn't any hint dropped. No pleading invitation. Because of an understanding of his or her fear, you stepped in and extended a statement of strength. And how about your children? Or a very close friend? Let's not assume others don't need it, even though they don't drop hints.

2. *How can the levels be penetrated?* I'll answer that with three "progressive" answers.

- It always takes time.
- It usually involves pain.
- It occasionally can be addressed verbally; i.e., "I sense you're hiding. As I talk with you right now, I sense that you're not really helping me see what's going on. Something is being held back."

That explains why it has to be a close relationship. You don't walk up to a stranger and say those words. You say them only to those with whom a deep level of love and acceptance has been cultivated.

3. *What essential techniques need to be remembered?*

- Talk less so you can feel more.
- Be sensitive to the timing.

- Watch your wording.
- Do everything in your power not to judge (we can say we're encouraging, but we're really preaching).
- Examine your motive.
- Guard against sarcasm.
- Don't hide behind a layer.

Remember the primary principle: Words that encourage are inspired by love and directed toward fear.

I close with a story that could be my own, but I prefer to use another's. You should have little difficulty identifying with it.

My wife and I had drooled over a planned sailing vacation for more than a year. Sacrificing a few pleasures and hoarding our pennies helped us to afford a week on the west coast of Florida at a sailing school. A week of sheer joy— rich time together, fun on the water, and rejoicing in God's blessings—rewarded our long anticipation.

When the week was over, we returned to the wintry climate of our northern home. Moving quickly from tropical paradise to snow-covered streets proved to be a major culture shock. I was mature enough to accept the loss of paradise without slipping into a sulk or depression, but I did feel a grudging reluctance as I dragged myself back to work bundled up in overcoat and gloves. An appeal to "rejoice evermore" or to "fight the good fight" would not have moved me at that moment. I was mildly down.

Eavesdrop on two conversations that took place shortly after my return home:

Fred: "Looks like you got some sun."
Dan: "Becky and I just spent a week in Florida. Great weather. We went sailing for a week."
Fred: "Jet set life, huh? Must be doing better than most of us. Too bad the tan won't last up here." (Fred then laughed a decidedly sarcastic laugh.)
Dan: "I know, but it was worth it just to get away, relax, and spend time together. It's hard though to get back to the grind of . . ."
Fred: "'Grind!' At least you got away! Well, look, we better figure out when we can get together to work on that project that's due . . ."

Before the conversation I was mildly discouraged. Afterward I was moderately discouraged—less inclined to return to my responsibilities, more affected by the realities of a sometimes unpleasant life. Why? Fred is a friend of mine. He is not typically unkind toward me. Nor did he seem especially vindictive or angry during our interchange. Yet his words were discouraging.

Fred was wrapped up in his world, unconcerned about the effect of his words on me, insensitive to what I was feeling. He never acknowledged my emotions, he battered them. Rather than express understanding, he scorned my sluggishness. He failed to give me a perspective to help me carry on; instead he reminded me of my duties.

Listen to the other conversation:

Jane: "Hi, Dan! Hey, good tan! When did you get back?"

Dan: "Just two days ago."

Jane: "How was it—a good time?"

Dan: "It was great! Just what Becky and I needed to unwind. Makes it hard to come back though. After eighty-degree days, below zero is hard to take."

Jane: "I'll bet! Probably hard to believe you were even there. How's Becky taking her reentry to the real world?"

Dan: "Better than me [sic], I think. Her schedule up here is tough, but a little more flexible than mine. I feel the contrast between having nothing to do for a week and having to meet time demands again."

Jane: "So you're the struggling one now."

Dan: "I'm not proud of it, but I am."

Jane: "Your school and work schedule is really pretty demanding of your time, isn't it?"

Dan: "Becky and I had so much undisturbed time just to be together—and up here I'm lucky if I get any quality time with her at all. I'm afraid our commitments to other things might damage some of the closeness we feel with each other."

Jane: "So it's not just missing warm weather and sailing that's getting you."

Dan: "I guess not. Maybe the trip helped me realize that my priorities were out of line, and now I'm afraid I'll get them fouled up again."

He concludes:

The contrast between the first and second conversations is dramatic, but not overdone. They happened just that way. Jane made an effort to understand me. She esteemed another's concerns greater than her own. She responded to my needs rather than to hers. Her encouraging words prompted me to evaluate what my struggles really were. With a better grip on my real problem clarifying the challenge that lay before me, I felt a renewed sense of commitment to keep my life in order. Jane had stirred me to love and good deeds.[6]

Yes, no doubt about it, doctrinal knowledge is important. We need to know what we believe and why we believe it. A church stands firmer amidst stormy times when its members are doctrinally sound. But no amount of doctrine will replace our need for encouraging relationships built on love and understanding.

Knowledge may strengthen, but relationships soften. A healthy church family has both.

1. Hebrews 10:22 *urges* us to draw near to the Father! *Urges* us to find cleansing and renewal through the blood of Christ! Then, when we have been cleansed and sense the nearness of our God, verses 24-25 *urge* us to pass that supernatural encouragement along—family style! But it begins with that vertical relationship between you and the Lord, doesn't it? Have you "drawn near" to your Father today, confidently claiming the blood of Jesus as your passport into His presence? Hear His invitation in these verses and respond with all your heart.

2. Hebrews 10:24 suggests "let us consider" how to stimulate and encourage one another. In other words, it takes some careful, creative thought—it doesn't happen automatically. I like the way the Amplified Bible renders it:

    And let us consider and give attentive, continuous care to watching over one another, studying how we may stir up (stimulate and incite) to love and helpful deeds and noble activities.

    Think of three individuals whom you would like to encourage over the next few weeks. Now, do what the text says . . . *consider*. Think and pray it through. Seek discernment from the Holy Spirit to discover practical, appropriate methods. And then perform a courage transfusion!

3. In this chapter we've looked at the awesome power of the "encouraging word." Scriptures like Matthew 12:36-37 and Ephesians 4:29 underline what Solomon wrote again and again in the Proverbs. If you have the courage, ask a close friend or associate or spouse to comment on the content of your casual conversation since they have known you. Are your words generally positive, "edifying," encouraging? What steps could you take to both "monitor" your speech and turn it in a direction that builds others and praises God?

WORSHIP:
LET IT SHINE!
LET IT SHINE!

t happened in Canada way back in 1961. A group of ministers had gathered for a special series of meetings. They had invited one of their favorite preachers. He was not a physically impressive individual or one known for his charisma and eloquence. But he was one who knew God and walked closely with Him.

From 1928 to 1959 the man had pastored what some might call a rather inconspicuous church in Chicago, the Southside Alliance Church. During those thirty-one years he had emerged, in the opinion of many, as the conscience of evangelicalism at large. The preacher was Aiden Wilson Tozer. He preferred, simply, A. W. Tozer.

There was a little surprise as that wiry soldier of the cross stood in front of those Canadian churchmen and announced his subject. And had I been one of the ministers, perhaps I, too, would have been surprised at the topic he chose—WORSHIP. I mean, after all, that is a minister's craft. That's like talking to a group of auto mechanics about car engines, like talking to musicians about the chromatic scale. But how much there was to learn! How long lasting those messages have become! So significant were they that they have been put into a booklet that is still available today, as are most of Tozer's works.

One line from his message on worship is as meaningful today as it was the day he said it, perhaps more: "Worship is the missing jewel of the evangelical church."

Even though decades have passed since Tozer first said it, I'm afraid the jewel, in most places of our world, is still missing. And the tragedy is intensified by the fact that there aren't many even in ministry who seem to be looking for it. The jewel remains hidden.

That is nothing short of amazing. We are able to find the contents of an Egyptian tomb and identify the remains, as well as the possessions, of an ancient king, Tutankhamen. We are able to locate and photograph the Titanic that sank as far back as April 1912, though it rests two miles deep in the north Atlantic Ocean. We are even able to locate and bring to trial most, if not all, Nazi officers from Hitler's army. But we still can't seem to find the missing jewel of true worship. And good preaching—even doctrinal preaching—is no guarantee of worship. In fact, a strong pulpit often means weakness in worship. Peter Gillquist puts it this way:

> A common complaint I hear over and over again is, "I just don't get anything out of worship." Often that statement is accompanied by another: "Our pastor is the best Bible teacher I have ever heard. When the man opens the Scriptures, I really learn. But our church has no sense of worship." There almost appears to be a pattern: the churches that are strongest on the preaching of the Scriptures are often the weakest when it comes to worshiping and giving praise to the Lord. . . . People say they feel like bystanders.[1]

An equally convicting statement has been made by Robert Webber of Wheaton College:

> Worship is the weakest area of evangelical Christianity. We are strongest in the areas of evangelism, teaching, and fellowship. We are improving greatly in the area of servanthood (application of the gospel to social needs) and the ministry of healing (counseling and care for the emotional needs of people). But depth in the area of worship is badly lacking. We hardly know where to begin because we have lost nearly all contact with the past.[2]

Stop and think. Many of you travel much more than I do. You've been to other churches, as I have. You and I have been in formal churches, casual churches, Bible-teaching churches, evangelistic churches, beautiful churches, small, lovely, and even quaint churches. We have seen discipling churches, growing churches, dying churches, busy churches, renewal churches, denominational churches, independent churches; yes, even those that call themselves "New Testament churches." But chances are good we can count on both hands (with fingers left over) the churches we attended that were *worshiping* churches . . . places where we genuinely sensed the awesome presence of Almighty God.

I don't mean to sound spooky about this (it is a difficult concept to articulate). I am simply referring to a place where there was balance. A solid message from the Scriptures, and yet an accompanying blend of music and prayer and quietness that exalted the living God whom you came to worship. And along with all that, appropriate, distinct themes of thought conveyed through well-chosen words—freedom from cliches, without all the inane side comments and program hype that never fail to interrupt true worship. I am referring to places where we encountered the presence of the living God and found ourselves, as Wesley expressed it, "lost in wonder, love, and praise." Places where we truly could "worship the King all glorious above." Where we genuinely could "gratefully sing His power and His love." Where we could easily envision the Lord, high and lifted up as we sang, "Our Shield and Defender, the Ancient of Days, pavilioned in splendor and girded with praise."

When we find such places of worship, we have discovered a missing jewel.

Where are those rare gems?

Ten years after Tozer made that statement in Canada, I found myself in Fullerton, California, beginning a ministry at the First Evangelical Free Church. I am at a loss to describe all the things that drew me to this marvelous family, but looking back I realize that it was here I found the freedom, the openness, the spontaneity necessary to forge out a fresh theology of worship. I never announced such an agenda. I certainly had no book to turn to or some authority from whom I could receive counsel. I knew of no other church that was doing what I wanted to do. I didn't go out and find a few people to add to our staff who were "experts" in worship. Had I known of such, I probably would not have hired them, because "experts" were not what we needed.

At the risk of sounding terribly pious here, I wanted God alone to shape my theology of worship, as He had not done at any other place I had ever served. Somehow I knew music had to be woven into the scene—yet not to the exclusion of a consistently strong message from God's Book. Music and message had to blend if this jewel were going to be found in Fullerton. I wanted our church family to delight in the Lord Himself. Furthermore, I didn't want worship itself to become a god, an end in itself . . . an emotional shrine. I wanted God to be God. I wanted His Son to be preeminent in our assembly. And the only vehicle I knew to bring us to Him, at least in our large corporate gatherings, was worship.

Some pastors want programs. Some churches feature guest celebrities. Some ministers choose to highlight television, others add emphasis on service. I wanted our emphasis to be *worship*. I felt that alone would do more to motivate and deepen our commitment than any other single ingredient.

Some of the Fullerton flock have been with us all through those years. I remember when I introduced spontaneous a cappella singing. How different! Today such singing seems so important, so beautiful. But in those days, at least at the beginning of them, a few were afraid we were on our way to becoming a charismatic church. I still remember the letters and phone calls. Fear is such an enemy of worship! We are not a charismatic church, but I was convinced we could learn from our charismatic friends. Thankfully, the Fullerton folks trusted me. They were flexible enough to say, "Yes . . . let's do that." In fact, some even got so comfortable with those innovations that when we *didn't* try new things, they chided me(!), saying, "Where is that a cappella singing we've learned to love? Let's keep trying fresh things, Chuck." The family grew closer.

And along with that, we began to dovetail the Lord's Table into a worship setting. And we gave music a far more significant role as we tied it together with the message from God's Book. How wrong to think of music as a "preliminary"! We began to weave singing into pastoral prayers, we developed a marvelous orchestra comprised of our own church family, and we began to bring the arts to the place where they belong, as an additional statement of worship. We even prayed through hymns and sang through our prayers. It became so enriching, so invigorating! The jewel began to sparkle as authentic worship replaced churchy meetings.

And all through the process of time, we were learning together. We made mistakes, and we shall in the future. But we were willing to flex. We were willing to shift and adapt and alter and change and give up and add to as we forged out fresh expressions of our praise. What were we doing? By means of fresh innovation and creative ideas, we were discovering the missing jewel! I never realized how much we were missing until we found it!

And now the one thing I fear, having come this far, is that somebody might plan to "package" it. You know, market the jewel. Once that starts, the spontaneity is lost and the Spirit is quenched. We haven't a corner on God's truth, nor a full understanding of what is involved in worship. All we know is this: We love our God. We want to express our praise and our adoration to Him freshly, fully, freely. We remain open to try new ideas, but our goal is always the same— to connect with the living Lord.

I have found that it is impossible to lead a group of people in something that is not a part of me personally. So I had to cultivate a *private* worship without talking about it, without spelling it out, without even confessing to the struggles of it. And I had to add to my discipline of prayer such things as meaningful times of singing, and to my walk with God quiet moments of silence. And even in the pressured times I had to work out a way for worship to fit. It was so delicate . . . even elusive.

Do you remember a line out of one of the songs in "The Sound of Music," sung by the Mother Superior? She did not know quite what to do with the young, creative, energetic nun Maria (played by Julie Andrews), so she asked, "How do you hold a moonbeam in your hand?" In many ways, the true, deep experience of worship is like trying to hold a moonbeam in your hand. There is no way you can define it or contain it—all you can do is let it shine. The same is true of worship.

I promised myself that if I ever wrote a book on doctrine, dealing with theology from a practical viewpoint, I would not conclude it without addressing the importance of worship. And my suggestion to you regarding worship? Don't be afraid of it . . . don't ignore it. It's a moonbeam. Let it shine! Let it shine!

THE MISSING JEWEL REDISCOVERED

How am I to enter into the experience of worship . . . how am I to let it shine? I think I have found something of the answer, thanks to God's Book and God's family.

Tucked away in the hymnbook of our Bible, the Psalms, is a grand statement of invitation. I'd like us to think about that ancient hymn, Psalm 95, for just a few moments—to relive in our minds the truth that has been preserved for centuries.

If we struggle with the concept of worship as "too elusive," we must be equally concerned about making it too mechanical. I deliberately resist suggesting something like "Five Steps to Worship." Or, "Worship Made Easy—Here's How!" I have no plan to package it so that you are able to read this chapter, then pass along several "transferable concepts" of worship. But perhaps you will grasp what I'm driving at as you digest these thoughts. Like the Scottish people say, "Some things are better felt than telt."

I want you to "feel" what this is all about, according to Psalm 95. I want you to experience the emotions flowing from the psalmist's pen as you read this passage. By the way, if there are precision-minded engineers reading, please, please, don't take this psalm so literally. It's to be understood symbolically. And if you don't have the ability to do that, talk it over with your wife! I've met more wives who are poets than husbands. Let's see if this psalm will help us get a handle on the moonbeam called worship.

Its Identity and Meaning

> O come, let us sing for joy to the Lord; let us shout joyfully to the rock of our salvation. Let us come before His presence with thanksgiving; let us shout joyfully to Him with psalms (Psalm 95:1-2).

But why? Why should we come before our God with thanksgiving and joyful shouts? Why take the psalmist up on his invitation? Because our God is great. He deserves our highest praise.

> For the Lord is a great God, and a great King above all gods, in whose hand are the depths of the earth; the peaks of the mountains are His also (vv. 3-4).

The psalmist interjects that illustration to show us the infinitude of our God. From the deepest place on earth, which would be in the bottom of some sea, to the highest peak in the Himalayan mountain range—earth's highest spot—from depth to height, our God is greater. And Someone that awesome, that great, is deserving of our silent praise as well as our vocal praise and melodious praise and shouting praise. Our God is great! He is above *all* other gods, He is great . . . greater than the ear-splitting depths and the dizzy, towering heights.

> The sea is His, for it was He who made it; and His hands formed the dry land (vv. 4-5).

Have you been out at sea? I mean out in the midst of one of earth's oceans? What awesome sights . . . how frightening they can be!

I will never forget crossing the Pacific Ocean during my days in the Marine Corps. Our troop ship seemed so enormous all the time it sat docked at San Diego. But once we got out of the harbor and the farther out to sea we went, the smaller we became. Until finally, at the heart of that vast ocean, we felt like a flimsy matchstick. A storm struck, which only added to my fears. When those swells reached thirty to forty feet in height (the water was just as black as the ace of spades) and the sky became filled with angry clouds, and the wind was howling, I gained a new respect for the sea. The bow of our ship drove its nose into one swell after another as the ship sank and rose . . . sank and rose. A stinging blast of salty mist blew across the deck as cold ocean water swept over the decks. Talk about scared! My prayer life was enhanced on that ship.

It was there—in the midst of the raging Pacific Ocean—that I first found Psalm 139.

> *If I take the wings of the dawn, if I dwell in the remotest part of the sea, even there Thy hand will lead me, and Thy right hand will lay hold of me* (Psalm 139:9-10).

Why? Because the sea is His. He made it. Neither waves nor winds intimidate Him. There is no swell that causes our God to suck in His breath out of fear. There is no depth that causes Him to lift His eyebrows in amazement. He made it all! The vast sea is His. And the vast land masses were formed with His hands. How glorious He is in strength! How deserving of our respect! So we aren't surprised to read:

> *Come, let us worship and bow down; let us kneel before the Lord our Maker* (Psalm 95:6).

The most basic meaning of worship is the thought of being on one's face. And to intensify such a position of abject submission, an ancient worshiper would kneel, place the palms of his hands on the ground, and remain in the prone position, with his face hidden before God. Try *that* sometime!

> *For He is our God, and we are the people of His pasture, and the sheep of His hand* (v. 7).

In worship we become preoccupied with the Lord. We don't watch something happen, we participate in it. It isn't like going to a ball game and seeing a few players knocking themselves out on a field. It's coming to a place in one's life, either alone, with a few, or with many, where one "connects" with the living God. It is almost as though you could reach out and touch Him.

The best definition I've come up with, and perhaps the one with the fewest words, is this: *Worship is a human response to a divine revelation.* God has said something, and I respond to it. God is doing things, and I respond to them. On occasion, the appropriate response may be absolute silence as we meditate on our God. On other occasions the best response may be in the loudest possible voice of praise. It may be as you drink in the majestic strains of a pipe organ.

Just yesterday, sitting in the worship center of our church and listening to the moving strains and melodious harmony of a hymn being played on our pipe organ, I "connected." You will understand better if I mention the lyrics:

> Like a river glorious is God's perfect peace.
> Over all victorious in its bright increase;
> Perfect, yet it floweth fuller every day,
> Perfect, yet it groweth deeper all the way.
>
> Stayed upon Jehovah, hearts are fully blest;
> Finding, as He promised, perfect peace and rest.[3]

I felt it. The message passed through my mind. At that moment I was lost in the wonder and praise of my God. I could envision a river, with its mysterious currents, moving and deep. I could sense the peace, I could feel the rest and relief from all anxiety.

An amazing thing about worship is that you don't care what anybody else thinks. You couldn't care less what someone else thinks about you as your heart is lifted up in profound awe. Seems like everything else is blocked out as you are being "touched" by God. Yes, touched—not literally, but symbolically, figuratively. How important is touch!

Several months ago I heard about a man who sat in coffee shops all over the world and watched people. He was conducting an experiment on touch. He counted the times people touched each other during an hour's span. He kept a record of his observations, and his observations were revealing. In Puerto Rico there were one-hundred-eighty touches an hour in the coffee shop. In France it was reduced to one-hundred-ten an hour. When he came to America, it dropped amazingly to only *two times an hour*. In England, not even once! When I heard that, I thought to myself, He should have gone to Italy, ohhh! I often say to people, "Italians don't simply hug and kiss you, they *frisk* you." I mean, they are all over you. I love it! Those Italian meals . . . aren't they the greatest experiences in the world? Food is flying, words are flying, arms are flying. There is laughter, openness, such fun! A real Italian meal is sort of a survival of the fittest. They're touching like crazy. I don't believe I've ever been around a true Italian who didn't touch.

I wonder how many Italian Christians really worship? You see, it isn't simply touching one another, though there's nothing wrong with that. It is being open and willing. One of the greatest hindrances to worship is resistance to *anyone* touching me. Some Christians don't want anyone to touch them . . . to probe their personal affairs. That is often blocked off. But you see, in worship, there is no place that is free from His touch. Resistance pushes Him away. And so worship is a response—an active, open, unguarded response to God, whereby we declare His worth in an intimate manner, leaving Him room to touch us, to flood us with His peaceful presence.

Its Significance and Purpose

Let's leave Psalm 95 and give some thought to several reasons worship is so significant. What happens when that "connection" occurs? Whether it's in a gathering of thousands, or when I'm alone in a closet of prayer with Him, or perhaps with a few, what happens?

1. *Worship magnifies my God.* All else is eclipsed in His presence.

2. *Worship enlarges my horizons.* I begin to see beyond the self-imposed fences.

3. *Worship eclipses my fears.* I soon forget those things that gnaw at me when I worship.

4. *Worship changes my perspective.* It is nothing short of remarkable. An attitude on Friday is so different than on a Monday, because sandwiched between a Friday and a Monday is a worship service in which my whole perspective changes.

I was leaving a worship service late one evening several Sundays ago. I had parked my pickup alongside the curb. One of my friends spotted it as he was leaving the meeting and tucked a brief note under the windshield wiper. At first my stomach turned when I saw something under my windshield wiper. But when I realized it was a note, I stopped right then and read it. It spoke of a change of perspective that had occurred in his life. It wasn't something I had done or said. I can change no one's perspective. It wasn't the mortar, or the brick, or the carpet, or the pulpit, or the sound system. It was the living God who had invaded that man's life and touched him deeply in his churning place and calmed his spirit. And he didn't know anything better to do than to thank one of the people who had been present at the same experience of worship. I understood. He was refreshed, which brings me to the fifth reason worship is so significant.

5. *Worship refreshes my spirit.* How can we possibly describe this?

6. *Worship enhances my work.* When I put worship to work in my life, when I see worship as a response to God woven through the fabric of my day, it's amazing how my attitude toward tasks changes. Life takes on a melodious dimension that sets our hearts to singing.

At this point I have to say more about music. I must address it. Few things bring out the beauty of worship like music. God gave us song! His longest book in Scripture is the ancient psalter—the hymns of the Hebrews. Then why are we so resistant to giving it a prominent place, especially music centering its message on the Word of God? As I stated earlier, music is not simply a "preliminary." Music is not tacked on. Nor is it a "filler." It's not something we do while getting ready for the important part. By the way, I cannot say enough about the importance of having just the right person giving leadership to the church in the realm of music. I have one of the very best in Howie Stevenson, but there are other great ones available. And I suggest that we not view these gifted people simply as "song leaders," but as *worship* leaders. A worshiping church is a singing church, since music is vital to worship. In fact, Psalm 92 begins:

> *It is good to give thanks to the Lord, and to sing praises to Thy name, O Most High; To declare Thy lovingkindness in the morning, and Thy faithfulness by night, with the ten-stringed lute, and with the harp; with resounding music upon the lyre. For Thou, O Lord, hast made me glad by what Thou hast done, I will sing for joy at the works of Thy hands* (vv. 1-4).

I wonder why it is that the song has dried up in our voices? Why are there so few who sing, including the pastors . . . I mean really sing heartily to the Lord with full voice. Stop and consider. I wouldn't doubt if fewer people than ever sing in the shower any more. How many of you in a business or profession hear your partner humming a song? How many do you see singing out joyfully on a freeway? (Now that's a new one.) No wonder our singing is limited to Sunday! I have asked myself—why?

I've come up with a couple of answers.

The pressures of life squeeze out our song. Song requires a free spirit within . . . creativity, relaxation, freedom from tension. But so many live their lives in submission to that pressure, the song is squeezed out of them. What a loss!

Someone else sings for us. You get in the car, on goes the radio with its blaring music. There is background music in our offices, in our homes, even on airplanes, in grocery stores and department stores; they all have "mood" songs. There's piped music in restaurants. And would you believe in elevators? You can't even be alone to hum a little tune to yourself in an elevator without this dumb elevator music coming through. Why? I had a flight attendant tell me it was to deaden people's fears. I don't know about that . . . some of that music is pretty scary by itself.

Let me encourage you to start singing again. Yes, even when you're alone. Add it to your time with God. Get up with a song, not someone else's song. Before anything in the day has a chance to squeeze it out of you, express your praise in a song. If you can't create one, find a hymnbook. Buy one for your own use. Use it. Right along with your time in God's Book, sing the songs back to Him.

SOME OFTEN-OVERLOOKED FACETS OF THE JEWEL

There are at least three facets of the missing jewel of worship that are easily overlooked. By my mentioning them, perhaps you may find fresh motivation to cultivate a greater love for worship.

1. *Worship is sought by God.*

In chapter 9 of this book we spent quite a bit of time in John 4. You'll recall that Jesus spoke to the woman at the well:

> *You worship that which you do not know, we worship that which we know, for salvation is from the Jews. But an hour is coming, and now is, when the true worshipers shall worship the Father in spirit and truth; for such people the Father seeks to be His worshipers* (John 4:22-23).

I appreciate Professor Zane Hodges' comment: "This utterance on worship is timeless and absolutely definitive. The time has come!" For what? For true worshipers to worship God! But have you ever noticed the two essential ingredients?

> *God is spirit; and those who worship Him must worship in spirit and truth* (v. 24).

Our worship *must* be in keeping with the revealed Word of God. That's truth, the Bible. And our worship *must* be in spirit.

Now this is where things tend to get a little sticky . . . hard to describe. Spirit is in the unseen realm. It probably would include the realm of imagination—mental pictures in our inner connection between His Spirit and our spirit.

To appreciate a great piece of music by Beethoven or Bach, I am not required to read the score. But I do have to enter into the feeling of that music. I have to let it capture me. I have to be open to that. In order for me to enter into the spirit of a song done by the church choir, or by some fine soloist, or through a statement of praise given in testimony, I have to enter unguarded into the *spirit* of that moment—without resistance. I say again, as long as I am resistant to such a thing, I will not enter into the depth of worship. I *must* worship in spirit!

Frequently, I find that I am in the midst of people who are afraid of feelings. Most often I find this among Bible-believing evangelicals, the more rigid brand. The same ones who are in love with the truth are often afraid of the spirit . . . so fearful of being carried to an extreme, they won't even let a little crack appear in the door of their emotions. The consequence is nothing short of tragic: sterile, cold truth without the warmth of feelings. And worship takes a back seat. I find few settings more uncomfortable.

May I give a word of encouragement to seminaries today? Most of the men and women who study in theological graduate schools don't arrive at those institutions with an understanding of worship. I encourage you who serve in such places to help your students leave differently. I suggest you commit yourself to introduce to each seminarian a primary understanding of the basics of what worship is about. His or her theological training is incomplete without such a grasp. How? Start at the most obvious place—the chapel. Cultivate a chapel service marked by quality—fine music, good speakers (even if it means having fewer chapels), with a constant emphasis on quality worship. You might invite worship leaders to visit your campus a time or two each year. Include the ministers of music as well. Expose your ministers-in-the-making to those outstanding models. What a contribution to make on young lives! Especially since worship is sought by God.

2. *Worship has been practiced in the past.* If I had the time to trace where worship appears in history, according to Scripture, I could literally take you from Genesis to Revelation. Do you know the first appearance of worship in the Bible? It will surprise you. The first time worship is mentioned is in Genesis 22 when Abraham is about to sacrifice his son Isaac on the altar. The old patriarch says to his friends down at the base of the mountain:

> *Stay here with the donkey, and I and the lad will go yonder; and we will <u>worship</u> and return to you* (v. 5, emphasis mine).

If we consider Job in the same context of the patriarchs, the suffering saint mentioned worship after he lost everything. Sitting in sackcloth and ashes he said:

> *. . . Naked I came from my mother's womb, and naked I shall return there. The Lord gave and the Lord has taken away. Blessed be the name of the Lord* (Job 1:21).

Prior to that confession the text says, "And he worshiped the Lord there" (v. 20).

Yes, it's possible to worship on a hospital bed. It is possible to worship though bankrupt, bruised, and beaten. Worship doesn't require comfortable surroundings, organ music, and the soft seats of a church pew. You don't have to have an orchestra. Those things may help enhance it, but worship is just as appropriate when we are all alone with our thoughts . . . as Abraham and Job were.

You may think I'm weird, but when I look at the fluid lines on a Michelangelo piece of sculpture, and I take the time to study that eight-foot masterpiece of white marble depicting David, I worship my God. He gave the genius that gift. He, through the hands of that gifted artist, sculpted that statue for mankind to appreciate. When I hear the loving strains of a hymn, I worship. I'm not worshiping the hymn, or the player, or the singer. I am worshiping God, the Giver. There are dozens of such experiences awaiting our worship.

3. *Worship is needed in the present.* Turn to Romans 12. Worship is not only something to be enjoyed as a recipient, it is something to *do* as a participant. That is my whole chapter in one statement. Worship is not dreamy and passive. It is a verb. Action is in the term.

I urge you therefore, brethren, by the mercies of God, to present your bodies a living and holy sacrifice, acceptable to God, which is your spiritual service of worship (v. 1).

Do you serve on a board or a committee in your church? Believe it or not, that's to be an experience of worship. Do you teach a class of children or teenagers or adults? That is your worship . . . your "spiritual service of worship." Do you sing in a choir? Do you play an instrument in the church orchestra? Do you sing as a soloist or as a part of an ensemble? That is a statement of worship as you minister the gospel to others. Do you work behind the scenes, not seen by the public, as you give time to youth or to adults or to children? That is your worship. Do you give regularly to the work of God? Is your giving marked by sacrifice and consistency? Do you realize God calls that your "spiritual service of worship"?

It will revolutionize your whole concept of Christian service if you begin to think of your involvement as an act of worship.

SPARKLING BEAUTY OF THE REDISCOVERED JEWEL

A. W. Tozer was right. Worship has been the missing jewel of the evangelical church. But I would like to add: It need not *remain*

missing. Let's make a difference! Let's risk innovating . . . let's cultivate a renewed appreciation for and participation in active, fulfilling worship. I love the way my friend, Dr. Ron Allen, refers to worship as our celebration of God. Read his words thoughtfully.

> What, then, is the essence of worship? It is the celebration of
> God! When we worship God, *we celebrate Him*: We extol Him,
> we sound His praises, we boast in Him.
>
> Worship is not the casual chatter that occasionally drowns out
> the organ prelude; we celebrate God when we allow the pre-
> lude to attune our hearts to the glory of God by the means of
> the music.
>
> Worship is not the mumbling of prayers or the mouthing of
> hymns with little thought and less heart; we celebrate God
> when we join together earnestly in prayer and intensely in
> song.
>
> Worship is not self-aggrandizing words or boring clichés when
> one is asked to give a testimony; we celebrate God when all of
> the parts of the service fit together and work to a common end.
>
> Worship is not grudging gifts or compulsory service; we cele-
> brate God when we give to Him hilariously and serve Him with
> integrity.
>
> Worship is not haphazard music done poorly, not even great
> music done merely as a performance; we celebrate God when
> we enjoy and participate in music to His glory.
>
> Worship is not a distracted endurance of the sermon; we cele-
> brate God as we hear His Word gladly and seek to be conformed
> by it more and more to the image of our Savior.
>
> Worship is not a sermon that is poorly prepared and carelessly
> delivered; we celebrate God when we honor His Word with our
> words, by His Spirit.
>
> Worship is not the hurried motions of a "tacked-on" Lord's
> Table; we celebrate God pre-eminently when we fellowship
> gratefully at the ceremonial meal that speaks so centrally of our
> faith in the Christ Who died for us, Who rose again on our be-
> half, and Who is to return for our good.
>
> As a thoughtful gift is a celebration of a birthday, as a special
> evening out is a celebration of an anniversary, as a warm eulogy
> is a celebration of a life, as a sexual embrace is a celebration of
> a marriage—*so a worship service is a celebration of God*.[4]

Finally, let me ask you three probing questions that examine the
jewel in your personal life.

1. *Does your public worship sparkle with creativity and variety?* If you want that to happen, start letting the hymn speak to you. Allow your mind to meditate on the piece that's being played, even the prelude, the offertory, the postlude. Allow yourself to enter into the music, considering the words if you know them, praying your own words if you don't. Let the sparkle return. Let it shine!

2. *Does your private worship sparkle with quality and consistency?* Years ago, I was working closely with a man who was trying to help me understand private worship. He went through a very, very low time in his life. I went by his home one afternoon to find him, and he wasn't there. His wife said, "I think he's down at the office." It had begun to rain. By the time I got to his office down in the center of town, it was pouring . . . rain was really splashing down.

I made my way around the corner to this little, inauspicious office where he met with God. Before I saw him, I could hear him. I could hear him singing. He was singing the lines from that great hymn, "Come Thou Fount of Every Blessing."

I stood alone in the darkness and the rain, listening . . . pondering the truth I heard.

> Prone to wander, Lord, I feel it,
> Prone to leave the God I love;
> Here's my heart, O, take and seal it,
> Seal it for Thy courts above.[5]

As I stood outside that little bamboo shack, seeing the flicker of the candle in his room, I felt I was standing on sacred soil. His private worship was obvious to me. And I walked away having learned more in that brief moment than I could have learned in a year of instruction. I shall never forget his model. He worshiped publicly, because he worshiped privately.

3. *Has something taken the sparkle out of your worship?* If so, it's time to do some soul-searching. Probe deeply. Whatever it is that is stealing your joy and sucking the life out of your worship must be removed. Until that happens, I must warn you, you will continue to do little more than play church on Sundays. Anne Ortlund admits:

> When I was little we used to play church. We'd get the chairs into rows, fight over who'd be preacher, vigorously lead the hymn singing, and generally have a great carnal time.

> The aggressive kids naturally wanted to be up front, directing or preaching. The quieter ones were content to sit and be entertained by the up-fronters.

> Occasionally we'd get mesmerized by a true sensationalistic crowd-swayer—like the girl who said, "Boo! I'm the Holy

Ghost!" But in general, if the up-fronters were pretty good they could hold their audience quite a while. If they weren't so good, eventually the kids would drift off to play something else—like jump rope or jacks.

Now that generation has grown up, but most of them haven't changed too much. Every Sunday they still play church. They line up in rows for the entertainment. If it's pretty good, their church may grow. If it's not too hot, eventually they'll drift off to play something else—like yachting or wife swapping.[6]

Yes, Anne is right. All the stuff we do in place of true worship is a cheap substitute. It doesn't satisfy. It certainly doesn't sparkle.

If you love God, if you love His Word, if you love the doctrines revealed in His Word, then I encourage you to become an active participant in worship. Find the jewel and let it shine! Let it shine!

Root Issues

1. Looking for something to read when you finish this book . . . something that might help you cultivate your own private worship of the Lord? For an unforgettable experience, dip into the writings of A. W. Tozer. Classics such as *The Pursuit of God*, or *Worship: The Missing Jewel of the Evangelical Church* are available through your local Christian bookstore—or perhaps your church library.

2. Is the music of worship a part of your daily life? Choose a few choruses, Scripture songs, or perhaps a grand old hymn or two to commit to memory. Then, rediscover the joy of singing your praise and adoration back to the Lord. Why let "the professionals" on your stereo or car radio have all the privilege of making music for the King. Don't worry if you can't carry a tune. If your spirit is in harmony with His, the music will be beautiful . . . and God will be well pleased. Let it shine!

3. You may or may not be pleased with all the aspects of the "worship service" at your church. Nevertheless, you can worship—with all your heart! Make up your mind on Sunday morning that you *will* worship the Lord through every aspect of the service—through the singing, the offering, the praying and the preaching. Refuse to let distractions or wandering thoughts pull your attention and concentration away from the living God and His Word. Give yourself totally to the worship of your God and Savior during those brief minutes. Let that hour of worship set the pace for the rest of your week.

CONCLUSION

have two reactions, now that we have come to the end. *Whew!* and *Why?*

The first is an expression of exhaustion. What began as a rather simple and easy approach to the doctrines that lie at the roots of our faith evolved into a project that has required an enormous amount of discipline and determination. The tough part was maintaining relevance and practicality with each subject. Now I understand why most books on doctrine focus on theory, include long lists of Bible verses, employ a lot of scholarly jargon, and give little attention to the *application* of theological issues. It's easier that way!

I was tempted to opt for the theoretical approach at times, but I'm glad I didn't yield. The hard work, I think, paid off. I'm tired tonight, but my joy comes in imagining how the Lord is going to use these pages in the lives of some who would normally be disinterested and turned off by the oversized, stuffy-looking volumes on doctrine.

As I said at the beginning, my wish has not been to impress those who are already sharp, well-informed students of systematic theology. Nor has it been to exhaust every issue on the doctrinal spectrum. My deep desire has been to address some of the major points of interest in a way that would be interesting, understandable, and true to Scripture . . . especially for the uninitiated. I hope I have succeeded. If so, the *Whew!* on my lips will become a *Wow!* on someone else's. Nothing would please me more.

Of greater importance is the second reaction: *Why?* This is a question of purpose. Why have I taken your time and invested my energy doing spade work around these old roots beneath this giant tree? In a society that is so forward looking and technologically advanced, why is it important to return to our roots? I have been asking myself this "Why" question all the way through the book. It has been the answer that has kept me at the task.

Why? Because we are fast becoming a rootless generation that is giving less respect to those people who shaped our faith and less regard to those truths that solidify it. Riding on the highs and lows of emotional waves, many (most?) are awash in an uncertain sea that lacks biblical guidelines, moral absolutes, historical breadth, and doctrinal depth. We have become dogmatic about the value of wings and dreams, but embarrassingly soft on roots and truth.

Substance—time-honored biblical content—is increasingly conspicuous by its absence. Far too many in God's family have minds like beds which need to be made and remade rather regularly.

We need to be absolutely sure of certain things.

I'm not suggesting that we become closed-minded and stubborn, but at the same time we dare not live like little children "tossed here and there by waves, and carried about by every wind of doctrine" (Ephesians 4:14). We must cultivate more than just the ability to get along well with one another. Relationships, as significant as they are, have come dangerously close to replacing a knowledge of the holy.

How we feel and what we think are now considered more important than what God wants and what His Word says. At the nucleus of today's philosophy of life is a me-ism none can deny. The "I" has taken the place of "Thou." Because we adults have sown the wind, our young are sure to reap the whirlwind.

This was brought home rather forcefully in a one-page article entitled "The Modern Mount Rushmore." The author, Ralph Schoenstein, humorously yet pointedly presents proof of this from a classroom he visited:

> My daughter Lori, who is eight, told me last night that she wants to grow up to sing like either Judy Garland or Michael Jackson. "Try for Judy Garland," I said. "A girl needs a great soprano to be Michael Jackson."
>
> These two singers have become Lori's first hero and heroine. they are hardly figures for commemorative stamps, but many children have no heroes or heroines anymore, no noble achievers they yearn to emulate . . . One day last spring I stood before 20 children of eight and nine in Lori's third-grade class to see if any heroes or heroines were inspiring them. I asked each child

to give me the names of the three greatest people he had ever heard about.

"Michael Jackson, Brooke Shields and Boy George," said a small blond girl, giving me one from all three sexes.

"Michael Jackson, Spider-Man and God," a boy then said, naming a new holy trinity.

. . . When the other children recited, Michael Jackson's name was spoken again and again, but Andrew Jackson never, nor Washington, Lincoln or any other presidential immortal. Just Ronald Reagan, who made it twice, once behind Batman and once behind Mr. T., a hero who likes to move people by saying, "Sucker, I'll break your face." . . . And I heard no modern equivalent of Charles A. Lindbergh, America's beloved "Lone Eagle." . . .

In answer to my request for heroes, I had expected to hear such names as Michael Jackson, Mr. T, Brooke Shields and Spider-Man from the kids, but I had not expected the replies of the eight who answered "Me." Their heroes were themselves.

It is sad enough to see the faces on Mount Rushmore replaced by rock stars, brawlers and cartoons, but it is sadder still to see Mount Rushmore replaced by a mirror.[1]

When I first read those words, I thought of the analogy in Scripture that refers to our looking in a mirror. What is interesting is that the biblical writer pleads for a replacement of the mirror with the truth of God, which he calls "the word implanted."

Therefore putting aside all filthiness and all that remains of wickedness, in humility receive the word implanted, which is able to save your souls. But prove yourselves doers of the word, and not merely hearers who delude themselves. For if any one is a hearer of the word and not a doer, he is like a man who looks at his natural face in a mirror; for once he has looked at himself and gone away, he has immediately forgotten what kind of person he was. But one who looks intently at the perfect law, the law of liberty, and abides by it, not having become a forgetful hearer but an effectual doer, this man shall be blessed in what he does (James 1:21-25).

My immediate hope is that you have found enough solid substance in these chapters to whet your appetite for further digging around these roots. My ultimate hope is that you would not only look intently but that you would *abide* by these things. My fear is that you might become more fascinated with individual roots than the whole tree . . . and more intrigued by the hearing of the Word than involved in the doing of it.

That is why, at the end of each chapter, I have suggested ways to keep the doctrines out of the realm of sterile theory and in touch with the real world. Let us *never* forget that our Lord's goal for us is that we become people who obey, not merely study . . . Christians who yield our wills in greater obedience, not merely expand our minds for greater intelligence.

I don't make many absolute promises, but there is one I can make without hesitation. If you will devote yourself to a consistent study of the Scriptures, balancing doctrinal intake with practical applications of the truth, your life will take on new meaning. Furthermore, I can promise you that knowledge will replace ignorance and superstition. The mirror of me-ism will be broken by an unselfish spirit. Stability will return, displacing uncertainty and fear. And a depth you have never had before will mark your life, instead of superficiality and shallowness.

As important as wings and dreams may be, what we really need is a solid network of roots. Hopefully, this volume has convinced you that growing deep in the Christian life is not optional, it's essential.

By returning to our roots, we can become like that tree the psalmist mentions. It is a strong, stable tree, firmly planted by streams of water . . . one that yields seasonal fruit and has no withering leaves . . . one that stands the test of time, reaching full and enviable maturity.

NOTES

Chapter 1
1. Jaime O'Neill, "No Allusions in the Classroom," *Newsweek*, 30 September 1985.
2. *Newsweek*, 30 September 1985, p. 22.
3. C.S. Lewis, "Learning in Wartime," *The Weight of Glory and Other Addresses* (New York: Macmillan Co., 1949), pp. 50-51.
Chapter 2
1. Everett F. Harrison, *Acts: The Expanding Church* (Chicago: Moody Press, 1975), p. 264.
2. G.W. Target, "The Window" from *The Window and Other Essays* (Boise, Idaho: Pacific Press Publishing Association, 1973), pp. 5-7.
Chapter 3
1. James M. Boice, "The Marks of the Church," *Can We Trust the Bible?* ed. Earl D. Radmacher (Wheaton, Ill.: Tyndale House, 1979), pp. 80-81.
2. Paul Feinberg, "The Meaning of Inerrancy," *Inerrancy* ed. Norman Geisler (Grand Rapids, Mich: Zondervan, 1980), p. 294.
3. Roy Aldrich, "The Wisdom of the Word," *Bibliotheca Sacra* 124 (April-June 1967): 61.
Chapter 4
1. Alfred Plummer, *An Exegetical Commentary on the Gospel According to St. Matthew* (Grand Rapids, Mich.: Wm. B. Eerdmans, 1960), p. 172.
2. Bernard Ramm, "But It Isn't Bible Study," *Eternity Magazine*, February 1960, p. 3.
3. Ibid., p. 4.
Chapter 5
1. Charles W. Colson, *Loving God* (Grand Rapids, Mich.: Zondervan, 1983), pp. 13-14.
2. Charles R. Swindoll, *Improving Your Serve* (Waco, Tex.: Word Books, 1981).
3. Shirley MacLaine, interview, *Washington Post*, 1977.
4. R. Laird Harris, Gleason L. Archer, Jr., Bruce K. Waltke, *Theological Wordbook of the Old Testament*, vol. 2 (Chicago: Moody Bible Institute, 1980), p. 877.
5. James M. Boice, *Foundations of the Christian Faith*, vol. 1: *The Sovereign God* (InterVarsity Press, 1978), p. 24.
Chapter 6
1. John Powell, *Fully Human, Fully Alive* (Niles, Ill.: Argus Communications, 1976), pp. 17-18.
2. William Williams, "Guide me, O Thou Great Jehovah."
3. J. Robert Raines, *A Creative Brooding* (New York: Macmillan Co., 1977), pp. 345-46.
Chapter 7
1. Jim Bishop, *The Day Christ Was Born* (New York: Harper & Row, 1961), pp. 16-17.
2. W. Phillip Keller, *A Layman Looks at the Son of God* (Old Tappan, N.J.: Fleming H. Revell Co., 1977), pp. 56-57.
3. George MacDonald, quoted in a sermon by J. Vernon McGee entitled "No Room for Him" (Los Angeles: Church of the Open Door, 1967), p. 7.
4. Leslie Savage, quoted in a sermon by J. Vernon McGee entitled "No Room for Him" Los Angeles: Church of the Open Door, 1967), p. 7.
Chapter 8
1. C.S. Lewis, *Mere Christianity* (New York: Macmillan Co., 1970), pp. 40-41.
2. G. Campbell Morgan, *The Crises of the Christ* (New York: Fleming H. Revell Co., 1936), p. 79.
Chapter 9
1. © Copyright 1973 by William J. Gaither. Used by permission of Gaither Music Company. From *Alleluia . . . A Praise Gathering for Believers*.
2. Adelaide A. Pollard, "Have Thine Own Way, Lord!"
3. J. Oswald Sanders, *Spiritual Leadership* (Chicago: Moody Press, 1967), p. 141.
4. Charles R. Swindoll, *Strengthening Your Grip* (Waco, Tex.: Word Books, 1982), pp. 99-100
5. Clarence E. Macartney, *Of Them He Chose Twelve* (Grand Rapids, Mich.: Baker Book House, 1969), pp. 73-75.
Chapter 10
1. Billy Graham, *The Holy Spirit* (Waco, Tex.: Word Books, 1978), p. 24.
2. Merrill G. Tenney, Ph.D., *John: The Gospel of Belief* (Grand Rapids, Mich.: Wm. B. Eerdmans, 1948), p. 235.
3. Daniel Iverson, "Spirit of the Living God" (Moody Bible Institute, 1963).
Chapter 11
1. I.G. Moss, "How Did the Universe Begin?" *Nature*, 316, 8 August 1985.
2. J. Dwight Pentecost, *Things Which Become Sound Doctrine* (Grand Rapids Mich.: Fleming H. Revell Co., 1955), pp. 9-10.
Chapter 12
1. Mark Twain, *Familiar Quotations*, ed. John Bartlett (Boston: Little, Brown & Co., 1955), p. 679.
2. Michel de Montaigne, *Quote Unquote*, ed. Lloyd Cory (Wheaton, Ill.: Victor Books, 1977), p. 297.
3. J. Dwight Pentecost, *Things Which Become Sound Doctrine* (Westwood, N.J.: Fleming H. Revell Co., 1965), pp. 17-18.

NOTES

4. John R.W. Stott, *Involvement*, vol. I: *Being a Responsible Christian in a Non-Christian Society* (Old Tappan, N.J.: Fleming H. Revell Co., 1985), pp. 64-65

5. Charlotte Elliott, "Just As I Am."

6. Catherine Marshall, *A Man Called Peter* (New York: McGraw-Hill, 1951), p. 319.

Chapter 13

1. Frank S. Mead, "Shepherd of the Senate," *Christian Herald*, November 1948.

2. Peter Marshall, "Mr. Jones, Meet the Master," *Mr. Jones, Meet the Master*, ed. Catherine Marshall (New York: Fleming H. Revell Co., 1950), pp. 135-36.

3. Charles Wesley, "And Can It Be That I Should Gain?"

4. Ibid.

5. Billy Graham, *How to Be Born Again* (Waco, Tex.: Word Books, 1977), pp. 118-21.

6. Marshall, *Mr. Jones*, pp. 30-31.

Chapter 14

1. John Bowring, "In the Cross of Christ I Glory."

2. Billy Graham, *How to Be Born Again* (Waco, Tex: Word Books, 1977), p. 116.

Chapter 15

1. C.S. Lewis, *Mere Christianity* (New York: Macmillan Co., 1958), p. 104.

Chapter 16

1. J. Dwight Pentecost, *Prophecy for Today* (Grand Rapids, Mich.: Zondervan, 1961), p. 19.

2. H.L. Turner, "It May Be At Morn."

3. Billy Graham, *World Aflame* (Garden City, N.Y.: Doubleday, 1965), pp. 206-7.

Chapter 17

1. Joan Welsh, *Quote Unquote*, ed. Lloyd Cory (Wheaton Ill.: Victor Books, 1977), p. 81.

2. Arnold Toynbee, "Traditional Attitudes Towards Death," *Man's Concern With Death* ed. Arnold Toynbee et al. (New York: McGraw-Hill, 1968), p. 63.

3. Peter Marshall, *John Doe, Disciple: Sermons for the Young in Spirit*, ed. Catherine Marshall (New York: McGraw-Hill, 1963), pp. 219-20.

4. Jon E. Braun, *Whatever Happened to Hell?* (Nashville: Thomas Nelson, 1977), pp. 11-12.

Chapter 18

1. J. Kerby Anderson, *Life, Death, and Beyond* (Grand Rapids, Mich.: Zondervan, 1980), pp. 81-82.

2. A paraphrase of the composite experience described by Raymond Moody, Jr., M.D., *Life After Life* (New York: Bantam Books, 1975), pp. 21-23.

3. Anderson, p. 110.

Chapter 19

1. Gloria Gaither, "The Family of God," © 1970. Used by permission.

2. Dr. Paul Brand and Philip Yancey, *Fearfully and Wonderfully Made* (Grand Rapids, Mich.: Zondervan, 1980), pp. 59-60.

Chapter 20

1. Judith Viorst, *If I Were in Charge of the World and Other Worries* (New York:Atheneum, 1981), pp. 2-3.

2. William Pitts, "The Little Brown Church," *The American Song Book* (New York: Robbins Music Corporation, 1942), p. 91.

3. Bill and Gloria Gaither and Don Marsh, "God Has Always Had a People," *The Church Triumphant* (Alexandria, Ind.: Paragon/Gaither). Used by permission.

Chapter 21

1. Armen Keteyian, "Nobody Wanted to Believe What Happened," *Sports Illustrated*, 9 September 1985, p. 10.

2. William Barclay, *More New Testament Words* (New York: Harper & Brother, 1958), pp. 134-35.

3. Ken Medema, "If This Is Not a Place," © 1977. Used by permission.

4. Gordon MacDonald, *The Effective Father* (Wheaton Ill.: Tyndale House, 1977), pp. 68-69.

5. Lawrence Crabb and Dan Allender, *Encouragement: The Key to Caring* (Grand Rapids, Mich.: Zondervan, 1984), pp. 121-23.

6. Billy Graham, *How to Be Born Again* (Waco, Tex.: Word Books, 1977), pp. 118, 119, 120-21.

Chapter 22

1. Peter E. Gillquist, *The Physical Side of Being Spiritual* (Grand Rapids Mich.: Zondervan, 1979), p. 115.

2. Robert E. Webber, Foreword to *Praise! A Matter of Life and Breath*, Ronald Barclay Allen (Nashville: Thomas Nelson, 1980), p. 9.

3. Frances R. Havergal, "Like a River Glorious."

4. Ronald Allen, *Worship: Rediscovering the Missing Jewel* (Portland, Ore.: Multnomah Press, 1982), pp. 18-19.

5. Robert Robinson, "Come, Thou Fount," © 1966 Singspiration. Used by permission.

6. Anne Ortlund, *Up with Worship* (Glendale, Calif.: Regal Books Division G/L Publications, 1975), pp. 2-3.

Conclusion

1. Ralph Schoenstein, "The Modern Mount Rushmore," *Newsweek*, 6 August, 1984.

A GLOSSARY OF MAJOR TERMS

ne of the most helpful ways to understand the Bible is through a serious study of the doctrinal terms contained in it. While a knowledge of such is no guarantee of spiritual success, this knowledge does give the Christian a proper orientation to life and a needed discernment in this day of confusion and error.

This glossary can be especially helpful when you come across terms that you've never really understood. The cutting edge of your Christian faith is kept sharp by an understanding of the key terms—not only a definition of each but also their relationship to other key terms. Although there are less than 150 major terms defined in this glossary, you may discover that the ones you encounter most often are included.

The definitions are purposely nontechnical, designed to clarify that which can be confusing or misleading. Scripture references have been added to help you identify particular terms with a biblical setting. It is advisable that you take the time to look up each reference when you want to expand your understanding of the term.

ADVOCATE: One who undertakes in the cause of another. Both Jesus Christ and the Holy Spirit are recognized as advocates on behalf of the believer (1 John 2:1; John 14:16; Romans 8:26-27).

AGNOSTIC: One who believes that the existence of any ultimate reality (such as God) is unknown and probably unknowable. The Greek term *Agnostos* appears only in Acts 17:23, where it is rendered "unknown."

ALPHA AND OMEGA: The first and last letters of the Greek alphabet. This expression appears three times in the New Testament (Revelation 1:8; 21:6; 22:13) and in each case has in mind totality, infinity, and/or eternity. The expression is essentially the same as God's words recorded in Isaiah, ". . . I am the first and I am the last, and there is no God besides Me" (44:6).

AMEN: Originally a Hebrew word meaning "reliable, sure, true," it now signifies one's firm belief, "I believe it," "surely," "yes, indeed!"

AMILLENNIALISM: The belief that there is no sufficient ground for the expectation of a literal thousand-year reign of Christ upon the earth in the future. This belief holds that there will be a general resurrection and judgment of the believers and unbelievers synchronized with the second advent of Christ. Amillennialists believe Christ is now reigning in His kingdom.

ANGELOLOGY: Angel is derived from the Greek word Angelos, meaning "messenger" or "sent one." The angels are messengers sent from their Master. This is the study of the origin, activity, and personality of all the angels.

ANTHROPOLOGY: Anthropos means "man, mankind" in Greek. This title refers to the doctrinal study of humanity.

ANTHROPOMORPHISM: Derived from two Greek words, Anthropos (man) and Morphe (form), it is the term used to attibute certain human forms to God; for example, "feet" of God in Exodus 24:10, "hand" of the Lord in Joshua 4:24, "arm" of the Lord in Isaiah 53:1, and "heart" of God in Hosea 11:8.

ANTHROPOPATHISM: Ascribing human feeling or emotion to God; for example, "repentance" of God in Genesis 6:6, "anger" of the Lord in Numbers 11:1, and "laughter" of God in Psalm 2:4.

ANTI-SEMITISM: Hostility in thought, word, or action against the Jews.

APOCRYPHA: From a Greek word meaning "hidden." It is the title given to the thirteen books written during the between-the-Testaments era which contain, among other things, historical events of the Jews of that time. Conservative, evangelical Christians deny that they are inspired writings. They are not a part of the completed canon of Scripture. They are never quoted by any New Testament author. Also, the teachings of purgatory, prayers for the dead, and salvation by works are sourced in these books. The Roman Church declared them to be canonical in 1548 at the Council of Trent.

APOSTASY: The act of departing from one's faith; abandonment of belief in the basic doctrines of Christianity and the renunciation of the standards of the faith (2 Thessalonians 2:3; 1 Timothy 4:1; 2 Timothy 3:1-5).

ASCENSION: The doctrinal belief that the God-man, Jesus Christ, bodily left the earth forty days after His resurrection, thus ending His earthly ministry until His second advent (Acts 1:1-11). His acceptance into heaven by God the Father at this time verified the Father's satisfaction in the life and death of His Son while he was upon the earth.

ASSURANCE: Confidence that right relations exist between one's self and God. Do not confuse this with eternal security. See 1 John 5:10-12 for a direct statement of spiritual assurance.

ATHEISM: The denial of the existence of God. This is a biblical term used, for example, in Ephesians 2:12, translated "without God." It is a transliterated Greek word: A (negative prefix) and Theos (God).

ATONEMENT: An all-inclusive word that describes, in general, all that Jesus Christ accomplished by His death on the cross. The term is found only in the Old Testament, where it means "to cover" and carries with it the thought of putting sin out of sight, covering it over by blood. The New Testament counterpart for this term is *redemption,* as found in Romans 3:24 and Ephesians 1:7.

BELIEVER: A person who has received the Lord Jesus Christ as his or her personal Savior (John 1:12; 3:16; Acts 16:31). Synonymous with being a Christian.

BIBLIOLOGY: The study of the doctrines related to the Bible.

BLASPHEMY: Taking the name of God upon the lips in an empty, vulgar, idle, and trifling manner; an irreverent use of God's name in oaths and curses addressed to people or things. In Matthew 12:22-37 Jesus addresses Himself to this very issue, since the Pharisees attributed the work of God to the devil—a blasphemous accusation.

CANON: The collection or list of Bible books that are recognized as genuine, inspired Holy Scripture. The collection is complete with thirty-nine Old Testament books and twenty-seven New Testament books in the canon.

CARNAL: The term used to describe the fleshly state of a believer who is controlled by his sin nature rather than by the Holy Spirit. While in this state, no eternal rewards are accrued, Scriptural intake is nil, and divine discipline frequently occurs (1 Corinthians 3:1-4).

CHRISTIAN: The title of one who has personally received the Lord Jesus Christ as his Saviour. A biblical term, appearing three times in Scripture (Acts 11:26; 26:28; 1 Peter 4:16). One who embraces the teachings of Christ as the basis of his faith and practice. Synonymous with *believer.*

CHRISTOLOGY: "Christ" is at the heart of this major term. This is the study of the doctrines related to the second Person of the Trinity, the Lord Jesus Christ.

CHRISTOPHANY: an appearance of the Lord Jesus Christ in bodily form prior to His incarnation. He is most often referred to as "the angel of the Lord" at those times.

CHURCH: Two possible meanings: (1) the *local* assembly that is established for the purpose of fellowship, prayer, worship, instruction, and the administration of the ordinances (Acts 2:42), and (2) the *universal* Body of Christ into which all believers are placed as members at the moment of salvation. This universal Church was begun at Pentecost (Acts 2) and will culminate its growth when Jesus Christ returns in the clouds for His own (1 Thessalonians 4:13-17). A synonym of the universal Church is "bride of Christ." See Ephesians 5:22-27 for this analogy.

CONFESSION: With reference to sin in the believer's life, this term has in mind the admission of sins for the purpose of restoring temporal fellowship with the Lord. It is to be noted that the believer, technically, does not need to "plead for forgiveness" from God; rather, he or she simply and openly agrees with God that it is sin and humbly acknowledges it, then claims the forgiveness that is promised in 1 John 1:9. The term comes from a Greek word *Homologeo* meaning "to say the same thing." Hence, the believer says the same thing about sin that God says, namely, that it *is* sin and displeasing to God. When wrong has affected another person, the believer is to go and seek reconciliation through an admission of his offense and guilt— according to Matthew 5:23-26 and James 5:16. The transaction is not complete nor is the conscience completely clear until that part of the transaction is accomplished.

COVENANT: A compact, promise, or agreement between two parties binding them mutually to undertakings on each other's behalf. God made a covenant with Abraham in Genesis 12:1-3 and with others during biblical days. He also promised a "new covenant" through Jeremiah (31:31-33).

CREATION: The doctrine of the miraculous origin of the universe by the power of the Trinity apart from previously-existing matter. This act is described in Genesis 1 and 2 along with John 1:3 and Colossians 1:16-17 (note "Let us" in Genesis 1:26).

CROSS: The framework of wood upon which Christ was crucified (Matthew 27:32-50). It is also a synonym of the terms *sacrifice, suffering,* and *death* (Galatians 6:14 and Matthew 16:24). It is used symbolically for "death to self" in Luke 9:23.

CROWN: With reference to eternal rewards, the believer will receive yet future, tangible evidences of God's satisfaction in his earthly life. These rewards are described in the New Testament as "crowns." There are at least five specific "crowns" promised the believer for faithfulness in various aspects of living for God's glory while on earth. These crowns will be distributed at the judgment seat of Christ (2 Corinthians 5:10) after the translation of the Church.Ultimately, the crowns will be cast before the Lord Jesus in heavenly worship (Reveation 4:9-11).

DEACON: Literally, "servant." One of the categories of leadership within the local assembly. Most likely, the deacons were instituted in Acts 6 when the need for more time in prayer and the ministry of the Word for the apostles arose (Acts 6:1-7). The qualifications for deacons are revealed in 1 Timothy 3:8-13.

DEATH: Though there are several different deaths mentioned in the Bible, the idea of "separation" is seen in each one. Most commonly, this refers to the separation of the soul/spirit from the body when *physical* death on earth occurs (Genesis 5:5, 8, 11; John 11:14).

DECALOGUE: Another word for the Ten Commandments. Not a biblical term.

DEITY: The character or essential nature of God the Father, Son, and Holy Spirit.

DEMONS: The innumerable company of fallen angels who chose to follow Satan when he was cast out of his heavenly abode in eternity past. They are his personal emissaries who carry out his evil plan upon earth until their ultimate judgment and doom. They have the ability to obsess and possess animals and mankind, working havoc in and through the lives of their victims. They energize idolatry, immorality, and every form of human wickedness (1 Corinthians 10:20; Revelation 9:20-21), inspire false teachers (1 John 4:1-2), and exercise influential power over governmental leaders in the satanic world system (Daniel 10:13; Ephesians 6:12). Demons exist today, comprising the invisible forces of darkness and wickedness that wage constant warfare against the forces of right.

DEPRAVITY: Every human being is as bad off as he can possibly be in the sight of God. The person without Christ is totally and completely dead in his spiritual life. Apart from new life through Christ, he or she remains in this condition of spiritual death, totally unable to understand in experience the value and meaning of the work of Christ or the Word of God (Romans 3:10-18; 5:12; Ephesians 2:1-9; 1 Corinthians 2:14).

DISCIPLE: A pupil, learner, or follower. A *general* term sometimes referring to Christ's chosen twelve, sometimes to many others who listened to His teachings (but not necessarily believers). All believers, however, could be called disciples in that they are being taught of God through the indwelling Holy Spirit. Jesus describes the cost of genuine discipleship in Luke 14:25-33.

DISPENSATION: A period of time on earth in which believers are given the opportunity to fellowship with God through a specified way of life in accordance with certain rules of life . . . and unbelievers are made aware of their inability to have fellowship with God in themselves. Each dispensation begins with a unique blessing and opportunity, contains a test upon man's obedience, and ends in judgment. Grace, however, flows through each dispensation from beginning to ending. In *every dispensation,* however, salvation is based on blood and entered into by faith.

DOCTRINE: Derived from the Greek term *Didache,* meaning "to teach" in its basic sense. Simply speaking, it means "teaching" (John 7:17; Acts 2:42; 2 Timothy 3:16). See the list that outlines the major doctrines of the Bible in the introduction of this book.

ECCLESIOLOGY: Pronounced "ee-*klee*-zeeology." This comes from *Ekklesia,* meaning "an assembly, church." Basically, it comes from *Ek ("out") and Kaleo* ("to call"). The church is comprised of "called-out ones." This, then, is the study of the doctrines pertaining to the *universal* and the *local* church.

ECUMENICAL: Worldwide in extent and influence. The ecumenical movement has tended to handle differing theological beliefs by calling together the maximum number of denomimations and pleading for "understanding and openmindedness" among all in attendance. The heart-and-center of this movement is biblical compromise and the elevation of human cooperation beyond its safe and proper bounds. The World Council of Churches is the most significant example of this rapidly-growing movement. The term is actually a transliterated Greek word from *Oikoumena,* meaning "the inhabited earth" (Luke 2:1; Acts 17:31; Revelation 3:10).

ELDER: The title given to those called of God as overseers in the local, visible church. *Bishop* is synonymous with this term. Qualities expected of an elder are set forth in 1 Timothy 3:1-7.

ELECTION: Literally means "to call out." The sovereign act of God in choosing the individuals who comprise the select company of saints. This selection was made personally and individually by God before all ages of time (Ephesians 1:4; Romans 9:11-13).

ESCHATOLOGY: Prounced "*es*kah-tology." *Exchatos* means "last" in Greek. This, then, is the doctrinal study of last things, future events, the prophecies of Scripture.

A GLOSSARY OF MAJOR TERMS

ETERNAL: Existence without beginning or ending—infinite time.

EVANGELIST: The popular usage today refers to the one who has the divinely given ability to communicate the gospel with effectiveness, ease, pleasure, and clarity (Acts 21:8 and Ephesians 4:11).

EXPIATION: The removal of the penalty of sin.

FAITH: Belief, confidence in the Person and/or Word of God. Can refer to saving faith (at the moment of salvation), Christian doctrines (*the* faith) or to daily reliance, trust, and rest in the Lord (Hebrews 11:1, 6).

FATALISM: The belief that events happen apart from any divine purpose or plan by a sovereign force—God or some other. Commonly referred to as "blind chance." This is not to be confused with the doctrine of providence.

FELLOWSHIP: The active, exciting, intimate, Christ-controlled relationship between the believer and his Lord and also believer with believer (1 John 1:3-7).

FLESH: Mere human nature. The earthly nature of man apart from divine influence and therefore prone to sin and opposed to God. Same as "old man" and "old sin nature" (Romans 7:18, 8:9, Galatians 5:17).

FOREKNOWLEDGE: That which God knows with certainty will come to pass because He has decreed that event. It has to do not only with *what* will occur but *who* will be involved.

FORGIVENESS: The removal of charges against a sinner in view of proper satisfaction before God. There is also contained in this a change of attitude toward the one forgiven. Matthew 18:21-35 also applies this to earthly relationships between one person and another. It is the solution to resentment and bitterness.

FUNDAMENTALISM: System of conservative beliefs in the principles which lie at the heart of Christian truth. Fundamentalists adhere essentially to nine points of doctrine: (1) the inspiration and inerrancy of Holy Scripture, (2) the Trinity, (3) the deity and virgin birth of the Lord Jesus Christ, (4) the literal creation and fall of man, (5) the substitutionary atonement of Christ, (6) the bodily resurrection and ascension of Christ, (7) the regeneration of believing sinners, (8) the personal and imminent return of Christ, and (9) the bodily resurrection and assignment of all men to eternal blessedness or eternal punishment.

GOSPEL: The "good news" of the death and resurrection of Jesus Christ on behalf of sinners (1 Corinthians 15:3-4).

GRACE: That which God does for mankind through His Son, which mankind cannot earn, does not deserve, and will never merit. It is God's unmerited favor in spite of the response of humanity. It is summed up in the name, person, and work of the Lord Jesus Christ (John 1:14, 16; Ephesians 2:8-9; Titus 2:11).

HADES: A transliterated Greek word that refers to the temporary abode of the departed souls/spirits of all dead unbelievers, who are awaiting final judgment and eternal punishment in the "lake of fire." Synonymous with *hell* (Luke 16:23).

HARMARTIOLOGY: Prounced "*hah*-martiology." *Hamartia* means "sin, error, wrong." It comes from *Hamartano*, meaning "to miss the mark," which aptly describes sin. This is the doctrinal study of sin—its causes, categories, and consequences.

HEART: Biblical word for mankind's entire inner being—the seat and source of motives, thoughts, passions, and volition (Jeremiah 17:9, 1 Peter 3:4).

HEAVEN: Most commonly used to refer to the future place of abode for all believers in Christ. Called "third heaven" and "paradise" in 2 Corinthians 12:1-2.

HERMENEUTICS: The science of biblical interpretation.

HOLY: Separate from sin, pure, sacred, clean; set apart to God for His glory.

HOLY SPIRIT: Third member of the Trinity. Possesses personality and all the attributes of deity. Has functions distinct from the Father and the Son. He came to earth at Pentecost (Acts 2:1-4; 1 Corinthians 12:13) to permanently indwell every believer.

HYPOSTATIC UNION: The unique combination of undiminished deity and true humanity that has existed in the person of Jesus Christ since His incarnation. These two natures existed without confusion or loss of separate identity, and they were inseparably united without transfer of attributes. Christ was (and still is) both God and man, no less God because of His humanity and no less human because of His deity. Synonymous with this truth is the term "theanthropic" person when it is used to refer to Christ Jesus, the God-man (John 1:14).

ILLUMINATION: The act of being enlightened with the truths of God's Word. This act is related to the work of the Holy Spirit, who takes the truths of the Bible and causes believers to have an understanding of their meaning and application (John 16:13 and 1 Corinthians 2:9-16).

IMMUTABLE: Unchangeable.

IMPECCABILITY: The sinlessness of the Lord Jesus Christ. Since He had no sin nature or imputed sin, He never committed acts of personal sin. The New Testament reveals that He "knew no sin" (2 Corinthians 5:21), "had no sin" (Hebrews 4:15), and "committed no sin" (1 Peter 2:22).

IMPUTATION: Principal meaning is "reckoning to the account of another." A legal term, it refers to the act of God, whereby He credits perfect righteousness to the account of the believing sinner at the moment of salvation. The Bible also speaks of the imputation of Adam's sin to mankind (Romans 5:12-21) and the imputation of mankind's sin to Christ (Isaiah 53:4-6; 2 Corinthians 5:21, and 1 Peter 2:24).

INCARNATION: The act of God the Son when He took upon Himself the form of man and became flesh (John 1:14 and Philippians 2:5-8).

INFALLIBLE: Apart from error or contradiction. Not subject to mistake. Inerrant.

INSPIRATION: The term is translated from a compound Greek word *Theopneustos* meaning, literally, "God-breathed." The key verse on this is 2 Timothy 3:16. God so supernaturally directed the writers of Scripture that without affecting their literary style, vocabulary, intelligence, or personal feelings, His complete message to mankind was recorded with perfect accuracy . . . the very words of the original manuscripts bearing the authority of divine authorship (see also 2 Peter 1:21).

INTERPRETATION: The act of drawing from Scripture its meaning. The interpretation of Scripture is determined by a careful investigation of (1) the context, (2) the normal understanding of each word, taking into consideration, (a) the historical background, (b) literary style, (c) grammatical usages, and (d) geographical location of the writers. Technically, this is known as biblical exegesis.

JUSTICE: The rightness of God's dealings with His creatures, either in approving and rewarding or condemning and judging. God's attitude and acts based on His righteousness (Psalm 89:14).

JUSTIFICATION: The judicial act of God whereby He declares righteous the believing sinner at the moment of salvation (Romans 3:24-28; 5:1).

KENOSIS: This term is a transliterated Greek word found in Philippians 2:7. It has reference to the act of the Lord Jesus Christ at the moment He became human flesh. He surrendered the *voluntary use of His divine attributes* throughout His earthly life . . . but at the same time, He did not empty himself of His deity. His actions were always under the direct will of the Father, empowered by the Holy Spirit (John 8:29; Hebrews 10:7- 9).

LAW: Refers to one of two specific matters: (1) the recorded Word of God given to Moses on Mt. Sinai, or (2) the period of time (or dispensation) between the reception of the Law at Sinai and the death of Jesus Christ at Calvary.

LEGALISM: Conforming to a code or system of deeds and observances in the energy of the flesh, hoping to gain the blessing and favor of God by such acts. Legalism invariably denies the principle of GRACE and exalts the PRIDE of man. The entire book of Galatians was written as a magna carta against such attitudes and practices.

LORD'S SUPPER: An ordinance of memorial that signifies the death of Christ. The two elements (bread and juice) represent the body and blood of our Lord. The local church is to observe this memorial regularly and in accordance with scriptural instruction (1 Corinthians 11:23-34). It is to be offered to all believers with emphasis upon partaking with all personal sins having been previously confessed (1 John 1:9; Proverbs 28:13; 1 Corinthians 11:28).

MARIOLATRY: The worship and veneration of Mary, the mother of Jesus. This practice obscures the preeminence of the Lord Jesus Christ and elevates Mary into a place of unscriptural prominence. Such worship ultimately results in her becoming the mediator between man and God, which is heresy.

MEDIATION: The work of one who reconciles persons at variance with one another. Christ is the only Mediator between God and man (1 Timothy 2:5).

MEDITATE: The act of pondering over Scripture for a period of time, for the purpose of allowing this continued reflection to result in a deeper and more meaningful understanding of that portion (and related portions) of God's blessed Word (Psalm 1:1- 3; 63:6).

MESSIAH: Title used throughout Scripture when referring to the Lord Jesus Christ, the "Anointed One," and especially His relationship to the nation Israel.

MILLENNIUM: The biblical teaching about the millennium is found in Revelation 20:1-10. This particular term is never used in Scripture. It has reference to a literal period of 1,000 years when the Lord Jesus will personally reign as

King of kings and Lord of lords over this earth. Often called the "kingdom," this will be the time when God's promises to the nation Israel will be completely and absolutely fulfilled, such as those appearing in 2 Samuel 7:8-29 and many of the minor prophets.

MISSIONS: The primary task of the Christian church since its inception has been the proclamation of the gospel of Christ to the ends of the earth. This call to world wide evangelism springs from Matthew 28:18-20 and Acts 1:8. The church's mission therefore, is the propagation of the gospel of Jesus Christ to all people across the street, across the States, and across the seas.

MONOTHEISM: The belief in only one God.

MYSTERY: Specific information hidden or withheld in the past but now revealed to believers today. Most often has reference to the information concerning the universal Church and God's plan for her (Ephesians 3:8-10).

NATURAL MAN: Terms used when referring to the unregenerate (1 Corinthians 2:14).

NECROMANCY: An attempt to communicate with the spirits of the dead for the purpose of comfort, receiving information, or ascertaining a knowledge of events of the future. This practice is condemned in many Scriptures, since it is connected with demonic influence and/or human deception. (Compare 1 Samuel 28:8-25 with 1 Chronicles 10:13-14).

NUMEROLOGY: The study of the significance and meaning of numbers in Scripture.

OMNIPOTENCE: The unlimited power and ability of God. He can do all that He wills to perform—nothing is impossible with Him (Luke 1:37).

OMNIPRESENCE: God's presence is universal. He is everywhere at once (Psalm 139:7-12).

OMNISCIENCE: God's knowledge is eternal and infinite. He knows everything. He never learns nor is He ever informed by mankind (Psalm 139:1-4).

ORDAIN: Commonly used when referring to setting individuals apart to a particular calling and service.

ORDINANCE: A ceremony instituted by the Lord for public observation and regular participation in the local assembly. Two ordinances remain for the local church to observe: (1) the Lord's Supper, and (2) baptism.

PARABLE: A short, simple story in narrative form from which a moral or spiritual truth is drawn by comparison. The contents of the parable are drawn from nature; the social, domestic, or political life of the people; and even from current events of biblical days. Parables often separated the believers from the unbelievers, i.e., unbelievers would be unable to grasp their meaning and significance. This method of instruction was used by Christ after the rulers of the Jews attributed His supernatural ability to Satan. It was used most often in His private ministry (Matthew 13:10-13).

PARACLETE: A transliterated Greek term used only by John in the New Testament. Literal meaning is "one called alongside." It is a reference to the Holy Spirit, our Comforter and Helper (John 14:16, 26; 15:26; 16:7), and also Christ, our Advocate (1 John 2:1).

PARADISE: Location of the soul/spirit of the redeemed after death (Luke 23:43; 2 Corinthians 12:4). It is now located in the "third heaven" in the very presence and abode of God.

PENTECOST: A term derived from the Greek *Pentecosta*, meaning "fiftieth." It applied to the fiftieth day after the Passover ceremony. To the New Testament world, it is significant because it was on the day of Pentecost that the Holy Spirit came in a unique manner and brought to pass the inception of the universal Church (Acts 2). This occurred fifty days after Christ's resurrection.

PNEUMATOLOGY: *Pneuma* (pronounced "nooma") means "wind, breath, spirit" in Greek, the most common title used in the Greek New Testament for the Holy Spirit. This is the study of the third Person of the Trinity, God the Holy Spirit.

POSTMILLENNIALISM: The belief that the world will become increasingly better as the Holy Spirit empowers believers with spiritual strength and authority above and beyond the evil powers of the world system . . . until the "golden age" of the kingdom is ushered in by this great revival of spirituality. Christ's second advent will occur *after* this millennium, hence *post-millennialism*. Only rarely do conservative, evangelical Christians accept this belief.

PREDESTINATION: The belief that God has foreordained *all things* which come to pass, including the final salvation or reprobation of man (Romans 8:29-30; Ephesians 1:3-6; Acts 4:27-28; 13:48).

PREMILLENNIALISM: The belief that Jesus Christ will return before the establishment of His kingdom upon the earth.

PROPITIATION: The doctrine of the satisfaction of all of God's righteous demands for judgment on the sinner by the death of Jesus Christ (Romans 3:25; 1 John 2:2).

PROVIDENCE: The belief that the events of our lives are not ruled by chance or fate but by our sovereign God and loving Lord who works out His plan and purpose in the lives of all His children (Romans 8:28; Ephesians 1:11).

PURGATORY: The alleged place of *temporal* punishment in an intermediate realm after death where souls and spirits undergo penal and purifying suffering. Those who go to this place are the ones who die "partially sanctified," encumbered with some degree of sin. While here, they suffer until all their sin is purged away and afterwards are translated to heaven. Money, prayers, masses provided by relatives, etc., aid in alleviating the suffering soul in purgatory. This belief is both unscriptural and untenable, for it never appears in inspired Scripture . . . only in 2 Maccabees 12:39-45, an apocryphal and uninspired book, but accepted by the Roman Church as late as the sixteenth century.

RANSOM: The price paid by Christ on the cross by which redemption was made possible (1 Timothy 2:6).

RAPTURE: The translation or meeting of the universal Church in the air (living and dead believers) with Christ at the end of this present era known as the Church Age (1 Corinthians 15:51-55 and 1 Thessalonians 4:13-17).

RECONCILIATION: The removal of the barrier of sin between God and man by the work of the Lord Jesus Christ on the cross . . . with the result that no barrier to fellowship with God remains. Mankind is now reconciled to God (2 Corinthians 5:14-21).

REDEMPTION: The payment of the price of sin by the sacrifice of Christ whereby He purchased the believer out of the slave market of sin and set him free, never to be under the yoke of sins's penalty again (Ephesians 1:7-8).

REGENERATION: The work of the Holy Spirit in salvation whereby He gives a new life and nature to the believing sinner at the moment of salvation. The new birth (John 3:1-16) is the beginning of this new nature that becomes a part of the believing sinner the instant he or she receives Christ (see also 2 Peter 1:4).

REMISSION: A sending away or passing over of sin . . . synonymous with forgiveness (Romans 3:25; Hebrews 9:22).

REPENTANCE: The act of changing one's inner attitude toward something or someone. From the Greek *Metanoeo*, literally, "to change the mind." Expanded, it means all that is involved in turning *from* sin and turning *to* God.

RESURRECTION: The belief in a bodily rising from the dead and the joining of that body with the soul and spirit. At the time of resurrection, the body will be fashioned anew so as to endure throughout eternity. Christ was bodily raised in this manner. First Corinthians 15 is the key chapter in the Bible on resurrection.

REVELATION: The supernatural act of God whereby He gave His Word to writers of Holy Scripture. This is no longer performed, since the canon of Scripture is now complete. God's inspired, written revelation is now completely contained in His Word. More generally, this can refer to God's making Himself known through nature (Psalm 19:1; Romans 1:18-20).

SANCTIFICATION: The state of being set apart unto God. "Saint," "sanctify," and "holy" are all from the same Greek root word, *Hagiazo*, "to dedicate, separate."

SATAN: The originator of evil who at first dwelt in the very presence of God the Father as the "angel of light," "Lucifer, Son of the morning," but who chose to rebel against God. He was cast out of heaven, made his dwelling over this earth, becoming the "god of this age," and actively participates in leading mankind into sin against God. He will ultimately be judged and doomed to eternal punishment along with his myriad of demons (Isaiah 14:12-14; Ezekiel 28:12-15; 2 Corinthians 4:3-4; Revelation 20:7-10).

SECOND ADVENT OF CHRIST: The personal return of Jesus Christ to this earth in power, judgment, glory, and authority (Revelation 19:11-21). This will occur at the end of the tribulation period, prior to the establishment of Christ's earthly kingdom, according to the premillennial point of view.

SECURITY: The doctrine of the eternal security of the believer is the teaching that once a person has received Christ as his Savior he is forever secure in God's family—never subject to being lost or rejected. This is based on the character, promises, grace, and power of God (John 3:16; 5:24; 6:37; 10:27-30; 1 Corinthians 3:15; Romans 8:1, 38-39; Ephesians 1:19-21; 4:30; 1 John 2:1-2).

SESSION: The doctrine of Christ's present position at the right hand of God the Father, sitting in authority as our Representative and Advocate (Ephesians 1:20-23; Hebrews 10:12-13).

SOTERIOLOGY: Pronounced "so-*teer*-eeology." This comes from *Soter* ("so-tare"), meaning "savior, deliverer." This logically follows the doctrine of sin. After sin occurred there came the need for salvation. This is the study of all the doctrines having to do with salvation and the Christian way of life.

SPIRITUAL GIFTS: Divinely-bestowed abilities or skills given to every believer at the moment of salvation which enable the believer to perform his or her service in the Body of Christ (universal Church) so that the Body functions with the maximum amount of effectiveness (Romans 12:6-8; 1 Corinthians 12; Ephesians 4:11-12; 1 Peter 4:11).

SPIRITUALITY: The state of the believer who is controlled by and walking in dependence upon the Holy Spirit (1 Corinthians 2:15; Ephesians 5:18).

TEMPTATION: Solicitation and enticement into evil prompted by the world system, the flesh, or the devil . . . never by God (James 1:13-15; 1 John 2:15-17).

THEOLOGY PROPER: *Theology* is from two Greek words *Theos* and *Logos*, which when combined, refer generally to the study of all Christian truth—all the doctrines. However, by adding *Proper* to the title, the subject is narrowed down to the study of the first Person of the Trinity, God the Father.

TONGUES: Reference to one of the spiritual gifts mentioned in the New Testament. It was used mainly as a means of spreading the gospel during the first century before the Scriptures were in the language of the people (Acts 2:4-11). Specific guidelines for tongue-speaking and interpretation of such were given to the Corinthians in 1 Corinthians, chapter 14.

TRIBULATION: A period of seven literal years upon the earth (Daniel 9:24-27) following the rapture of the Church and ending with the second advent of Christ. The events of this era are contained in Revelation, Chapters 6 through 19. It will be a time of unprecedented evil, anguish, affliction, and trouble upon the earth due to the unrestrained activity of Satan (2 Thessalonians 2:7-8).

TRINITY: The Godhead, consisting of the Father, Son, and Spirit, who are one in essence and attributes, yet three in distinct work and purpose. They are coequal, coeternal, and coexistent (2 Corinthians 13:14).

WORD OF GOD: The Bible or Holy Scripture (Luke 24:27; Ephesians 6:17; Hebrews 4:12).

WORSHIP: A human response to divine revelation. More specifically, the act of personal adoration, meditation, and respect directed toward God and His Word. Worship includes such things as praying, giving, singing, reading, and meditating when these are directed toward the Lord. The Book of Psalms helps us know how to worship as it directs our attention to the Lord our God.

SCRIPTURE INDEX

423

SUBJECT INDEX

Also available by Charles R. Swindoll:

Books:
Come Before Winter
Compassion: Showing Care in a
  Careless World
Dropping Your Guard
Encourage Me
For Those Who Hurt
Growing Strong in the Seasons of Life
Hand Me Another Brick
Improving Your Serve
Killing Giants, Pulling Thorns
Leadership: Influence that Inspires
Living on the Ragged Edge
Make Up Your Mind
Recovery: When Healing Takes Time
Standing Out
Starting Over
Strengthening Your Grip
Strike the Original Match
Three Steps Forward, Two Steps Back
Victory: A Winning Game Plan for
  Life
You and Your Child

Films:
People of Refuge
Strengthening Your Grip

Booklets:
Anger: The Burning Fuse of Hostility
Attitudes
Commitment: The Key to Marriage
Dealing With Defiance
Demonism: How to Win Against the
  Devil
Destiny: Choosing to Change the
  Course of Your Life
Divorce: When It All Comes
  Tumbling Down
Eternal Security: The Assurance of
  Our Destiny
God's Will: Biblical Direction for
  Living
Hope: Our Anchor of the Soul
Impossibilities
Integrity: The Mark of Godliness
Leisure: Having Fun is Serious
  Business
Moral Purity
Our Mediator
Peace. . . . In Spite of Panic
Prayer
Sensuality: Resisting the Lure of Lust
Singleness: Biblical Advice on
  Staying Single
Stress: Calm Answers for the Worry
  Worn
The Lonely Whine of the Top Dog
Tongues: An Answer to Charismatic
  Confusion
When Your Comfort Zone Gets the
  Squeeze
Woman: A Person of Worth and
  Dignity

... *W*hatever he does prospers.